SO IT GOES

Bob Ellis divides his time between screenwriting, film directing, broadcasting, song writing, acting, mob oratory, regular journalism and ceremonial speech writing, a rigorous round of dining out and theatre-going, and his family in Palm Beach, north of Sydney.

His screenwriting credits, *Newsfront*, *Goodbye Paradise*, *Maybe This Time* and the Paul Cox collaborations, *Man of Flowers* and *My First Wife*, all won major Australian prizes; as did his historical miniseries co-written with Stephen Ramsay, *True Believers*; his musical play, *The Legend of King O'Malley*, co-written with Michael Boddy; and his children's films, *Fatty Finn*, *Top Kid* and *The Paper Boy*. To this, he adds his three directorial feature films, *Unfinished Business*, *Warm Nights on a Slow Moving Train* and *The Nostradamus Kid*.

His political books, *The Things We Did Last Summer*, *Two Weeks in Another Country*, *Letters to the Future*, *Goodbye Jerusalem* and *First Abolish the Customer: 202 Arguments Against Economic Rationalism*, his collection of *The Inessential Ellis* and his comic novel, *The Hewson Tapes*, are regarded in his native land as small classics. His position as a war correspondent, social commentator, theatre owner, documentary director, dispirited collaborator with Werner Hertzog, nightclub turn and political mover is possibly unique.

Bob Ellis' hobbies are eating, conversation, film-going, cricket, reading and exploring the Ring of Kerry. He is now in his fifties, overweight but healthy, and a curiously happy man.

SO IT GOES
BOB ELLIS

ESSAYS, BROADCASTS, SPEECHES 1987–1999

VIKING

Viking
Penguin Books Australia Ltd
487 Maroondah Highway, PO Box 257
Ringwood, Victoria 3134, Australia
Penguin Books Ltd
Harmondsworth, Middlesex, England
Penguin Putnam Inc.
375 Hudson Street, New York, New York 10014 USA
Penguin Books Canada Limited
10 Alcorn Avenue, Toronto, Ontario, Canada M4V 3B2
Penguin Books (NZ) Ltd
Cnr Rosedale and Airborne Roads, Albany, Auckland, New Zealand
Penguin Books (South Africa) (Pty) Ltd
5 Watkins Street, Denver Ext 4, 2094 South Africa
Penguin Books India (P) Ltd
11, Community Centre, Panchsheel Park, New Delhi 110 017 India

First published by Penguin Books Australia Ltd 2000

10 9 8 7 6 5 4 3 2 1

Cover design by George Dale and Guy Mirabella
Author photograph by Lorrie Graham
Printed and bound in Australia by Australian Print Group, Maryborough, Victoria

National Library of Australia
Cataloguing-in-Publication data:

Ellis, Bob.
  So it goes: essays, broadcasts, speeches 1987–1999.
  ISBN 0 670 88971 7.
  1. Australian essays – 20th century. 2. Speeches, addresses, etc., Australian.
  I. Title.
A804.3

www.penguin.com.au

This book is dedicated to my daughter, Jenny Ellis

And so it goes,
The leaf, the rose,
And Old Tom Cobley, I suppose.

Thomas Shapcott, 'Old Tom's Song'

Acknowledgements

Many of these pieces, some in earlier versions, originally appeared in the following publications (some kind of expression of gratitude), the *Sydney Morning Herald*, the *Age*, the *Courier Mail*, the *Australian*, the *Good Weekend*, the *Sunday Age*, the *Sunday Mail*, the *Daily Telegraph*, the *Adelaide Advertiser*, the *Weekend Guardian, Encore, Amnesis, GQ*, the *Labor Herald*, the *Financial Review*, or were broadcast on Radio National, or were speeches made at various Labor, Green, Independent and ATSIC functions. 'James McAuley' first appeared in *Overland*, 'Palm Beach' also appeared in *The Inessential Ellis*, and 'John Hargreaves' in *Goodbye Jerusalem*. Other pieces are thus far unpublished or written for this book.

The author and publisher wish to thank copyright holders for permission to quote the following material: David Moran, page 17; the lines from Hemingway's *Islands in the Stream*, page 44; James McAuley's 'Gnostic Prelude', page 178, is taken from *Collected Poems 1993*, Angus & Robertson; *Bastards from the Bush*, page 278, © Seedwillow P/L; Kenneth Slessor's 'William Street', pages 394–95.

Particular thanks to Chris McGillion, David Crossen, Wendy Harmer, Greg Lenthen, Brad Norrington, Tess Livingstone, Kay Dibben, James Button, Paul Austin, Steve Foley, Tracy Prisk, Jacquie Mooney, Carrie Schofield, Ramona Koval, Anne Summers, John Sharp, Gary Orr, James Fontayne, Andrew Valder, and especial thanks to Rose Creswell, Jane Cameron, Bob Sessions and Sandy Webster. Undying gratitude, too, to my wife and minder Anne Brooksbank for months of sorting, typing, editorial amendment and forgiveness beyond the call of duty.

Contents

Introduction

An actress long accustomed to working on the stage eventually, it is said, with some trepidation did a big role in a film. This took her four months, and after a year, when the film was finished, she came to the premiere. And she looked up in a kind of wonder at herself on the giant screen, and after it was over she said, 'Did I do all that? All I remember is the waiting.'

This present book to me has come as a similar shock. Did I do all that? All I remember are the deadlines. It was work done while other, larger work for the stage or screen or politics was pending, or overdue. Occasional, minor work required of me by editors with a set ephemeral subject – love, beaches, courage, Fred Hollows, Elvis, my favourite year – that somehow unleashed in me some spurts of meaning in a tumble of words that were sometimes worth reading, and sometimes not, or a speech I was asked to do on a particular night to a particular audience of strangers on a particular topic – reconciliation, May Day, a state schooling – that got the cadences going. But it's work as well that includes a fair deal of my better writing, writing that changed the way some readers looked at things, work that was read out in Parliament, or put up on a fridge or a noticeboard, or talked of in a schoolroom.

It's a chronicle, too, of my ongoing struggle with a number of sorts of writing – the half-hour speech, the three-minute speech, the five-minute broadcast soliloquy, the thousand-word gossip column on the latest film premiere, the 800-word opinion – all a test of my power to say, at that length, anything worthwhile.

For to write really well you need three thousand words, maybe five thousand words, just to get your arguments up and pulsing. Fifteen hundred words are the comfortable, or semi-comfortable, minimum. A thousand are a struggle. Five hundred impossible. Yet seven or eight hundred words are now the norm in most newspapers and magazines, and three hundred in the tabloids.

And very few good authors can serve these limits with honour. The big names of the past – Mailer, Muggeridge, Vidal, Tynan, Orwell, Lippan, Mencken, Macaulay, Hazlitt, Johnson, Addison, Swift, Browne – had two, three, five, ten thousand words to play with, conjure with. And there are therefore no big names of the present, big in that same way, because they do not have that crucial elbow room for the thinking heart to gather its eloquence and energy and power. Word limits, in short, are the new censorship of the writer's power to move the reader. Prove that I lie.

To overcome this, or to try to overcome it, I re-created in broadcasting what I suppose I must call the evangelistic rant, and this form I like the best of all that I've used in this book. I like second-best the diary column, in which the rambunctious toper Ellis, a person who is not me but a fictional barfly bearing my name and some of my past, speaks uncensored to a daunted, restless listener. The third-best is the quiet reflection, genteelly worded for the kind of responsible reader who doesn't like slang or bad language or Rabelaisian metaphor: short-back-and-sides writing I call it; though it too can pack, sometimes, as in the piece called 'Christmas', the odd philosophical rabbit-punch.

And so it is (or so it goes) that to some of you it will seem this book is by three different people – the stump orator, the set-'em-up-Joe raconteur in the pub, and the sober, thoughtful college tutor. All, I suppose, reflect me in some way.

If you are looking for a laugh, and you probably should be, go straight to 'Broadcast News' or 'Metropolitan Distractions'. If you are, however, a wholly serious person, one keen to learn more of the wide world and the pilgrimage of one mind through it in our time, go to bed with a cup of cocoa and read from the beginning.

And if you too have thoughts, heaven help you, of taking up essay-writing yourself, please don't. It's too hard, too testing, too ill-paid, too wrecked by deadline, and too late in the millennium, and in the story of humankind.

For journalism as now practised is no longer a forum for differing, reasoned, passionate opinion. It is filler, which goes in between the advertisements which are most newspapers' only purpose, when that purpose is not the lame echoing of the current owner's views or vendettas or hot flushes or superstitions. Great various organs of contesting thought, like *Nation Review* or *Nation* or *Esquire* or the *Listener*, are gone now. Learn to live, if you can, with their absence.

And read this book.

BOOK ONE

Overture

Palm Beach

I'd lived for sixteen years round Sydney without knowing Palm Beach and took maybe six months more to yearn for it, having lived there, moved away and half moved back. I'd like to die there on the hill that overlooks all that altering water and the lighthouse and the golf course and the wharf and the seaplane, feeding in my latter days the selfsame lorikeets I met first in my thirties (since lorikeets, too, have three score years and ten and they, too, are creatures of habit that go and come back and know when they are home). They numbered thirty-eight in the good years, clustering and screeching round our plates of honeyed bread, and now, because of our absence, only two – but the two, I hope, are spreading the word that the Welfare State is back and our old friends will cluster and bicker as they used to on the verandah that for them and my children is a sacred site that draws us in dreams, like a magnet, home.

For years at night a blind possum came to us for apples and bread, somehow surviving his awesome journey by braille up the jungly hill. Sometimes he came in the day, not knowing the difference. My little daughter cried for him and his phlegmatic valour and asked if there was a way to make him see again and we had to tell her there was not, eye transplants for possums being at a distance that even Socialism would not bridge.

Our Palm Beach hill offered bandicoots too, and mynah birds, none of which, for love or sunflower seed, would recite for me the Gettysburg Address – the bastards – and in the good days a white duck, called Duck, we lost to an eagle and in a welter of grief at length replaced by having children. There were year-round native flowers and a sky-high cactus we told the children was a beanstalk and a *Monstera deliciosa* that pushed a wall down and miles of beautiful murderous morning glory and acres, it seemed, of lantana we would hack at, cursing in vain. Lantana, like Americans, does not seem to understand why it is not welcome and keeps triumphantly arriving anyway.

There were and are a lot of Americans in Palm Beach then and now, and a lot of pot smoking I can vouch for, and schoolyard heroin and modern painting and guitar plucking and surfboard polishing and wave cracking and beach crawls past the topless dollybirds at the North End and resident film directors holding court. On our hilltop lived Weir and Noyce and Elfick,

3

and nearabouts, in their bambooed gardens, Deling, Cowan and Ricketson. Only Ricketson, the first and the last, is left now, his waist-length blond hair trimmed for a stodgier age, but he still holds parties on his verandah for visiting auteurs and rock stars who marvel at the unchanging, calm, subtropical heat and the view.

Captain Goodvibes is gone too, evicted after decades from a lovely big crumbly stone house with (maybe) a better view than ours, a view he painted without end, hard blue, soft green with birds and boats, his Eden lost. In that same house lived Vladimir Petrov for the first seven years of his exile, convalescing, as all of us at Palm Beach do, from the twentieth century, wishing we'll never have to get back to it, knowing we will.

Like the Christmas holidays, Palm Beach is what some Australians have instead of psychoanalysis. Ten minutes over that view is a holiday, a week is a supernumerary lifetime. The calendar slows down, the water glimmers, boats sail through the glimmer, the seaplane takes off and lands among unruffled windsurfers, hang-gliders float by the lighthouse, up and around . . .

I stand over the view sometimes, pleased that forty thousand years ago people experienced the same panorama – Lion Island, Barrenjoey, the Hawkesbury mouth, all the way up to Clareville one way and Woy Woy the other – and drank it in as I do now, deeming it as I do now a sacred site for which, as I do now, they had a particular affinity: thirty-six thousand years before Khufu and Enkidu and Methuselah they stood here, moved as I and as much at home.

We left it of course, for insufficient reasons, fearing the breathalyser, the schoolyard heroin and the deathly midnight gauntlet of the Bilgola Bends, yearning for harbourside parties and opening nights at the Nimrod and cocktails and arguments at Kinselas, and came to roost in Wahroonga, which is roughly like moving from the Côte d'Azur to upstate Scandinavia.

Still, even in Wahroonga the kids found school friends (and can even get to play with them by making appointments three months ahead in between their Bible, Moog and judo lessons) and moving back will be hard. We left after eight years there – only months before Mike Walsh, with his Avalon cinema, civilised the arid Sundays with Fellini and *Fantasia* and Woody Allen and the Japanese restaurant opened and the infamous beachfront development, Flamingos, that I would not campaign against because I dreamed of martini lunches and writing novels on the bar stools in the afternoons.

And only a year before a good stern headmaster came to Barrenjoey High and smack went out of fashion and Patrick Cook moved there, and Bryan Brown and Rachel, and Tom Keneally came back from Manhattan. Patrick Cook lives there four days a week now, on a ridge that looks to water both ways, and in that setting his conversation is even better, his barbecuing superb and his heart maybe for the first time calm. I miss it all very much but had to leave to find out why.

There's another Palm Beach, of course, of retired capitalists and gangsters and weekend advertising men and boating fools and golfers and indoor bowlers at the RSL and water police that sneak around the corner and fish for bream on the quiet, that I know not of, though the smell of barbecues and bare midriffs occasionally wafts up the hill and tantalises me with suburban possibilities. Wives are being swapped down there and bridge played for high stakes and mashie shots perfected and fish netted and real estate fortunes concocted, and I am up here above it, inhaling no more than a sacred glimmering view. Still, I've made my choice, like everyone.

Everyone's view in Palm Beach is the best and everyone finds there what they thought they wanted once, peace of heart, a tan, a weekend solace, a boogie board, a diet, a nut religion, a new beat, a second wife, a perfect wave, an adoring bimbo for the summer vac, blond happy children bereft perhaps of an urban future but full of a past they would not replace, and good things they can brightly see down latter years by merely closing their eyes.

Such visions and revisions, I think now, are worth keeping as facts, and as home, and as heartland. I'm going back if I can. And when I'm old and surly and filthy, in a mouldy shack with a view, limping daily down to the RSL and cursing in the long afternoons the advancing hovercraft-loads of commuting Japanese coming home from the office to fifty-storey condominiums all around me, I will know even then I'll have won a victory, somehow, nonetheless. Sacred sites are probably worth the battle. The heart has its reasons and Palm Beach is reason enough.

July, 1987

On Being Burned Down

In the months that followed our fire, on the edge of sleep, a waking dream would rise up to taunt me – the flames, the rushing, the shouting, my nakedness, the tangled hose, the hour-long wait for the firemen's water to flow. *This time*, I thought, *this time it'll be different, I'll get the hose untangled, I'll get the photos out, the videotapes, the diaries.* And soon I'd be fully awake again, and I'd know there was no way back, no erasing rescue, no resurrection out of the ash and wind of so much that was loved.

5

Fire moves very quickly and its angry, mythical, animal ferocity is real, and it leaps like a tiger from trees to fronds to roof to house, like a sentient, awesome beast that has made up its mind. And I tugged and tugged at the tangled hose – left so not by us but by a Christmas lodger – and attacked with a feeble trickle, thumb over nozzle, what might (only might) for ninety seconds, no more, have been contained.

And the house filled up with smoke, and the getting out of the children, the dog and cat (we forgot the white mice and the neighbour's budgie, and the goldfish in the heat-broken tank were already dead). And the unbelief, and the coughing and shrieking and running about and furious recrimination (it starts early) *made us forget*, somehow, the precious album photos and videotapes in the room beside the room already alight. *The purpose of life is to remember*, a character in the movie I'd just finished had said, and I called it to mind as everywhere that night in firelight memory was going, going, gone.

And we got to the house next door and on the verandah, balefully drinking their magnum champagne, watched all our past go up into the sky. Shakespeare's letters went up like this, I thought, and Byron's memoirs, and the cremated dead of Auschwitz – up, up and gone.

Within hours there were blankets and soup and toys from the neighbours, from people we hardly knew, and rooms for us to sleep in and someone to drive me to town where I launched my latest comic novel at ten the following morning (in a cinder-smudged shirt and borrowed oversized shoes, with three camera crews in prurient attendance), and patient volunteers who sifted, hour by hour, the ash and wreckage and prised apart the blackly gummed and melted photos and kept them preserved in freezers, charred edges forever encircling our goofily smiling yesterdays. *There is so much goodness in the world*, I thought, *uncelebrated, kept out of mind till days like this. Where does it hide in the meantime? Where does it go?*

We got through the experience, I suppose. The children didn't go mad or feral (but one came close), after losing everything they loved, and little Tom was told in the schoolyard 'I'm glad your house burnt down', and he didn't much want to go back to that school again.

We rented a house across the road and the kids caught the same school bus and the dog took the same beach walk and Max the cat would go by moonlight and sit in the ashes, trying to will the house back into being. I felt the way he did for a while, till, after insurance wrangles, we built a new house over the ashes and could look out at the same view as before.

And the charred blue jacarandas, the ones that arched over the Pittwater view, grew back in different shapes and they were a comfort framing our life as before. Old friends.

And the mind has a steel door that *once you have slept* closes out forever so much of the pain. You are first numb, then thankful, thankful nobody died (though Tom remembered the mice and the budgie, and was pensively sad for four or five months), and soon it hardens over into *this too shall pass*, and of course it does.

A simple foam extinguisher would have fixed it and, of course, we didn't have one. Or (perhaps) an untangled hose. Or a wind that had blown, however gently, the other way.

It's all so random. A CD-player survived, and some middling jazz records, and two thousand books, great heirlooms among them, went. And charcoal drawings and landscape paintings done by my wife in her student days; beautiful things. And the final conversations, on cassette, I had with my dad when he was dying. And Richard Beckett's worsted jacket, given me at his wake. And all the videos of all the children's infancy, and childhood, and a trip to Ireland when they were so very little, reading poems on Yeats's tower, *I sigh that kiss you, For I must own, That I will miss you, When you have grown.*

The idea that these things *no longer exist*, have gone into air, into thin air, and there were no miraculous exemptions (my pen, I hoped, would come out of the ashes, my Filofax, the Scrooge McDuck doll, but no), made finally firm in my mind the atheism I had toyed with down the years. Randomness. Cruelty. Death. Destruction. Loss of remembered happiness. These were the only certainties. There was, therefore, no God – or not a God that cared a damn.

I believe this, but I also believe in quiescent human goodness, that habit in the tribe, of healing for the wounded, comfort for the anguished. We are seeing it again this week, and we will see more of it, I fear, in the dreadful bushfire summer to come.

December, 1997

Success

I grew up in an Australia that seemed, then (in John Howard's picket-fence fifties), enduring, unchanging, provincial and kindly – and Anglo-Celtic, of course. I will die, I know, in an Australia I find increasingly strange.

Friendship meant something more then. And neighbourhood. And country. And family. Family was a big three-volume novel of quarrel and gossip and loyalty and surname and recurring noses and disputed wills and homes where, when you went there, they had to take you in.

It is not like that now. These days the one true test of a friend – that you can ring him up from the watch-house and ask him to stand you bail – will find few takers. People have become, in what is perhaps the awful shift of the twentieth century, replaceable. Divorce, and the thousands of miles you go from home town to eventual place of work, has made them literally, perhaps necessitously, back numbers you leave behind in what in past times would have been your whole life, as unfinished business. We start with a roomful of people who we think are the world. We end in a kind of emotional supermarket, with prices on everything.

This change, which is instantly recognisable to anyone over fifty, has a cause, I believe, and one that few have noted before. It has nothing to do, happily, with the worldwide spread of identity-eroding multiculturalism. (Lord, let not the soul of Pauline Hanson enter this bosom, not this week.) It is something else.

Put it this way.

In the year 1922 an old man could die unvisited in a single room in a mouldy boarding house yet feel content. Content because he knew that in his life he had done his *duty* ... to his country, his party, his school, his family, his neighbourhood, or his religion. Or all of the above. And he could then pass on into the great dark justified, in a way complete.

It is not like that now.

For over the intervening years and generations the idea of Duty has somehow faded, and somehow been replaced with the idea of Success. You now die justified only if you have been a Success. And the measure of Success has so altered as to exclude from its embrace almost everybody.

A few years ago a successful man was one who, say, had run a small business with four employees for thirty-five years, raised three children who had gone to college, served two terms as an alderman on the municipal council, and retired at sixty-two to a flat in Surfers Paradise.

It is not so now.

Now a successful man, to be called a successful man, must own billions, and control the broadcast rights to Outer Space. He must be as famous as Michael Jackson or as renowned as Stephen Hawking, or must star at the very least in a show named after him, like *Seinfeld*, on worldwide television.

And because this definition excludes well over 98 per cent of us (and each year leaves many, like Alan Bond and O.J. Simpson, and Helen Demidenko and Paul Keating, uncertain of their current status), most of the world then tends to think it is a failure. And because the prevailing fantasy, touted everywhere in the media, is that anyone can make it – look at Sid Vicious, look at Madonna – most of the world falls into a despondency.

Most of the world then beats its wife, or wants to. And some of the world buys a handgun. And some of the world then arrives in a McDonald's in

Texas with its handgun crying, 'Call me a failure, will you?' Blam blam blam blam blam.

Or in a cafe in Port Arthur.

Images of success and famousness taunt us nightly from the television (even the weather men are famous) and ask us 'What have you done with *your* life?' And there's no answer to that, except, perhaps, to find someone to blame. My father raped me when I was eight – I *think*. Yes, it's all coming back . . .

Or to crash your way out of oblivion with a repeat-action shotgun. Stephen Sondheim, in his wonderful short opera *Assassins*, explores this. Is your life a darkness and a despair? Do you feel a nobody? I have here the solution for you. *Why don't you shoot the President?*

It's no accident that the killers of John Lennon and the Kennedys and Abraham Lincoln and Yitzhak Rabin, and the ones who went blam blam blam at President Reagan and President Ford and Governor Wallace and President Truman and President Roosevelt – both President Roosevelts – and President McKinley were all in their middle or late twenties, and at that stage in life when you realise, at last, that you're not going to make it big. Murder is a response to a feeling of lack of success. It is almost nothing else.

So Success has a lot to answer for, in a way that Duty never did. Duty kept you warm at night, and righteous and, if wrapped up in religion, bound for a better world. Success is of the earth, a nightly torture, a waking hell. And the reason the world is so unpleasant now. Why aren't you a silverchair? You're already fifteen.

Japanese high school students pressed by exams and young Aborigines hang themselves for want of it. Young men in Mosman and Toorak take heroin for want of it. Everyone young for want of it is forming a rock band, hoping for the big break, real soon . . .

It affects women less I'm sure, for whom successful childbirth is proof of something, and loving descendants, but they have to tiptoe round the want of it in their men every afternoon and night.

The man out the back in his toolshed, polishing his gun.

Down with Success, if it can be downed. And bring back duty. Or re-define it. Its absence is wrecking the world.

September, 1996

Fred Hollows

I

'Turn right at the marihuana,' we were told, a little mysteriously I thought, when we asked the way to the Hollows Lens Factory in Kathmandu. The driver of the *tuk-tuk*, a small, obstreperous, deafening conveyance that is best described as a cross between a tricycle, a lawnmower and an umbrella, immediately understood.

After twenty minutes of boneshaking and beeping risk to life and limb, we arrived. There was a dirty bridge, a filthy river, two burning corpses, a number of golden splashing children, a temple of carved penises, a monk on a hunger strike, twenty hectares of marihuana growing as untended and unremarked as paspalum and, before the factory, a brick wall being pulled down by the same Nepali workmen who had laboriously built it the day before. All of Asia, I decided, in three hundred yards. It was enough marihuana, I thought, as I stood there under its flourishing greenness amazed, to pay off my entire mortgage, but my fifteen-year-old son, more worldly wise than I am, said it wasn't worth the risk.

They were tearing down the wall to make room for the big expected audience for King Birendra of Nepal on Tuesday. He was opening the Hollows Lens Factory in the company of Prime Minister Girija Prasad Koirala, his sworn enemy, the two of them together for the first time on any stage.

We went in. The austere brick corridors were crammed with elderly, blind, silent people who looked like Bible illustrations, often two together, man and wife, sometimes lying stoic on a single stretcher, holding hands. Upstairs, in conditions of what I felt was unseemly conviviality, eye operations were occurring, two every fifteen minutes in adjacent surgeries, one of them televised, before a buoyant audience applauding, arguing, punching the Coke machine, and eating sandwiches. At one point the power went off, pitching the surgery into darkness, and then operating ophthalmologist Dr Sanduk Ruit kept his hand steady on the needle in the probed pupil till it came back on. A movement of more than one tenth of a millimetre would ensure lifelong blindness and Ruit, as ever, was patient in the dark.

Ruit is legendary. A burly, broad-faced Nepalese fortyish man of much calm leaderly magnetism and of such acknowledged and celebrated surgical genius he had turned down repeated offers of millions from America, he did thirty-seven or forty operations a day, seven days a week, for no charge, and had been doing this for twelve years. As Fred Hollows's principal disciple in Asia (and in his last years, his closest friend), he had inherited, or acquired, Fred's determination to open the eyes of the Third World.

'A difficult, arrogant, cantankerous man,' he said, between operations, with love of his great unruly rumpled mentor. '"If you don't do it this way, I'm going to kick your arse." Very direct, very Australian in that way. Very much the teacher in front of the classroom with the bamboo in his hand. But he understood, and he taught me to understand – I was much more of a colonial once – that Third World countries must spend the money they get in aid properly, in learning to do things themselves. So much money we get goes *back* to the First World in the pockets of Western doctors taking fees – what he called medical tourists – and what is the good of that? It should stay here. I am much more of a Nepali now. Fred made me that. Fred used to say, "If you give a man a fish, you feed him for one meal. If you teach him how to fish, you feed him for a lifetime."'

Watching Ruit work – and the gory shock of the operation soon gives way to something different, to an abstract fascination, cut and scrape and stitch, and push, ever so delicately push, the new lens in under the skin of the eye, an abstract, almost artistic fascination of the kind one has for a great guitarist concentrating on his music, John Williams perhaps or Segovia – is to participate in a kind of secular miracle, like a moon probe.

'It's such a small organ, the eye,' he says, 'and what a big role it plays. Close your own eyes, and see how big.' A man whose eyes are cured of blindness is no longer a passenger, he explained, no longer a burden, no longer a social difficulty. He can earn money. He can relate. Everyone about him is happy; the entire mountain village is happy. There are no unfortunate side effects to curing blindness. It is a process, almost the only one, with no downside.

Not charging for his thirty-seven or forty miracles a day puts a financial burden on Ruit's own life that he wears with unpretentious, courtly, good-humoured grace, his voice retaining its musical sly chuckle always. From seven in the morning to four-thirty in the afternoon, he explains, he works for the Hollows Foundation for free (Mike Lynskey, the red-bearded, shrewd and watchful minder of Hollows's last years on earth finally persuaded Ruit to take a modest salary in June after months of negotiations); from four-thirty to nine he works for himself as a general practitioner for money – not much, but some. That's seven days a week for Fred, six nights a week for himself. Between four-thirty and nine on Saturdays he has to himself, and with his family. This is his reward. He has had no holidays, and no week-ends, for twelve years.

'Why work so hard?' I asked. 'Why not thirty a day instead of thirty-seven?'

'If I do thirty a day,' he responded with a kind of deep, amused simplicity I can't begin to decipher, 'seven less people can see.'

The cost therefore, because of all this, to each of his patients (walk in, walk out, like a dental surgery, with no expensive stay in hospital) is five dollars all up – necessitously and regrettably as much as this, he emphasises, because of the price of the processed plastic in the lens. Next day they take the cotton wool off their eyes and they can see. It has to be this way, he says, it is part of Fred's philosophy, the whole technique has to be this cheap, was contrived to be this cheap, in order to make it accessible to people who otherwise could not afford it. He is meanwhile teaching others the technique – something so simple, Fred said, that any steady-handed plumber can do it, and requiring seven years in medical school before you are *allowed* to do it is ridiculous.

And so the good news spreads, through the equivalent of a barefoot doctor movement, and all over Asia and Africa eyes are opening, and joy abounds. Soon, with relief, he will be only teaching, no longer operating, in ten more years perhaps, and the one million cataract cases of Nepal will by then be less. No-one knows why there are so many. It might be to do with diet or altitude, or ozone holes (cows in the Falklands develop cataract where cows in the tropics do not), or sunlight itself; so many Nepalese live in the fields and in the streets, and never go indoors.

The semi-medieval people in the mountain communities regard Ruit and his colleagues as miracle workers, as demi-gods. They come up and want to touch him, ask him to bless their children, ask for a lock of his thinning hair. 'The hard part,' he says, 'is explaining to those whose blindness *cannot* be treated – who do not have cataract, or whose cataract is too far advanced – that there is no hope. "You did it for my friend," they say, "why will you not do it for me?" That, I think, is the most difficult part of the work, by far.'

'The most difficult moment for me,' said Dick Litwin of Berkeley, California, a cheerful grey-bearded man with a close resemblance to Allen Ginsberg, 'was when I was operating in a tent by hurricane lamplight in the Himalayas and the needle was in the eye and I looked down at my bare hand – our hands have to be bare, you know, because the work is so delicate – and saw it was covered with crawling mosquitos. Now I couldn't slap them. I couldn't move my hand. These are moments, as they say, that wonderfully focus the mind.'

All who have been on the eye camps with Ruit and with Dick – travelling surgeries in pitched tents in the high mountain villages far from the twentieth century – speak of them as almost religious experiences. 'That such good is achieved tells wonderfully in the mind,' Dr David Moran, a bald ophthalmologist, part-time poet and choir music fanatic from Port Macquarie, said. He, like the others, had the confident serenity of those that know they have paid their dues on earth, increased, not reduced, human happiness.

And part of it, of course, is Asia itself, and the particular magic, long celebrated in the West, that is Nepal. I and the others hung about on the unofficial days with Tim McCartney-Snape, a long, lean, freckled sombre conqueror twice of Everest with many of the physical attributes of a llama and a mild, magnetic personality akin to that, I thought, of Lawrence of Arabia, among the dusty medieval jostling marketplaces and the monkey-crawling temples, the temple of the living goddess and the rest of it, climbing the Himalayas by night under bright stars through calmly drifting fireflies, absorbing the surrounding peace and the unconcern that is part and parcel of a belief in eternity, a belief that life is forever and the present dusty starvation but an interlude on an endless journey with a good guide.

You begin very quickly to share the stoicism of the locals – two-year-old children totter untended and unharmed within inches of roaring traffic on crowded footpaths – and all our Western civilisation very quickly, all our obsession with cleanliness and safety and predictability and insurance pre-miums, becomes in the light of Asia a pointless collage of silly neuroses. You do question your values in Kathmandu, the way you are supposed to, the way most Westerners always have, among the mountain peace and the green terraced hills and the intricate ivory statuary and woven carpets and the squatting black baleful bulls in the public thoroughfares, and the temples with painted eyes on them that watch and follow you, the prayer wheels and the Buddhist monks that share their temples, amazingly, with Hindus, and the visible family love spilling out on the dusty streets, the love of children, the care and respect of the old, the crowded mutual fondness, the abiding married love, the unbruised faith, the unconcern with death as the bodies daily burn by the sacred river and children swim in the ashes a few yards down.

It must be hard, I suggested to Ruit, to get such a people interested in their earthly future, to get them to worry about health and all that, to convince them that earthly consequences were at all important, that they should, in short, get their eyes checked.

'It's difficult,' he said, choosing words with care, 'but as democracy comes, and with it literacy, it gets easier. And it gets easier as the word spreads. A man who was blind last week and can see this week is a damned good advertisement, you know?

'But I don't want Nepal to change much. Already the art and the sculpture is worse than it was two hundred years ago. There is so much we must preserve, including those values we derive from being . . . a little poor, the great family feeling, the sense of dependence on each other. We must be developed in a way that fits all these things, and keeps them, and doesn't hurt them.'

2

The opening of the lens factory took place, among brass bands and mar-quees and microphones, in the space reclaimed the day before from the demolished brick wall, a few yards from the nodding marihuana, with the King observing Ruit operating (Ruit had the prickly feeling of Fred being in the room then, behind him, watching him work, one of the faces in masks behind him, vigilant, critical, surly, vociferous, ultimately, though grudgingly, approving) and the Prime Minister, who had himself been cured of cataract by the Hollows technique, speaking suddenly and mov-ingly, departing from his text, to Gabi on the stage beside him, of the enor-mity of Fred's loss and his greatness and how he shared her grief. But the day was oddly dry-eyed, Gabi serene and proud, Fred's two brothers Bruce and John, each of whom had lost a son to AIDS, jocular and buoyant and very Fred-like and buccaneering and ultimately drunk and all of his dis-ciples clustering in among the band music and the soft drink and the sodden finger food and the royal snobbery (Gabi has become a kind of royalty in Nepal too, as she has at home), all of the Hollows diaspora for-gathered for perhaps this one single time, rejoicing in his memory, such a recent memory, it seemed somehow longer since he died than a mere sixteen months, and all of them full of the kind of sharp, no-nonsense honesty of which he would have approved.

All agreed on his foul mouth, bad temper, lack of basic organisational skills, impatience, political ferocity (bawling out Bob Hawke to his face on the day he was made Australian of the Year), unreconstructed Marxism, residual Christianity, pioneering zeal, primitive humanism ('What is the patient's *name*?'), convivial companionship with gaolbirds and low-life and poets, intolerance of bureaucratic fools. David Moran recalled occasions in the surgery when Fred didn't know which eye, right or left, he was there to work on. 'He never went anywhere without an entourage,' he said, 'and an eyeball is a pretty small place to take an entourage.'

Mike Lynskey remembered how in one fearsome week Fred's brain tumour was operated on in Sydney on the Monday (laser treatment through holes bored in his head) and he flew to Hanoi on the Tuesday, and on the Tuesday afternoon faced down the entire Vietnamese medical establishment, told them they were doing it all wrong, they were bloody awful ophthal-mologists, and converted them, turned them right around in one visit, his only visit. That night Lynskey found him in his motel room with his singlet covered in blood, protesting he was all right, fuck off, there was work to do. Till his last four months his hand stayed steady on the operating table; full of carcinoma and radiation and breathlessness and pain-suppressants and occasionally whisky, this fierce, tough, tactless, driven man had the manual dexterity of a worker in silk tapestries to the very end. He was among other things, as recalled by Hugh Thomas, a tall bald ophthalmologist from Melbourne, a brilliant surgeon. He couldn't handle matches in the end, but after his medication he was back at the operating table, deft as ever.

Hugh remembered him at night in the Australian outback round a brightening campfire under the stars passing whisky round in a Johnny Walker bottle-top and talking, talking all night unsleeping about life, the universe, the world economy and what a man must do on earth for those he could help, how you could make a difference. 'A good man to go mountaineering with,' said Tim McCartney-Snape. 'In the end, a more than adequate conversationalist.'

Lynskey recalled protesting feebly when Fred stole a whole swag of medical equipment from Prince Alfred hospital and put it in the back of a truck. 'They're not going to arrest a dying man, Lynskey,' he rasped, and drove off at speed.

All agreed on his charisma, his capacity to inspirit others with a desire to follow him up a mountain and over the top and down the other side – the sort of childlike, bellicose, impatient charm that successful politicians have, the capacity to hypnotise and cleanse from the mind of the hearer all but his own priorities; I suppose it's leadership I mean by this. 'He was my elder brother,' said Ruit, 'my father, my teacher, my scourge. Hearing he had cancer of the kidneys, and knowing this was not a good cancer to have, was I think the worst moment of my life, and I wept then. Not when he died, because he had to, but when I first knew he was bound to die, and soon.'

A man aware, with humour, of what he was doing too, and how he seemed. 'God, sometimes, Lynskey,' and here his affectionate minder fell into a perfect gritty mimicry of the famous whisky voice, 'sometimes, some days I wish I didn't have to be outrageous. But that's my job.' A man who knew better than anyone what his imminent death meant, what it meant poetically and tactically, and what it meant as public relations, as politics, as legend. A brilliant career move, some said. It was a chance for him, and he seized it, to as it were run for office, and run hard. To use all the tricky and manipulative levers of politics – the interviews, the stunts, the public controversies, the Banjo Paterson readings, the angry shouting matches with the mighty of the earth, the vivid fraternisations with the wretched of the earth to achieve – and the words though true seemed inappropriate, too pretentious for Fred – a noble cause.

Sainthood is a funny thing I decided, back at the hostel looking at the famous propaganda photos of him in his half-moon spectacles and the withered old people with opaque eyes under his care, since Fred was a person I knew, though not well, for twenty odd years before he was renowned and someone I would not have picked in a pink fit as an Albert Schweitzer or a Jonas Salk of our time. And here it is happening. Already, as with Lenin, the theological disputes are beginning: did Fred really say that, or perhaps what he meant was, yes, he must've meant that, the Fred of my vision would never have said that, it must be a misquote.

And his stature is growing, almost daily. The Minister for Health in Vietnam, himself a former ophthalmologist, a tiny, impressive, tranquil man with war medals in a glass case in his minuscule office in Hanoi (he was a decorated hero of Dien Bien Phu), called Fred one of the most impressive men he had ever met, an acquaintance that included Ho Chi Minh. Fred lurched up to General Giap in a restaurant unintroduced and they were soon singing 'The Internationale' together and drinking heavily. These are not small tributes.

Nor is the esteem in which Australian ophthalmologists are now held in Nepal and throughout Asia. Les Douglas, the Australian ambassador in Kathmandu (now headed back to Canberra and hating the idea), is known as a genuine hero by the Nepalese, because he got the lens factory up and moving so fast. There is an Australian straightforwardness that appeals across the cultures (the Vietnamese unreservedly like Australians and, perhaps for historic reasons as well, unreservedly detest Americans) to people who also value honesty. The Hollows factory will soon be making other goods – CDs and surgical equipment, video cameras perhaps – and will soon be self-supporting within the capitalist system. None of this is trivial. None of it is temporary, or patronising. It is, in David Moran's words, the most unsordid partnership of West and East in, probably, two hundred years.

In his last year Fred would talk to Ruit about his fear of death. He had tubes sticking out of him and he'd say, 'Oh shit, I'm scared.' Sometimes he wanted a quick death and sometimes he wanted to live as long as possible, however painfully, because his work was important. He was an unbeliever, and bore no hope of heaven, even a Marxist one. From his youth, McCartney-Snape said, he was very much a mountaineer, with the ability such men have to live life in a raw state, face up to the void, to take fear like a drug and go through it. Ten days before his death, when he knew his time remaining was days not weeks, he was still reading the medical magazines and arguing about their contents, keeping up, while simultaneously organising his funeral. 'Don't let them turn me into a Catholic, Hardy,' he said to his Marxist old friend Frank Hardy. True to his word Frank used the mighty occasion to lecture from the rostrum of St Mary's Cathedral, thrillingly and hilariously (it was Frank's last major gig as well, and he sensed it), an audience that included Whitlam, Keating, Hawke, Howard and Hewson on their failure while in power to implement the communist revolution. Then Fred was buried in Broken Hill, among the grief and laughter of those Aboriginal companions he always felt so close to, people near the edge.

And that was that, a chapter over, a mountain climbed, a journey ended and a long sleep of the kind he rarely had in life. He was always up and about, thinking, planning, cat-napping, up again. Fred, who kept open house and fed whoever turned up, had may kinds of friends and many kinds of tributes when he died but one of the best I think was by the occasional poet and thoughtful eye surgeon David Moran, who in phlegmatic extremis wrote one night in Kathmandu, a lovely, sometimes frightening town:

> *I am in Kathmandu – alone. It is 3 a.m. It is*
> *dark. The power is out, as usual. There is a*
> *candle but no matches. My torch battery is*
> > *flat.*
> *It is very cold and quiet in my $10 hotel*
> > *room.*
>
> *I am sitting on the toilet in the blackness*
> *shivering. I have terrible diarrhoea, a*
> > *twisting*
> *wrenching griping diarrhoea. It seems likely I*
> *will vomit soon but my body's decision on this*
> > *is not yet final.*
>
> *There is no-one to comfort me or tell me I'm*
> > *not*
> *going to die. I want my mother but she is*
> > *dead.*
> *At least her spirit is close to me. I want*
> *my wife and children but they are far away.*
>
> *Don't worry David, it's all in a good cause.*
>
> *You bastard Hollows, you got me into this.*

August, 1994

Elsie at Eighty-six

My mother turns eighty-six this week. She has had two hip replacements and lives in her own house, *stay in your own house, Else*, all her friends, now dead, would say to her, *stay in your own house as long as you can*, and she moves on a walking stick from room to room cooking, vacuuming, keeping it clean.

A nephew and his family live in the town, and they visit. Her oldest girlfriend Jean is eighty-seven and is a thousand kilometres away, but they see each other often and talk a lot on the phone. Nurses who are friends now come each day and her neighbours are superb in the way that country town people are and caring. I see her four times a year and one of her grand-daughters (and her great-grandson) is moving soon to a beachside place near her. She still occasionally drives to town and a loving neighbour, Wal Buckley, helps out.

She has a life. She watches the TV in her bedroom, listens to Macca, reads biographies, talks on the phone and sleeps a good deal. Her house has a sunlit view and a garden she is proud of. She misses her husband Keith, my dad, who died in 1989, and she still counts the birthdays of her daughter Margaret who was killed in 1953 when she was twenty-two. Margaret would be sixty-five now, and a grandmother probably too. Mum is aware that she has, or had, a lot of cousins in Parkes, where both her parents came from, and wishes she had sought them out. Her ancestors came to Australia in the 1810s and it's a pity to lose touch. Her siblings, Edna, Minnie, Harry and Covey, all are dead and there is no-one much any more to write her lovely copperplate letters to. Her mind remains unimpaired and her memory keen, and she loves our phone calls, and her grandchildren's voices. *Mustn't keep you, this is costing you money.*

She and Keith bought the house, new built in 1946, when he came back from six years of war and she left her mother's house (at last) at thirty-four. He built the garage and the verandah extensions, an aviary for me and Kay, a chookyard, a toolshed, a storeroom. We kept budgies for a while, a wallaby, a sheep, a kelpie mongrel, Rover, and lots of cats and had visiting friends always sleeping over. We both had bikes and would ride long miles over surrounding green hills and ride to school at Lismore High.

There are lots of memories in the house, *keep your own house, Else*, but of course she'll have to sell it now, or soon. She hates the thought, and so do I. Selling their houses destroyed her sister Edna and her old friend Dot when they went into nursing homes. There was no longer the sustaining fantasy of a house to return to and they soon wilted and despaired, and died. *Keep your own house, Else.*

But the mathematics are such that she will have to sell it. She has $14 000 in the bank and the house is worth $160 000 probably, and the entrance fee to a good nursing home won't be under $50 000, wait and see. She'll have to sell it. And have nowhere to dream of coming home to.

The New Mathematics. Where did they come from?

Else remembers the casualty lists of the First World War. She remembers the funeral processions of the Great Flu Epidemic of 1919 going past her house in Murwillumbah, and the horsedrawn ambulances up to the hospital, the dead and dying. She survived the Depression, which ended Keith's banana farm, and the Second World War and his years in the Air Force, the death of one child and the moving away of two others, one a thousand kilometres, one two thousand, and the death of Keith, and if the purpose of life is to remember, she deserves her memories, her small green patch of life on earth, and this government is taking them from her soon and that's not right. She deserves better, and so does her generation. They have suffered enough. They paid their taxes when taxes were high and they went to war when their country called them and they went to Changi and to hell and back and they lost their brothers and husbands and copped it sweet and they have suffered enough.

I love that house. The bed I slept in as a boy is still there, and the lowboy beside it and the pawpaw tree. My daughter Jenny might have lived in it when she went, as is her plan, to Southern Cross University. My dreams take place in that house, and the view from its back verandah is part of my mind.

I can distort my young family's life by paying to keep it, of course, I have that choice, *good to have a choice in life*, to ease Mum's lonely exit from the world. I can take my kids out of their chosen schools or put Mum into a noisome concentration camp, four beds to a room and bullying staff and lots of moaning in the night, and thereby save the house, her dreaming, from oblivion and strangers' hands. No-one should have to make choices like that. There are old people I know who will kill themselves rather than make it. And old people you know.

What a mean and cold-eyed government this is, tormenting the weak (the blacks, the kids, the arriving migrants, the single mothers) in their extremity, blaming them for the Black Holes of the entrepreneurs and the bad arithmetic of the tax department. And for what? To impress four sadomonetarists in Moody's with our Economic Correctness (as if such people mattered) and the slavishly balanced budget of a country now *therefore* paying foreign companies for its local phone calls? To defend our shores with hourly obsolescing bombers and submarines at a cost of $10 billion a year against invaders no-one can name? To avoid at all costs the bleeding obvious, which is one per cent off every department's budget, this year, next year and the next year, which would put it all into massive surplus by 1999?

Ask any economist.

No, don't bother. It won't make any difference. They prefer the cruelty. They must. When you look at the figures, there is no other explanation.

They should lay off my mum at least, and her generation. This wasn't the deal they signed when they paid in good faith their taxes in the thirties, forties, fifties and sixties. They've paid enough. They've suffered enough. They've battled enough. And it isn't fair.

February, 1997

Love

> *What is love? 'Tis not hereafter;*
> *Present mirth hath present laughter;*
> *What's to come is still unsure:*
> *In delay there lies no plenty;*
> *Then come kiss me, sweet and twenty,*
> *Youth's a stuff will not endure.*

A plausible theory I read once (in Penelope Lively's slim sweet novel *According to Mark*) is that love is a virus that passes like the flu. It infects, takes hold, brings night sweats, is treated, subsides and at last is gone.

This seems to me to fit all instances, in youth and age. But so too does the theory that love never dies, but returns in a kind of glowing flashback every seven years or so, and can be enjoyed again for a night, a week, exactly as it was.

Love fits a lot of definitions. The best I know (from *The Reader's Digest 1955*) is 'fullness of response'. This allows it, as it must, to change, transform itself, in an hour or so, into hate, stalking, pursuit, a suicide pact, a murder. It evokes too that claustrophobic enclosedness, that hot obsessiveness, best seen in Hitchcock's *Vertigo*, or in Shakespeare's poison sonnet on the troubling adjacent subject of lust.

Th' expense of spirit in a waste of shame
Is lust in action; and till action, lust
Is perjured, murderous, bloody, full of blame,
Savage, extreme, rude, cruel, not to trust;
Enjoyed no sooner, but despised straight:
Past reason hunted; and no sooner had,
Past reason hated, as a swallowed bait,
On purpose laid to make the taker mad:
Mad in pursuit, and in possession so;
Had, having, and in quest to have, extreme;
A bliss in proof, and proved, a very woe;
Before, a joy proposed; behind, a dream.
All this the world well knows; yet none knows well
To shun the heaven that leads men to this hell.

The sexual component of love seems mostly to presage its undoing: Hamlet spurns Ophelia, mocks her, bids her go to a nunnery once he has bedded her ('I did love you once.' 'Indeed, my Lord, you made me believe so.'). Michael Douglas in *Fatal Attraction* satisfies himself, then is haunted and stalked by a kind of disease that will not go away. That most erotic of films, *Betty Blue*, starts with a vivid, limbs-clenched consummation, then goes on to chart a nightmare, as the hero finds the beloved is mad.

Love without sex as a rule is better, or seems so in retrospect. One girl I loved first when I was sixteen – if loved is the word – and took out, courted, proposed to, met again, courted again, for seven years, I found in Canada in 1968 and got at last to bed in Toronto. And because the relationship was built on a kind of hovering pleasured incompleteness – a kiss, a fumble, an intense long talk at night by Bondi Beach – once pushed to its logical end it was soon, in another year, over. Love is best in youth *because* of all that incompleteness. The boy in *Cinema Paradiso* who waits for ninety-nine nights beneath the window of his beloved to the music of Morricone best reminds us of what it was like, and the heart soars and tingles.

Oh do not call it love though thousands praise
These primy thoughts of thee on edge of sleep
That fill with naked thees my hidden ways
And mock me like so many counted sheep.
Oh do not call it love though I do sing
Archangel-sweet of slumbering on thy breast
And half-convert the nations of the West

To worship at thine icon in the Spring.
Oh do not call it love and do not weep
Though I do plunge the world five fathoms deep
In adoration of thy bridal trove
For love requires a giving back to keep
The barren age at bay in one joint sleep;
And lacking that, oh do not call it love.

The above, amazingly, was written by me – in imitation, I suppose, of Shakespeare or Donne – to an unhad beloved, still unhad, when I was young. I had long thought it burnt but it turned up, and there it is. It's a measure of what fruitfulness comes with unconsummation, what sweet sorrow. It's a measure, too, of what it was like for us who are old now when, in our youth, the *custom* was unconsummation, and yearning, and letters, and phone calls with long pauses, and lingering on the doorstep, or those comic half measures in the front seat of the car that we saw with such glum recognition in *The Last Picture Show*, that best film of what it was like in the fifties. *Behave now. All that can wait till after we're married. Aw, Emmy Lou . . .*

Love is a word that covers too many meanings, too many, as the novelist might say, wild shores of the heart. The Inuit have, I think, twenty-eight different words for different *kinds* of snow, but no one word for snow as a generality, and it were best for us if we had more words for different loves, and none for the generality.

There is puppy love, and carnal love, and shipboard passing love, and old love returning (Rick and Ilsa in *Casablanca*, Beatrice and Benedick in *Much Ado*), the love of pets, the love of brothers, the love of grandchildren, and these need no explaining. There is love unconsummate in old age between a widow and a widower, finding and looking after one another in their last extremity. There is enduring love between those who dwell together, and have children together, and go through buffetings and trials together, bonding (as the dull word is) into that super-loyalty that is wedlock, married life. There is the love of a mother for a baby at the breast. *That* is fullness of response. That is greater love than all. She will turn her back to the bullet to shield her baby. She will do it instinctively.

A great unspoken fact of love I think is its situationality, its proneness and vulnerability to geography. As a student you share digs or a tutorial group with someone, and you see them often, and soon you are in love. An arranged marriage of the Greek or Jewish kind grows eventually, ineluctably, in a shared house with children, into something like love. To spend time with someone – to go, for instance, on a camping trip with them, or a sailing trip, or even a train journey – is to begin, somehow, to love them. To know a person is to love them. You cannot stay forever bonded to the girl who left for England eight years ago, and writes a letter now and then. She has to be here, or you have to be there, in the room. You have to engage.

Is love replaceable then? I think so. I have seen too many pleasured widowhoods, in my aunties, in my mother (whose great love, Wal, died on Monday night), to think that anything else is true. When asked the difficult question of who of a widow's three dead husbands will be her husband in heaven, Jesus of Nazareth, giving it up, said there will be no marriage in heaven. It improved the religion's popularity immensely, I imagine – beyond the pearly gates, the orgy. But what else could there be. Each new love was true, and it passed into death, and was replaced.

Since the publication of the first Lancelot–Guinevere stories in the thirteenth century we have been obsessed with stories of adulterous love, and this leads me to believe (and I have no proof) that at least as a *yearning* it is an almost universal fact in married lives. For David and Bathsheba, for Antony and Cleopatra, for even Henry VIII's long, seven-year quest for the enjoyment of Anne Boleyn, there is a sympathy in women readers that suggests at least a knowledge, a participative dreaming of the dangerous chase that shows what we loosely give the name of love to be more promiscuous, more adventurous, more game than some in pulpits and courts would have it, and there is a lot of it about (prove that I lie), and much enjoyed and contemplated, and much in old age remembered, and as Yeats put it, in 'When You Are Old':

When you are old and grey and full of sleep,
And nodding by the fire, take down this book,
And slowly read, and dream of the soft look
Your eyes had once, and of their shadows deep;

How many loved your moments of glad grace,
And loved your beauty with love false or true,
But one man loved the pilgrim soul in you,
And loved the sorrows of your changing face;

And bending down beside the glowing bars,
Murmur, a little sadly, how Love fled
And paced upon the mountains overhead
And hid his face amid a crowd of stars.

May, 1999

23

Ancestors

A broadcast

Over Christmas I learned, because I finally asked of my mother in her caravan in her eighty-seventh year, a little of my forebears Percy Ward and Margaret Clark, who married in Parkes in 1897 and eventually begot my mother in Lismore in 1911. They each of them had eleven siblings and in Parkes their families, the Wards and the Clarks, were known to each other as neighbouring clans as far back as the 1850s.

When, however, Margaret and Percy, my grandparents, left Parkes for Lismore in 1910, they saw precious little of their twenty-two brothers and sisters ever again. My grandfather visited his mother once a year, but on her death his pilgrimages ceased, and my grandmother, by contrast, never saw her eleven brothers and sisters, most of whom she loved, from 1911 till her death in 1959. I grew up within reach of all her family, two aunties and an uncle, six cousins and a younger uncle's grave, in Murwillumbah and Lismore, people you could walk down the street and stay with for a week if you liked.

But then I moved to Sydney, a further dispiriting exile from Murwillumbah, which was an exile from Parkes, which was an exile from London, and far from home, far from that good village whose beckoning window light we all of us hitchhike towards, in dream, in dark, forever in vain. My mother had a hundred cousins in Parkes that she never met, and my wife, who comes from Melbourne and lives in Sydney, has a sister and mother in Adelaide she sees every two years, and a brother in Perth she sees, on the average, every five years, the $500 return fare being too great a price on love.

This tragedy of familial estrangement – all the lost intimates we might so easily have had, and kept, and cherished and laughed with and wept with and dined with down the years of an unending saga of blood ties and family scandals and Christmas dinners and disputed wills and black sheep and school medals and overcrowded funerals with the same nose all round the room – is lost in the Australian diaspora of unendurable distance, and so much kin knowledge with it, and so much convivial enjoyment – go ask your uncle, he knows about these things – as my children are having this week with their Perth cousins, who are of similar ages and whom they barely know.

Australia, at the start of its present chapter a land of convict exile, has a lot of internal suburban exile too, a lot of little Siberias far from love, and it is the common tragedy of *almost* all of us that, in Sandy Stone's immortal mutter, 'You know, there are people you love and you never see them, and there are people you can't stand, and you see them all the time.' In a country where Sydney is as far from Perth as Dublin is from Teheran, and Hobart is as far from Darwin as Cairo is from Copenhagen, it could hardly be otherwise.

No government has ever addressed this loss and this derangement of gene pool unique, I think, to Australia, in the way it should – with, say, free train travel or free petrol or free phone calls one day a week, and we are all of us exiles now, each of us a stranger in a far land, wearing out his welcome in the prison of his days, amid alien tribes, learning new manners, catching up. No-one writes, and phone calls are few, and school reunions disaster areas because too long delayed, the shimmering distances taunt our exile from the towns and folk we loved, and all our lives become, in this tyranny of time and space, unfinished business there, and here, and where we go to meet.

Home, said Robert Frost, is where, when you have to go there, they have to take you in. It sounds pretty wonderful to me.

January, 1997

The Irish Potato Famine

A Radio National broadcast

The memory of Ireland is long and long, and lavishly reiterated in pubs and in song and if in their memorious reckoning the Battle of the Boyne was yesterday at noon, the potato blight and the potato famine and the consequent migration across the planet of a sad and glorious and angry nostalgic people and their jokes and their claddach rings and their wakes and tin whistles began at ten past four this morning and are still going on as day draws in.

There were nine million Irish in Ireland in 1841. There are four million now – less now and throughout this century than the population of Sydney, and there are five million Irish or their descendants in the city of New York. Some that left were Keatings, and some Kennedys, and Reagans and Richardsons and Breretons and Carrs and Beazleys and Faheys and Mc-Clellands and Murphys and Kellys and Bourkes and Gairs and Chifleys, and Dalys and Youngs and Langs and Lawrences and Calwells and Cullens and Shanahans and . . . so on. Without the blight we would not be what we are, and nor would the world.

The potato famine lies deeply buried, encased, cut off, in the English memory, much like the million poisoned Aborigines in Australian memory, or the lost Apache and Navaho hordes of North America. Numberless hundreds of thousands died because a subject people ruled by absent English landlords and deprived of the soil they had tilled for millennia and living now in hovels, disenfranchised of right and religion and language, and working small peasant holdings and raising families of fifteen were then deprived of the one thing, the potato, they could survive on, and given no succour by the English – forbidden, in fact, at gunpoint the harvest wheat they had sown and grown and reaped for the English year after year, and unable on a wage of ninepence a week to buy it – they died like flies. There are bombs blowing up buses because of this in London even now, as the day draws in, and rightly so.

Such was the trauma of the migration and exile that followed, worse than the Babylonian exile of the Hebrews, worse and further and more numerous and murderous, that even now it is usual for Australian Irish *not* to want to go back, the ancestral dreams are too terrible to walk among again. There is a great wound in their history that they dare not revisit lest the tears become unstoppable and the anger homicidal, and rightly so.

A man deprived of his country may turn to drink, and this has occurred. He may obsessively embrace or re-embrace his persecuted religion, and this has occurred. He may rigorously invade and reorganise local politics, or the larger politics of his new found land, and this has occurred. He may give himself over to song and sorrow and womanising and lengthy confessional and literature and grief and Guinness and the murmuring name upon name in his cups and his dreams of heroes and martyrs – Emmet, Wolfe Tone, Parnell, Michael Collins, Bobby Sands – and this has occurred. A man deprived of his country may do many things but the one thing he may not do is forget. And Ireland's memory is long and long.

And a hundred and fifty years down the track a man begotten of the loins of Galway is calling, as did Ned Kelly, and his political sire Jack Lang is calling for an Australian republic, and a man begotten of Kentish England is opposing it, or wittering *not yet.* And thus the whirligig of time brings in his revenges, or some revenges, and history is shaped and takes its form. The vegetable microbe *Phytophthora infestans* casts a long shadow, and the people it might have ruined roved the earth, and changed it for the better.

Day draws in, the IRA are back, and the story, and the great aching song, continues.

February, 1993

Shakespeare in Bowral

I went down to Bowral a month ago and experienced over two pleasured weekends a part, not all, of the Shakespeare Festival there. *King Lear* in Corbett Gardens. *Hamlet* in a Mittagong gymnasium (with a resurrected naked Ophelia slowly drenched in blood at evening's end). A grunting and eye-bulging Samurai in a version of *Macbeth* called *Crown of Blood*. A beautiful green-shaded BBC *Twelfth Night* and Al Pacino's rough-cast Richard III in the Empire Cinema. Matthew O'Sullivan's enthralling meditation *Shakespeare's Journey* in the Federation church where the young Don Bradman sang high and sweet once in the choir. Trefor Gare's pratfalling monodrama *The King's Player* (part Stoppard, part Marceau, part circus clown) in, yes, the Bradman Museum. *Shakespeare, Shylock and Hanson* (the trial scene, with brutish redneck interruptions) in a farmyard corral. *The Sonnets* in gentle erotic duet in a stately house among green hills. Tim Page's brash cabaret *From Bard to Broadway* (the modern songs and comedy routines, like those in *Kiss Me Kate*, derived from Shakespeare in tumbling bawdy collage). A fresh, arousing *Taming of the Shrew* in the park, round the Springett cupola, under southern stars . . .

I had a terrific time, although I missed *The Musicke* and *The Proposal Scenes* and *A Great Reckoning in a Little Room*, a suspense drama on Marlowe's murder, and although every uttered line I heard was at least half known to me I never once nodded off, or even yawned.

A few things should be said.

One is that the architecture of Bowral – Victorian, Federation, Georgian sandstone, its autumn parks and white picket fences and art deco coffee houses and pensive bookshops and melancholy churchyards and weeping-willowy creekbanks – makes a celebration of great poetic writing possible in a way that the concrete-and-fibro structures of, say, Penrith or Kogarah, and their seedy neon streets, cannot.

This in turn means, of course, that the Economic Rationalists (and it's not, I think, too long a bow to draw), who regard all such elaborate architectural display, with its wasteful scrolls and columns, as culpably extravagant, are, as always, wrong again. Because Bowral shows not only that money can be generated by aesthetic pleasure and architectural beauty but also (not that such things matter any more) by human joy and civic pride. (Extravagance, indeed, nearly always brings, with tourism, riches once unimagined, discuss: I cite the Taj Mahal and the Sistine Chapel – and the Big Pineapple – and rest my case.)

And so in Bowral, too, there will soon be galleries and theme parks and costume exhibitions and Shakespeare Summer Schools and an actors' academy and, yes, *jobs for young people* as ushers and scene shifters and cleaners when the mines and cement works and slaughterhouse close for good and the drought-seared farms are cut up in blocks for sale as nouveau suburbs. There is money, in short, in snob standards and the brandishing of high culture and, as the tourism figures for Rome, Stratford, Bayreuth yearly show, there always was. And the Economically Correct are wrong, as always; they who would for sure have made Will downsize his plays to three characters, or two. *Caesar and Brutus and Antony. Why any more? Hamlet and Claudius, with Claudius doubling as the Ghost. Why any more? Save money. Save money.*

The second thing that should be said (and *asked*) is why he is *genuinely* popular and not just snob-popular (watch the little kids in the park who run around at interval but when the play is on sit silently absorbed). One theory is that he has only one theme; and it's the most universal theme there is.

This is that we are each of us given a role, and it's a role that we fail to play very well, and tragedy (or farce) ensues. Thus Hamlet, an adequate moody student, is a poor avenging assassin. Brutus, an adequate moody philosopher, is a poor coup leader. Lear an adequate anointed king but a poor elder statesman. Macbeth a good serving soldier but a disastrous usurping murderer. Viola a poor boy. Malvolio an able butler but a fatuous gallant wooer. Othello a brilliant field marshal but an over-watchful spouse and the too-trusting boss (like Whitlam) of his crafty lieutenant. Falstaff a jovial tavern roisterer but a raucous, unwelcome palace consultant. Orlando a superb wrestler but a fat-headed love sonneteer. And so on. Shakespeare revives our pained memories of being made to stand up in class and recite, or sing on stage, or catch a football and run for the tryline with it, in vain. The terror. The shame. The crowd's catcalls. *Oh that this too too solid flesh would melt. Howl, howl, howl . . .*

There's a third thing that should be said, and it's this. Shakespeare not only had the largest vocabulary of any good English writer, he also had the biggest *emotional* vocabulary, and his work is a gigantic trove of emotions that, but for him, we might not now still know of, nor feel so keenly even yet. Courtly love. The love, not necessarily homosexual, of man for man. The scalding, envenomed love of old lovers when they meet again. The radiant sorrows of kingship. That sense of honour that is worth dying for, by one's own hand. Ambition that will dare all, defying the gods. Young love so strong it must, like Juliet's, end in death. The love of a man like Antony for a dead ally he must bloodily avenge. The desire to howl and curse under bad weather. The welling fear of madness in oneself and others. The guilts that materialise as ghosts over dinner.

And so on. The list is large; he gave us a Sistine-size canvas of emotions that without his word music might now be lost to us, a tonal range of emotional melody we might be otherwise deaf to. It's fair to say I think (and this is not a long bow either) that people unacquainted with Shakespeare live starved and meagre lives.

Some schools would ban him for political incorrectness, but they miss the point, which is that with his great enlargements of those fitful things we sometimes feel – in the cool of the night, in the stirrings of youth, the carps and cursings of age – he maps and enumerates our species as no other. No politician, and no businessman, who evades or ignores him is worthy of his trade. And no human being that lives without him, and his majestic illuminations of our life on earth, lives well.

April, 1998

The Stolen Children

From Lindsay's voters by the end of the week we might know better, perhaps, which things are those that matter in white working-class Australia, and if jobs, tolls, teeth, tax, health, Short, Skase, guns, euthanasia and broken promises outweigh the stolen victory of Jackie Kelly and the rumour of Asian tuberculosis, and if the rise in racist incidents across Australia is, in political terms, of no account.

Or if what Senator Herron and Wilson Tuckey said twelve days ago is resented, applauded, or even remembered. Twelve days is a long, long time.

Some Aborigines were fortunate, they said, to be taken as babies from their grieving mothers and raised in white culture, and sent to white schools far from their grubby origins.

Well, it may be so. It's a possible scenario. It stacks up. Had Azaria Chamberlain, likewise, been kidnapped at birth her eventual fate – alive, in the care of adoring captors – would have been quite different too.

This might have been what happened. She might have been taken that night, from the tent in which her brothers lay deeply sleeping, by person or persons unknown, with the nearby foraging dingo (if there was one) a cruel coincidence. She might have been happily raised by now, be sixteen and relaxed and bright and bubbly, like my daughter, Jenny, who was born a day before her, far from Adventist grimness, a happy child. (I grew up an Adventist, and I know how narrow and threatening that cast of mind can be.)

So what is wrong with this plausible scenario? Of a child, though kidnapped, happy and cared for? Living another, different kind of life?

For the child, perhaps, not much. For the *parents*, though, it involves a level of suffering unimaginable by anyone who has not been through it. Never knowing where she is. Never knowing what happened. Not knowing what she looks like. Or what her children look like. Or what her name is now. Had Lindy that legendary night cried out instead, 'My baby! Somebody's taken my baby!', that would have been her fate, and Michael's fate.

I know something of what this is like. My sister Margaret was killed and our surviving family, blaming and counter-blaming, and sobbing far into the night, *Marg, Marg, Marg,* and standing by her grave each weekend, was broken to pieces and never reassembled. But losing a live child to unknown abductors is, I imagine, worse.

Some Aboriginal mothers lost suckling babies to forced adoption. Some, like Lois O'Donoghue's mother, had other children, and they were stolen too. Some had to face astonished husbands who came home and found their adored babies gone. *Why didn't you look after her, woman? Why didn't you fight?* Husbands who then drank heavily and beat them night after night. *Where's my baby? Where's my little baby, you bitch?*

All kidnappers of children believe the child will be better off with them. It is what such people do. I myself have often wished that children I've seen ill-used by ignorant parents could come with me. But it's not my *right*. It's not my right to take them. Deep in the human spirit is a belief – irrational perhaps, economically irrational for sure – that if you bear a child and push him through your loins into the world, you have a right to keep him and watch him grow and know what he looks like. It's hard to justify but that's the way it is. We call it human nature.

Lois O'Donoghue grew up in an institution that also, in another building, eventually housed her mother. Her keepers knew the relationship and made sure they never met lest Lois be infected by a godless, heathen heritage. They met when she was in her twenties – and they spoke different languages.

(Yet Senator Herron says she was fortunate. And Senator Herron is an honourable man.)

This process of ethnic cleansing, the ethnic cleansing of kidnapped babies by people of good Christian conscience determined to exterminate Aboriginality from children of mixed blood, distorted the lives of 100 000 children in the 1920s and the 1930s – when Hitler was dealing with his ethnic problem rather more straightforwardly – and in the 1940s and 1950s, when I was a boy, but it also did a good bit more. It engulfed and shattered and poisoned and shortened the lives of their 200 000 parents, their 100 000, maybe, surviving grandparents, and their communities and their cultural pride.

It is the common quality of racists to believe they are not racist. They think they are merely being realistic, or rational, or scientific – easing a culture bound to die out anyway into its inevitable oblivion. Inculcating proper Western values into those who, without them, are only sad parasites. Locking them up for their own good. They drink. They fight. They can't hold their liquor. It's a scientific fact. They would benefit from being brought up in another place, in a good Catholic orphanage, and not be tainted by a savage culture.

It was in just this way that reputable scientists once thought Jews were Neanderthals. And Japanese genetically bandy-legged and unable to see at night. And the black slaves of *Gone-With-The-Wind* America cheery smiling halfwits unable to cope unaided with white man's freedom.

One vast construct, the British Empire, was built on thoughts like these. From a likewise racist construct, the Third World, flow many kindred thoughts, as we daily bombard its often happier communities with that mindless jackal avarice that has made of the West an ethical quicksand and urban America, each night, a civil war. Racism is more common than you think, and in London and Jerusalem and Rwanda, as in Surfers Paradise, its abusive cries are heard and its fists are out and ready.

Racism is not just political incorrectness. It is war.

It's hurting Australia now, and the damage done is building swiftly – and only when Nelson Mandela (for instance) declares he is taking his country out of our Olympic Games or the first honeymooning Japanese is kicked to death by a teenage gang on a Sydney street will we see how cruel and wrong it is.

There used, for instance, to be five million Aborigines, probably, in 1788, when Governor Phillip came. Pauline Hanson seems to think there are still too many. *If it's their country*, she cries, *where do I go?*

If we keep up the good work, I guess, there'll be none of them left very soon and we, and she, can relax and be comfortable.

And it's not of great value, our Prime Minister has said, to talk very much any more of the Stolen Children. It was all a long time ago. And there's very little we can do about it now. Much as Mr Netanyahu might say *there's not much point now in dredging up the Holocaust. It was all a long time ago, and we can't bring back the dead.* Or Bruce Ruxton might now say *forget about Gallipoli. It was such a long time ago.* Or President Clinton might say *Gettysburg? Schmettysburg. A regrettable old schemozzle, best forgotten.*

That's if they were political morons, they might. Or racists. Racists being those (let's say it) who would never compare an Aboriginal tragedy to a white one. People like you and me.

Because racism never knows itself and it lives in the silence as well as the noise. And it's everywhere we look, and read, and hear. Everywhere around us, on beaches and streets and country roads, and wherever ordinary people meet and have drinks and murmur of things in general. Murmur and then begin shouting.

And I am today at last ashamed to be Australian.

How about you?

October, 1996

On the Punishment of Paedophiles

Things said by Franca Arena and things done by David Yeldham in the past week of our national history go to the heart of how we live, and speak, and punish one another in a democracy.

Declaring my interest, I had a brush with paedophilia in recent years. It involved a cricket coach of young boys, one of them my son, who police revealed was having affairs (if that's the right phrase) with several pubescent boys, to their parents' rage and anguish, and who ended in gaol serving three years and in some danger of being beaten to death one summer evening by moralistic fellow prisoners. I knew him socially and liked him, had him in my house and found out eventually that he'd made a pass at – and been rebuffed by – my tall, handsome son, who thereafter lost all interest in cricket, a game that was for a while his religion; a small loss perhaps, perhaps not. And while I know this man did awful things to vulnerable youngsters, distorting the lives of some, perhaps forever, I also believe he does not deserve to be beaten to death, or raped and given AIDS, or whatever the current, unspoken penal custom is. That seems too harsh.

I may be wrong. But in all our debates of recent years – on racial vilification and sexual harassment and marital rape and the defrauding of the nation by offshore companies of billions – there has always been a lot of emphasis given to the concept of *crime*, and what it is, and who is guilty of it, but little about the concept of *punishment*.

Do this exercise. Imagine a middle-aged male member of your extended family. Imagine he is a paedophile. Imagine he has done life-long harm to, say, two young men. Now prescribe his prison sentence.

I do not believe this is easy.

Part of the reason is the suspicion present in all of us that the paedophilic impulse is not, in the end, easily controllable. That it may be something that comes like a virus, and goes, and comes again unbidden and is no more the bearer's *fault* than influenza or genital herpes or certain kinds of schizophrenia. And that there is, therefore, no appropriate *punishment* for it except perhaps a year of home detention with an electronic bracelet and counselling in depth. Or something of that order.

There is as well the feeling that the one word paedophilia is a black hole that contains too many things. For it can mean, on the one hand, the repeated penetration of an eight-month-old girl whose bowel function is thereafter forever deranged or, on the other hand, giving oral sex on Mardi Gras night to a young man in rouge and feathers who proves upon constabulary interrogation to be seventeen years and eight months old. It can also cover the sort of boarding school romance long celebrated in literature of a lonely boy and a sensitive teacher who opens his mind, *while no doubt also behaving improperly*, to music, art and life's possibilities. The kind of relationship extolled by Oscar Wilde in the dock in a speech for a while applauded but now no longer. And a hundred years after the hounding to death of Oscar Wilde by English hypocrisy, the verdict now would be the same. The boy was under-age. Gaol the pervert. Burn his books in the public square.

(Gaol too and burn the later works of Socrates and Michelangelo and Leonardo and Shakespeare and Marlowe and Byron and Strachey and Coward and Rattigan and Isherwood and Auden and Chaplin and Waugh and Greene and Tennessee Williams and Errol Flynn and Brendan Behan and – yes – Frank Thring and Donald Friend and Stuart Challender and Peter Allen and John F. Kennedy. They stand condemned. Their partners, I imagine, sometimes were under-age.)

There may be a system of punishment – and we should quickly find out what it is – that covers the different gradations of sexual crime, from the drunken rape of an eight-year-old daughter on the night of one's retrenchment from a job of last resort, to a brief, well-paid encounter with a male prostitute aged seventeen in Manila, or a grope on a beach by a sixteen-year-old boy at a fifteen-year-old girl. There may be such a system, but one thing is certain: the present practised system of capital punishment by parliamentary libel and Royal Commission vagueness is not good enough.

I once gave a speech to the Evatt Foundation, at some political cost, on what I called Sexual McCarthyism; the meaning is self-evident. As in the 1950s, it now requires, in the 1990s, the mere public naming of a person in a context of sinister allegation to ruin him or her for life. No detailed proof is required to achieve this end, no crime of great substance either. The brushing of the nipples of two freshettes while dancing at a college ball will do, or jogging in a park with a person of criminal record; and ruin surely follows – before the trial, before the verdict, before the policeman's knock at the door. The stain will not be washed off, by all the waters of the rough rude sea. Your name has been spoken; the bone has been pointed. Your only proper response to the bone is to kill yourself and leave a note of decorous apology, or to give yourself up to violence in Long Bay, where sticks and stones will break your bones and names will really hurt you.

This, as a system of crime and punishment – no, let's call it sin and punishment – is *disproportionate* surely, like the stoning to death under Mosaic law of those caught picking flowers on a Sunday.

There should surely be in all of this a question of *harm done*, the most important question. For just as a drunken driver may one night kill a pedestrian or may miss him by inches, and is therefore punished in accordance with the harm he has done, so surely should a sexual offender be punished in a way that reflects harm done. If he has provably made frigid or otherwise distorted lifelong the emotional development of a prepubescent girl once under his power, then fair enough, there's a powerful argument for giving him years and years. But if, on the other hand, he has merely added an amusing anecdote to an adolescent life that is full of other event – or, as in the case of Blanche D'Alpuget, an arousing half-romantic episode of some remembered pride – go easy on him. Just a little easy.

Let him who is without sin, as a famous Nazarene associate of prostitutes known as Jesus ben Joseph once said, *cast the first stone.* To which a notorious paedophilic spreader of fatal venereal disease, William Shakespeare, once pensively added, *Use all of us 'gainst our deserts and who should 'scape whipping?* Not too many of us. *Romeo Montague, I hereby arrest you for the crime and mortal sin of the sexual penetration under the age of consent of one Juliet Capulet, thirteen, of Verona W4 . . .* Give us a break.

And give ordinary varying humanity a chance.

November, 1996

Kids These Days

I have a twenty-year-old son and an eighteen-year-old daughter, and among their friends are some of the finest people I know. Their stoicism, their grace, their humour, the wily courage with which they have greeted the stacked deck that history has dealt them, undercuts any pride or smugness I might have, because they are better people.

I had a choice of careers, and they have none of that. I knew if I quit a job on Friday I could certainly have, if I wanted it, another job on Monday week – I did this twice – and to them this is inconceivable. I knew I could strive in my life to do the kind of work that suited me, and I had a fair chance of getting that kind of work, and to them that is a preposterous fantasy. I knew I would certainly make enough money to buy a house and raise a family and put them through university, and they dare not even think of that.

And yet they look forward, with a kind of joshing hope, to the one life they will have on this earth, in an era not of their choosing. They look forward to, at best, an uncertain series of part-time jobs in different parts of the world and an abiding *hobby* – in music, surfing, writing, ecological protest, iridology, fly-fishing, late-night conversation, romantic love – that will give their existence meaning for a decade or two, and then who knows? Perhaps they will own a few acres then, and will be growing and sharing radishes when the Great Bust comes. Perhaps they will be busking. Perhaps, at last, the song they wrote this year will be a hit, or the computer game they are still perfecting, or the better beer they are hoping to brew by then. Or perhaps they will be starving, or dead of chemical misadventure, but ... them's the breaks.

If courage is grace under pressure, they have it. They have done their 110 job interviews, and have been turned down. They have dressed up, and pretended, and come away rejected, and had a drink and got up the next morning. They have auditioned for NIDA, and narrowly missed. They have mixed martinis in a boutique bar that soon went broke. They have fossicked for gold beyond Kalgoorlie and found none.

And now we are lecturing them on Mutual Obligation: they must be thrilled with that. For they have put in the hard yards, in thirteen years of imprisonment in schools in crowded classrooms with overworked teachers, in obsolescent courses that led nowhere. They believed us when we told them this misery meant, at the end of it, fulfilment in life. A job. A career. A family. Continuity. Hope of personal triumph. And now they have done the 110 job interviews, and found we were lying. At least one half of that Mutual Obligation is ours, and we have not delivered. And they do not trust us any more, or believe anything that we are saying. And why should they? We have told them lies.

I love these young people and their courage and their grace, but I know now, having watched them, that we are losing more and more of them year by year – to drink, to heroin, to a kind of rootless euphoria that keeps them hitch-hiking with a surfboard, a guitar, a smoking habit, a dream of the Good Place they will not find. To the sullenness that follows thwarted love. To the crazier political movements. To sudden bursts of petty crime and AIDS in gaol. To suicide in the spare room of a friend.

And part of our Mutual Obligation is to understand that this is not their fault. Illiteracy is at least in part the fault of the bad schools we have given them, or of moving from school to school as their parents lose their jobs and move on. Lack of career ambition is at least in part the fault of us not giving them any real hope of career, as I once knew it, or of choice of work, as I once knew it. The accusing finger points, and it points at us.

Or it points at those economic fashions that are ripping all hope from the modern world – and restoring slavery under the usual euphemisms of work-for-the-dole, or privatised prisons, or illegal immigrant labour, or unpaid overtime, or the free-market cargo cult that asks us to freely compete with slaves by becoming slaves ourselves, and to cop the sack from more and more places of work as the only hope for full employment at some time as yet unknown in the pig-flying future.

I love these young people – or I love the friends of my children that I know – and one by one I see that I am losing them. They might have done well in the end, had they survived. They might have had children themselves, that they would have loved. And they probably will not. I mourn them already. And I hate the society that is inch by inch eroding their self-esteem and wasting their talents and their stoicism and grace and is now persecuting them for merely being born with hypocritical word games – mutual obligation, tough love, compassion with a hard edge, downsizing, workplace efficiency – worthy of Georgian England, where nine-year-old children were hanged for stealing purses to feed their parents and siblings, and prayers uttered up from the gallows for their souls.

It is time the lying stopped, and the hypocrisy and the tyranny. It is time, and time already, for a Sorry Day for our young. They are better people than we will ever be, and we are wrecking most of them, and slowly killing some of them, day by day.

February, 1999

Death and Dying

Pharaohs took their servants with them, and golden chariots and jewelled headdresses the locals quickly thieved, as they voyaged forever through the darkness, their bandaged bodies preserved, in pyramids they spent their whole reign building. Romans elected their rulers to godhood, and burnt their bodies, like Julius Caesar's, on piled-up furniture in the public square. Indian princes were burned on ceremonial platforms, their young wives in the fire, squealing, beside them. American fundamentalists from the Deep South viewed the corpse in the church, and required its appalled grandchildren to kiss it goodbye.

Russians carry their dead rulers exposed down weeping streets through falling snow. Communist dictators in China and Russia lie preserved, with ears and noses rotting, for the reverent peasantry to shuffle past, amazed. Lenin, who died in 1924, is there to be gazed on still – if it is indeed him, and not a wax dummy. Stalin lay beside him for a while, but soon lost government approval, and was rapidly moved and buried under a tree.

Charlie Chaplin's corpse was stolen, and Peter Lorre's too. Abe Lincoln's body was 'kidnapped', ransomed and re-interred. It was dug up again by scholars ten years ago and 'still looked', Gore Vidal said, 'pretty much like Lincoln'.

Corpses do not lie easy. They are often exhumed to see if they were murdered (arsenic, it seems, took Napoleon out), or if they were, like Jefferson, slave-abusing child-molesters who could be so proven long after death by their genetic coding.

Some lie cold and unclaimed on slabs or in aluminium drawers for years. Many these days are burned in crematoria ('It's more hygienic,' old folk would say, 'isn't it?'), in part because their kinfolk will move to another town and leave the graves untended, full of weeds.

In part to get death out of the way. Put it out of mind.

This has been the obsession of many cultures in this century, since the Afterlife became a doubtful hypothesis. Californians annually spend millions preserving their dead Pekingeses *exactly as they were*. Or beautifying with cosmetics, and puffing up with chemicals, cadavers ravaged by cancer and glad, at the end, of the rest. Some take the ashes up to a high mountain, and they blow all over the bereaved ('I've got Mum in my eye') before mingling, theoretically, with a landscape dear to them.

Death is never easy for the bereaved. Of a person who is ninety the saying 'she had a good innings' is no comfort when you have loved them. You want them still to be there. In every century but ours little children would lose from the room they shared a brother, a sister, who wasn't there any more – but seemed to be there some nights, in dreams. In moonlight, a wisp of hair over the eye could seem, for a terrible waking moment, to be them. It seemed wrong they were gone. And little private religions were built up from nothing to comfort the loss.

It's probable all ideas of an Afterlife began this way: *Mummy, will I see Jackie again? Yes, love, you'll see him, and he'll be just as he was, and we'll all go and live with him in this wonderful place* . . . It's not a bad thing to tell a child. It's not a bad thing, perhaps, to believe as an adult.

But the trouble is, no-one believes it much any more. There are few true believers in nursing homes, few resurrectionists in the terminal wards. Most of them are worried only about the pain, and not losing their mind, and their dignity, to the drugs that ease the pain, and not being left alone by their fraught loved ones when the big day nears. Few say, 'Well, I'll be seeing your father soon.' Not any more.

This has led in turn to a new kind of religion, that is to do with preserving life. Diets, exercises, rigorous regimens of meditation, getting in touch with your inner child, male bonding, primal screaming, retrieved memory and suchlike try to put off the moment when the organs, as they must, break down and the darkness nears. *Vitamin E will do it. Crushed cloves will cure AIDS, it's already been proved.*

And it's all to do, I suppose, with the shortness of life. Twenty-eight thousand days; 4000 weeks from kindergarten to crematorium, if you go at eighty-four, seems all too short a stay. *I haven't read* Don Quixote *yet. I haven't seen the lakes of Sweden. I have to make it up with my daughter. No, no.* All of us feel round fifty that a decade has been stolen from us somewhere along the way. *I haven't sailed the South Pacific in my own little boat. I must find the girl I loved when I was fifteen, and tell her so.*

. . . And we make our arrangements as best we can, and blame whoever is handy. Try late divorce, new young wives, new addresses, new religions. Do a university course in our seventies.

But the dread day comes. And before that, we know it's approaching.

'I suppose it's an experience we all have to go through,' Don Bradman said, 'but it's not one I'm looking forward to.'

'I don't mind dying, not really,' Woody Allen said. 'I just don't want to be there when it happens.'

'It's hard to imagine, lying dead in the box,' says Tom Stoppard's Rosencrantz. 'I mean, it's not the same as lying asleep in a box. It's something totally different.'

For me the hard bit is imagining that after this I will have no *memory*. I could lie in darkness alone forever, I think, if I could remember my life and think about things. But not to have that power to think, and remember. To not be. It's unimaginable.

And what cannot be imagined cannot be.

So in different ways we have come to deny our own death altogether. Or we blur its meaning with new definitions, new buzz words and medical jargon. Brain death. Terminal condition. Inoperable carcinoma. Semipermanent coma. A condition requiring increasing levels of palliative care.

Or we endlessly fudge, because we cannot bear its meaning, the euthanasia debate. We try to convince ourselves, successfully sometimes, that there are things worse than quick death by lethal injection in the presence of a daughter, a lover, a hospital nurse. Things worse than needing to convince your mum to die now, die quickly, before we have to sell, to pay the hospital bills, the family property.

We need a new terminology, too, for the thing itself, and its bringing on.

In the old days we said passed over, gone to heaven, gone to Jesus, gone to his rest, sleeping in Abraham's bosom. Now we say we made him comfortable, increased the level of his palliative care. We told him he'd had a good innings and we turned up the tap. *It's all right, Mum. Is it all right? Yes, it's all right. Oh, that's good. That's good. I'm glad.*

It's a question of words in the end – how well we say *I've loved you all my life*, or *It's good to have been your daughter*, and how well in the church we say the words and sing the songs that end the tale of a particular soul's trajectory through a given time on earth. Words that say thank you adequately, so long, farewell, it's been a privilege.

And this process is not as bad now as it was. The dead are not always now captured by ministers of religion who did not know them in life and say ignorant things about them in the pulpit after death. It's more common now for the family to say things, and for old friends to tell funny stories, and some old home movies to go up on the screen, or a prerecorded message to be played, *keep the faith, life is joyous, comrades*, to break through the grief and get the survivors back, as it were, to home base, to that calm of mind where life goes on.

It's more common now, too, for the memorial celebration to happen before a death, for people to come to a gathering with food and make speeches while the mortal subject of them sits in a wheelchair and hears how much he is appreciated and makes a speech, perhaps, in return. This, though harrowing for some, is better than a lot of hypocrisy in church, the secret mistress unable to attend, the first wife hugging her supplanter, the worn-out rituals of a religion long rejected. It is seeing the man himself, the woman herself, or some facsimile of them, in the flesh, or what is left of it, and saying thank you, safe journey, God speed.

We are not here very long, and that which we love goes from us faster than we expect. And we are always caught on the hop by the death of one we had long meant to visit, and now, quite often, it is too late.

My sister has been dead for forty-five years. I didn't say much to her the last time we saw each other, in Stockton that December. I was nine, and she was twenty-two. I have tried to say things to her since, but I doubt if she can hear.

It's important, I think, to get it said, and say it soon. To make peace, to kiss it better. No memorial indulgence, no golden chariot pulled by black horses with tossing manes through thinly falling snow will ever be as good as those clear words said, 'I love you. I'll miss you. It was good for the world that you were here.'

March 1999

Christmas

As always the school choir sang, and the church setting was beautiful. The star by night, the shepherds on the hill, the three wise men, the frankincense and myrrh, the unbreached virgin's Ghost-sired baby in the straw among the munching cattle on the clear winter's night, the trumpet-playing angels rejoicing among the stars over Royal David's city, and the God-light beaming down on the holy manger, all were sung of as always, high and clear, and the children's faces shone in the candlelight. A story not wholly believable was read out from the carved lectern by grown men and women and we, like them, somehow believed it. Or we half believed it. Or did we?

Well, we went with it anyway. We shared in the emotion. It came in the music, and the magical feelings undiminished from childhood, and we ... well, we *somewhat* believed. And we gave our responding voices to the under-pinning story. How a Creator God made sinful man and when he therefore sinned the God decided to kill him and the God's only Son said, no, kill me instead, and the God said, right, it's a deal. So he killed his own son instead, and if sinful man believes in this grisly deal (no, call it a holy covenant), he'll die, but he'll come alive again and live forever in bliss and happiness standing on a Sea of Glass and singing Holy Holy Holy to the God who made and loves him, and wanted to kill him, but killed his son instead.

Only his son's not really dead. He came alive too, and he begs his father daily to be merciful to us poor sinners because the loving God is still outraged when we have the feelings he gave us, and we act on them. He's so outraged he'll burn us all in Hell, put us through the suffering of Tjandamurra O'Shane for billions of years if we don't believe in this palliative concern of the Son and eat his body and drink his blood. And so on.

I'm uncomfortable as I write this – late at night, as Christmas comes – because I too still half believe it. (Lord, Lord, I half believe. Help Thou mine unbelief.) And I really want to believe it.

We all of us have our sustaining fantasy, Martin Cohen once said. We know it's not real, but it's what keeps us going.

Christian redemption is like that. The afterlife. The expectation of romantic love. Or the perfect holiday. The fulfilling retirement. The grateful child.

Martin Cohen is a wise man I was at university with. He's a film producer now. His insight, I think, is very important.

Because it explains the universal process we are in. The irrational hope we all go to in some way, the light at the tunnel's end. The sustaining fantasy. The star of hope. The town called Hope, as President Clinton says, in his happy, weepy, affable way.

And we all do have them, and they may be large or small. We all believe, or half believe, that we will get through old age without a crippling illness and not end screaming for euthanasia. We all believe, or half believe, that our old age will be spent in contemplative reading, or listening to music, or educative travel, or visits from our grateful children. A wheelchair and a shattered memory are not in our calculation.

In much the same way we believed in youth we would always be young and attractive and bound for endless promotion and free of debt. And in childhood we believed our playmates would always be there, and Santa would come at year's end with the presents we really wanted.

It goes back a long way. The ever accessible breast. The happy hours on grandfather's knee. Noni on television. And it gets us up in the morning and it brews the coffee and turns on the shower and gets us on the train. Like the Life Force it keeps us going. The half belief that Tattslotto will yield up its fruits to us this week or the Crown Casino, or our party will win the election or our teenage children are just going through a phase. That though we still smoke we are personally exempt from science's findings and our lungs will not decay. That Mr Right is out there and we will find him somehow, or our mistress will not make trouble, and our wife will not find out. That we can go home to Greece or Ireland in our old age and the home village will still be there. Sustaining fantasies. And necessary perhaps.

Some come in the form of religions, others as diets, or exercise regimes or novels from Mills & Boon. Some, alas, are national cultures.

America for instance is a whole society built on this dangerous wishfulness.

Americans believe you can change your life. That the nose job, or the night course, will make all the difference, between your present status as a waiter and that of a billionaire. That there is a genius in you that only needs to be let out. That every change of address, or spouse, is a new start, a new chapter in your personal growth. That hard work, and really wanting to succeed, ensures fame and renown and maybe even the presidency. It's a deeply deluded country where, of course and not unusually, 92 per cent of the rich are the children of the rich and 98 per cent of the populace are not rich at all, and never will be.

Some sustaining fantasies are very dangerous. Hundreds of thousands of Rwandans this Christmas are walking home to Rwanda to share again their villages with their families' murderers, believing peace has come. A big noble heroic dream whose end is, possibly, a thousand more years of bloodshed. I fear for them.

The strangest one of all is the Afterlife, whose contradictions are many. One of them is that although the dead are alive and better off than we are, and although they still love and remember us, they can't get in touch with us and say hello, or they somehow choose not to. With technology being the way it is, they could surely send us a fax: *having a great time, wish you were here*. And somehow they choose not to.

And yet I half believe the dead are alive too (Lord, help Thou mine unbelief), because the alternative is too desolate to countenance – the mis-carriages, the road-accident victims, the war dead, the sisters, the uncles, gone forever.

The sustaining fantasy is a needed state of mind. Like Vitamin C or mother's love or marital sex, we need it daily. It's the fuel that moves us down our days. Perhaps we shouldn't question it. Perhaps it is the answer, and not the question.

I half believe that. I really do.

December, 1997

On Turning Fifty

A speech

The human tendency, I once wrote, is to first discover where the party is, and then contrive a moral reason for being there; and it's a little distressing, I think, that one or other of these mileposts to the grave, these anniversary shivoos of our worm-bound mortality, of our coming hither and our going hence, our wedding and childing and manning and kinging and breaking and burying, must be invoked before we dare, in our classic Anglo-Saxon fashion of deferring pleasure until it is properly earned, to have a gathering like this of old and past and passing friends and new acquaintance and old carnality and grief, of what Les Murray once called our Witnesses, people who knew you when you were still young and vulnerable, before the shell formed over you, whose price is above rubies, whom you must seek out.

The party should be easier than that, more Irish, more Italian, more Polynesian, more sudden in its contrivance, less morbid in its excuse. At my present age, I grimly note, Shakespeare had retired, whilst I feel yet an apprentice, a mere horse-holder outside the great Globe of the world, still taking preliminary notes. I feel a decade has been filched from me somewhere, perhaps by my handsome and mocking gene pool, and I want it back. I do not feel happy to be so placed, between the conception and the last reality, under falling shadows on a high hill under lowering time, with a view of pelicans floating into the blue. Forty I will accept, but this is ridiculous; and yet it must be borne, and not lamented in the Hemingway Kilimanjaro fashion of the ghosts invoked, of the stories underwritten, the days unconsummate, the curtains unrisen, the songs unsung, but fifty is a cold wind to sing under nonetheless.

My thanks to Les Murray, who is my two-ton Jiminy Cricket, and to Francis James, who is my Holy Ghost and remedial speech instructor, for being here, and Leyland Minter, who knew me when I was seven and has been since then unusually patient with my sinfulness and my neglect; to Annie for reasons numberless and fine and rare, not the least of which is her cooking; to Roy Masters, the secret, sly Machiavellian cause of my failure at rugby league at Lismore High; to Bill Marwood, who in the same school brought me day after day and year after year the excitements of Shakespeare in, alas, my algebra class; and Richard Brennan, who, in the corner of every room I have ever been in through my adult years, was always watchfully, judgmentally, diary-keepingly, caringly there; and Captain Robert Lawrence, VC posthumous cancelled, who lately wrestled me and my fibrillating heart into a hospital I feared, in the middle of a love scene on a mountaintop I would rather have stayed with, as I would with life itself; and to the faces many, undimmed and beautiful and patient too in these long years with this one loose, fool, cantankerous man.

In a play last month at the Playwrights' Conference it was correctly said that we all start out with love of everyone, and it is only accident and mistiming and bad wording by which that love is dimmed. Be less guilty therefore at how much you once felt for those whom, in your coming hither and going hence and your aching adolescence and beyond, you met and warmed to, for love is the rule, truly, and only vile and gnawing time and cruel misprision or accident make of it an exception. Love is everywhere.

I will close, I think, with Hemingway's marvellous dying fall, planned for the end of the yet unfinished *Islands in the Stream*, as the hero, bloody, mortally wounded and fleeing in his boat from the coastguards of Cuba, and imagining the life he might *still* have with his second wife and his two surviving children, remarks to the coming darkness: *I wish there was some way of passing on what I've learnt though. I was learning fast there at the end. I know now there is no one thing that is true: it is all true.*

May, 1992

Old Friends

I see Rex Collins every six or seven years, when he comes dutifully home to Australia to visit his daughter or I for different reasons (the latest a documentary) go to Toronto, a beautiful city, and stay with him a few days there.

This is the thirty-eighth year of our friendship (we met while failing to sell encyclopaedias together in 1961), yet the time we have spent together, all in all, might add up to a month, maybe five weeks, and our occasional bursts of letter-writings – for fiftieth birthdays, emotional crises, family deaths – never last long. We are busy. We have other lives.

And yet our intimacy continues. We call each other by our surnames, mockingly, lovingly, as always. We tell each other of our deepest concerns. We make jokes, fall silent, talk again. No time seems to have passed since we first met, both lonely bush-born students fond of jazz and good movies and keen to be, soon, significant writers, great novelists, like Hemingway and Salinger, and we drank a lot of coffee and talked about big things. We will both be grandfathers soon, but we seem in our own minds to be just *beginning*. It's all so short, so stupidly short, we agree. And our lives in our final decades are not slowing up, they are crowding.

He has kept his Australian accent for all of his thirty years in Canada, but he has become, I know, more North American in his opinions and our views are different now. His work as a clinical psychologist has made known to him a lot of human tragedy and he is less tolerant of my Leftish generalisations than he used to be. He knows life is very specific and there are no magic potions, no giant enveloping bandaids, for what is wrong with people. Many live in a hell derived from luckless childhoods. Some just get by in a world they find increasingly strange. Most go to bed of a night-time fearful of the morrow. There are more bad things to know than we read back then in those old encyclopaedias.

I differ from this view, believing many of life's ills are curable, or fixable, by governments governing, by public education, by the income taxes that buy civilisation. Kosovo, I argue, cannot be solved by the free market acting spontaneously in its usual feeding frenzy on a level playing field where the fit survive; ethics must underpin what happens, ethics and mercy, all of what happens.

And so we rub along, debating, not squabbling, but sometimes, courteously, avoiding debate. We have long phone calls now and then, my midnight, his mid-morning lull between patients, or in those dreadful times when a girl-child has run away, or a house burnt down, and we conspire to speak in a language that avoids our differences, the way adults do, or old friends. Friendship, I wrote once, is a conspiracy of things not said, in order that love may last.

I feel guilty about Collins sometimes, in the usual old-friend way, and the guilt I suppose is a bond. We wrote scripts together once, and nothing came of them, and he wrote a novel, and it was good, and I took a long, long time to read it, and he became discouraged by my tardiness in finishing it. And he drifted into teaching, and Canada, and clinical psychology, a late second marriage, step-children, and now he's all that stands between a good few sorrowful souls and suicide. One of them is a Holocaust survivor, female, who lived like Anne Frank in an attic from when she was three to when she was six, forbidden to cry, laugh, run about like a child lest she reveal their presence, and she has vivid dreams now, and is formidably depressed, and Collins ministers to her depression, as best he can. I would have wished

45

a less lugubrious and testing and burdensome fate on my old friend. We could be writing a comedy series together, or going on Mediterranean cruises, or hiking in the Himalayas together.

Or maybe not. The likelihood is, of course (and friendship is like this), that had we continued to collaborate, to be business partners, co-producers, quarrelling co-auteurs, we wouldn't be friends now, any more. Some sore point of difference would have started one of us blaming the other for the failure of something, some now forgotten trifle, and a slamming door, or a hung-up phone, would have ended something precious that is now, through distance, and through fond infrequent contact, preserved.

So our friendship is a time capsule, really. We talk of old events, and old acquaintance, no longer part of our lives. We drink deep from our common pool of memory, and memory of loss. For us it is always high summer, and the sixties, and a future opening for us like a sunflower and there are miles to go, and worlds to conquer, before we sleep.

He played some Beatles melodies on his home piano last Friday night, before we parted. We drank red wine. We embraced. We will see each other a few times more, I suppose. The letters, the phone calls, will swell for a while then fade, then swell again on a seventieth birthday, a child's wedding day. The enormity of our old age will go swiftly by. And then, a message on a wreath in one of our two cities. And nothing more.

Except for this . . .

April, 1999

BOOK TWO

Faraway Places with Strange Sounding Names

Vietnam, 1995

The pool game in the Apocalypse Now, a bar patronised by Australians on the dodgier side of Saigon, grew less absorbing as the shots made by hefty Townsville blondes awash with margaritas worsened and the midnight neared, and Tet neared too, and we moodily downed our Tiger beers and set off through the back streets towards the Q Bar, which Lynskey falsely alleged was nearby, and rickshaw drivers swarmed around us like fireflies in the intermittent throbbing neon, and teenage hawkers of chocolate and gum, and the occasional very clean sister. No sense of physical danger was anywhere apparent in this infamous town: I had felt more threatened in Kings Cross, where capitalist melancholy was in its latter stages, and occasionally flared into knife fights: here it was in its infancy, and not much more than a shouted haggle over the price of a GI dog tag, or a cigarette lighter made of captured mortar shells, reft the warm and balmy midwinter night.

'Shh, they think they won the war,' P.J. O'Rourke, the sardonic American apostle of right-wing Republican values, wrote of post-socialist Vietnam, and it's a fair point, but there is something very communist here, too, as in Cuba and in China. The reverent queues at dawn at the Ho Chi Minh mausoleum. The buoyant, eager children in clean uniforms in the earnest, hygienic schools. The scarcity of hookers on the broad and glamorous Parisian streets and the absence, it seems, of drugs and child prostitution. The cheerful, friendly pride of a nation which, after all, tweaked the nose and broke the spirit of the most powerful nation in world history at the height of its power, and in a hail of bullets raised the Vietcong flag above its embassy.

The Q Bar was depressing too, though the bar girls, teachers in their day jobs and middle-class in their deportment and hungry for occidental husbands, proved better at pool than their Queensland soul sisters, and my morose American companions, none too eager for sex, played them a number of games and drank deeply. Soon tiring in my late middle age of the all too familiar small-town fifties coquetry, I took a rickety taxi home through safe uncrowded streets, all marked in Western lettering, to my small hotel, where the concierge slept soundly on the marble floor, and I lay awake, exhausted but exhilarated, and amazed at the events of that waning summer-breathed winter night.

Course followed course, more delicious than seemed humanly possible (none of it, tactfully, dog), at the dinner for Professor Nhan, Vietnam's Minister for Health, and the skilfully translated joshing tensely flowed between the alcohol-primed combatants on either side of the table. The professor, a small man with calm eyes in his pensive sixties, was a decorated hero of the Battle of Dien Bien Phu by which the French had been evicted, after a century, from their Asian empire, and among his fellow tipplers was Normie Rowe, the nuggety Australian pop singer who had been a draftee in the war against the North, and Stephen Ramsey, the solemn, scholarly film director who in 1968 had gone to court to fight, in the end successfully, his conscription marble in the birthday ballot. The professor and Ramsey got on pretty well, predictably, the older man recalling what a boost to their morale it had been when Whitlam removed the Australian troops and it seemed for the first time they were winning; but when Normie by pre-arrangement got up to sing to him, and tuned his guitar, the table fell apprehensively silent.

He sang 'Bring Him Home', a great high-soaring song of anguish from Les Miserables, *in which he had starred, a plea to God by Jean Valjean to save his adopted son from the fires of revolutionary battle. It had a lot of high notes in it, perfectly struck, and I looked at the faces around the table and after a verse or two the attending women were in tears. The professor, the small calm revolutionary hero, looked apparently unmoved at his burning cigarette held upward between his finger and thumb. The song ended. There was applause. The professor then lifted his expressionless gaze at mine. 'Do you know anything,' he said, 'by the Beatles?'*

Behind its massive gates the US embassy loomed, unvisited still. The doors, the desk, the biros, the blotters, the telephones are as they were on the day the rising helicopters with the people hanging from them and dropping out of the sky ascended from its roof into the dawn and chuttered off over the harbour never to return, all of them one after the other ditching into the sea. Nothing in the embassy has been touched, or even approached, including the safes reportedly stuffed with money, for fear of the booby traps the Americans may have left behind in vengeance for their humiliation. It remains as uninvaded and sacred as Cheops's pyramid, a perfectly preserved time capsule, immaculate and ghostly for all foreseeable millennia. No-one will ever go there. It has a curse on it, like a pharaoh's tomb.

Capitulating, Normie then sang 'Let It Be' to the professor's table, and 'Twenty Years Ago', a Vietnam veteran song. The professor was moved. The table relaxed. Normie sang some more. The bracket ended. There was applause. Normie sat down and with a certain mischief said, 'In our country we have a game called football in which it is our custom to kick the shit out of each other on the field and after the game, in the pub, to buy each other a beer.' He raised his beer. 'To our two great cultures,' he said. The professor paused a long time, thinking I suppose of a million dead, and the Agent Orange and the bombs and the devastated landscape and the rest of it, then with an unchanging expression, raised his glass also.

Every metre of the footpath in Saigon boasts a new small business; a Lilliputian restaurant, a bike-chain shop, a florist, a gallery of gorgeous tapestries or wooden carvings of Scrooge McDuck, a dispenser of bicycle air. Busyness is everywhere and from dawn till late at night the streets are thronged with motor scooters and bicycles (where are they all going?) cheerfully weaving in and out of each other's pathway like intermingling shoals of tropical fish, beeping and yarning as they go, babies riding pillion, a whole billiard table on the front handlebars. Again, you feel no danger: they go mysteriously out of each other's way. The cheeriness is almost alarming; what have they to rejoice for? These are the toiling masses indeed, crowded as maggots and happy as meadowlarks; is this, I wondered, what we were in Vietnam to save them from, with more bombs than fell on Europe in World War II? Or is this what they learned from us since? Or would they have found it out without us?

   Being pedalled on a cycle through a warm tropic night is as good as it gets, I decided, floating like a ladybird about a foot above the ground through the looming beautiful faces: you know these people know who they are, and where they are going. They have been this for millennia, and only the ignorant ejected invaders have got it wrong.

'I know why the Americans and the French couldn't leave Vietnam,' P.J. O'Rourke wrote. 'They fell in love with the place.'

The pleasure boat proceeded up the Mekong Delta. It was like a series of South Sea islands, with grass hut villages and wild bananas and citrus orchards and frangipanis, as wildly and absurdly beautiful as any P&O brochure. The idea that helicopter gunships came strafing over this paradise (to the accompanying music of the 'Ride of the Valkyries') seemed unimaginable. This couldn't be the actual Mekong Delta. It had to be somewhere else. We went ashore, into an underpopulated grass hut village, and visited the family of Dr Nhan, a female ophthalmologist from the Fred Hollows Foundation.

   'Were you ever attacked by American helicopters?' I asked her sister.
   'Oh yes. Many times.'
   'How many of you were killed?'
   'About half.'
   I imagined the American platoons coming through places like these. 'Okay,' the colonel would say to identical slender youthful faces, 'Vietcong

please step forward. We will take you away and shoot you. The rest of you, we're here to win your hearts and minds.'

How could you win a war like that? Cutting the ears off dead, courageous young men for the body count and then giving chocolate to their relatives as you burned the houses they had lived in for hundreds of years and moved them weeping south in lorries. What levels of racism would you need to make you believe it even remotely possible? American levels, probably. And the religious fervour of John Foster Dulles. These are the heathens. They must be converted. And if they refuse, they must be burnt at the stake.

Gina Jeffries sang 'My Shoes Keep Walkin' Back to You' to the annual general meeting of the staff of Quac Tong Hospital. Her big sweet unvarying smile and large doll-blue porcelain eyes and general facial resemblance to the Little Mermaid added to the strangeness of the not unfriendly occasion. What, the overworked Vietnamese provincial medicos wondered, was she trying to tell them? She seemed a nice person. Then, on Normie's insistence, she went into the audience. She picked the shyest young man and sat on his knee and sang to him. The room around her erupted into shouts of embarrassed joy and giggling. Then the young man got up and seized the microphone and sang a song. Then Normie and Gina sang 'Waltzing Matilda' and, somehow, all joined in. It was an astounding happening, unbelievable if there had not been a videotape record to prove it. The Vietnamese seemed so accessible, so cheerful and forgiving that my heart surged in guilt. I wanted to make amends. To an entire country. We all did.

The fashion parade and barbecue at the Australian Embassy, with the diplomat's wives doing the modelling in the manner of *Prêt-à-Porter*, and doing it very badly, included among its introductory entertainment Captain Matchbox eating fire. The Australians present, numbering thousands, cracking coldies and wolfing sausages, looked gross and barbaric and low grade in comparison with the surrounding delicacy of the polite and reticent Vietnamese and filled me with shame. How much like Americans, in that context, we looked. The coarse, acquisitive, money-seeking invader, his stomach lined with offal and flatulence and his brain free of thought, overweight, over the limit, over here.

The Kochin Tunnels are now a theme park ('Disneyland for Victor Charlie' is the popular local phrase), with slide lectures in an adjacent marquee on the glorious Tet Offensive, given by a veteran with clockwork gestures and cadences, and souvenir stalls where captured American backpacks can be bought and hammocks and dog tags, and shoes made from American tyres, or tiny toy aeroplanes made from American bullets, or bloodstained postcards that got sent home to Indiana, New Jersey, Hoboken.

Then we went down the tunnels themselves, a terrifying experience, much like crawling up the alimentary canal of an unwelcoming stranger. Half an inch on either side of you as, on hands and knees, you crawled gasping and whimpering maybe a hundred metres round Stygian corners and up stairs aching for light.

It was here the Vietcong had lived for ten years, and rested between guerilla operations, under manholes covered by leaves in forests the Americans daily bombed. Those that took part in the Tet Offensive, nearly all of whom died in the next thirty hours, had crawled at a steady pace for a day and a half before they emerged in downtown Saigon, and came out shooting. And they took the American Embassy and died on its roof. And history changed.

Never such courage as this. Never such patience, fanatical patience. More. Never such love of country. Whatever. It was hard to treat it with scorn. And nobody ever has.

On the streets and in the villages the busyness continued, and the sun gorgeously set behind palm trees. An industrious, cheerful, absurdly beautiful country wherever we went – bound, I decided, to overtake South Korea in five years and Japan, maybe in twenty-five.

No signs of the bombing in Hanoi any more. The classic French architecture restored, all back, and by the moonlit lake a saxophone playing, and Ho Chi Minh, in his final sleep, a sacred object for which the queuing started each day before dawn. Religion everywhere, diligence, duty, family life, the work ethic, a kind of dusty crowded cleanliness of purpose. A sense of the future, a sense of excitable hope. I rejoiced that at last there was a stopover place on the way to England where you could alight without queasiness and look with interest over a country, and a people, uncorrupted yet.

April, 1994

Eritrea

A broadcast

I'm in Eritrea, far from the madding world (unaware, as an instance, of Haiti's fate and having as rare a time as I've had in my life), in the dry heat and sweet honesty of a people humbling in their courage and goodness. One goes a long, long mile to a more inspiring destination, Orwell's Catalonia perhaps, before it was traduced, or Danton's Paris before the Great Terror. Their curious mixture of sophistication and lack of guile, an innocent knowingness, together with a kind of humorous puritanism (no-one is unfaithful to his wife, and no-one fails to laugh about it) may come from the Coptic religion but I'm not sure. Their faces, which are European but black, and their mode of dress, watch chains and waistcoats and pork pie hats, give me the impression that there are the basic stock, flourishing by the Euphrates, out of which all Europeans, Indians, Arabs and Jews mutated. It feels like coming home, to one's true kinfolk, after sad long years of persecuted exile, shamefacedly, under mongrel invaders. These are the people we should be, and were once, back when the world was wide. Poetry rises in the heart, and for once it feels like truth, and in among the familiar sewer smells and dusty streets and Old Testament marketplaces of the Third World something else in the bruised wake of their largely unknown war is going on, something unfamiliar.

All of them told the same story. We fought for our freedom, I did not expect to live, I had given my life to my country, I was a dead man, a dead woman already. We lived on bread and salt and water, and lentil soup as a luxury once a month maybe, under bombardment in the field for seventeen years, against weapons supplied by first the Americans and then the Soviet Union and a genocidal policy of driving us into the sea, burying sometimes ten of our fighters a day, in the time of the drought fifty a day, calling out over each buried corpse, 'Victory to the masses.' On Wednesday we would have the coffee ceremony, and talk and relax, though the shelling went on. We learned to sleep while standing up, while walking even, sometimes only three seconds of sleep, sometimes five minutes, while walking under shellfire, sleeping anyhow, men and women side by side for years, one in every three of the fighters were women, but no sexual contact, sleeping always back to back, not only on moral grounds but as well because sexual contact would mean children and any children we had we could not keep or leave, they would have to be killed when we moved to the next battlefront. So there were no children, and there was no sex, in those seventeen years.

Everyone I talked to had killed people, and their faces showed the soft grief of men and women who had paused at the gates of hell, and sometimes gone on in.

The great purifying this holocaust has brought them, this trying in the fire, like seventeen years of the Australian bushfires last January, has along with their culture and their genes and their religion produced a nation of people recognisably heroic, Homeric in their stubborn courage. In one day I interviewed, it seemed, Demosthenes followed by Lincoln followed by Boadicea and Sir Lancelot and got drunk that night with Che Guevara who was very agreeable company. All the heroes have agreed to work without wages, and only basic food and shelter, for three years, for their country. Think about that.

I have no doubt that I sound like a fool taken in by wily serpentine foreigners but all I say is true, as Tom Keneally and Fred Hollows, both heroes of free Eritrea, found with the same amazement as I.

It is all very humbling – the punctuality, the courtesy that is also honesty, the absolute lack of corruption, foreign hucksters with brown envelopes are sent back home on the plane, the absolute straightforwardness. This latter quality I think is due to the lack of casual sex. So much of our deviousness and male bluster in the West is a cover-up of the humiliation felt by men when sexually rejected, or cast off, a feeling they must revenge. In Eritrea the question does not even arise, so all dealings man to man, and woman to man, are absolutely straightforward and in no need of consolation. Because there is nothing to hide.

And of course, the absolute self-sacrifice, the *un*individualistic belief that one is part of a whole that is good. I spoke to a woman, seven of whose sons and one of whose daughters went at her wish to fight in the war, who did not see them for seventeen years and did not know till the last bullet flew and a week, a fortnight thereafter, if any of them had survived. Six sons came back, and the daughter, and they all now live in their parents' house, a house at which I ate, as an honoured guest, very well. They went away teenagers and came back middle-aged, living poorly, on no wages, working hard, sacrificing still for the free Eritrea that is coming, that is yet to be. I gave them, she said to me, I gave them freely. It is better to live for an hour as a free person in courage than for a lifetime as a slave, in shame.

I watched too, for hour after hour, the uncut footage of the battle of Masawa, the thousands and thousands fleeing on foot, carrying one item of furniture, a table, a chamberpot, parents carrying children, fathers carrying grandmothers, mothers looking for daughters in the rubble of the bombed marketplace, howling children asking where's my mummy, where's my mummy, and the corpses, and the corpses, and the pieces of corpses, and I thought how wicked all news reporting on the television is now, because it takes all human suffering as read, an inevitable somehow, and talks of other things, the politics, the shakedown. Mother after mother, corpse after corpse, mutilated child after mutilated child, in the uncut footage tells a different story, of life itself, and the weight of life cut short, not the CNN myth of moderates and hardliners, free marketeers and reactionaries, cardboard villains and American interests, but death and war and blood, the song of freedom and the cancerous curse of power.

I am going back, of course, to help set up a film festival, a film school, a feature film about Fred Hollows, and maybe a deal to export their excellent beer to guilt-struck Balmain lefties as the Eritreans in turn rebuild their shattered cities and ruined railways and burnt orchards and repair the mutilated limbs of the children playing daily in the undetectable minefields left by the Ethiopians and pretend to be right wing enough to satisfy the IMF. I have found, old fool that I am, a kind of new Jerusalem, and it's nice to know it's there, maybe only for a brief shining moment, like Dubcek, or Catalonia, the workers' Camelot we dreamed of in our youth, but it's there.

February, 1994

Ireland

I've had an odd year all in all, one Will Shakespeare or Kim Beazley might call 'passing strange'. My house burned down. I was overwhelmed that night and others with the kindness of neighbours. I stood behind Paul Keating as on election night he said (in a nod of thanks, I like to think, to me) 'the true believers'. I played Brendan Behan and Oscar Wilde. I visited Ireland, my adopted heartland, twice. I saw my film, a sad comedy, ignored in France, adored in Scotland, loved by women in Sydney, and hissed by idle feminists in Melbourne. I saw Russia, a place I love (and have lately visited four times), going up in fascist flames once more, amid effusive worldwide applause. I ached for Woody Allen, grieved for Anthony Burgess, pitied Michael Jackson and my friend Peter Collins and, oh yes, I stood for

Parliament – against Bronwyn Bishop, a great and beautiful woman free of malice and earthly ambition, and very litigious.

But let that pass.

The nicest thing I did was to take my two teenage children to Britain, Ireland and Italy. I saw them wonderingly stand in the Sistine Chapel and under Michelangelo's *David*, mix with the assassins in Stratford on Avon's marvellous promenade version of *Julius Caesar*, and search the long dark ripples of Loch Ness for dinosaurs.

Mostly, though, what I most loved was Ireland's west coast, whose heavenly physical beauty and joyous, eloquent people remain for me a measure of what we, as human beings, have lost this century, of what we all once had.

Let me explain. Under grey, ever varying skies in which God still hovers, men in grey cloth caps walk along narrow lanes by grey, broken stone fences into an infinite grey and white and changing, shimmering distance whose magic haunts the mind like a dream of Narnia. And by night they sing in pubs, and dance to fiddles as though it is the last night of the world and all the world's gladness had to be undergone tonight, before midnight . . . and this is just another night in Ireland, where the moon is always full.

The human race, I like to say, overstating it perhaps, is living in exile on the west coast of Ireland, and some rough beast has taken over the rest of the planet. It is as if the world's race memory resides there, and as if by a time machine, that memory can be visited.

Let me explain.

I have no Irish ancestry that I know of (though a grandfather's surname, Ward, is everywhere in Galway, a town in which I oddly, spookily feel at home), and I have suffered inconvenience at Irish hands. I was blown up by the Irish once, or nearly, in Piccadilly in 1974, and was irritable for days. It is furthermore the farthest, least convenient place on the planet for me, with perilous narrow roads, no public transport to speak of, rickety little hire cars, uncertain accommodation and weather that is treacherous and cold. The people are priest-ridden, superstitious, provincial, prurient, massively unemployed, unusually poor, tremendously talkative, and full of Guinness.

But that's not the point.

The point is that in their society (and here I take a deep breath) lies the secret of human happiness. No country that I know of is happier, or more human. Some Caribbean island maybe, full of dance and rum and clear oceans and boisterous polygamy. But . . . I doubt it.

What Ireland has is . . . well . . . lots of things. The women, for instance, have dignity, identity and status whatever their social position. Barmaids and waitresses have stature. It is acknowledged. It is assumed. This is partly because they know they are under no sexual threat. The gallantry of Irish men is ingrained. It comes with the Virgin Mary, and large families with one adored, heroic mother. It is unthinkable a woman might be molested. Wooed, yes. That is different.

The net result is unlike almost any other society (Russia is one, and possibly Spain), the women react to the men as equals. They joke with them and mock them, as in our society only other men do. This is remarkable.

So is their relationship to language. To them speech between people is a sensuous physical act, like swimming or (yes) making love. It is a joint exploration of unknown territory. The words have hugeness and meaning, and their tongues waft over them like hovercraft, caressing without touching. Talk is an act of love. It has the zaniness and playfulness that lovemaking has. No-one who has experienced it can fail to be astounded by it, nor fail to try it on themselves, sometimes for days on end.

But you have to be there to keep it up. Ireland is a tonic for the tongue and the mind that is irreplaceable. You have to go back. The vital medicine is nowhere else.

And the reasons for this are unfashionable. It is a uniculture. Few Vietnamese are among it, or Pakistanis or West Indians to enrich its cuisine or distort its gene pool in interesting ways. The same ten faces appear throughout Ireland as they have since 2000 B.C. They therefore have a sense of self, and of history, and of the epic story of the people of which they are now an honourable object.

This allows them to be hospitable, in a way no-one else is, because they know who they are, and they do not feel threatened. Having beaten back the hated English for eight hundred years, and having kept their culture and their religion, and even, for those who wish it, their language, they know this battle can be won.

So when they greet you it is as an honourable stranger within their gates to whom, at will, and often, they can accord love. They understand the most basic of all human truths, which is that friendship is a gift, and it can be given instantly. And so, with astonishment, by us, it is received.

The overwhelming sense of all visitors that the grey-haired shrewd mannerly lady running the Bed and Breakfast place is like a close relative of theirs *within minutes* is universal, and so is the belief that there are families, big families, all over Ireland, you can book into for life, and be welcome in.

This is because of the other unfashionable reason. The families are very big and the story of each an epic, a soap opera, a Dickensian canvas of bickering and territoriality and mad uncles and crazy voyages and young love. Left-wing thinkers would have us believe that 80 per cent of the Irish ought to have been aborted, because the families are too big. I do not agree. I have met some of that 80 per cent and I am glad that in uniculturality and overfecundity and song in pubs and lack of breathalysers and a sense of self, and history, and friendship, they have found the secret of life.

I will be back, every year, if I can, and maybe forever, hopefully, maybe. Who am I kidding? Life could not be that good, at all, at all, and that's a fact.

December, 1993

Dingle

I once imagined a television series called *In Search of the Earthly Paradise* where I or Phillip Adams or Peter Ustinov or Sam Neill roved the planet in quest of that Good Place from which we are all exiles. On my list (and better travelled people might make different choices) were Cambridge, Yalta, Nantucket, Ubud, Barbados, Llangollen, Barcelona, Kashmir and so on, but the clear winner (or it was clear to me) was Dingle, where I am now.

It's midnight and the pubs are emptying young happy people full of Guinness and good music into the narrow ascending streets. The high green fields that climb to the brink of the sky hover like a memory in the rainy night. The fishing boats bob on the harbour. Sheep huddle on the hills and there are lights in the small white houses. As always the pub music has been magnificent and the various artists, farmers, policemen, millionaires and tourists have mingled and yarned in promiscuous equality making friends, and assuming friendship in ways that other, staider cultures cannot imagine.

The landscape (used by Lean in *Ryan's Daughter*) is overwhelmingly beautiful and yes, you think, yes, this is home, this is where my childhood should have been, this is where my old age must now be.

My friend Patric Juillet lives here now, running two restaurants, one already so famous that President Clinton is coming to eat at it, raising a new family and writing a trilogy of novels about his varied life and now and then attempting to put a film together. His last place of residence was Los Angeles, where, after riots, earthquakes, bushfires, floods, mendacity, and ignorant madmen shouting formulas – jeopardy! journey! – without end and without result, he didn't see the point of continuing and he came here first to convalesce and then to pleasure his remaining days with human simplicities and tribal convivialities long forgotten elsewhere. His agent warned him against it, saying he had to live in L.A. and suffer along with everyone else if he wanted to be taken seriously, and he thought about this, and it didn't take long. He made a choice, and moved from the worst town in the world to the best.

The Irish understand something very basic that's been forgotten elsewhere, and it's that friendship is a gift, and it can be given *instantly*. And so there are no hoops to be jumped through. There is another whole human being before you, greeting you in amiable equality and inviting you to sing along, discuss the universe, rejoice in creation or the snooker scores. You are who you are, and you are welcome in my house, and in my town, and it's probably the way most people were before the Capitalist Imperative (sell, compete, make a killing) made adversaries and suckers and tyrants of us all. They understand that, small or great, we are all God's creatures and we all have a story worth hearing.

And so on. This, in Dingle, is added to a landscape like the outer suburbs of heaven (ask anyone who's been here) and a tradition of art and music routinely of such excellence that you think you must be dreaming, and the kind of instinctive hospitality (the policeman on the beat says, 'God bless you, sir', and he means it too) that makes you think there may be something in Christianity after all.

Patric and I talked of making films here. He was my co-producer on *Unfinished Business* and *Warm Nights on a Slow-Moving Train*. We agreed the possibilities here are almost dizzyingly various. Any kind of children's adventure film, or adult romance, or holiday comedy, or IRA thriller, or costume drama (like *The Field*, or *Widow's Peak*) would go equally well here – in the soft mist and the yearning distances, the grey mud and grey water that rises up into grey sky over fields so achingly green. (I'm missing it already, and I'm still here.) Pierce Brosnan and Patrick Bergin and, amazingly, Gregory Peck came from round here and fed into the unending fecund miracle that is Irish acting. And the Irish government will go halves in any reasonable co-production – one co-starring Bill Hunter and Stephen Rea and Toni Collette and Max Cullen and Ken Branagh and Ben Mendelsohn and Jackie McKenzie and Tony Barry . . . It's easy enough to imagine, and not too hard to do.

I was in England for the landslide election (which I alone predicted to be a Labour majority of 171–189, and it was 179) and I heard that my friend David Puttnam will be put in charge of some great film corporation to be set up by the new government. As both he and Blair are fond of Australia, it may be a partial solution (English–Irish–Australian co-productions perhaps) to our coming misery when Costello abolishes our cinema infrastructure this week. Appalling to think he has an Irish name. It just shows how wrong it is to ever leave Dingle, the earthly paradise, or Ireland, for the various chapters of hell we know as the world.

May, 1997

Cannes 1

Ellis, awake again, his mouth like an Ayatollah's armpit and his destiny possibly in ruins, went looking for his missing brain along the *plage*. Food, he thought, I must have food. His mind, scraped clean of thought, throbbed in the Mediterranean sunlight of the Côte de merde. His tuxedo jacket, rank with sweat, hung off his bowed shoulders like an ecological effect. Around him, all-night revellers, fresh from Scott Fitzgeraldish yacht parties and rich as Croesus, murmurously consumed $200 business breakfasts in beachside cafes. All were handsome, blithe and making further redundant millions with grace and élan. Ellis hated them deeply.

In the night, one felt, there roamed among the untenanted cafes and quays of this brightly chattering hedonistic sewer a ghost, sour-hearted and lizard-visaged in a snappy transparent tuxedo, a cigarette holder in his thin, spectral grasp. It was Somerset Maugham, long a snakey senior citizen of these parts. He looked out at the sea, in which, in hundred-foot effigy, stood Arnold Schwarzenegger, a moonlit roving phallic pistol in his mighty paw. 'Bah humbug,' said Maugham and moved on.

Think of it, thought Ellis, as a form of dieting. Unable to afford food, one should for the sake of one's health eschew it, and walk a lot. Up and down . . .

As arranged, the two determined Hollywood agents arrived at the Petit Carlton at 2 a.m. to meet Stephan Elliott who was drunk. 'Don't decide yet,' they said with baritone gentleness, 'do it in your own time, your own mind space, but think of us. We can show you career options that maybe, just maybe . . .' 'I'll sign your contract,' slurred Elliott abruptly. 'Pardon?' smiled the startled Californian primates, out of their depth. 'On one condition!' shouted Elliott. 'Yes?' they said. 'That when I meet Mike Ovitz,' shouted Elliott, 'he's wearing a dress!' There was a pregnant Californian pause. 'I think we can deliver that,' said the agents, who were puzzled, then, to find Elliott doubled over with mirth.

In one of the cafes Errol Sullivan and Andrew Pike were breakfasting on heat and plotting their acquisition of *The Piano*. Sitting down genially beside them, Ellis quickly ate the remains of Pike's croissants, and all of Sullivan's strawberry jam. The two moguls looked at him amazed. 'Save your money,' growled Ellis, his mouth full. 'It's a film of which the hero is a sexual harasser, the villain a marital rapist.' He chewed determinedly and sipped

Andrew's coffee. 'And the heroine a deaf-and-dumb nymphomaniac who owns a piano. The sisterhood of Glebe and Carlton won't stand for it. Save your money. Believe me. Trust me. I mean that sincerely.' He lurched off again into the brazen sunlight, their pitying eyes following him. Ellis was clearly in need of sleep, but the French had deprived his hotel bedroom of all curtains and the sun, in brazen conspiracy, rose at 4.30 a.m.

Ellis, queuing in rainy London for tickets to Arthur Miller's Last Yankee, *was suddenly and sickeningly accosted by the Doug Anthony All Stars – all twenty of them, it momentarily seemed – who swarmed around him like woodmites, hectically demanding he see their opening night, on free tickets, in the same theatre, after the Miller.*

Ellis did this, albeit inwardly cursing their impudence in depriving him of a night of, say, Shakespeare and, as the eldest member of the close-cropped and ear-ringed audience, laughed himself silly at the hearty necrophilia and joyous bestiality ('I fuck dogs' was the recurring refrain of one of their simpler, less disarming songs) that seemed to be passing the English by. The show's climax involved a beer shower to Esther Williams choreography, all over Arthur Miller's stately sloping stage. Shouts and thumps were then heard from the wings, and a foyer full of expectant first-nighters were swiftly evicted by humourless large Cockneys into the street. You've got to watch it in Europe, Ellis decided, if you are Australian and not yet housetrained. Like them. Like me.

Ellis proceeded sombrely up the red carpet into the Palais de Festivale, three hundred Frog wallopers holding back his fans with signal and some-times violent success. Ellis after twenty-five years' absence had come to again hate France. A region free of lavatories and full of cops and narks and rules (anything not forbidden is compulsory), with a brown-stained Mediterranean no-one any longer swam in, in just fear of plague. It further boasted, among the neon, lung cancer, plastic bread, paleolithic cheeses and milk reconsti-tuted from cattle corpses killed in luckless crossfire at Verdun, a furious Festival bureaucracy bent on stopping any ticket holders from seeing any films (as in Kafka, each officer passed you on to the next and the ninth arrested you for going where you were sent), scions of a green-skinned, imperious, corpulent, idle race ('You have to get up pretty early in the afternoon,' as Patrick Cook memorably wrote, 'to outwit us French.'), whose very accent is a form of self-congratulation, who did not care, in their affable, nicotine-stained way, if you lived or died.

Ellis went into the film *Frauds*, which was chosen with Gallic cunning and greeted with uniform Gallic dismay. It was just the French style, Ellis deduced, sending you broke in another way. Having built you up with flattery they then, with gelid remorsefulness, cut you off at the knees. I hate them, thought Ellis, so much.

I will swim out to that Russian billionaire in that yacht, thought Robert Lawrence, drunk in moonlight. His name is Dennis. He gives five-figure cheques to all who ask for them at 2 a.m., after surviving his vodka toasts. The yacht gleamed on the foul dark water. Lawrence took off his jacket. Out in small boats, the French were waiting for him with nets.

May, 1993

Cannes 2

Later, speeding across Ireland with two hitch-hikers called Kelly and Murphy, mellifluously unravelling the universe and sharing his Guinness through the mists and rainbows and black hills and waterfalls of the Ring of Kerry, Ellis looked back on the horror of Cannes with a kinder eye. Its vulgar multitudinous glamour, purring avarice, fraudulent bonhomie, pre-posterous prices (three initial gin-and-tonics at the Majestic cost him $72), traffic jams, lurid blue weather, hubris and hype added up, he realised, as over a black sea a black sun descended into Galway Bay, and the Guinness foam cascaded into its dark depths and the Irish stew simmered in its fat, to a cold bath of international reality. This was the hubbub over which your voice must be heard. The makers of *Frauds* understood this (and by causing the festival's worst traffic jam with the arrival of Phil Collins, proved they did) and Ellis hitherto had not. He thought mere quiet quality was enough, but the world was getting too crowded for that. If your name was not also a brand name (Weir, Disney, Puttnam, Stoppard, Andrew Lloyd Webber, David aargh Williamson) you were nothing. Ellis imagined his name in Broadway lights, then shook his head.

In wet winterish cold Ellis, first arriving ticket seeker at the National Theatre box office at 8 a.m., sat down sniffling on chill concrete and began reading A Dance to the Music of Time, *Anthony Powell's masterly thirteen-volume chronicle of the workings of divine providence on certain Old Etonians through the entire twentieth century. He had reached page eighty-nine of Volume One, he bitterly noted, before a second ticket seeker, a mysterious rich tuxedoed Pole, resident in New York and affiliated with the CIA, joined him furtively in the queue at 9.20. Their conversation, over cardboard coffee held in blue hands, increased their irritable puzzlement with one another until the doors crashed open at 10 a.m. That night they saw the play,* Tom Stoppard's Arcadia, *from adjoining front-row seats (with unwelcome, close views of Felicity Kendall's tonsils), and agreed sombrely that the time spent queuing for it was*

more exciting than the time spent watching it. How many further naked emperors,
Ellis wondered, in how many more new suits of imagined gold lamé, would waste
his fleeting time before the flames of North Shore Crematorium soon, too soon,
engulfed him? He gnawed on salt beef and pickles at Rabin's in Soho and pondered
the imminence of Cannes and the climax of Jane Campion's oeuvre with trepidation.

Ellis came out of *Broken Highway* in a rage, accompanied by much of
civilised Europe, gasping for oxygen and howling in vain among the quenchless catacombs of the Cannes Festival Centre for alcohol, coffee, a game of
Russian roulette, anything. Once more had the addled judgement of the
perfidious French appalled and baffled humankind, and humankind, especially the Ellis sector of it, wasn't happy. A work resembling something
rescued from the gnashing shredder of a soused juvenile Eugene O'Neill
(acts one to three seemed missing, people were already shouting portentously
about Death on doomful shipboard in the first two minutes), yet nonetheless
parading wondrous monochrome photography worthy of Gregg Toland, it
put Ellis into cheese-munching despair on the drizzling *plage*. When, dad
blast them, he wondered, would the long-promised raves in *Variety* and
Screen International appear, and swell into triple figures the overflow audience
from the adjacent laundromat of *The Nostradamus Kid*? Cursing, starved and
bilious, he invaded the Carlton's marble corridors to have it out loudly with
Screen International, and found their office abandoned, furnitureless, empty.
They, like history, had moved on and the Frogs, deaf to his literate English,
had dished him once again.

In the Majestic bar Sly Stallone shot past at shoulder height, craving invisi-
bility, inches and possibly booze. Robert Altman sat in Falstaffian affability
three tables away, administrating with ease the awed adulation of three gulping
fans. Liz Taylor, rattling with jewels and awash with brainless congratulations,
scarpered into a stretch limousine accompanied by the dim whiff of six dead
husbands. David Puttnam, grey and sere and shrunken, dwindled at a brisk
walking pace into the swirling melee. By the pool yet another half-clad phal-
anx of motivated beauties beamed at yet another swarm of shrieking shutter-
bugs. Beyond them, abaft the strangely tedious fleshy nakedness of the *plage*,
the beachfront avenue thronged, as always, and the traffic jammed. Ellis, sitting by the hour over his $16 cafe latte, decided that this mountainous Euro-
pean patience with delay, as the traffic amassed and the queues lengthened and
the gendarmes roved and snarled, was entirely explicable. Here, unlike
Australia, they had destinations worth getting to, and the long waits therefore
didn't matter much. In Australia, by contrast, where no destination was ever
worth the journey, we were always in a frazzled hurry, to be there, at the next
place, and the next, anticlimax succeeding anticlimax down through life. He
began to ponder the worthwhileness of living in colonies, and enduring their
emptiness and guilt and drunken bluster, when the true, originating culture,

the unforced joy of life, the destinations, were all here. In Europe. Home. He looked into the sunlit multitude, trying to pick by their appearance the future superstars. It was absolutely impossible. They could look like Dustin Hoffman. Anyone. How could you possibly know?

May, 1993

Toronto

In Toronto, which is like America with all the bad bits taken out – a mild-mannered metropolis of coffee houses and bookshops and grand yet unpretentious architecture and underground stations and museums and restaurants and a multicultural populace free of prejudice, at once literate, honest and kind – I slowly and gently sense, as I did in Wellington, and Edinburgh, and Dingle, that this is a place I could move to and change my name, and feel in a week I'd never lived anywhere else; and I wonder, in passing, how many such places that are so much better than Sydney (a transit lounge of thieves, I call it, where you can't any more trust anybody even to be there for lunch on Thursday, let alone to be your friend for life) there are in the world, unadvertised like this one, yet modestly perfect, unfraught and civil and physically beautiful and umpompously wide, and how wrong we are not to seek them out, how wrong we are to go whoring in rouge and nose-rings 'round pestholes like Burbank and Crows Nest and Cannes, believing that bluster and wisecracks and millions, and exciting lies, make up for anything.

Excitement is overrated, I've decided, in this my middle age of shrunken gonads and limited expectations. 'If you want political excitement,' Bob Carr said lately of his dull triumphant campaign, 'go join the Shining Path guerillas.' Go sit in a ruined house in Kosovo, he might have added, with a belt of ammunition and a virtuous cause and three hours to live, and my very best wishes to you for the Easter Offensive and may you earn your just reward.

I'm moved to these thoughts by John Ralston Saul, whom I'm here to work with on a television series that will be like *The Ascent of Man*. He's the author of (maybe) the best book of the past fifty years, *Voltaire's Bastards*, which explains the fix that humankind is currently in with more lucidity and learning than anyone since Gibbon, adverting to Renaissance art, political structures, corporate economics, Tin Pan Alley, the slow sad shrinkage of the concept of God, the arrival to take His place of the concept of the Hero, and the Board of Directors, and the Shareholder who must grow fat on human misery; the invention by Cardinal Richelieu of the nation state, the Jesuitical managers of the modern corporation, the fate of the earth, the iniquity of Levis jeans, and so on. He's a mild, long, sandy fellow, with an unremarkable receding face like Garry McDonald's and impeccable manners, who has a fair grasp of most things that have happened thus far on earth, and his view is that excitement comes from the simplifications that come in turn from the needless planting in our brains of national and personal myths, and these myths may be the root of all evil, for the world is *complex*, and only by living with complexity (the way his bifurcated Canada does), and not attempting to solve too much, can we cohabit as humans in a civilised way, with libraries and museums and lasting marriages and Foxtel re-runs of *The Simpsons* and better Satchmo CDs and hot sour soup and King Island cheese and Kilkenny beer and so on. Excitement is more trouble than it's worth, discuss. Excitement is an adolescent construct, like the driving of souped-up hotrods real fast and real loud up the wrong side of the street, and we should let it go, and cultivate our garden, dandle our grandchildren, read Charles Dickens aloud by hurricane lamplight under a full moon in August, and so on.

Which is another way of saying, I suppose, come to live in Canada, and by cripes it's tempting, the Good Village from which we are all exiles, the Good Dinner Table carrying what Les Murray calls the Common Dish. The Good Village is not home to a decisive battle of implacable ideologies and obsessed crusaders. It is not a place where autumn reminds us of our mortality, and life makes only a kind of middling sense.

It's probably another way of saying, too, that our species is born with expectations of unassertive limits – the neighbourhood, the extended family, the town, the district, the local memory of things past, and not much more than these – and the Hollywood or Manhattan craziness that many are in, *I must change the world for the better and change it entirely and make billions before I'm thirty while I'm up.* And the mobile phone, and the laptop computer and the personal jet, and the Internet site and the facelift, and the handsome teenage children snorting coke on the yacht – all this is an error of proportion and emphasis that leads, as a rule, to tragedy, and in the quietude of Toronto, among the squirrels in the autumn park, in the great inclusive open library, at the orchestral concert, the revered live theatre, the chess game in the firelit room over mulled wine with an old friend, lies our unremarkable salvation, and elsewhere madness lies, if we are not careful.

My current plans, therefore, to cover Israel's election, and there witness an assassination or two, and to film with Saul in Kosovo under American bombardment, and to make Imax films of Tasmania from helicopters in pelting snowstorms, and to debate with Peter Costello on world economics in Madison Square Garden, and to go parachute-jumping with the delectable Kate Lundy, and interview her in mid-air, are probably therefore on hold. Or maybe not. The barricades will beckon while ever I live and breathe, and the mountaintop, and the long night of the soul, but maybe, maybe, there comes a time to ease up, cut back, let go, cultivate the garden, write a scorching memoir or two over mulled wine by lamplight under a full moon, while the possums devour the garden and the teenage house-guests wreck the kitchen and quaff the wine . . .

It's a life choice, certainly.

Watch this space.

April, 1999

New Zealand

In New Zealand, where I've lately been, they read a film script overnight, and apologise for not being able to do it that very afternoon. In New Zealand they find you the ideal locations in a matter of hours, and give you their photos of them free of charge. In New Zealand they commit to a project straight away, and work like beavers to get it made.

In New Zealand, too, coincidentally, they make each year a film or two that intrigue or enchant the known world. *Desperate Remedies. Once Were Warriors. Heavenly Creatures. The End of the Golden Weather. Smash Palace. Bad Blood. The Piano.* More Oscar nominations per capita attend New Zealand than any other similar, midget country. Campion, twice, and Dryburgh for *The Piano*, for *Heavenly Creatures*. Hardy and Stevens for *Breaker Morant*.

The most profitable film of all time, *Jurassic Park*, stars a New Zealander, Sam Neill. The three most waywardly interesting actors in the Antipodes, Bruno Lawrence, Bruce Spence and Kerry Fox, are New Zealanders. The funniest man in the Antipodes, John Clarke, is a New Zealander. The funniest cartoon feature yet made, *Footrot Flats*, is a product of New Zealand. The most popular Australian miniseries, *A Town Like Alice*, was made by a New Zealander, David Stevens. The most esteemed Australian play put on in New

York, *The Sum of Us*, was written by a New Zealander (David Stevens). The best Antipodean film yet made, *Angel at My Table*, derives from New Zealand. The most successful Australian politician, Sir Joh Bjelke-Petersen, is a New Zealander. The most remarkable talent in Australian theatre – playwright, director, teacher, screenwriter, film director, singer, actor, heart-transplant recipient, twice – Jonathan Hardy, is a New Zealander. The most respected Antipodean world statesman, David Lange, is a New Zealander. The most respected Australian of all time, Fred Hollows, is a New Zealander.

And they will win, the bastards, the America's Cup.

I do not, in saying all this, exaggerate much. They must be doing something right, the bastards. I wonder what it is.

Being born there helps, I guess. The hills. The towering fjords. The desolate beaches. The snow. The sheep. The madness under pale stars. The tongue-waggling warriors. The bubbling mud. The winds. The earthquakes. The Maori drag queens. The voluptuous Polynesians intermarrying with wily Scots. The proud tradition of bizarre provincial homicides. The attractive mixture of tight conformism and stark lunacy.

Every New Zealand film leaves reality for a while. In *Heavenly Creatures*, where the girls enter a dream world of medieval castles and giant butterflies. In *Once Were Warriors*, where the mild social worker abruptly turns into a menacing warrior chieftain. In *The Piano*, where the eponymous instrument lies for days on a windswept beach but does not lose its tune. In *The Sum of Us*, when the paraplegic father sits up in bed and rudely addresses the camera. In *Foreskin's Lament*, when a footballer grieves his fate in a soliloquy worthy of *Hamlet*.

The whole country is like that. The rules do not apply. Aeroplanes land safely in Wellington's perpetual multi-directional hurricane. Actors make a living by pursuing, simultaneously, fifteen other trades, packing more into a year than seems possible. Grant Tilly, for instance, is an actor, producer, director, teacher, conservationist and artist. His pen-and-ink drawings of the soon-to-be-demolished wooden buildings of Wellington, published in successive annual volumes, are a national treasure. He also, as a party trick, pushes forty pounds of meat into his face in about three minutes. Acts as well as Brando most nights too. Feels underoccupied weekends.

The Maori Wars, you will be astonished to hear, were won by the Maoris. Social climbers in New Zealand pretend to Maori blood. So sanguine are they of their bifurcated culture that they made, without civil ructions, *Once Were Warriors*. Imagine us making a film about Aborigines and domestic violence. Imagine that.

We have a lot to learn from the New Zealanders. Their directness of approach and jovial ferocity of intent, bugger the budget, let's make the film, shame us yearly more and more in the marketplaces of the world. Our pampered bureaucracies and productless world-travelling producers shrivel in their cold clear light – as will soon, I fear, our footballers.

As long as we beat New Zealand? Not bloody likely.

I was in Wellington on St Patrick's Day. I wish I still was.

May, 1995

The Former Soviet Union, 1988

I spent eleven days in October with my old friend Roy Masters, the prominent football coach, in the Soviet Union for reasons not clear to either of us, and had a good clarifying time hanging round Odessa, Yalta, Kiev, Leningrad, Moscow. Like most people I felt illuminated by the experience, astounded at what I saw and anxious to go back very soon – in my case to write a film set in Kiev, which is close to Chernobyl (60, 120, 180 kilometres or 'twelve hours on the train', depending on which nervous patriot you believed), a story of love in passing on holiday, called *The Girl from Perestroika*. (Vulgar plot summary: Jack Thompson goes to Kiev in search of his Ukrainian roots and finds one. Glasnost Mon Amour.)

I want to return to Russia a little less than I want to return to the west coast of Ireland and the West End of London, but not by very much. Russia fills up your mind with questions and leaves you deeply angry not at the propaganda that you heard but how much you believed.

We constantly met busloads of puzzled, admiring Americans, often in their sixties. One of them when asked what he thought said, 'Well, everything they've told us about this country is wrong. They're a nice people. It's a good country. It's got its faults, a few of them. But Jesus, why we're spending 200 billion a year on ways of blowing these people up. These people. I really don't understand.'

This was a fair summary of our feelings too. Later on in London, where we stayed with Doug McClelland in his ambassadorial mansion at Hyde Park Gate, Doug said he'd not gone to Russia yet for fear of being disappointed. He needn't have worried. He won't be.

How to put it into words. Well, there are for instance poker machines in the Soviet Union, and highly arousing near-nude nightclub acts in its tourist hotels, and medieval apothecaries and octogenarian usherettes and parrot-torturing acts and what they call Heineken bars where you can pick up girls

69

of dizzying beauty and theatres devoted to satire and musical comedy and Chekhov and Italian opera and Shakespeare and street stalls that sell beer (never vodka, since the edict) at 7 a.m. and cities as beautiful as Paris and Venice and art galleries agog with Rembrandts and Van Goghs and Picassos and vulgar concrete resorts like Surfers Paradise and a 40 per cent divorce rate and medieval artisans employed lifelong to forge anew old statues and murals destroyed by German bombing and the entire population looks as if it's been personally dressed by Pierre Cardin and it's very warm in October and it's entirely run by women who are the most liberated on earth and have somehow achieved a balance between femininity and strength. I hope I've attracted your attention by now.

People look at you oddly when you say these things. Has he been brainwashed? Has he not, the silly bastard, read the famous long essay by the Blessed Blanche D'Alpuget in the influential colour supplement on the average ten abortions of the average Russian wife? I knew he was Left but not that left. God knows I'm a socialist myself, but . . . *Soviet Russia*?

Well, it's all true. I have this football coach as witness. There are gaps in the fabric of course. Not all the nozzles on the showers are firmly affixed. You never know till late the day before when tomorrow's plane is taking off. You can't buy film, cassettes, many foreign newspapers (though the monetarist right-wing European *Financial Times* is inexplicably available everywhere), nor watch Sky Channel, nor easily get your clothes washed. The unchanging Intourist breakfasts (cheese, black bread, yoghurt, omelette, juice) get a bit wearing, as does the lack of taxis, the opening and closing times of the apathetic travel bureaucracy and the street-smart persistence of the slim young money changers with their appalling American accents (official rate two American dollars to the rouble, unofficial rate three roubles to the American dollar) and so on.

But . . . it's a functioning country, not a cartoon. With breakfast television with rock-clips instead of commercials and newspaper headlines saying The Russian Dream: A Home of One's Own. You are not, or we weren't, prevented from moving unaccompanied around any of the cities, in the punctual trains and trolley buses, or loitering round the squalid Third World railway stations buying conversations with American cigarettes or handfuls of lollies, nosing about. The one KGB man we met for certain was very altruistic, dragging Roy into a lift and with great intensity urging him not to change any more money as the penalty, even for tourists, was seven to ten years in prison. Soviet prison.

And the tourist guides (all female, all startlingly beautiful) were very frank. You do not see the elite, one said, but they are there. They go past in black chauffeur-driven cars with drawn blinds and you never see them but they are there, and so are the KGB. All expressed exasperation with the housing shortage (five years' waiting for a flat of adequate size and so on while you lived with your ructious in-laws, making love in the small room next to theirs). Why, we asked, in a country as big as a third of the planet was there a shortage of building materials? There are enough trees. There's a good deal of sandstone. 'Yes,' said one of them, 'is mystery.' One, asked for the reform she most craved, said, 'An exportable currency.' All of them yearned for travel (Tahiti loomed large in their dream life, London, Paris; one had got as far as India and yearned for even more) but all equally wanted then to come home. Home was real and meant more than it does to us. So many had died for it, twenty million in the last war. Mother Russia was real, felt, believed and true.

We saw outside Kiev a statue of Mother Russia, fist raised, garbed like Boadicea, 100 metres high. A tribal divinity truly, one you suddenly understood. Underneath her was a war museum.

All over the western Soviet Union are war museums, and monuments to battles fought on these very streets, partisans massacred here; the town mayor executed here. The war is very real, they do not want another and they never did. The foremost Big Lie of the twentieth century is that they did, and do: billions and billions of dollars spendable on schools and crèches and hospitals have been wasted in the West on this wicked avaricious lie, rockets built never to be used, great land armies at the ready never to be deployed, playing cards and drinking Coke down long and weary decades in the service of this lie. Thank God this year the lie began at last to fade.

Russia is . . . what? Another country. A big and various one in a process of modest change. Interesting to visit. The people are very honest. They pursue you down the street to return the wallet you have dropped, as they do in England. You should go there. It will greatly assist your peace of mind.

November, 1988

The Great World, 1968

Some years in memory take on a bright legend that has little to do with what happened to you as a person but much with what happened to the world. The year 1968, for me, was both – the mingled clichés of a London that swung and a Europe in revolution and an America riven by assassination, riot and a cruel, far-off war, and the sexual opportunities unleashed by the

Pill, were coincident for me, at twenty-five, with my first journey overseas; and I lived a bit of it, saw some of it up close and was never the same.

I travelled with a girl I loved and would marry, on money taken early from her meagre inheritance, and we bought a van we slept in and travelled England, Scotland, Ireland. Carnal, unhappy, young, quarrelsome, discovering Cornish clotted cream and the Isle of Skye, the Narnia shapes of Connemara and the wonder of Irish conversation, taking a photo (now burnt) of a road sign saying 'Fairy Crossing – Slow'. We saw a peasant countryside unchanged since the century's turn, and visited Yeats's grave and Yeats's tower and Joyce's tower and the lake isle of Innisfree and experienced a country whose rock-grey beauty and bogs and blazing green and Arthurian coastline under ever-changing pale grey light so many died for, and understood why.

We took photos and photos and photos, lost now. We discovered English theatre and the miracle of great acting and the engulfing enormity of Shakespeare superbly performed, and Gielgud, Richardson, Scofield, Olivier and Guinness in their fading prime. We saw the famed Peter Brook production of *Oedipus* that ended in a maypole dance around a giant golden penis to a trad-jazz black band playing 'Yes, We Have No Bananas'. We discovered pork pies in pubs and sausages on sticks and pale ale and the Nosh Bar where you got unforgettable salt-beef on rye and pickles at all hours. We sat long hours in the House of Commons when there was still great oratory there – Powell and Jenkins, Foot, and Benn and Wilson, the English language up on its hind legs and fighting mad. We experienced the miracle, since lost, of a confident, prosperous, eccentric England still sure of the power of its heritage, still flaunting an architecture – Dr Johnson's house, the Old Curiosity Shop, the Wig and Pen Club – we somehow remembered, as we did every other street name.

We saw something, too, of Swinging London, though we missed the famous party one entered by climbing stickily through an enormous clinging red vagina, and we underwent, by mutual agreement, a fair few carnal adventures and an orgy or two, in the fashion of the day. I appeared in a film with Germaine Greer and Richard Neville and Gary Shearston called *Trouble in Molopolis* and wrote and spoke the narration of a documentary on the Opera House, called *Autopsy on a Dream*. I might have stayed and sought work, but I was scared and buffeted by then and aching for home.

We crashed the van on the way to Stratford on the day Bobby Kennedy was shot and, though it was repaired, it, and we, were never the same. We rushed through Europe – a series of rapidly flicking postcards of Sweden, Holland, Italy, Athens, Hydra. We stood amazed in the Sistine Chapel, wept at Pompeii, sighed at Salzburg, stood in the rain at Venice, ached to be home.

We were detained by police at Checkpoint Charlie for driving from West to East Berlin (still a heap of wartime rubble) with a van inadvertently full of contraband paperbacks, and warned by amiable communists with shoulder holsters (Germans make good communists, I remember thinking: they follow leaders, they raise fists, they sing along) and sent back sadly West.

We split up and Annie went to find the world's oldest woman, then 119, in Bulgaria (and did) where the van broke down for good, and I went on to America. I'd meant to see Bobby Kennedy elected there as President and I visited his grave instead – a little white wooden cross, like the grave of a dog, with 'Bobby' written on it, hard by Jack's eternal flame. I travelled by Greyhound bus to Chicago beside a self-confessed mass murderer (he liked to lock up honeymooning couples in cupboards, he said, and suffocate them) who turned up again in Chicago Central Bus Station claiming I had stolen his wallet, and I somehow talked him out of killing me. I saw Humphrey speak and Nixon speak and spent election day in New York watching black Americans line up by the hour to exercise their democratic rights with patience and civility, and I went to sleep believing Humphrey had won, and woke up and he hadn't.

And then I flew home and went back to work in the ABC. Theatre I'd seen in London informed the play I then co-wrote with Michael Boddy, *The Legend of King O'Malley*, which transformed (the histories tell us) Australian theatre. I began to write, and travel, and travel more, and knew for the first time why the best writers are always travellers. I saw what actors could do and began to realise they are the best, most selfless and least rewarded craftspeople of genius on earth. I left the ABC within two years and have been a freelance jack-of-all-disciplines since.

I'm glad what changed me was Europe and not – as was the case with so many – India, which drives the young and vulnerable crazy with its glowing and jangling simplicities. I'm glad I missed the major drugs. I'm glad I melded through shared odyssey and pain my summer love of Annie into a long life together. I'm sorry I didn't see more; or stay a few months longer.

No-one can know now the enormity travel was then. There was so little money, and if you went, it was for decades, not months, and into another life – as Clive James did and Bob Hughes and Germaine, to our country's cost, and a lot of other people who might have done well here, and are still there and unknown. To be able to go and come back as I did was a startling spiritual rarity – to taste, learn, come back and go on, do more.

For me, 1968 was a good year, though it ended The Beatles and Bobby and Martin Luther King and caused Charlie Manson and smothered the Dubček Spring and the Paris student uprising and saw the slaughter of Tet and the coming of the Blue Meanie Nixon and the end, therefore, of much of what it had come to mean. I remember it through the tumbling clouds of the years as a lighthouse to which I still, as the dark draws in, aspire. My favourite year.

January, 1997

BOOK THREE
Family Matters

Elsie at Eighty-seven

My mother turns eighty-seven this week. She's home now, after spending most of the last three months in different hospitals – one of them, Greenslopes Repat, far away from her living friends (though a dead one, Gladys, lived a few streets down from it, and lately died there) – and my sister Kay and I are tending her now, at home. And sleeping interrupted sleeps in the unchanged bedrooms of our childhood. And grappling, of late, with big decisions.

Else's problem, not uncommon, is unruly blood pressure and, around 4 a.m. on some nights, a wildly pattering heart. I know now why most old people die at 4 or 5 a.m., unpeacefully, in their sleep. They die of bad dreams: a surging pulse, a stroke, a sudden shocked and howling quietus, because the dreams – and some have Death or the Devil in them, wrestling for their souls – are harrowingly real and the brain doesn't know they are only dreams. This, and the maladroit drug mixtures pushed at her suffering by overworked doctors, and doled out, sometimes, by weary nurses in the wrong proportions, or so it is said, as the prescriptions vary. My vigilant sister saved her life more than once last week – or so she believes – by correcting the dose at the last minute.

It would all be easier if she was a vegetable, or a blathering fool. We could let her go then, I guess, or maybe we could let conventional medicine do its murderous worst. But her mind is fine, her memory clear and her conversation keen and thoughtful. She can walk, with difficulty, with her two new hips, on a metal walking frame. And she is afraid, profoundly afraid, of dying, of being extinguished. If there are no atheists in foxholes, there are also few resurrectionists aged eighty-seven in terminal wards these days. They have seen too much of the world. They know how it ends. And Elsie has been alone at night in an empty house of old memories for ten years now, and she can't stand the dark any more.

And this is our mother, and we don't know what to do.

A nursing home, for various reasons, not least John Howard's innumerate confusions but mainly the horror (waking in the night in an unfamiliar room to hear the cries of the mad), is out, or probably out for now. So too in the end, though with misgivings, is the sharing out of her last years between us – in Yarrawonga, eight hundred miles from all her friends and known places, and in Sydney, five hundred miles. And rebuilding our houses, I guess, with ramps and handrails so she can totter about, get up in the night without falling down. These are the choices you make when you go, as a student, away from your country town and choose, for whatever cause, to not come back, across those tyrannies of distance that sever us from love. And the childhood bedrooms we should sleep in more often. And the back-yards we should sit in, looking out at a view of the town.

We will, I suppose, work it out, with a roster of neighbours, paid or not, who sleep over one night a week, and a paid nurse maybe two nights, or a fifty-year-old student maybe two nights, and frequent visits, a week or two at a time, from Kay and me, and our children and spouses and cousins and nieces. There will be ways, oh yes, there will be ways of seeing her out.

And we'll get her a lot of Talking Books because reading is harder now. And satellite television, thank heaven (literally), is accessible in Lismore, with twenty channels at all hours to prattle her back to sleep, old movies, documentaries, *I Love Lucy*. And she can call her surviving friends on the phone, and earnestly talk of those lesser things by the hour that old girls talk of. The heat. The grandchildren's prospects. The murderers of Princess Di. And we will talk to her too, at all hours.

And this is adequate, I suppose. This is fair enough, at the crumbling final edge of a good innings, of a life that saw and survived a remarkable century. This is fair enough, I suppose. These are her dues.

But doubts form, and thoughts flow, especially now, near dawn, when I sit and write these poor fumbling words to myself and watch the dark.

One is how seriously wrong we all have been in following the fashions of this vapid century. Having smaller families. Pursuing that phantom Career across thousands of miles, that sterile goal of self-esteem that soon, in a moment, is gone, is a mocking void. In the old world we would have stayed Home, and frugally lived in a fibro house a few blocks away, and our five or seven or fourteen bicycling children would have called in on their grandma Elsie once a week and their grandpa Keith, when he lived. And our bloodline, our clan, would have kept its most primal thing, its Address, its own native country, its heartland. And Else would not now lie awake in a long loved room, in an empty house, in her eighty-eighth year, through a single earphone listening to a perfect stranger read a book, and waiting for the dawn; that, or her final fibrillation, or the phone to ring.

This reasoning is flawed, of course, for to do it would mean not having met my wife, nor Kay her husband, nor those pleasures of travel across the world we both have had. Yet a lot of what we learned there, across the world – in Ireland, Eritrea, Nepal, Samoa, New Zealand – adds up to no more than the obvious, that family matters, and must be better served, and in some good places it is; but not here, not now. For we have outgrown the goodness of our forefathers. We have learned, and learned with great skill and long practice, how not to care. We have learned with chill glad relief that everyone is expendable, parents too. We have learned to make money. We have learned to cope.

And the work isn't there in Lismore, we argue, anyway. Kids have to go away now to seek work as I did, and Kay did, or they lose the dole. One job presently listed by the local CES is for a young female. In a massage parlour. In Melbourne, a thousand miles away. Go seek it, girlie, the message is, or lose the dole. Go quickly, go now. So my kids will stay, for better or worse, in the city. And my mum I guess will die in the country alone.

I will write a book soon, I have promised myself, called *An Etiquette for the Dying* – on how to behave on your deathbed, and round the deathbeds of others. It will contain some things I have lately learned, from Else and Keith and John Hepworth the writer and Francis James, my great eccentric hero, about that ultimate challenge of mannerly grace when time is so short and the visitors crowd with smiles and falsehoods and lame good cheer. We have much to learn of these matters, I think, in this racked agnostic age. We have to learn, above all, how not to lie, and yet be kind. And this is hard.

And I wish my mother Elsie well. And I wish her, in her final extremity, a final certitude of love. And I wish her, however dim and shallow it seems, a happy birthday.

Good on you, Mum. Sleep well.

February, 1998

Beaches

It wasn't until I had gone for thirty-nine years to the same cement-brick shack between the lagoon and the sea for Christmas with my extended, quarrelsome family (a tent and a caravan on the lawn, four cars, a trailer with a motorboat on it, a frog in the well, cicadas loud at night and sandflies everywhere) that I began to realise what beach and ocean and fishing and swimming and hot Christmas nights are for.

They're what we have in Australia instead of psychoanalysis.

For we meet again the people (parents, brothers, cousins) who have bruised us most and we walk by a roaring surf alongside them shouting and gesturing, working things out. We beat them at Monopoly or Scrabble and dunk them under breaking waves. We give them over Christmas dinner the hard time they deserve. We get pretty drunk. We sing along with Bing Crosby, daring them with the high notes. We get it all said. And then we are at peace for another ten months, till the need in the soul for another Australian beachside Christmas purging comes again.

In all those years, and it's fifty years this Christmas, the experience for me had been had in Fingal, on the Queensland border, across the River Tweed from what used to be farmland just a heartbeat ago, at Banora Point, just down from Coolangatta. In all those years the beach out the back has been unpatrolled and every day of surfing a test of nerve in the long, long breakers that stretch white and curving for three or four miles to Cudgen Headland to the south. There were strong rips most years, and a shark sighting only once, but lots of jellyfish lazily floating in the uprearing water, and blue-bottles lethal at its edge. One year was plagued with what looked like corn-flakes in the water for three weeks. One year had a drenching rain every day for six weeks, when they were filming *Coolangatta Gold* across the water and a local Aborigine, it is said, pointed the bone. Many times there were flickering and blazing lightshows of lightning above the grey horizon, heaven flexing its muscles, amazing the children who will remember the spectacle all their lives.

And the fireworks every year over the pine trees, and the honking of horns and 'Auld Lang Syne', and the teenagers fighting and the beer cans rolling at sunrise on the blowing sand.

I go back a long way before what is there in those border cities now of course – to the 1940s, when Surfers Paradise was a weatherboard village with a big weatherboard hotel and a big bright billboard of a squealing little girl with her knickers coming off in the jaws of a growling dog and a zoo – my first zoo, with wallabies in it, and monkeys and shrieking parrots – in Cavill Avenue and paint-flakey boarding houses and empty, sandy blocks of land by the beach, for sale then for ten or fifteen pounds each. My father, a commercial traveller-for-hire in those days, used to sell them. Why didn't you buy one? I asked. I didn't have the ten pounds, he said.

It was different then, uncrowded, and pleasures were simple and lives were long. My sister Margaret stayed in the Stella Maris Guesthouse at Kirra Beach and each boarding house had its war cry (Stella Maris ya! ya! ya!) and its own house team in the beach volleyball contests and the beach cricket and the surfboard races, in those far-off blood-warm summers that seemed without end.

For time was different then, with no TV at all, not even in black and white, and radio news infrequent, at 7.45, 12.30 and 7 p.m., and days and days of conversation and nights of – I guess – heavy petting and early engage-ments and skinny-dipping and bucks' nights and shower teas and debutante balls and 'pashing' in the back row of the pictures and furtive penetration at the drive-in, and the kind of friends you made on the beach in the dump of a wave and kept as jovial intimates down all your days. Life was more local then, and your town and the next town, and the farms in between, were your country, country in the ways that Aborigines use the word, your particular portion of life on earth, your dreaming.

And the beach meant so much. It was your first glimpse of the edge of the world – its blue rounded rim pushing out into the sky – and your first adventure against the elements, your first fear of death when you were dumped and rolled over and over with salt in your nostrils and sand in your mouth and hair. It was where you first saw a lighthouse up on the rocky headland winking at night and the lights far out on the ships in peril on the sea. It was where by lantern-light you came with your father chasing soldier crabs as they ran in corporate formation this way and that, or pumping yabbies by moonlight from the sand-bars on the Tweed, and where by the hour you baited hooks (with poor little living things with arms and legs and faces) and waited and waited and occasionally dragged in a wriggling flat-head. 'Lizards,' my father would call them, and throw them back.

It was where you would fall asleep in blazing heat and wake up pink and aching and peel your own skin off your shoulders and look at its transparency: Is this me? Is this all I am? It was where you learned your first awkward balance on a surfboard, and fell off and clambered weeping back and got, after so many failures, a sense, maybe, of the limits of the world. It was where you came back a half hour later and saw your sandcastle awash and realised at once that awful thing, impermanency. It was where you could look at the bumpy shapes of girls under their swimmers and think at night about your future at night with this one or that one, in bed, in pyjamas, looking out at the moon moving between the palms and sandhills.

We had enormous sandhills, Lawrence-of-Arabia sandhills, in Fingal in those years, till a mining company came one winter with steam shovels and trucks and permits and took them away. We would ride trays and surf-o-planes down the sides of the sandhills and do cartwheels down them and meet among them at night for our first groping, tentative essays into kissing, pashing, love.

Sand on female skin, a kiss with suddenly bumping teeth and the rolling roar of water and insects dinning added so much to young love back then. It felt eternal, fated. It felt like something meant to be. But another summer on, and she wasn't there. She had moved to another state, and her ghost was on the sandhill under moonlight for a while as you grieved her vacancy. A summer on, and the sandhill wasn't there. And so it goes. And the same sea, roaring, mocks our impermanence.

And so it goes.

Wherever humankind has crossed plains and traversed mountains and come at last to the coast, it is always the same. They will settle, and swim and fish, and dream and write poems of the prospect of the sea and the sun coming up and going down in grey surging water and the seagulls heckling and the sails far out on the edge of the world. This may be no more than our ancestor the coelacanth, the fish that walked (and still walks, in coastal Africa) on six legs, reminding us in dreams that haunt our genes of our origins. It may be that throughout the millennia the sea was the only certain means (if you had a boat) of escape from the slaughtering invaders coming down from the inland mountains to pillage and murder your tribe, your family. It may be that it was from time immemorial the only certain source of food in any season, in drought or earthquake or deluging rain. Certainly we pay dearly, now, in mortgaged millions for its prospect – the water view – and the feel of sand between the toes as we walk at dawn with our dogs toward the lighthouse, the headland, the drenched and splashing rocks that we Australians, refugees all from a meaner world, adore so dearly and incurably and illogically, like a dream of eternity.

I write this at night in an uncompleted house above a beach I have walked on with dogs and children for twenty years, a beach very like the one at Fingal, with a lighthouse on a headland at its end, meeting each morning new strangers, old friends, in a way that in my taciturn country is mostly impossible, or hard, in the other places where people walk. The beach and the water, with its hints of eternity, of journeys outwards and death's near-ness and life on earth's beginnings, unlocks your capacity for friendship like no other place. I walk alongside people with whom I differ politically, talking amiably and skirting round the sensitive bits, throwing sticks for the dogs, hands in pockets, barefoot, nodding, being old and tolerant as once in such another place with other more urgent friendships I was young and fierce and romantic and, oh yes, cocksure. I am again *myself* here, or what is left of me, unlocked, unburdened, psychoanalysed, unrepressed, relieved, unfearful in this unaltered setting of what it is I will say or hear. The beach is like that. It is heartland. It is my country, my orchestra, my canvas, my manuscript. It is where I am. It is home.

December, 1998

Jenny Leaving

My daughter Jenny did her final school project last month, and is now preparing to go to the University of the West, the Richmond campus, two hours' drive from our home. Because of the distance she will live in a room in the college there, and come home on some weekends. Her special quarters in the house, a loft with attached verandah in her favourite canary colours, with pot plants and her sketches, will be waiting for her, as always. The little kitchen we were going to provide her with will not be built, nor the extra room for her guests.

For she is going now, one way or another, and that is that. She will be back for visits, and there will be monthly family dinners, perhaps, in restaurants and nights out at plays, a coming trip to Bali with her mother. But, unstoppably and inevitably, Jenny is going. Leaving. And braving an uncertain world.

We will have less of her left than we had planned. Many of the photos were lost in the fire, and all of the videotapes of her as a baby and a little girl. Her special toys burned and many of her drawings. She will take her Celtic harp and the guitar and play in coffee houses in Richmond or in town.

We are not too worried about her. She has immense personality and charm and courage and, though her ambition is disparate, much realism about the world, along with a beguiling, buoyant capacity for hope. Jenny will be okay. She may marry, of course, a grazier's son, or one of those earnest Greenies with whom she will study her worthy tree-hugging course, Social Ecology, in the next few years. Or she may pursue her music and marry a drummer and live poor and restless and die broke. But she will always have loving friends, and entertaining parties, and children (I hope) to love her as her parents do.

But now she is going, and bit by bit the house is emptying of her presence. Jack, our eldest, encouraged, has found a studio in town he shares with some fellow musicians, and sleeps in some nights. 'Jack is leaving too, isn't he?' Jenny said yesterday, in part to comfort herself with the example of his absence. Tom, the youngest, will be here for a while, but the years are not many before it will be just us and the dogs and the phone and birthday cards and Christmas dinner.

We had hoped to buy the block of land next door and offer it to one or other of the children to raise their family next to us, the ever available babysitters. But it was passed in at much more than we could afford at the auction last week and thanks to the Abbott and Costello court case and the damage it has done to my power to earn, and thanks to a few poor decisions I've made, and the interest hikes of the eighties, and the recession we had to have, it will never be in our reach.

And Jenny is going, very soon. And, life being local, her life will soon occur away from us. Those animal loyalties that grow with familiarity will be directed towards those tutors and colleagues and room-mates and boy-friends that will be her family soon and we will be the past, the loved past yes, but that which no longer impinges much on what she decides will be her future course.

And this is normal. This is what happens. But oh the little girl I miss, and carried sleeping up the long stairs in moonlight all those years. The baby girl who lay asleep like a starfish on the big double bed, occupying its whole width. The baby girl who said, 'I not a girl, I a wombat'. The little girl who wrote music, and became a Buddhist, and a vegetarian, and meditated out on the front lawn at sunrise, the schoolgirl who draws now marvellous charcoal nudes. Going too.

And this is what happens. This is normal.

I wish I had done more for her, and this is normal too. I especially wish we could have seen together Topol in *Fiddler on the Roof* singing *Is this the little girl I carried*, but money was short and the trip to Melbourne inconvenient. I would love to have gone with her to more painting exhibitions, more concerts, more films and plays. She didn't see *Titanic*. She will see *Elizabeth*, for the costumes, and *Antz*, for the computer puppets. And so it goes. I would like to have spent a summer in Tuscany with her, looking at statues and paintings. But real life intervened, and that was never to be.

The hard bit is to realise how little you can do to a loved life without being a tyrant. They will go their own way unless you command, imprison, order and shout. And so they will miss out, sometimes, on the best you can give them. They will learn in their own time. And they may not, in this dread world, learn enough.

If I had the money I would buy her an art gallery to own and paint in, or a puppet theatre in an inner suburb. But that, I suppose, is never to be. I remember on his deathbed my father wishing he could have done more for me, left me more to go on with, and me responding that it didn't matter. It does, of course, it does to the parent a lot, if less to the child. To hold, to carry, to encircle, protect, to clutch while crossing the road and carry quickly out of the fire leaving all behind to burn is what parenting means. It is animal. It is human. It is us. It is me.

And Jenny is going, and those loved encircling days will soon, or pretty soon, be the legendary past for her, and then, though later, for us. We will not rise in the morning aware of her presence in the house. She will not be there to call to the phone, to tell a joke, to invite for a walk, and a run, on the little beach with the dogs. The dogs will miss her, she was their mother, and so will I.

On my sister's grave is the message *We miss you, Marg*, and nothing else. I miss you, little Jen. I miss you already.

December, 1998

Expulsion

A while back two schoolgirls were expelled from Castle Hill State High for buying and selling a small amount of marihuana in the toilet block, an offence committed by tens of thousands of secondary students, I suspect, in any year.

Then they were reinstated on the order of the Minister, persecuted on their return by chanting gangs of students, and defamed on air by their male school captain and their headmaster as persons unfit to cross again the threshold of that worthy old school. They should seek their education, it was said, somewhere else.

It occurred to me at the time that they should probably sue the school captain for defamation. Then it occurred to me – rather more significantly – that any act of expulsion is *in itself* an act of defamation.

It certainly has the same effect. Your good name becomes soiled, your career prospects lessened, your self-esteem shrunken, your hope of ordinary friendships diminished. Like being sacked from a job (and I know full well what this is like), it is a devastating blow to the ego and reduces through life your capacity to hope and seek the better. It marks you down in your own mind lifelong as a potential failure, a possible criminal.

Yet headmasters have the power to wreck young lives unpunished (and unsued) – after, for instance, as happened up my way, catching two girls smoking tobacco not in the school grounds but in the local shopping centre while wearing the school uniform when they were of legal age to do so if they liked.

They were expelled. Neither sought an education elsewhere. One went fruit-picking. One got a job, locally, in a pastry shop. They never got the HSC. They weren't *attentive* students, but they could have got the HSC. The year was 1993.

Other kids up my way were expelled for truancy, a curious logic, and their lives likewise diminished if not wrecked, their friendships disrupted, their mood made momentarily suicidal. The kids of divorced and warring parents, usually, with enough trouble in life already, punished by the system for their bad choice of parents, or a recession we had to have.

I met this particular deputy headmaster once and regard him, perhaps unjustly, as emotionally stingy and unforgiving. But what he did is only a fraction of the dreadful things that happen to our children. We force them like indentured labourers into religions and institutions (like boarding schools) emotionally wrong for them. We make them work unpaid in the family business. We torture them with custody arrangements after divorce. We drag them all over the map according to our convenience. We promise them a career if they go through thirteen years of educational imprisonment, then jeer at them (or some Education Ministers do) for expecting one. *Clean out toilets, you young fools. It's a tough world.*

And we react with amazement when they attempt suicide or go on drugs or burgle rich homes for the price of a fix. We react with amazement when young Aborigines, finding they can get suspended from school by merely holding up a middle finger at a teacher, opt to do so, preferring life, however brief, in the dusty outdoors to an Anglo-Saxon fierceness they cannot comprehend or live by.

Expulsion is the worst thing that can be *legally* done to a child. It's a penalty more severe for a minor offence, I suspect, than any other in our society – like a ten-year sentence for double parking, or five hundred lashes for avoidable errors in spelling. Or decapitation, as happens in some places, for adultery. Kids in their teens are still discovering what the world is, and after their expulsion begin to think it's cruel and unchangeably unjust. It's a short step from that to drugs, crime, chronic unemployment or, even worse I suspect, a kind of jaded idleness, hitch-hiking with a surfboard to God knows where.

A couple of examples of young people I know. A boy expelled at seventeen in his final year had lately watched his well-loved brother slowly die over three years of a rare heart disease and end his struggle three days before he might have had a heart–lung transplant. Then he watched in the next year, as the sole surviving child, his traumatised parents acrimoniously divorce. Then he turned seventeen. And one morning he came up behind a girl he knew in the school library and gave her – by way of greeting – a single pelvic thrust from behind. Not realising the likely consequences, she complained to the Head, who expelled him without appeal or any consideration of his recent distress or what expulsion might do to him. He went through hard years after that – exam failure, TAFE, drug abuse, terrible fights with his parents and girlfriends – but has narrowly survived and found his way into a course he likes at a provincial university. He got through it. But he didn't deserve any of it, I believe. He should, I believe, have been better treated.

Another, the son of a famous man, at that time estranged from his wife, topped classes at one of Sydney's best-known schools, and was mocked for it by his father, the famous Australian. No teacher helped the boy through all this. One day before an excursion the organising teacher was forty minutes late and the waiting kids grew restless. The boy was one of them and in boredom he climbed a tree. He was put on suspension, pending expulsion, for climbing the tree. Francis James and I intervened with the blustering pompous headmaster, and he grew nervous and the boy was belatedly reprieved. But over the four weeks of his suspension he lost all respect, all enthusiasm, for things in general, for life itself.

Big deal.

The boy was eventually expelled for being drunk and abusive on *muck-up day*, the last day of his life at school, and forbidden to sit the HSC among his friends, and travelled long miles to do it among strangers. He did badly, of course, dropped out, worked shifts in factories, joined a thrash band, contemplated suicide, took drugs, got through it, and prospects for gold now near Kalgoorlie. He will survive. He may even get in as a mature-age to uni, become an academic.

Think about that. The genes of his famous father didn't help, and they didn't matter. The heinous crime of tree-climbing outweighed all that. Tree-climbing had to be punished.

These are stories I know first-hand. You will know others.

Punishment, says Ken Buttrum, the Director General of Juvenile Justice who is my second-oldest friend (we went to a *good* country high school together in the 1950s), punishment is now thought to correct all things, but of course it corrects very little 'because the threat of it frightens only those with something substantial to lose. And meanwhile, of course, it rides roughshod over our human rights, particularly those of children.'

Australia has the worst youth suicide rate in the Western world. Think about this. And in an era of divorce, job insecurity, the breakdown of religions and general spiritual trauma, expulsions go on as if it were still 1891. Kids expelled for truancy. Think about that. For smoking tobacco. For climbing trees.

In a just society the emotional history of moody, torpid students would be taken into account, and lawyers provided by the state would plead for clemency. In a just society only offences that harmed others (like chronic classroom disruption, or serious violence to fellow pupils or teachers) would be grounds for expulsion, and truancy wouldn't be one of them. In a just society pupils expelled and so defamed could sue.

And perhaps they can. Perhaps the girls in Castle Hill could try it, on their school captain. Then he might see what it's like to be young and isolated and scared and lonely and thought a villain by your peers. And justice then, maybe, reasonable merciful modern justice might prevail.

September, 1997

Divorce

A few years back I witnessed a divorce arrangement that did the right thing by all concerned. It was a rare experience. It went like this.

The marital home was not sold but kept. In it the two children, boy and girl, lived as they had all their lives, in the same neighbourhood, with the same playmates, attending the same school and swimming at the same beach. For four days a week the wife, who was doing a university course, lived in the house and looked after the children. For three days a week the husband, a film director, lived in the house and looked after the children.

Not far from the house, a suburb away, was a flat. Husband and wife lived alternately in this and on the four days and on the three days pursued their other lives, the husband with his new girlfriend, the wife with her studies.

And thus it was the children were able to keep that thing most precious to children, their address, and their sense of neighbourhood and parenthood. They were not made to travel miles across a city to eat at McDonald's and go to the zoo with a gloomy parent with only edgy things to say to them. They were home. This was Mummy. This was Daddy. This was their address, where they came from, there they stayed. Where they slept each night in the same beds, knowing who they were.

This arrangement shows by its contrasts, I think, what awful things are done to children by divorce – disruption, dislocation, confusion, sadness, ache and guilt, did Mummy and Daddy break up because of me? – by the yearning for how it was before. The address. The far-off lost contentment of life as it was. Like ET all children want to be Home.

'We're only staying together because of the kids' was a common phrase in country towns when I was young in the fifties. I used to think such couples cowardly. I don't any more. I think they behave correctly, some heroically. And I now suspect that the Murphy No-Fault Divorce Law was a noble experiment that has failed and if divorce is to occur at all it should be on the one-house model I speak of, or something pretty close to it, with ground rules that are fixed and firm.

For a lot of lives are stuffed up by divorce, and not too many improved. Children of divorce, dragged back and forth across the map, grow scared and neurotic, mistrust friendships and sexual contact, do badly at school, lose jobs and drink too much or shoot up drugs and fail in their marriages too – after wedding parties when fourteen step-parents make speeches each in turn. And they do not deserve to end like this, because a man once sought a younger woman for his bed, and met one at the office, or because a woman once sought to escape her caged and claustrophobic life and ease her soul of its intellectual frustrations. It isn't, actually, fair.

My son had a friend, call him Mark, when he was little. Mark's father left his mother for a younger woman when he was four. The little boy grieved, felt guilty, got through it. Then his father went *back* to his mother when he was five. He was overjoyed. His Daddy was back. It was going to be all right. Then when he was six his father left again, for the same younger woman. I saw that little boy change in his soul after that second betrayal into someone with criminal tendencies. I do not believe the father's sexual satisfaction (or whatever it was) was important enough to distort another life, to embitter and criminalise it, make it a life (as he did not, but he came close) that would end in gunfire at a filling station, or a heroin overdose. I believe that fatherhood asks more than that.

Nor do I believe a mother has the right, as a court lately ruled, to take her children thousands of miles from their father merely because her sexual satisfaction (or whatever it is) lies in Tasmania or California or Bechuanaland. To hell with her sexual satisfaction (or whatever it is). There are greater things at stake here.

Put it this way.

Forty-three per cent of Australian children suffer through a process of parental divorce. Some do it twice. Many watch their mothers go successively to the bedroom with five or six or fifteen male callers. Many attend their father's remarriages. Some are sexually abused by new step-parents. Many are punched and insulted by new step-brothers. All change address, many five or six times. Many change schools, two or three times. Many more live alone with a single, fraught, impoverished and occasionally shrieking mother, and slowly learn to hate her.

It's a punishment they do not deserve when their only crime is being born. It's cruel and unusual punishment for a life they did not seek, and could not help.

If divorce is to happen, there should be ground rules that include a right of grandparents (say) to seek the children's custody from the court. The children should stay in the one suburb and go to the same school whatever it costs. This is the one time they need close friends, and it's the one time they lose them. The court should understand that children's happiness lies not just in which parent keeps them, but the neighbourhood, the friendships, the streets and beaches they have come to know as the world.

And so on. It's no accident, I think, that Ireland, which has very little divorce, is a happy society, and the USA, which has a lot of divorce, is an unhappy society to the extent of 28 000 gun murders a year. It's no accident that more kids from broken homes commit suicide. It's no accident that kids who change address a lot (kids that are known as army brats, for instance) more often end up on the dole or in gaol. It's no accident that kids from broken homes themselves divorce, and the cycle starts again.

It's my belief that divorce is not a human right, it's a privilege. It's a licence to harm another human being irreparably. It's a method of destroying children's hope in the goodness of the world.

So it shouldn't be entered into lightly. And neither – in the words of the Book of Common Prayer – should marriage. There should be two years' notice required by law of anyone wanting to marry, and one year's proven cohabitation. Every high school should teach what marriage is – among other things an ongoing battle over how money is spent.

For lives are at stake here, young lives. Children are not just genetic baggage, they have rights. Among them I believe is the right not to be stuffed around and emotionally wrecked by the self-indulgence of their immature progenitors. They have a right, a human right, to their sense of identity, to a surname, playmates, friendships. They deserve better.

And if they do not get it they might, with justification, tear society apart.

November, 1996

Moving House

In all of our lifetimes the three most upsetting things we go through, a recent survey shows, the things that wound and scar our lives the most are, in order of suffered grief, a death in the family, a divorce, and moving house.

The third one may surprise a few of us. Because we all move house routinely now – once or twice in childhood, four or five times after leaving home for college or a new job out of town, two or three times more after marriage, in search of better-paid work or a larger dwelling, once more in retirement to a seaside flat, then a last melancholy surrender to a nursing home.

Since this is all so regular and common, and it happens to almost everyone, how can it be so bad?

Well, think back. Think back, and remember, as far as you can.

There was a world you were born in, with particular aunties and neighbours and fences and corner stores maybe, and playgrounds and playmates and a swing and a grandmother who babysat and a particular bed with a particular ceiling above it and a particular window beside it and a particular view of the yard. And this was your universe. It was what you knew as reality.

And then abruptly, suddenly, there was inexplicably a garage sale, and the bed went, and the tricycle, and the little desk and the still remembered one-eyed doll. And then a long car ride, and the houses going by. And all of that universe was gone. And there was a new place, with a different door and hall. Do you remember how frightened you felt? And how you cried?

Most of us don't. We have most of us walled it off, excluded it from our past. But it's in there somewhere and worse than anything – except I guess those two other things – a vivid erasure, a cruel betraying, a lopping off, an amputation of the beloved and legendary past.

Our identity is very much a product of where we are – a certain street, a certain school, a certain football team, becomes a defining adjective we live by, a badge, a flag, a jumper, an emotional fingerprint some would say. Take all that away, as a house-move does, and we become quite literally dislocated. Disoriented. Floundering. We become, for a while, a little crazy.

This is not too big a word for it. Most of us who once left home for college will remember a period – six months, a year – of serious emotional instability when we didn't know who our friends were or what the future was or what the world was up to. Many of us survived it, though some did not, and are dead now, or mad, or broken in their hearts in other ways. Had we all returned each evening to a familiar street, and a familiar bedroom, and a familiar backyard and neighbours, we would not have been so upset, so vulnerable, so despairing. We know that now.

And the result, a kind of crazed and questing fury, and in some a kind of suicidal mischief, is found too in the children of divorce who have often in one afternoon lost a parent, their address and those intricate emotional supports that are their schoolfriends and playmates, and lost them for good. If they had kept their address, their neighbourhood, their emotional bonding to where they are and who they love, their sacred sites and blood relatives, it would have seemed less bad. They might have survived it all then. Children of divorce who move away from their neighbourhood as well do not survive, or not often, into true adult maturity and calm of mind. Prove that I lie.

Well known to experts in mental disturbance is the Army Brat syndrome. The children of army personnel would move every two years, as a rule, to another army town. And they were as a rule, unsurprisingly, found by their new (always new and usually wary) schoolteachers the most unruly, the most unstable, the least controllable, the least literate and the least academically adept in every successive school.

They had moved, you see. They had lost their Address, lost it once again. And they had left even more of themselves behind. Throughout life such kids have a pattern of moving again and again, every two years usually, of changing partners, changing surnames, discarding each successive self and moving on and never settling. Children of preachers and schoolmasters and upwardly mobile bank managers show a similar pattern, and the children of divorce.

We aren't meant to be like this. And the ever-changing, ever more frantic economic rationalist world of constant sudden unsought crisis and repeated crushing trauma is warping and wounding and wrecking and driving to teenage suicide, we now hear, more and more of us. And taking our homes away.

Many of us can't resist, of course, and can't fight back these tides of corporate greed and onrushing avarice that routinely close down communities and cripple whole regions and send people out, and down the highways, and across the oceans, desperately, frantically, seeking lives elsewhere, anywhere, quick, quick, move on. I'm late, said the rabbit, I'm late.

But some of us can. And we should have a care, and take some thought, before we breezily move a growing child from the world he loves, or she loves, from his Address, or her Address, to a world of strangers and unknown hills and unfamiliar belligerent skies. It is worse than taking away a beloved little dog, and gassing it. It is worse than that. It is worse than letting a child befriend a particular lamb or duck and then making her eat the pet for dinner. It is worse than smashing a particular toy, a toy she loves, before her eyes and making her sweep it up.

For it is taking away their world, and so much of their Self that there is not much of it left to keep, and go on with.

We should let them keep their primal memories, if we can, their legendary places. We should let them revisit them when they are old. We should let them sleep again in their middle age (as I do, thankfully, often) in the same bedroom beside the same window and its view of the same backyard. And they will love you more for it, and come to see you more often, when you need them to come, when you are old.

For we are all of us familiarity-seeking animals, and heartland-seeking animals, who crave common tribal names and tribal tales, and home teams, and home towns, and homes, and nests of kinship and friendship and neighbourhood we journey from and return to in our lives on earth with glad renewal. We mark out our territory, what Aborigines call our Country, as surely as dogs do and new-hatched ducklings who know what they first see, even if it's an elephant, as Mother. No economic fashion, no tide of political history, will change that. We are what we are.

And we should, if we can, stay home. Among our kin. And in our Country. Stay as long as we can.

January, 1998

What Jenny Did Next

Thank God He Met Lizzie, a film of great warmth and thoughtfulness and carnal wit, is about love of course, and what love is, and where one day it went, and why – one of the very few local films (*The Year My Voice Broke* and *Flirting* are two of maybe ten) ever to go near the subject.

Guy, a lawyer, turns thirty and meets Lizzie, a doctor, who is also thirty, and bright and beautiful and the perfect choice. They marry and at the wedding party, organised by Lizzie's North Shore mother-from-hell, a nightmare of clunking good intentions – sugary Bacharach ballads in bad performance and speeches of moving sincerity and wedding guests hell-bent on loveless fornication at evening's end with someone, anyone, they meet at this ritual of happy endings – Guy begins to think, wistfully, sadly, of the girl he should, perhaps, have married.

Jenny.

Impossible, randy, eager, untidy Jenny.

All men have their Jenny, the girl who wanted everything, love everlasting, babies, the whole catastrophe, too soon. All women have *been* Jenny at some stage, going night after night through the *mechanics* of procreation and ruefully, woundedly taking the Pill in the morning, and regarding the bathroom mirror with red-rimmed grimness and feeling used, and yet in love.

And so it goes. The film affirms the pattern of loving that is now, post-AIDS, the prevailing one. It involves a first, or second, love that is in effect a first marriage, wedlock without a ring – live-in, faithful, at first arousing,

93

in the end routine, domestically contentious, full of wordless quarrels mysterious even to the participants. It occupies all of one's twenties and all of one's romance and ends on the stroke of thirty because of the children, long postponed (and ofttimes aborted), that the man in his guilt can't face – children from this girl anyway. And so they split, and she ends childless perhaps, perhaps not, but certainly, gravely wounded as she limps through her thirties to the decade of grief and menopause – and pet cats and baby-sitting nephews on bitter-sweet weekends. And he marries Lizzie.

Of course he marries Lizzie. Lizzie is a good match – cool and blonde and willing to widen the boundaries, the very *definition* of marriage to take in, well, incidents, minor adulteries, his and hers, holiday incidents one needn't worry about, Lizzie can bestride all that. Lizzie will be there. Loyal and steady, but somehow loveless, Lizzie will be there. At your deathbed side, with the needed hypodermic, Doctor Lizzie will be there.

Jenny however . . . Jenny is discarded, and lost, and feels a barren mess, and a modern one, the sour fruit of contraception. In medieval times Jenny at thirty would be having her eleventh child and at forty-two her seventeenth and be busy at fifty in a fecund womanly way with them all (or all that survived), and her thirty grandchildren too. Jenny now at fifty is talking to a cat and chain-smoking and dining with girlfriends and planning trips to Venice via Hanoi and wondering who will look after the cat, and studying the Tarot, and macrobiotic gardening.

Jenny has been under-used. Both used and under-used.

In Ireland they live in the old way still. No woman regrets her many children and they rub along, somehow, in the great three-volume novel that is the extended, quarrelling, singing, abundant contentious extended family. Everyone has a hundred and fifty cousins and the families gather and the Guinness is drunk and the stories are told. Or that's the way it was till they let in contraception (wisely, oh yes, begorrah, wisely) a few years back. So things henceforth will be better, I guess, in Ireland. The smaller family has arrived, and greater happiness with it. The last eight children of each Irish family were not needed, and better unborn, discuss. You've met a lot of them. Imagine them not there. What a relief.

In five hundred years from now the thing most known about our time will be men's power on marrying to forbid their women the children they wanted, in some astonishing cases any children at all. By then it will be known that love must procreate or end. Like the shark in *Jaws* it must move forward or die and children, or perhaps a business partnership, are (with exceptions all of us have met) its only way of moving forward. Strange that this is not known, or even thought of, now. We talk of orgasms instead. Orgasms are what we have instead of children, grandchildren, tribes, communities, clans. What a contemptible trade-off. What a con. In the place of another human being, a momentary loss of oxygen to the brain.

In these unmarrying times there should be some rules I think, rules that give Jenny a chance in her life to avoid her probable destruction, her probable spaying, her Hanoi-and-tabby-cat sad sole quietus. One rule I invented for myself, in 1964, and kept to, is not a bad one and it's this. *If you're a man, it runs, and you live with a girl, and it's constant and loving and feels good, give it two years. And at that point either cut out or commit for life. For you do not have the RIGHT to take (as so many do) a girl's best years and leave her adrift and smashed at thirty or thirty-two.* It's not fair. For you will survive. And she will not. She will shrivel, and strangle many of her better selves in loneliness. And it will be your doing. She will hate you, and she will be right. You will, in the old-fashioned phrase, have used her, and cast her aside.

And one day, as in the film, Jenny will walk past you in the street, with hatred and grief and oblivion in her eyes. And you will know the wrong you have done her, and feel quite ill until, well, maybe, your three-martini lunch.

Better to leave after two years. Give the girl a fair go.

Fecundity and the craving for it in women is the fact least thought of in the feminist revolution, and the idea that it can be shrunk down to one child at thirty-nine (or three miscarriages, and no child) is as foolish as any other premise of economic rationalism: downsize, downsize, discuss.

Conduct an experiment. Find a woman, any woman, with five children, a woman of any social class, and ask her if she regrets having had her last three children. Then find a woman, any woman, with one child, and ask if she regrets not having more. The first will always be no, the second always yes.

And yet in our culture children are always looked on as being the problem – when they are of course the solution, the consolation, the joy, the advancement of love, the solace for death, the sole guarantee of a listening ear in old age and a bed for a week or so. There are children daily sloshed into buckets who would have loved you and it's a crying pity and I mourn for them, as I would for victims in war, and I curse (in vain) the trendiness that numbly and hourly slaughters them.

Guy, in short, has a lot to answer for. For he has come in his mind to that most awful of truths (and it is a truth) that *Jenny is replaceable*, and he has used it first to enslave her body and scramble her mind (*children? you must be joking*) and then (of course) to leave her out with the other empties on the day he turns thirty and moves on.

I don't think much of Guy. I'm like him, or I was, and however much he puts the SNA in front of his name I don't believe him. He has been a tyrant where it counts, in the countdown of ova that would have been useful citizens and their mother's joy.

October, 1997

Heroin

When my son Jack was twelve a neighbour offered him heroin, and Jack had sense enough to say no. Had he said yes and become addicted and died at twenty-nine like Bob Carr's brother, after going into a terminal coma at twenty-eight, I would have murdered my neighbour, I think, and thereby added my family's name, and Jack's, to the numbers that are always growing. I'm glad I didn't have to, and all my kids are through the worst of the danger years now, touch wood. Why I didn't summon the cops to put in gaol a neighbour and a friend is hard to say. I'm part of a culture of pardon, forgiveness, denial up our way I guess, and I didn't find out about it till long after he had moved, and himself stopped using. But because of that culture, and because of merciful fools like me, more and more kids are hooked, and eventually, stupidly die.

No-one takes up heroin in his thirties; it comes with youth. Like tobacco it's a habit born of adolescent boredom or self-distaste or else that urgent feeling of immortality that all youth has. Like tobacco it mostly, though not always, kills you, and it mostly does so sooner.

An inner-city headmistress I know tells how she has tried to help smacked pupils through the HSC, and she knew when she looked in their eyes that their lives were already over; poor kids, they were dead already. Because one morning, or one afternoon, someone like my amiable neighbour made a twenty dollar profit on a deal, and with the money maybe bought some for himself.

It's likely both pusher and user lack stimulating jobs. It's probable both did badly at school, and didn't read books much, or had reading difficulties. It's pretty certain both are the children of divorce, or domestic violence, or incestuous assault. But it's also just possible sometimes that they're just kids, like other ordinary kids, pressured or shamed or dared one afternoon into giving it a try – and undergoing that rush of all the pleasure centres from which, I hear, there is no road back.

Some politicians think it's good not to do anything radical about all these young deaths lest youth 'get the wrong message'. These deaths are an affordable statistic in short – or keeping them alive a waste of money that is better spent on gaols and cops on the beat and bars on windows and work-for-the-dole. These lives, in society's balance, are an affordable expense. They are, in the World War One phrase, expendable.

Well, it's a point of view, and one we have heard before. Child pick-pockets were hanged in the eighteenth century. They were not worth saving. They were expendable.

But you judge a system of belief, and the government it elects – you have to – by how many people it kills, in needless wars and road accidents, bad hospitals, ambulances that never come. Industrial deaths caused by harsh new laws. The suicidal melancholy joblessness brings. The dead in buckets flung into furnaces after abortions, abortions that are safe for the mother but fatal for the baby. Killing people, as a rule, is wrong. And death a bottom line we should not forgive.

There are different ways of saving lives from heroin, however, and inject-ing it free in safe doses to known users is only one of these. Another (I have told politicians who listened with interest, then glumly shook their heads) is to lock up the *users*, for months on end, in padded cells where they can go cold turkey, and not let them out till they name the pushers, and lock up the pushers till they name the suppliers, and so on, and so by depriving it of *customers*, kill the trade.

Too hard, perhaps. Politically unaffordable. Better to let kids die.

Throughout this century our governments have killed off surplus job-seekers by sending them off to war, and maybe this is just another way of doing that. It may be economically necessary. It may be unavoidable, or, as they say now, inevitable, an inevitable part of world-wide restructuring.

But it isn't fair.

Because heroin isn't comparable with anything else. It's heaven on earth for twenty dollars at your first injection, and a wee bit less than heaven the second time, and less than that the third time, and a ceaseless gnawing hunger thereafter for the first, fine careless rapture, irrecoverable now, that out-weighs all else there is in life – sex, family love, the movies, music, religion, travelling the world.

It's a hunger that can't be fought, or erased from the memory of the senses. It can only be held off by a drab and tedious truce with addiction for one year, five years, ten, that will never satisfy, never bring joy, never bring happiness in the measure that first rush did, that can offer only as cure a lifetime of grim and seedy anticlimax lit with lightning flashes of remem-bering how it was.

And the victims are everywhere – the parents, the children, the lovers, the neighbours who found the young corpse in the bathroom and wish they had visited sooner. It fills the companions of the dead teenager with ineradi-cable guilt. What could I have done more to help them? They surely could have been saved.

I vary in my view of what can be done. I think sometimes it might be better for all concerned if my former neighbour, an addict himself, had been hanged, and every pusher so treated by the law, and every tourist returning with plastic bags of it inside their brassieres. And I think sometimes that anything, anything that prevents a *death*, and this includes safe injecting rooms, is better than anything that involves one, like hanging pushers as they do in Malaysia and Thailand.

At the very least we must find alternatives for our youth. Free Internet parlours open at all hours where video games against aliens can be played by the ill-at-ease. Free reading groups for adolescents in concrete buildings with dancefloors and skateboard ramps attached. Pubs where no-one over thirty is admitted.

And jobs above all, however economically irrational. Jobs they must get up early for, that give them money to spend on CDs and the ordinary elements of personal pride. It was once said the Devil finds work for idle hands. And heroin does too. The work of a short, climactic lifetime. A lifetime briefly fulfilling, and often thrilling, often painful, always exciting.

And over very soon.

Because the heroin trade is the worst thing there is. It's worse than murder because it is a living death, with torture added in, sold to gullible kids for the price of a cinema ticket and a box of Maltesers. It further tortures those already troubled in their lives. It tortures their families, their children, their surviving spouses, with an ongoing anguish that does not end in a death by overdose, that always haunts the survivors with guilt. What did I do wrong? How could I have saved him? What was I doing that night? Why wasn't I with her?

Oh sweet Jesus forgive me.

A government, of course, that further torments youth by praising the makers of big money while keeping youth in jobless poverty, keeping them unskilled and unschooled and shamed and despairing of their lives, is an accomplice in the heroin trade. For that and prostitution and burglary and armed robbery are the only places where the big money is – if you start out poor and are not Mel Gibson or silverchair.

Tim Costello can see this but apparently not his brother, or John Howard, or Peter Reith. Heroin is economically rational. Smack and global economics go hand in glove. One is the cause of the other.

Prove that I lie.

For a kid with a good fulfilling job and an income and the price of a night out feels less like a hit than one under stress from long hours in an empty room. A kid with a girlfriend or a young man with a pregnant wife is less likely to do something stupid with his life. Ordinary intelligence can work this out. John Howard can't. His mind is too tangled up with the ethic of punishment, and the undeserving poor. And sin, the sin that properly ends in hellfire.

There are lives in flames round him and he doesn't care. Or he doesn't care enough.

Prove that I lie.

May, 1999

Boredom

Like some others of my generation my great fault I suppose is impatience: I want things now, now, quickly. This I think is because my mother, like some others of her generation, believed in four-hour breastfeeds and so I would have to wait and wait and grow restive, then plaintive, then scared, then frantic, and ever since then I have hated waiting.

This at any rate is my excuse for my being, and my forties generation being, so quickly bored and for wanting to leave the table, the room, the house, the playhouse, the church, the political party, the relationship, the marriage bed, the faith of our fathers, now, now, fast-forward, fast-forward, cut to the chase. Later generations will have a different excuse but this is mine, and the condition is common.

For the fear of boredom, I know, rules most of our lives. New fashions, new pop songs, new pop stars, new diets, new boyfriends, new wives, new alcohol mixtures, new cheeses, new drugs of choice, new Monica jokes on the Internet, new political trends, new cult religions, new Elvis sightings, new cancer cures, new hopes for life on Mars or the moon, new proofs that aliens are among us, or used to be, and that JFK killed Marilyn, and that Michael Jackson or Madonna is making a comeback, show how bored we are with what we already have or know, and how hungry for what is now novel and strange and unsettling. When I was a boy in the 1940s the radio news was broadcast three times a day. Today it is on the hour every hour, or the half hour, on CNN the quarter hour. In the sixties political sound-grabs took forty-five seconds. Now they take five. We are, it seems, obsessed now, and for no good cause, with *what happens next*. Now, now. Fast-forward.

And what is happening now is never enough. We drift in our minds away from the conversation we are in to watch, to no purpose, moving pictures on silent television screens. We scream aloud at red traffic lights. We drum our fingers on banking machines: *it's been ten seconds, come on.* We play loud music at parties lest mere conversation bore us; we have to shout to be heard, and that is more exciting.

And we choose our friends or discard them for the brevity of their discourse, and hold it a mortal sin to talk too much. To a verbose friend on the phone we are never at home, or in a meeting, and soon he is not our friend; or not our close friend anyway.

And this is fair enough, is it not, since life is too short and our time on earth so limited. We have to get on, to cut to the chase, to get to the bottom line, now, now.

. . . Yet I worry sometimes that I, like much of the world, am wrong in thinking this. For some of our great experiences in life on this earth are inextricably interleaved with boredom. Family funerals. Wedding breakfasts. Political orations. High school concerts. Bushwalks down the Franklin. Five-day cricket matches. Twelve-day South Sea cruises. Climbs up live volcanoes in Vanuatu. Chess games. Week-long folk festivals at Woodford. Jazz on a summer afternoon. A book by Joseph Heller or A.S. Byatt, or Ralston Saul or Tolkien. A symphony by Sibelius or Mahler. A recitation on Bloomsday. Queuing up for a Wyeth exhibition. The first fifteen minutes of a Shakespeare play. A twelve-hour theatrical event by Peter Brook. Conversation with friends round fires all night in the desert under the stars. For we become during such an experience part of the whole of something larger than ourselves, something shared, like a great song, something immense and unlikely and exalting that lifts us out of our selfishness and out of our puny impatience and sets us down on a higher plane of being and sometimes – not always – makes a better person of us; a nobler person of us, maybe.

Boredom ennobles, discuss.

It certainly ennobles nurses, and the nuns in hospices who hear the dying eke out for days their last fragmented thoughts in the gathering dark. It ennobles great musicians who practise hour after hour on the same piano in their eighties. And ballet dancers, up on their toes every day at the studio. And historians, mulling through the faded manuscripts of monarchs and ministers long dead and forgotten. Or sculptors like Rodin at work in clay.

A fear of boredom for many is a fear (I fear) of the ingredients of excellence or high aspiration, or inspiration. Perhaps the long, long learning of their thousand-symbol alphabet is why the Chinese are usually, as academic achievers, ahead of most of the world. They have gone through boredom to the better place that waits them, on the other side.

And a fear of boredom is often also the fear of love. Most of us will find excuses, month after month, for never visiting an ageing aunt or grandmother, in her solitary flat or nursing home, for fear that she will talk to us – repetitively perhaps, repetitively almost certainly, but with the directness and earnestness of one who loves us and cares for us, and always has. We cloak under pretended fear of being bored this darker fear of obligation, of ties of blood and kin, of human affection unstinted, and the fullness of response that is love. And coming away from that love we feel much, much better. The boredom was worth it, we find to our surprise, and it nearly always is.

With Foxtel's twenty-four channels, alas, this dread new power to change the subject unpunished is almost infinite now. We can escape from any obligation, any tug of love, into another world. We can surf the shallow alternatives to our world all night if we like.

And this is, of course, exactly what we were like as little children, wriggling in church while the sermon lengthened. Can we go now, Mummy? Can we go outside please? Are we there yet, Mummy? Are we home yet? And a hatred of boredom is a sign of enduring infantility perhaps, the Me generation out for new thrills, now, now. Fast forward.

The net result, however, is a life so shallow or skimmed it is barely a life at all. Americans, who have had television for fifty years now, cannot, we are told, hold attention on anything for more than eight minutes, the time between television commercials. Fifty per cent of them do not read a book after high school, not one, or not right through, in the rest of their lifetimes. Eight per cent cannot read at all; the time between commercials wasn't long enough to learn. Fifty-one per cent do not bother to vote. All that queuing up and filling out forms and making moral choices. Too boring. Fast forward. Fast forward.

It's possible that boredom and a full, rich experience of life go hand in hand. Those who go walking in the Himalayas for days and weeks, like Tim McCartney-Snape, have depths and glimmers and echoes that others more impatient never show. And Nelson Mandela, whose battle with boredom in his twenty-seven years of solitary imprisonment was epic, and whose victory over it, whose triumph because of it, still shines on his face.

We should take more time over things than we do. We should listen longer, and longer still, before we look at our watch. We should endure more public speeches (Noel Pearson's especially, Rabbi Brasch's, Tim Costello's), whatever their length. We should hear more boring, hypnotic music like Phillip Glass's, and J.S. Bach's and Stephen Sondheim's. We should linger all day over paintings by Turner, and Manet, and Rembrandt, and stay till closing time. For something may then take us over, when the third or fourth yawn is done, that is quite remarkable. We might find ourselves transported, engaged, uplifted, pleasured in ways we had not thought were ours any more to reach for, let alone attain.

We should give this a try now and then. Or else we will never know it is possible.

Boredom ennobles, discuss.

Discuss it fast. Now, now. Fast forward.

December, 1998

The Last Days of Jean Gray

My Auntie Jean died last week. She had for years been wandery, and would tell the same few stories over and over, and would ask the same questions. In her ninety-first year she lost herself, and didn't know any more her daughter Robyn and grand-daughters, except as agreeable smiling strangers. She posed in a photo with a great-grandchild, and knew, Robyn said, that the baby was somehow linked with her, but didn't know how.

I saw her the day before she died – skeletal, sere, asleep, in a week-long coma, one eye half open, moaning and muttering in response to the fondness I then, too late, poured out, or maybe not. There is a theory they hear you. Maybe they do. I kissed her goodbye the next day, and her face relaxed, and I left, and drove south. In an hour she was dead.

There was a good roll-up at the chapel the following Tuesday, of the Stockton people she had coached in hockey and served with on church committees for sixty years, and a superb service in an older English by a chaplain in his seventies, more like a nineteenth-century man, who knew Jean well, and had rubbed along with her in her latter years. We sang 'Abide With Me' and 'The Lord's My Shepherd'. And then she was burnt. And that was that. And I drove south again.

On the journey I thought of the ten or twelve times I had visited Jean in the last five years of her life on earth – in the old people's hostel she liked, in a room across the corridor from a woman she had known for sixty years – and how the visits got shorter and shorter, because I was bored with hearing what I already knew and with being asked what I had already answered, by a person who was now just a thumbnail sketch of the complex, cantankerous, alert and difficult Auntie Jean I knew. The 'whiting out', as they call it, of the brain cells reduced her, month after month, to a kind of querulous intermittent ghost, forever tolling the same old themes. Her mother's forsaken Jewishness. The fire that burnt down the house in Maitland. My father's womanising. Her daughter's (supposed) ingratitude.

Reacting humanly, I came to see her less and less, avoiding the visit once or twice when I was in the area filming, and once when I was passing through. She would not, I reasoned, remember I had been there anyway. Not for long.

What is the duty we owe, I wondered, to people who are no longer themselves? These bleak, wraithlike mementoes of personalities past and gone? It is hard to say. As a question it ranks with the number of times each year we should go with flowers to the grave of a cranky relative with whom we have quarrelled. Or how we should behave with the children damaged at birth who shriek and have fits and smash things and are yet of our blood and kin. What is it we owe to the damaged and old and crazed of our time on earth which in itself is brief and largely thwarted? What do we owe?

These questions arise more and more in a time on this planet where life inordinately lengthens and dementia grows in frequency and people begging for death are shown little mercy – and wills are cruelly altered, I guess, by minds grown mad in the final belief that their children are plotting against them, conspiring to poison them, steal their photo albums, sell their homes, and the rest of it. We are not as a species built for these morose old crinkled autumn leaves in their twilight concentration camps, drugged by day with their mouths hanging open, and calling out in the night for mothers who are not there. We are not built for these long farewells.

Honour thy father and thy mother, the terse commandment goes, but it's not that easy. The Chinese, the Japanese, manage it somehow, and grand revered old patriarchs have their faculties and their honour and their children's obeisance well into their nineties. And their own homes. But not here. We fear as agnostics Death so much we will not long look on its prefiguring – not as long, as a rule, as an hour at a time.

There is a partial answer to some of these matters, I now believe. Autopsies on three nuns who died in their late eighties showed in all of them advanced Alzheimer's, but none of them in their last years had shown the smallest evidence of it. They prayed, they taught, they studied, they tended the garden and performed their ministerial rituals and did the domestic work as they always had. They kept busy. They kept their minds occupied. And what brain cells survived unwhitened, it seemed, made up for the rest.

I found lately an old woman long since written off by her daughter as having 'lost it', and I talked to her about her life. Slowly she became lucid, and clear and detailed, and thoughtful and articulate and wise. I questioned her unpatronisingly, and drew her out. She rose to meet me at the level I lured her up to, and the years melted off her, and soon she was fine. There are triggers in there, I believe, in all of them, or nearly all, that bring the old agendas back to life. They are in there somewhere.

Somerset Maugham in his nineties had these lucid intervals of eloquence and wisdom, in among a chaotic daily onrush of garrulous raving and fouled furniture. It is remarkable what survives. Or survives now and then.

Old people, I have often thought, perhaps should write themselves letters, detailing who they are, and who their relatives are, and what their story is, and keep the letters by the bed, and at the nurses' prompting read them again each morning. 'I know that,' they'll say as they read. 'I know that.'

As to what our duty is to them, in their body's decay and their mind's adversity, I think it is fair to ask what else we are doing in those two hours a month. Watching again, on television, the news we already know? Eating Thai food? Being indecisive in the delicatessen? Walking the dog? Trimming the garden? There are two hours in a month to spend with the shimmering fragments of one you once loved, who once loved you and did much for you, and who knows you sometimes.

Aren't there?

Maybe one hour a month.

For they are irreplaceable, these people, in however diminished a reality you find them in their final fading out of the world and time, and they will never be there – as thumbnail sketch or full portrait or fading ghost – in your world or your sight again.

Be nice. It's not too hard.

October, 1998

Elsie at Eighty-eight

My mother Elsie turns eighty-eight this week. She can still walk, on stick and walking frame, and without them round the old familiarities of the house, the house I grew up in, but she doesn't leave the house much, she watches television in her bedroom and sleeps, and chats to the nurses who come early and late, to help her into the shower and whatever it is nurses do.

She sometimes cooks for herself, sometimes has Meals on Wheels. Her nephew Barry, now sixty-six, visits for an hour on Friday nights; on occasion her grand-daughter Leisa, who lives 100 kilometres away, visits with her baby Koah, a nice little fellow with big black eyes, her first great-grandchild.

Her mind is clear. She is in good health now, the best in years, since the chiropractor, the one I'd been urging her to go to for five years, finally fixed her heart fibrillation, and her medication was reduced, and her panic and mental confusion subsided, and she was herself again. 'Why didn't you see him five years ago?' I asked in retrospective frustration. 'He was there all the time.'

'I didn't have *time*, Robert,' she said. 'I've been *sick*.'

All thought of travel, even 15 kilometres to the chiropractor, scares her now. She might not, she suspects, survive the journey. She talks on the phone to the few friends still living – Jean Wright, Jean Rowe, Dorrie Ward – and Irene and Bob and Daphne and Phyllis and Hammer and Val, neighbours these fifty years, who drop in.

And Wal Buckley of course. Wal Buckley is very special.

Wal is a neighbouring widower who, about a year after my dad died, began to visit Elsie and run errands for her. A sort of courtship occurred, and he would come up every day, and help with the housework and garden and watch television with her. Soon he became indispensable. When she was ill last, during the fibrillations and panic attacks, he would stay all night, in the spare room, in case she had to be taken, quickly, to hospital. Wal survived Changi, and plays darts at his club, and grew up in an orphanage, and is lean and reclusive, a determined walker.

And Wal six months back was operated on for stomach cancer. And now it *seems*, though it has not yet turned up in the blood tests, he might have secondaries. Elsie has been hobbling down to see Wal at his place, to comfort him and assist his two daughters, who are staying with him. Wal had the hiccups for a whole week this month. I urged her to get him (of course) to the chiropractor, who I believed could cure them. She said he wouldn't survive the journey.

The hiccups have now been fixed by a doctor's drug, and Wal is improving, a little anyway. He eats, hungrily. He is walking up to Elsie's again, a little fraily. He might not have cancer at all.

If he does, it may be the end for Elsie of the companionship and support system that have sustained her through her eighties. She is bound now, I think, to live to at least ninety-five like her grandmother, though her mum and elder sister made only eighty-five, a sister and brother seventy. And what will become of her?

She hates the idea of a nursing home. She enjoys her back garden. She knows her house. *Stay in your own house, Else,* her long-dead friends would say, *as long as you can.* She has her photos on the shelves – my dead sister Margaret, my live sister Kay, her children, mine, Dad when young, his father – the crockery cabinet, the original watercolour of lilies in a vase, the lounge room, the verandah extension with its view all over Lismore and the hills beyond. The bars in the bathroom and toilet she holds onto. The

Reader's Digest Condensed Books she has kept for fifty years – *The Surprise of Cremona, The City of the Bees.* This is her universe. This is where she should live.

It's not as bad as it might be. She can stay, after plane flights, which she doesn't seem to mind, with me and Annie for three months in Palm Beach, with Kay for three months in Yarrawonga. Irene and Bob have been sleeping overnight during Wal's illness. A mature-age student might accept free lodging, and look out for her at nights. The story is not over yet.

But the loneliness grows. Jean Wright, whom she's known since she was three, is eighty-nine, and poorly, and an implacable 100 kilometres away. Jean Rowe is inaccessible, barely even ringable, in Tamworth; phone bills cost so much. My daughter Jenny visited her over the holidays. I'll be there in March. But the void grows.

I'd hoped Wal would see her out – he's only eighty-two, and determined to maintain his health – but it seems doubtful now. And it's hard to imagine the mighty change that is coming – death, moving out, the loss for me of the little bedroom of my childhood that I still sleep in when I visit, the same lowboy, the same built-in reading lamp. So much of our life is a fantasy of continuity. Of things being there forever.

I do not want Elsie to die. But her life is dwindling. It is turning into *things* – mementoes, not people – and that's a pity. Her brain is almost maddeningly, determinedly, clear and curious. There is no great comforting censorship by Alzheimer's of the past, of identity and remembered loss. She remembers everything. She has questions. She needs to know things.

I should, I suppose, begin to put on cassette her memories – of World War One, the Depression, the six years Dad was gone in World War Two, the move from her mother's house to Lismore in 1946, the fifties, the sixties, the world that changed, for her, from horses-and-sulkies and bikes and paddle steamers and church to colour television and *The Midday Show* and grandchildren who went to rock festivals instead of church camps and travel overseas. But to do that is admitting she won't be here long, and I don't want to do that. I'll procrastinate as always, because I can't bear thinking she won't always be there.

Happy birthday, Mum. Keep well. I'll see you soon.

February, 1999

BOOK FOUR
Headliners

John Ralston Saul

The long summer day and night that I spent with John Ralston Saul and the subsequent meals that I had with him in other people's houses after his public lectures were among the best I can remember. It's good to talk in middle age about *everything* for hours on end, the way that students do, with a man who has mastered the subject; or nearly.

We swam, walked beaches, drank beer and coffee, drove here and there in my elderly blue Volvo. He kept a road map in front of him (a habit picked up from his dad, an army officer) to keep up with where we were – in bushland, cliff edges, suburban roundabouts. His obedient acceptance of what we would eat, drink, look at, were all of a piece with his mild self-mocking Canadian accent, his Woody Allen cadences, his tallness, his unremarkable sandy, spindly, hair-challenged looks (you see his face in duplicate most European summers, bicycling in the Alps), his undiluted hopefulness about humanity's future in a world beset by deaf unthinking tyrannies.

Forget the sound bite, he says. Hold public meetings. Start up newspapers. Think up new slogans. *Jest* about their failings. *Shame* them into change. Simply say *no* to what cannot be borne, the way France lately has to the free trade snare, the way Russia will soon when it defaults on all its debts and the Third World then does likewise and no atomic war then occurs – nothing much, in fact, except the ruin of the IMF, and about time too. Remember that all periods of national expansion, national prosperity, national creative energy throughout history have followed a repudiation of debt.

Do not be afraid of the obvious. Do not hedge your options round with fashionable masochistic doctrines of obligation to the current fiscal fashion. Just do what must be done. Abjure ideology, for ideology is just a way of saying everything is inevitable, which is wrong, and democracy a pesky obstruction of the historically foredoomed, and government a needless wasteful burden – when government, in fact, is the only big voice people have and democracy the only way of raising it.

What at first can seem irresponsible is quickly made convincing by the swoop and range of his mind. From Richelieu to MacNamara, Plato to Mussolini, from Sun Tzu to the Gulf War, from the artistic triumph of

Raphael to the maze and murk of modern art, he works out plausible causes for what happened and why things lately are getting worse and worse (in this unadmitted world depression that since 1973 has been daily denied by those selfsame corporate courtiers that daily ensure its prolongation) and why the cure, though dauntingly unclear (for nothing is inevitable, and nothing ever was), must urgently, intricately, be found. Can democracy survive the present shrinkage of good public education? No. Can *civilisation* survive when all private contracts now seemingly outweigh the Social Contract? No. Can we win back the words – like freedom, like rationality – that our enslavers now use as propaganda? Perhaps, if we are swift and clever.

Being a Canadian helps, he says, because it is a country built on the acknowledgment of unbridgeable fractious differences – English versus French, Indian versus cowboy, igloo versus bungalow, informed Canadian civility versus ignorant American bombast – and the realisation, enshrined in its federal structure (the first such tactful constitution since ancient times), that things are very *local* and no one cure fits all diseases. No one cure makes sense, in fact, in two adjacent *villages* let alone the world. It has taught him, too, that empires are not always overt, with gunboats and governors and fluttering flags and grand parades of tanks. An empire may merely command the airwaves, or the currency, or the national debt, or the cinema culture, or the stock exchange or CNN, or those international corporations (built without shame, run without conscience, attuned to no local need) whose budgets now are bigger than those of many small countries.

Refreshingly, he does not villainise, for as a former oil executive himself he knows the kind of man that shapes and subserves the corporations and finds no particular malice in them, they are decent loyal servitors of their anointed masters the stockholders, no more, as one might wish. But he abhors their historical ignorance (history did not start yesterday, he says, history is old, and its lessons can be learned) and the many small political surrenders that daily made their marauding structures possible. Villainising does not help, he says. All men mean well. What we have to do is attack the problem, not rub salt in the wounds of its authorship. We have to do it now.

He spent time among outback Aborigines while he was here. He swam daily, fearing bluebottles, at Coogee. He filled Wollongong Town Hall and enthralled them for two hours with his darting insights, not drawing breath. He sought my wife's recipe for fish in coconut milk. He constantly asked big questions, of me, Noel Pearson, his tireless wily host Les Robinson – about Australia's history and fault lines. Don Dunstan's pioneering administration – in film, theatre, architectural preservation, Aboriginal and homosexual rights, the multiculture – intrigued him with its prescience. He wanted, as always, to know more.

He saw in Canada and Australia the obvious similarities, and more. Both countries were untamed, he said, yet feigned an ordered European tranquillity while bushfires, blizzards, avalanches, earthquakes, inundations, yacht race catastrophes and colliding icebergs showed how unruly our two vast regions were, and why solutions that suit the manicured-garden cultures of Europe do not suit ours. We have enormous areas and thin populations, and so need different rules. We should find out what they are.

And thus it is that people of all kinds are listening to and reading him. Native tribesmen. Academic ecologists. Government bureaucrats of the Sir Humphrey sort, all over. Corporate executives who privately tell him they absolutely agree but, alas, what can they do, their hands are tied. And as in a Capra movie, the halls are filling, the printing presses pounding out his books in many translations. His historic effect, like that of G.B. Shaw, and Bertrand Russell, Orwell, Heller and Bob Dylan, Noam Chomsky and (yes) Voltaire may well (just may) be educationally immense, and politically and economically and ecologically seismic. I await his next visit (in August) with a kind of amiable, apocalyptic suspense.

January, 1999

Gore Vidal

After it all I asked myself why so many of my friends (thirteen, I think) had refused my offer of tickets (I bought the last five in the house) to Gore Vidal's one Australian lecture – his last, almost certainly, here ever – and came up with the answer 'fear of excellence'. For all that refused knew well he was not just a Man of Letters but, in our time, a Prince of Letters and that was pretty scary. Screenwriter, dramatist, New Novelist, historian, political philosopher, actor, stump orator and, almost certainly, the deftest essayist in the English language since George Bernard Shaw. One's ego tends to shrivel in such golden glare; one tends to stay home, watch Galaxy and think of lesser things.

Vidal attempted, for instance, a novel in which one character meets in one lifetime Zoroaster, Buddha, Confucius and Socrates, and he brought it off; and a six-volume saga of United States history since the War of Independence (involving deep-etched portraits of Washington, Jefferson, Lincoln, Henry Adams, Teddy Roosevelt, D.W. Griffith, Charlie Chaplin,

Woodrow Wilson, Hearst, F.D.R., skilfully mixed with ongoing fictional characters) and brought this off too. His essays on Maugham, Dawn Powell, John Horne Burns, Henry James, Edith Wharton, Mishima, Calvino, Burroughs are classics now; his personal memoirs of Eleanor Roosevelt, Jackie Kennedy (his semi-half sister), Tennessee Williams, Orson Welles, Ronald Reagan (the Acting President) and Truman Capote ('Truman never told the truth,' he said, 'and Tennessee never told a lie.') teeter on the edge of the definitive. His double act with Noam Chomsky about America the Imperial Marauder has altered the way we think of the world.

His Broadway plays, *Visit to a Small Planet*, *The Best Man* and *An Evening with Richard Nixon* (science fiction, comedy, political fiction, political documentary), made money. His screenplays, *The Left-Handed Gun* (on Billy the Kid), *I Accuse* (on Dreyfus), *Suddenly Last Summer* (a favour to Tennessee) and *A Catered Affair* (a present for Bette Davis), touch (at the very least) high excellence in that form. His work on the Philco Playhouse helped pioneer (with Paddy Chayevsky, Sidney Lumet and John Frankenheimer) television drama on earth. His contribution to *Ben Hur* (a sweaty homoerotic reunion scene) was very effective. His novel *Messiah*, on a fundamentalist death cult, predated Jim Jones by thirty years. He pioneered the homosexual novel in English (*The City and the Pillar*, *A Thirsty Evil*). He has mastered in his time the anti-Christian Roman emperor novel (*Julian*), the post-modernist sex-change novel (*Myra Breckenridge*), the end-of-the-world novel (*Kalki*), and the Internet Black Farce (*Live from Golgotha*). He ran for Congress as a Democrat and in Duchess County in 1960 outscored in the vote Jack Kennedy. He appeared effectively in *Bob Roberts* as a senator like Eugene McCarthy, and in *Fellini's Roma* as himself. He is, by repute (and also demonstrably), the most accomplished conversationalist of his time and his literary feuds have good punchlines. When Norman Mailer, for instance, slugged him in the CBS Green Room he remarked, 'I at last encountered Norman's tiny fist. As usual, words failed him.'

It was therefore with some trepidation I co-wrote with Bob Carr the letter that invited him (again) to Australia (he opted out last time after being sent customs forms to fill in) and with some amazement read his acceptance, and with stark fear approached the harbour wharf where I would meet him. I need not have worried. Though large, florid, stiff in movement, jet-lagged after eight hours in Bangkok Airport and unamused by the boat captain's loud unceasing commentary on the harbour's wonders, he proved, well . . . generous and courtly; the memorable eyes of his photographs were large, including, assessing and kindly.

He spoke of Lincoln being lately dug up (again) and 'looking still pretty much like Lincoln'; of Lincoln's probable syphilis and Mary Todd Lincoln's consequent howling madness and death; of the excellence of Mark Twain's Pudd'nhead Wilson; and the mediocrity of Updike, 'who stood for everything I detest'; of having met in their decayed old age a few of Proust's original characters, elderly duchesses in musty hotel rooms, and a conversation with Gide about his lover Oscar Wilde of which he recalled, now, nothing any more. He explained with patience to John Bell, who was on the boat, why Coriolanus (which Bell disliked) could be a rewarding role. He recalled meeting Lady Fairfax in Venice and being dizzy with boredom at her conversation (about her son Warwick, the genius) and how, thus goaded, he sourly predicted the boy would be broke in six months, and of course he was. He didn't recall having said of Australia in 1974, 'I have seen the past, and it works: Cleveland Ohio, 1945, I'd put it, and it's looking great', but he was pleased to think he might have.

His voice, an iron-and-violet light baritone, unforced and East Coast mandarin (somewhere between F.D.R. and Olivier's James Tyrone), was clear and emphatic and bore no gay inflections; he seemed in personality and in body language more, Carr said, like a heterosexual English aristocrat with a new young wife. His long liaison with Anaïs Nin and the plot of *Two Sisters* (in which a character called Gore Vidal successively beds, and loves, and loses, a brother and sister, twins) argues at least some variety of response in these matters, one he would argue is common to humankind. I asked if his illegitimate son in that novel had any basis in fact. 'Yes,' he said, 'it was a daughter, but I never discovered finally if she was mine; her mother was, among her other virtues, a dedicated liar.'

Bob Carr, ever the dutiful young reporter, shepherded him off the boat ('This man,' Gore said, 'should be your first President.') and I saw him briefly at the opening of Writers' Week the next night ('I've never been to a writers' festival before,' he said, 'and I was uncertain what I should bring. A series of writers' blocks perhaps: labelled *Joan Didion 1976–81*, and so on.'), then I went to his lecture-and-interview at the Town Hall and to supper afterwards with him (and Carr and Schofield and Pounder and Freudenberg and Evan Williams and Richard Hall and, by accident, Geoffrey Rush), which added up to one of the better nights in my life.

He mimicked expertly, and with an exactitude as deft as Mike Carlton's, Katharine Hepburn, Eleanor Roosevelt, the Duchess of Windsor, the Duke of Windsor ('A P.G. Wodehouse character, utterly harmless, no intelligence at all.'), Marlon Brando (who, he said, when acting on stage would have a woman between act one and two, another woman between act two and three, and another after the curtain 'and that was just the matinee'), Princess Margaret, Ronald Reagan and J.F.K. He explained the facts behind the Dallas murder (a Mob hit by Joe's old boot-legging partners after Bobby in a hot flush of righteousness began arresting the Holy Family's former providers). I asked if it was true his close friend Princess Margaret was known at Buckingham Palace parties to sing unasked 'I'm Just A Girl Who Can't Say No'. 'Well,' he said, 'that was *part* of her repertoire.' He was fond of Princess Margaret, he said, and amazed us by revealing her family was Jewish (via Prince Albert, bastard son of the House of Hanover's randy tailor).

He hated the word 'arguably' and preferred in his writing verbs, not adjectives: verbs advance the story. He improvised, while Hall boggled, a perfect verb-heavy paragraph in the style of Dickens. He upheld his view that Lincoln was the US's greatest prose writer, but yielded with amusement to Freudenberg's plea that Ulysses S. Grant get a close second place. He and I did contesting Olivier imitations; I lost.

The night was long and pleasing (and at one point disorderly when Pounder kissed him on both cheeks to his visible dismay) and then prolonged when he invited the Premier and his wife to a further hour of ironic chat and whisky in his hotel. He favoured whisky after midnight and suffered no hangovers, once alarming the throbbing Kenneth Tynan by 'speaking in perfect fucking sentences at 7 a.m.'. His memory for names was fading, he said, but he woke each morning to find the mislaid ones all lined up, smiling, at the end of the bed.

He was guilty, he told the Town Hall, of intervention in world history. When casting his play *The Best Man* (in which presidential aspirants resembling Richard Nixon and Adlai Stevenson connive and bicker in hotel rooms at convention time) he rejected out of hand one Ronald Reagan, who wanted the Stevenson role, because he was too 'gee willikers' and 'gosh all Friday'; too innocent, in short, to be plausible as a presidential candidate. This meant that during the play's run, from 1960 to 1962, Reagan had nothing to do at all and was tempted therefore into politics, and ruining the world.

His likes and dislikes were unpredictable – George C. Scott, not Olivier: Ramona Koval, not David Marr; Jack, not Bobby (Jack was marvellous company, though swinging wildly in personality – pacifist, warmonger – because of the daily varying drugs); Henry James and Edith Wharton, not Ernest Hemingway and F. Scott Fitzgerald; and so on. He hated Martin Scorsese's *The Age of Innocence* (which he offered to adapt for free) because he got the people, his people, East Coast old money and their poorer cousins, so very wrong.

Carr found magnetic his intimacy with legend. His blind grandfather, Senator Thomas Gore, for instance (who pretended to look at speech notes lest his condition become known and prove a political setback), knew Robert Lincoln, son of the president. Vidal knew General Douglas MacArthur, who was 'superintendent at West Point when I was born. My mother would park her grey Plymouth in his parking space and there was nothing he could do about it because she was the daughter of the powerful Senator Gore. There was an unsmiling bald major in his outer office. His name was Eisenhower.' In another demi-monde, he once had sex with Jack Kerouac (to Kerouac's

retrospective annoyance) and spent long afternoons immersed with Orson
Welles, 'like two Talmudic scholars' in successive sea-changing memoirs by
Rudy Vallee, his neighbour in the Hollywood hills. And so on.

I saw him once more at a lunch with the Carrs before he flew out and I
tried to work him out. He was, I decided, very like a Shakespeare character Jacques, perhaps (I told him so, and he did some lines in character), or
Hamlet, with a lemon slice of Iago. He yearns, I think, like that thwarted
lieutenant, to have led great armies in time of war. 'Nineteen-seventy-six,'
he said sadly to Carr, 'that should have been my year. The presidency.' He
admired, he told me, the rogue survivors of history – Aaron Burr before
Alexander Hamilton, Gore before Wilson, Teddy Roosevelt before William
Jennings Bryan – and found most martyrs 'tiresome'. He believes in success,
endurance. He felt shamed, I suspect, by his grandfather's eyeless eminence;
after such an example, and such dark victory, mere sexual imprecision was
no excuse.

His mind roved easily over centuries and dynasties and came back always
to his first love, Washington politics. He mourned the Roosevelts, Eleanor
more than Franklin: her he adored more than any other person, an East
Coast puritan like himself, concerned with doing good.

He mourned, too, for what the security state and its maintenance had cost
the US. 'I look at Arlington,' he said to Carr one morning, 'and the graves
spilling out into the surrounding streets. This is the price of having an
empire.' The price, too, of money unspent on public education. 'The public
education used to be good. It produced people with knowledge. Now they
just get *USA Today* and CNN.'

He mourned most the loss of knowledge in the world and its replacement
with distractions, clever new toys he calls them. He loves the Roosevelt
America – literate, communitarian – that probably died at Chappaquiddick.
He is in his heart, he confessed once, an unreconstructed Scandinavian
socialist of the dullest, most hopeful kind. He believes, like his beloved
Eleanor, that human good is still possible.

On the pavement I asked him what he thought of Australia. 'A good
place,' he said. 'You do look after your needy. That old crippled couple,
the Whitlams, for instance, down to their last cup of caviar. And how
you care for them.' He got into the car, very stiffly. I was distressed to see
him go.

March, 1997

Andrew Olle

The astonishing news that the admired and famous broadcaster Andrew Olle was in a coma and, with two inoperable tumours of the brain, unlikely to live, affected Australia with a sense of loss which to a somewhat lesser degree resembled that of the first Kennedy murder: a young, handsome, urbane and highly intelligent man of boundless promise cut down in his prime with the best years of his life ahead of him unenjoyed. The switchboards rang all night and colleagues waited in vigil at Royal North Shore Hospital where Olle, forty-seven, lay sedated in, it was said, 'a sweet sleep'. And the nation grieved.

Like Michael Charlton, his famed predecessor at *Four Corners* – the esteemed *Panorama*-style television program now in its thirty-fifth year – Olle mixed in his personality an almost British dignity and a kind of telepathy with his audience. His lopsided, full-lipped smile of irregular teeth communicated volumes of ideological unease, and beneath his easy, light baritone voice lurked an always rational, humanist capacity for doubt that his audience came to share. No blustering politician ever got through his radar, or wholly survived his tactful tenacity (he was both impeccable and implacable) in seeking the truth. His own politics were a mystery to even his closest acquaintance and all sides felt the scorch of his probing gentleness. His off-screen personality, one of wary, smiling sadness, was such that he made few enemies, and politicians on all sides wept at the news of his collapse.

His own *annus horribilis* preceded his sudden passing. Removed from his beloved *Four Corners* to front the faltering *7.30 Report*, he worked long nights and rose at 5 a.m. for his morning radio program, whose climactic political dialogue with Canberra correspondent Paul Lyneham, famed for its rambunctiousness, became a national institution. Overworked and ragged of mind and irritable with technicians, he began suffering memory lapses on air whose cause no-one suspected. He was brutally removed from the still failing *7.30 Report* only two weeks ago and his morning radio program shifted to late afternoon and his friend Lyneham, also summarily sidelined, left the ABC in fury. Olle's death, though medically unconnected with these events, was an awful climax to this period of organisational change.

His mannerly personality belied his turbulent origins. The child of a fractured marriage and a bitter custody dispute that was won, unusually, by his father, an army major, he spent miserable early years in primitive boarding schools, from several of which he was expelled, and appeared at age eleven before a Children's Court on a charge of public vandalism. He left school in a scarred state at fifteen to work in a department store but was persuaded back to school by his probation officer, a man to whom, he later confessed, he owed a lot. His last expulsion occurred a month before his final exams, when he was found smoking tobacco at age eighteen by the nineteen-year-old housemaster of a school with high Christian standards. He joined the Australian Broadcasting Commission, the organisation that was to become his family substitute, as a news cadet in 1967, and briefly attempted Arts/ Law part-time at the University of Queensland.

Provincial broadcast work followed in northern Queensland; a cadet stint on the trail-blazing nightly political program *This Day Tonight* and the rural show *Big Country*, and three years on the commercial television program *Sunday*, whose high quality he helped pioneer. Such was his polite devotion to truth that the dictatorial Queensland Premier Joh Bjelke-Petersen refused to be interviewed by him. Returning to the ABC to front *Four Corners*, he clashed with Prime Minister Bob Hawke and New South Wales Prisons Minister Michael Yabsley in incidents now legendary. Equally effective on both radio and television, he had a passionate devotion to factual accuracy that sometimes wearied his producers. The exhaustless professionalism of his chairmanship on long election nights was both admirable and disarming. 'However it goes,' he would say, 'you can still rest assured that the sun will rise in the morning.'

He married young, raised three happy children, avidly followed football, gambled on horses, read many books, threw roisterous parties, kept early friends lifelong and somehow added his urbane personality to Australia's tribal memory. Like many buffeted children he had low self-esteem, and would be of all people most astonished at the grief now engulfing his nation.

December, 1995

John Hargreaves Dying

'Hurry, hurry, last days,' was how John Hargreaves, with his usual gallant wryness, announced the depth of his illness in early December: he was going blind now, after years of struggle, and he was in St Vincent's Hospital at last and I should try to see him, my agent Jane Cameron said, try and tell him how much he was loved. People were dropping in and leaving messages and I should at least do that. Do it, darling, quickly.

It was a hard appointment to keep. Johnny was from Murwillumbah where I was born and reared, and his first paid gig as an actor was in *King O'Malley*, which I'd co-written, where he played a carnival spruiker with marvellous lines he'd written himself – be a writer, I said to him; no, he said – and I'd seen his NIDA audition in 1970, when he did the final speech of *As You Like It* in the cross-dressed person of Rosalind, *because I am a woman*, not effeminately though but straight and confronting and clear, a genderless creature of Shakespearian moonlight, ready for whatever, and whoever, occurred. I'd seen his Biggles after that, in the show that opened the Nimrod Theatre, and his colonial gallant in *The Currency Lass*, the play that opened the STC, the first Australian play ever written, his Man of Mode and his Noel Coward in *Present Laughter*, his partying Don and his Vanya and his Cairns and his bent copper in *Scales of Justice*, and his extraordinary drooling and snickering and gibbering serial killer in *Wentworthville* where his entrance, at great physical risk, was through the actual upstairs window of the Stables Theatre; he hung outside on the drainpipe while the audience dawdled in, and then with a swift, astonishing panther leap was amongst us, nostrils flaring. I'd spent time with him too in foyers, at parties, on buses and planes, not that much, though a whole night once through to dawn at the Bourbon 'n' Beefsteak Bar talking, talking the way you do when young, in part about his sexuality. I'd seen him and briefly hugged him on the night he got his Byron Kennedy Award: he looked like a sere and shrivelled, smiling autumn leaf.

And so I rang on 8 December, and was told by the nun he was turning in for the night and he wasn't seeing anybody. I suspected I wasn't welcome and let it slide for a precious week. In that week Andrew Olle collapsed and, copiously motivated by the twice threatened loss, I arrived at St

Vincent's Private with his fellow NIDA student Denny Lawrence and collided with him coming out of the lift.

He looked bulky and strong and vaguely angry, with staring, unfocused eyes, but he greeted us with a kind of blank heartiness, and invited us out to dinner with him, in a nearby Cantonese, and walked there leaning on the shoulder of Kendall Flanagan, a heterosexual friend of many years who was now devotedly, obsessively looking after him.

We talked long and buoyantly. I came back the next night, and the next and we talked some more, while Kendall massaged his feet ('Kendall is massaging my feet,' he told Wendy Hughes on the phone, 'and Ellis is telling me *lies*.') and the hours rushed on, and I'm glad I did. If I ever write my long-planned book *An Etiquette for the Dying*, his example of jocular lambent grace under crushing pressure may light a candle to the world.

He joked; he gossiped; he sneered and pried and chortled and judged his peers, and described his hospital food as 'stewed cunt'. He spoke frankly of his HIV: he'd picked it up, he said, in New York in 1981; he could nominate the week but not the hour or the partner. He spoke warmly of the future, of the retina operation that Thursday that would hopefully bring back sight to one eye and allow him to work again; of the Jim McNeil monologue he planned to edit and perform as a one-man show; of his various intense relationships with women, Judy Davis one of them, Judy whom he regarded as in some ways the perfect woman, and his recent hard routine, essaying limited acting jobs while in remission; of his pleasure in country life and *Hotel Sorrento* and *Blue Murder*; of his continuing, buoyant, stoic, measured hope for a cure. 'If a cure for AIDS were bending over nude with a flower up my arse in Pitt Street for two hours,' he said, 'I'd do it.' He hated the disease (one he firmly believed was manufactured by American germ warriors) because it was slowly murdering, and not so slowly, all the wit in the world.

He had his operation on the Thursday and the trauma and the anaesthetic buffeted his few remaining T-cells. I went to Andrew Olle's funeral on the Friday and went away on holiday. Johnny's eyesight did not recover. He began to lose sense of where he was and to wish, as his pain increased, he could simply die and soon, too soon, always too soon ...

His alert, lean, humorous face fitted a slouch hat like no other. His nasal, sinuous voice bespoke all of his nation's bruisable, wry, self-mocking tenderness. His smile was a miracle of widening mischief. Like all Murwillumbah men he had that marvellous quirky, complex mixture of innocence and cynicism. Like most great actors he was a superb human being.

His loss is shocking, and irrecoverable, and still, though expected, as I write this two days later, unbelievable. I have lost an icon and an inspiration, and Australia an actor of genius. Damn and blast it all to hell.

January, 1996

Elvis Presley

Anyone who lived through all of Elvis will agree that he was more than just an entrepreneur. He was a landscape, a mood, a moral universe, a warm bath of youthful melancholy in which we steeped ourselves when the day darkened and our thoughts took on self-pity or adolescent fury. He was truly a god to us in the old Greek way, a highly flawed being who suffered in our sight, who stood at heaven's gallows in our stead, our voice, our advocate, our elected representative on Olympus.

He was one of twins and the other twin died and his yearning for this lost companion, vividly clear in his every expression, was one we believed was our loss too, the good big brother out there somewhere, reaching out to us from the dark. Brando and James Dean gave us our sensual gloom in the early fifties but Elvis, truly, gave us our voice.

He helped invent a new kind of music, one mixing rhythm and blues with white mainstream music, and the dates suggest he was there with it first because 'Mystery Train' and 'That's All Right Momma' predated 'Rock Around The Clock' by a couple of weeks. The sound hit white America square in the middle of its biggest wave of suburban hypocrisy, when washing the car and mowing the lawn and passing exams and going to church and cheering the home team were supposed to inhale into history's Hoover all that was learned and loved in the forties, in wartime travel, the novelty of working women, the free and guiltless one-night stands of men in uniform soon to sail away. It showed that youth was game and turbulent and ready and sexual as any wartime soldier on London leave. It threatened the new bland suburbs and their high school anthems and careerist greed with terrible things – with all-night parties and motor cycle gangs and heavy necking at the drive-in and high school girls who now knew more about contraception than their mothers. It admitted the unadmittable, that kids do it and like it and white weddings weren't such a big deal, not any more.

Rock'n'roll embodied all that, but Elvis was something more. His full-lipped leer and greasy sideburns and pelvic movements and coital bellow had something demonic about them, like a force of nature – earthquake, tornado, eruption – that was both containable and fated. He was the first white boy to sing like a Negro, with everything sexual that this meant. He moved, in Al Clark's words, 'like a knowing stripper, he knew exactly what he was doing, and he relished it'. The fearful television producers tried to domesticate him, filming him only from the waist up, making him sing 'You Ain't Nothin' But A Hound Dog' to an adoring bloodhound. They tried to turn him into something cute, and mild and amiable, but the kids knew; they knew what he stood for. That connection was made, and never broken.

It happened very early. While still an adolescent, he was a millionaire and a force in the land, a famous face of Rushmore enormity, like Orson Welles at twenty, the presiding Mephistopheles of American youth. But as with Orson it couldn't last and part of him knew it wouldn't, ever the tragic hero prescient of his fall. He had through life the classic working-class melancholy of the Southern white trash towns where nothing can be afforded but cheap liquor and marital violence and nothing is learned but pinball and mateship and souped-up secondhand cars. He never grew. He stayed as he was, a bit of a hoon, a small-town mug lair and so went through a lot of sadness that quicker learners – Bob Mitchum for instance, or Johnny Cash or Springsteen or McCartney – were able to evade. He was amiable Southern white trash to the end, with an entourage of similar slow-witted small-town boys who played the pinball machines in his mansion and took to their beds the girls unchosen by the King from his nightly line-up of doe-eyed groupies eager for his pouty lips.

His career occurred in three parts: before he was dragged off into the army and shorn, like Samson, of his menace for a time. The seven years of Hollywood movies, two a year, that made his fortune but stole the best years of his artistic development, and his last, leviathan revival as an overweight, adroit, already mythical performer. In the first part he sang in a boy's voice, in the last two in a big formidable baritone, the cured-ham voice of 'It's Now Or Never' and 'Surrender' that shrank his preppy piping rivals (Johnny Mathis, Buddy Holly) to the status of geldings, a voice that seemed aged in wood and old and worldly wise and belied his true condition, which was one, I believe (despite the celebrated fetishes, girls in white panties wrestling in foam and the like), of ongoing innocence. Or perhaps I mean lack of curiosity.

A *kind* of innocence anyway. He was always very polite, yes ma'am, thank you kindly ma'am, calling his interviewers sir, and gentle and hospitable in the Southern way. He famously loved his mother, the first celebrity so famed since, probably, Nero, and was shattered by her death when he was in Germany being a GI. He believed in his country, not evading army service as he might so easily (like John Wayne) have done. He accepted proudly from Richard Nixon a Drug Enforcement Officer's badge and campaigned to have John Lennon, a heroin user, thrown out of America. He volunteered for the FBI (and in some fantastical views is alive and working for them still) and believed in law enforcement. Far from the demonic tempter he was reviled as by the middle-class fifties – and as such the inspiration equally of Bill Clinton, Paul Keating and Tony Blair – he became in his last flabby years an almost establishment figure, upheld by the nation corporate, tamed and benign and fit for commemorative display on a stamp. He was, perhaps, a genuine Jekyll-and-Hyde, the mild-mannered host of daytime, the beast unleashed at night in song, the dull, puzzled witness next morning: did I do that?

In his army years in Germany he met Priscilla who was then fifteen and with her dealt most like a Southern gentleman, keeping her in his mansion for six years but not (it is said) having sex with her until they were married and going into a roaring vortex of grief when four years later she stormed away from him taking his daughter Lisa Marie. It was this enormous loss of an innocent vision of romantic love (it is also said) that soured and saddened him and made him the mean mother of his final years, the Roman volup-tuary fat with candy and pickled with drugs and whisky, shooting television screens with handguns and groaning long hours in his room of differing drug-fed maladies and rages.

'His final years' is an odd thing to say of a man who died at forty-three (the age that, say, Bobby Kennedy died) but he always seemed older than his years. When the Beatles met him (and Lennon repelled him with his genial chiacking), he was only thirty but already the grand old man. His iconic status was early and never shrank. He had only, it seemed, to wait out his time, to join the dots of his inevitable doom. He was a tragedy waiting to happen.

He suffered, like most Roman emperors, from flatterers and foolish strategic advice which, because he had talent but little judgment, he often took. 'Colonel' Tom Parker booked him into movies for the big easy money and not all of them were bad, Don Siegel's *Flaming Star* and Clifford Odets' *Wild in the Country*. But between shoots and shots and song rehearsals he indulged that sensual corpulent laziness of mind (he never, for instance, wrote any songs) that in the end was to bloat and waste him. With Priscilla forever waiting in bridal readiness back in Graceland and L.A. broads by the busload at his beck and call, he spent in bovine stupor and carnal pointlessness and chemical peril (popping amphetamines to lose weight in Hawaii, gorging on steak and fries in L.A.) those years from when he was twenty-seven to when he was thirty-four that he might otherwise have used to shape and deepen his art. He got into bad habits, in short, and they stuck.

So when he was older there was nowhere for him to go. He was offered the fading-male-superstar role in Streisand's *A Star is Born* that might have inspired and varied his later years but he turned it down, in fear, I suppose, of its echoes of himself. He never, like lesser stars – Cliff Richard comes to mind, Tommy Steele and Normie Rowe – essayed the Broadway stage, though what a Sky Masterson he might have made in *Guys and Dolls* and what a Javert in *Les Mis*. What a title role, indeed, in *Bye Bye Birdie*. And so it goes.

I think of him always with a sense of loss, a wanting his life to be different, and better, and longer. The girl that might have made all the difference, Ann-Margret, was in every way his equal, and a great igniter of his talent (their numbers in *Viva Las Vegas* still blaze and sizzle with horny excitement) who he used and cast aside. And that was a pity. He never became curious about anything. His head was formed in the clapboard, hot-rodding, redneck outlands and never became anything more. Or anything *much* more.

These words, as I write them, seem seriously wrong. A man that conveyed and meant so much to hundreds of millions of people across the planet, and hundreds of thousands of people across the planet believe is still alive, resurrected somehow, a cultish conviction every bit as remarkable (and, in its numbers, popular) as the initial cult of the resurrected Nazarene, a man whom thousands across the planet daily and nightly mimic in dress and voice and gesture, ballrooms full of them sometimes, and run as his clones for the House of Commons as the Elvis Presley Party and to Tony Blair's delight and bemusement pick up votes, a man whose fan club president signs off 'Elvisly yours', a man whose voice is heard more now than when he was alive, adds up, I think, to something more than these bare sociological excuses. There is tribal magic here, the corn god born anew each spring, of a rare and heady kind.

Because no-one thinks James Dean is still alive, or John Lennon or Bobby Kennedy. There are no Bing Crosby sightings. It can only mean that our need for Elvis, and what Elvis means, is greater; whatever it is that Elvis means. A more glamorous projection, perhaps, of our youthful bruised unease. Something like that. A need, at any rate, that his principal supplanter, Tom Jones, could never fill, then or now.

When he came back in 1969 he was *really* magic, looking better than he ever had or did again. He was Lucifer back from the underworld, Osiris reborn, in a series of swirling white capes and sequined jeans that made him seem, at times, like a homicidal matador. The fans, now middle-aged, flocked to him and exulted around him, throwing keys and panties, as others might have done if Che Guevara, say, had returned from Bolivia scarred but alive. But soon his performances became laboured, and when it was an old song, fat and contemptuous, puffed and flabby. And the last phases began.

Anyone wanting a whiff of what he was like should look at the opening sequence of *King Creole*. He leans with a kind of twitchy languor over the balcony, his eyes both menacing and lazy, his hips implacably active, singing 'Crawfish' to the rising noise of New Orleans at dawn. Later, in a nightclub, he stands bolt upright, legs moving and head tossing, singing 'Trouble' with the accent and stance and stubborn gaze of every kid who ever wanted to break a window. That's the way I remember him, and the way you should meet him.

Elvisly yours.

June, 1997

Mitchum and Stewart, R.I.P.

There are movie stars who are lucky and movie stars who are special. Among the lucky I would count (in no particular order) Tom Cruise, Tab Hunter, Bob Wagner, Kim Novak, Jane Fonda, Liz Taylor, Bruce Willis and Demi Moore. Bogart was special. Tracy. Wayne. Henry Fonda. James Earl Jones. Bergman. Hepburn. Both Davises. Both Grants – no, make that three (I've just read Richard E's diaries and they're superb). And Mitchum of course, and Jimmy Stewart – both, in a devastating double whammy (devastating for those of a certain age), gone from us – though always present, I suppose, as push-button ghosts.

I drank with Al Clark and Richard Brennan and Ross Matthews the day after Mitchum went and we're gathering on his eightieth birthday next month to toast him a bit and eat a meal and see *Rachel and the Stranger* in which he sings like Crosby. He was an interesting man, a published poet and Oscar-winning songwriter (*Thunder Road*) and the actor that Charles Laughton most wanted to see play Macbeth. A fatherless quarter-Indian who rode the rails in the thirties and as a Los Angeles bartender served whiskies to Raymond Chandler and as an assembly-line worker befriended Marilyn Monroe's first husband Jim Doherty and went home with him sometimes for ill-cooked meals that Marilyn, eighteen then and bigger in the nose than she was to be, often burnt. He got his start in Hopalong Cassidy one-reelers, an Oscar nomination for *The Story of GI Joe*, and, in his own words, 'never looked back'. He was a devoted family man and (in a not unusual combination) a tremendous womaniser (I remember with pleasure Edna O'Brien's flushed response on a Parkinson show to Mitchum's 'How is it, doll?'), a serious drinker of spirits and early fan of marihjuana, famously gaoled for it once, but was never out of work because, he explained, 'I work cheap.'

The character he provided, quintessentially in *Out of the Past* and *Heaven Knows, Mr Allison* (ruefully sobbing as he undressed the feverish nun), was working-class America's best image of itself – reined in, self-knowing, fond of the odd glass, graceful, sardonic, the graduate *cum laude* of a sinful past. In *Cape Fear* a woman goes to bed with him and afterwards he asks why. 'I just wanted to know,' she says, 'what it was like to know I couldn't sink any lower.' He reacts, characteristically, with one of his well-thank-you-kindly-ma'am-and-fuck-you-too inclinations of the head, a gesture that fitted him well to play an Australian, as he did unerringly in *The Sundowners*, giving in it, in a character that predated Jack Thompson in *Sunday Too Far Away* by fifteen years, the best rendition yet on film of *The Wild Colonial Boy*.

He dignified the underclass, who adored him for it, as for a moment Sylvester Stallone later did, and Johnny Cash and Bruce Springsteen for longer and John Williamson in our country. He was a one-off and, as Al Clark said, 'living proof, while he lived, that you can abuse your body to hell and live a long time if you've got a good constitution to start with'. And so it goes. I hope we give him a good birthday party.

Jimmy Stewart, who almost certainly topped himself (as he was threatening to do all last year), was different; not least in being the best, most naturalistic English-speaking screen actor probably ever. Only three other screen performers, and all to a lesser degree, emulated what he could do: Kristin Scott Thomas, Hugh Grant and Noah Taylor. This capacity to be wholly alive and seemingly spontaneous before the camera, he pretty well invented.

He was both subtle and theatrical, with twitches and yelps and hand flutters and heavy hysterics his friend and room-mate Henry Fonda, for instance, would have found undignified. He brought male neurosis to the screen and a tight-coiled feline readiness to do ill, to rage and threaten murder. You remember with a frisson his denunciation of his former pupils in *Rope* ('You're gonna die, Norman!') and his relentless dragging of Novak up the stairs at the top of which he plans to kill her in *Vertigo*. But he could be poignant too. His arrival in the devastated house of his dead children in *Shenandoah*, and his picking up of the surviving infant and his whimpering utterance, 'It's good to have a baby in the house' (or words to that effect), I rank very high (along with Brando's 'Stella! Stella!') in cinema acting.

He came from the other side of the tracks from Mitchum. WASP. Scottish. Semi-prosperous, with a shopkeeper father (who displayed his son's Oscar in his shop for forty years), he was a university graduate in architecture and a simple-hearted, eventually Goldwaterite patriot not far in his naivety from his Mr Smith, who put himself on the line for his country like Gable and Olivier and Niven and Guinness (while Wayne and Mitchum and Reagan skulked in Santa Monica), flying bombers over Germany and rising to the rank of brigadier general and because of his values losing a son in Vietnam. His film roles reflected this a bit – *The FBI Story* and *The Spirit of*

Saint Louis and *Strategic Air Command* and *The Glenn Miller Story*, though his left-wing friend Henry Fonda in what was clearly an ad lib in *The Cheyenne Social Club* accused him of voting Democrat all along and Stewart said, 'No c-c-comment', or words to that effect.

And so it goes. It's curious how little all this matters when an actor gives you so much of your memory – the jaded lawyer in *Anatomy of a Murder*, the suicidal good man who has quietly changed the world for the better and does not know it in *It's a Wonderful Life*, the voice of the doddery blood-hound deputy sheriff in *Feivel Goes West*. Like the very few Hollywood great actors (Newman, Fonda, Hepburn, Streep) Stewart returned again and again to the legitimate stage (the last time for a year in *Harvey*) and was of course magnificent on it, that extraordinary voice cutting through the footlights like a hot knife through butter.

And so it goes. The era is nearly done. Bacall is alive and working and Hepburn not dead and Sinatra sourly hanging on and Rooney still absurdly tapdancing and Ronald Reagan pretty well embalmed. But we will not see its like again. No-one will write of Arnold Schwarzenegger the way they wrote of Bogart. The actors mean less as the technology overwhelms them and television crowds them out of consciousness. They were all of our dream life once, of those then glad to be alive. And now no more.

And so it goes.

July, 1997

Frank Sinatra

Of the good things and the bad things that were said of Sinatra since his going last week (with his checked coat, I guess, slung over his shoulder), a couple are often missing. One was that his hostile, bully-boy, journo-punch-ing ways date not from the first rumours of his Mafia links in 1949 but much earlier than that, when the House UnAmerican Activities Committee went after him in 1945 as a likely communist. This was because he appeared in a film called *What is America to Me* and throughout the war kept publicly raising on stage the fate of the Jews in Poland and Germany, something no true American would do. And the harsh downturn in his career in the early fifties was in large part due to that, the downturn that his Oscar for playing

Maggio in *From Here to Eternity* rescued him from, much like the parallel downturn in those fraught, bleak years of the rising careers of Larry Parks and Zero Mostel and Melvyn Douglas and Martin Ritt and Ring Lardner Jnr and Arthur Miller, when Ol' Blue Eyes was not only Black (as Dennis Whitburn wittily observed in his fine play *The Siege of Frank Sinatra*) but Black because thought Red.

My first published work was about Sinatra, a feisty defence of him in the letters page of the *Brisbane Telegraph* when I was ten (ending with the passionate plea 'Give the mug a fair go'), an intervention in history that did much, I'm sure, to speed his resurrection, and I've thought about him a good bit since then. Among a lot of other things, for instance, he somehow legitimised what might be called the underclass of the promiscuous, gave dignity to people – both men and woman – who sleep around. Not just with the obvious one, 'Strangers in the Night', but much earlier, with 'Set 'Em Up Joe' and 'The Wee Small Hours' and 'All the Way' and 'A Very Good Year' and 'Summer Wind', he gave sex (if these are the words I want) its head in a way that jazz had never done for the nervous Updike middle classes, and when he sang 'Love and Marriage' (go together like a horse and carriage) you didn't believe him. He was every suburban woman's dream of a one-night stand, a man who 'knew how to make you feel like a woman', as one of his classier bedfellows – or broads, as he gallantly called them – Lauren Bacall, once said. None who saw it will forget the oomph and sizzle when he arrived on the piano stool next to Doris Day in her respectable suburban family parlour in *Young at Heart*, nor what a good match she was for him; Doris, we felt, would settle him down.

He was such a good actor too, reaching Bogart levels in *The Detective* and *The Manchurian Candidate*, and had he played all the parts of that curiously similar screen actor Richard Widmark, he would have done them as well. History (and his own famed impatience) denied him the great swan-song role like Fonda's in *On Golden Pond* and Wayne's in *True Grit*, but in another medium the album *Duets* is that.

His would have to be the most American of careers – the first singer little girls squealed and threw panties at, a husband of Ava Gardner (and Mia Farrow, when that looked more like pederasty), a founder of Las Vegas, a pimp for the Kennedys, a midnight solace for a month or two for Marilyn Monroe, the first big name to call Ronald Reagan 'dumb and dangerous' before in the long run supporting him, a hipster, a swinger, a playboy, a lounge lizard, a man's man, a pack leader, a Mafia don, a singing waiter, a broken-down nightclub stand-up, a washout, a comeback, a legend, the first big star to move round with a retinue of thick-witted bodyguards and fly his classy buddies in a private jet to parties overseas, the first public figure besieged for political incorrectness (when he called Australian female journos 'hookers' in 1976 and he was locked inside the Boulevard Hotel by angry service unions till Bob Hawke dropped by for a scotch and ice and sorted him out), a first-generation Italo-American whose mother was an abortionist and whose son Frank Junior's bloodied ear arrived in the mail a week after his kidnapping, a voice that as background went equally well with a cocktail party on Fifth Avenue, a gay bathhouse in San Francisco or a melancholy bar like Cheers in Chicago at four in the morning (and more, much more than this, I did it . . .), an elegiac voice as cool and sad as vermouth for all the lost seasons of love. And so it goes. You might say our lives will be poorer without him but he'll be around for a while – on CD, on cable, and on the summer wind.

May, 1998

Dorothy Parker

Some reviewers have responded to Alan Rudolph's film about the Algonquin Round Table, *Mrs Parker and the Vicious Circle*, by asking if these babbling underachievers, soused on bathtub gin and their own self-importance, are worthy any more, if they ever were, of our attention, or whether Mrs Parker herself was a good writer, or a nice person. They invoke her several suicide attempts, her bad taste in men – she married a morphine addict once and the same promiscuous homosexual twice – and the dog turds that littered the hotel apartments of her fading years.

But this is surely not the point, any more than a film on, say, Oscar Wilde, whose oeuvre was as insubstantial and self-puffed as Dottie's and whose mouth was a sarcophagus of untreated caries, can be said to deal with an indulged, unhygienic mediocrity.

We make drama for other reasons – about Willy Loman not because of his bad sales figures or his poor track record as a parent, about Hamlet not because of his foul treatment of women (he taunts one into suicide, and comes near to incestuous rape of another) or his lack of respect for the dead (he mocks a skull, and embraces a corpse in mid-funeral), but because they give us cause to reflect on larger questions, like how we live our life on earth and what we make of it.

Dottie's life and that of her support group at the Algonquin, a sort of cross between an adult crèche and a gong show for aspiring intellectuals, raise the (for me) large question of how bohemian you can be. How many passionate adulteries is the modicum? How many first-night piss-ups are enough? Was Eddie Parker wise to go back to the dullness of the Connecticut suburbs? Was Dottie foolish to persist in her Faustian struggle with the great metropolis? When does normal happiness begin? When is it normal to see a shrink? Do we have a right to ask? Did she?

Rudolph deals with these questions without ever patronising the people they are about. He juggles thirty-five flamboyant, articulate characters without ever stooping to caricature and gives us the inner landscape of the stylish bohemians of the combative, apolitical twenties more deftly and sympathetically than it is possible to describe. Each intriguing walk-on (Kaufman, Ferber, Ross, Fitzgerald, Harpo Marx) you want to see more of, know better. What could be a mere rag-bag of glib one-liners is marvellously hewn dramatic dialolgue.

And in Dottie, played with methylated, gloopy-vowelled semi-aristocracy by Jennifer Jason Leigh, he has achieved a screen original. Never at any point do we question her right to her booze, divorces, hungover melancholy, unceasing bitchery, bad fucks ('Don't worry,' she says to one dud performer, 'I don't review rehearsals.') and royal, enduring self-pity ('I do not like me any more'), because she is so complete as a human being – as Margot Channing is in *All About Eve*, or Sally Bowles in *Cabaret*. She is the living, accusing embodiment of Les Murray's dictum that art is not born in you, it is grafted in you through a wound.

And Campbell Scott as Benchley, the greater love she dare not lay for fear of losing, is another. Here is Twenties Man complete – pencil-moustached, brilliantined, self-doubting, loyal, zany, sad to his core, a good friend in trouble to all but his wife, a beaming portrait in soft charcoal that ranks very high in the cinema of likeable gallant wimps.

Mrs Parker succeeds because it is humanist not feminist, and deals unjudgementally with the mess that men and women make of their random bumpings in the night. It's possible that the cure for Dottie, who miscarried as often as she suicided, might have been six kids in Schenectady and quiet Episcopalian Sunday dinners behind a white picket fence. You never know. And it's the great achievement of this fine sad film that it convinces us how much we never know.

June, 1995

John Mortimer

It's hard I think to stand in a room near someone you've admired for thirty years and know it may be your last chance to meet him, and know as well that any conceivable word of praise would only weary him. It was thus in the Playhouse bar I stood near John Mortimer last month and after an hour of desultory loquacity with Cate Blanchett and Leo Schofield and Jim Spigelman and his watchful brood, one of whom, too young to know any better, was equally in awe of me, I went up in my shorts and sandals and sunscreen looking like a moron – I had been to the Second Test with my sons – to the stately corpulent Jacques of English populism (or Jacques as Sydney Greenstreet might have played him) and like a fool praised Rumpole and wearied him in thirty seconds.

I should have mentioned other things – *Bunny Lake Is Missing*, in which a Scotland Yard Plod played by Lord Olivier confronts a mildewed boarding-house roué played by Noel Coward with the sharp, improbable question: 'Who the devil are you?' Or *John and Mary*, a glum romantic comedy about a one-night stand's next morning, interspersed with the spoken thoughts of the disillusioned bonkers, Dustin Hoffman and Mia Farrow, two shortarses whose buttocks *seemed* to appear in the film's early light but proved after howled complaints and legal muttering to belong to slyly added body doubles. Or his wonderful, much underpraised miniseries *Will Shakespeare*, starring Tim Curry as the wary, thick-vowelled eponymous, or his superb sad playlet *Dock Brief*, about a mouldy barrister buggering up a murder defence, and that character's deftest interpretation, by not Peter Sellers but John Meillon at the Q Theatre in 1967. I should have spoken of the lovely ornate miniseries *Brideshead Revisited* and asked why his adaptation was rather longer than the book, and what Olivier's ten-minute death-greeting soliloquy, omitted to the good Lord's anguish and cursing from the final cut, was really like.

And so on. Which of Guinness and Olivier and Redgrave he preferred as his dad – for twenty years an utterly blind yet still formidable divorce lawyer – in *A Voyage around My Father*. How he liked Peter Finch's portrayal of him in *The Pumpkin Eater*, the weepy monochrome classic his fecund, plaintive first consort Penelope confected with Harold Pinter.

But no, I instead like a fool praised the Rumpole books, those rich wily hybrids of Holmes and Wooster ('Let us be thankful for small blessings,' Clive James once wrote. 'The first of these is Rumpole.') – not *Clinging to the Wreckage*, not *Paradise Postponed*, not *Collaborators*, the play he co-wrote with Penelope as off-shore Hollywood hack work, not his mock-solemn with-a-splash-of-lemon interviews with British politicians or his London one-acters or autumnal poetry readings, and by so summoning that vulgar uncorkable genie with the choko proboscis and stubby cigars I lost his flickering good will: I meant to be smoother, and I'm sorry. I should have put on trousers. Or compared him to Gore Vidal who also spent big parts of his boyhood reading great verse aloud to a blind forebear. 'You're so very kind,' he said, and moved off and bought whisky.

Mortimer's rare achievement is a body of work that can be readily enjoyed by any literate person of any social background in the English-speaking world, a success that Maugham and Greene and McMurtry and Heller have managed and few others – a middlebrowness uninsulting to highbrows – plus a tone of voice as distinct and lifeworn and self-saddened as Raymond Chandler's. As a Labour-voting champion of smoking and buggery and fox-hunting, the jury system and Cockney thieves and Enoch Powell and Michael Foot, he like most large talents cannot be boxed and labelled though his own self-image as 'a middle-of-the-road liberal anarchist' is probably about right.

But whatever the mix and the flavouring we're lucky to have him, couplets and puns and fusty lawyers' stories and all. 'You're a great man,' I said, 'and you may moreover be as well a fine fellow.'

'Thank you,' he said, momentarily beaming.

And so it goes.

The good and great are not ours to keep, I fear, however we hoard their signatures. We should only enjoy them, at whatever dim distance, and pass on.

January, 1998

O.J. Simpson

A lot of people die in unexplained knife murders in Los Angeles in any year. There were seventeen last year. In 1969, one of them was Sharon Tate, the pregnant film-star wife of Roman Polanski, the director.

Curiously no-one accused Polanski of her killing, despite his violent past as a street kid in Warsaw and the taste he showed for bloodshed in a number of murderous films he made.

Why, I wonder, was this so? Was it, perhaps, because he was white?

Some would say it was because his wife was pregnant and it was inconceivable, whatever he felt about his wife, that he would also kill his unborn child. Yet many of the same people had no difficulty accusing O.J. Simpson, another film celebrity, of slaughtering his wife while his children lay sleeping upstairs and leaving her mutilated corpse where the children might find it next morning. No difficulty either in believing that she did not scream for help, or try, as she had before, to phone the police. She watched silent, it seems, as her jealous husband struggled with and killed her friend, then silently submitted, and yielded herself up, to his subsequent knife attack on herself.

As a dramatist I do not find the scenario likely. What is much more likely is that Nicole Brown and Ron Goldman surprised in her home two intruders, with two weapons, whose cold steel at her throat ensured her silence while Goldman was killed, or ensured that the two of them could be killed simultaneously.

Why did they do it, these two unknown attackers? Well, they might have been burglars in the house of a sleeping mother, surprised by Goldman's arrival. They might have been after Goldman, or after money for drugs. They might have been thrill killers. They might have been kidnappers, intent on capturing the rich and famous O.J.'s children, surprised by their mother's arrival and then fleeing in panic at the persistent sound of the howling dog.

None of the scenarios are unlikely. But none of them were explored – by a police officer confessedly racist and a forger of evidence, and displeased by black men who marry white women, and unnerved by blacks in general.

I think it unlikely that a big, strong man with a history of wife-beating would arrive with and wield a knife. He might beat her and beat her and so cause her death. Or he might simply shoot her. Few husbands kill their wives with knives. For the damage done that night there had to be two killers, two killers at least.

One man delivering sixty stab wounds to two people? The first thirty while one of them just stood there? I don't think so. And neither did the jury. Why would they?

And a man who deliberately puts on a glove to commit an undetected murder and then drops it near his own house? No. He would soak it in petrol and burn it. Of course he would.

It follows, therefore, that the glove was planted. It also follows, probably, that other things were too – hair, bloodstains – by motivated white men of Los Angeles, keen to find a big bad black man whose deeds would make them seem less villainous after Rodney King. They had done, according to Detective Sergeant Fuhrman, this kind of thing before.

It fits. The jury's racist thesis may be right. It also fits that Fuhrman did the murder or one of his colleagues.

The story continues.

April, 1995

Clinton

'President Roosevelt, will you kindly tell the court how, despite being paralysed below the waist, you nonetheless for eight years managed copulation with your amanuensis Missy Le Hand? With the female straddling? Could you draw a diagram please?'

'President Harding, can you explain why you also wrote sonnets to the mistress you kept in a White House cupboard, when she was already yours for the taking? Would you read, perhaps, these three of them to the court? Speak up, please.'

'Are you telling the court, Mr Lincoln, that having contracted syphilis in a whorehouse in Chicago you then had intercourse with your wife Mary Todd only ten years later? Cured, you say? How irresponsible were you, Mr President! Is it any wonder two of your sons are dead, and your wife almost certainly going mad?'

'What age was your mulatto mistress, your slave, Mr Jefferson, when first you worked your will with her? Fourteen? Was she not in fact *thirteen*?'

'You had an affair, General Eisenhower, with your personal assistant for a *decade*? While she was in your *employ*? Oh, a technically *unconsummated* affair, was it? Could you tell the court precisely what that is?'

'I have a long list of questions, President Kennedy. I have set aside eight days.'

'You, Sir Robert Menzies, had congress with Lady *Who*, *across a desk*?'

'You, Sir Winston Churchill, had sex with Ivor Novello? Which of you was the active partner, and which the passive? Did you change places? Surely you remember that?'

. . . Kenneth Starr, I imagine, would have thought such questions fair and appropriate, had any of these great men fudged his private life under oath. But I doubt the American presidency, or any congruent high office, would have long survived his panty-sniffing prurience. And I doubt such investigation (of F.D.R. for instance, at the height of World War Two) would have been for the public good.

It's a very Anglo-Saxon thing. The French and Latin peoples care less about these private matters. Mitterrand had a mistress, and an illegitimate daughter he tenderly acknowledged in his last dying days in office. Franco was an active predatory army homosexual. Julius Caesar was cheerfully famed as 'a husband to every wife, a wife to every husband'. Cleopatra dutifully, as a good Egyptian queen, had sex with her brother. A number of popes had mistresses, and bastard offspring they gave castles to. In Asia, it mattered little that Mao Tse-tung had four wives and many teenage girlfriends or General Sukarno priapically demanded five hookers a night from his overseas hosts, and got them too. It was noted, but it didn't matter.

From ancient times the ordinary people have murmured of the bed games of their masters – in part, I suppose, to shrink down to size men grown too grand in the mind. From Suetonius's time, and the time of the author of Genesis, historians and biographers have included carnal matters (including Lot's wily dealings with visiting angels in Sodom and, later, with his daughters) in their final assessment of the dead.

To do this to the *living*, however, and in such lavish and slimy detail (President Clinton was clearly, lividly angry still at Ken Starr's proddings and sneerings when, two hours out of the dock, he spoke his defiance to the watching world), is actually, frankly, straightforwardly, not fair. No less a figure than Jesus of Nazareth, whom some called the Christ, said famously in his defence of, yes, an accused and sobbing prostitute, 'Let him that is without sin cast the first stone.' He too in his time was called a winebibber, whoremonger and companion of tax-gatherers and, by one Gospel author at least, an active homosexual – consort, it was said, of John, 'the disciple whom Jesus loved'. Think what harm Ken Starr could have done with a fearless late-night cross-examination before the yawning Sanhedrin that Passover Eve, to his 'character', his following, his cult and his cause.

What else was Clinton, a working politician, *supposed* to say under oath? 'Sure I did, and let me tell you how'?

Give me a break.

Much of life as we live it on earth, and most of friendship, and most of parenting, depends on things unsaid. You do not tell the children over breakfast how last night their mother sat on your face. You do not tell your boss, even in court, and even under oath, how much you detest him. Nor, in most foreseeable circumstances, should you, I think, be forced to, by even Kenneth Starr, the Torquemada of Tumescence. 'What do you mean, Mr President, by *uncompleted sex*? You mean you did not go the full Monica? And she did not *inhale*? What kind of a man are you?'

But now with presidents, as five years ago with princes, this shadow line has been crossed. And it's a pity. And no good will come of it.

It was not as if the fate of America hung on an admitted or unadmitted affair between a fifty-year-old man and a twenty-year-old girl. There was no such consequence involved. And it was not as if either of them was accused of any illegality, except the perjury they were being tempted into. What did it matter?

One more thing should perhaps be said, or perhaps not said, I guess, and it's this.

Anyone who's ever held or run for political office knows how *tense* you get, after effusive hours of chat with people you do not wholly like, and eating ethnic food that gives you the runs, and fudging facts you wish were other facts, and if you're away from home for days on end, and there's something soft, discreet and female in your reach, what else do you do? (I do not speak from experience – oh no – but, having once run for office, I can vividly imagine that experience.) And if Marilyn Monroe walks into the room with no clothes, with lips parted, and you are a thousand miles from home, what else do you do? Tell her to go away?

I doubt many men so placed – Richard Nixon perhaps, Brian Harradine certainly – would bid the lady clothe herself and begone.

It's important to realise what species we belong to, and not cast stones. Jesus the companion of prostitutes would not. And nor should you.

August, 1998

Princess Diana 1

And so things change. A vapid adventuress has been transformed, in death, into the brightest legend of our time. In death she is exalted, and will not be struck down.

There will be no Queen Camilla, now, for London crowds, as in the eighteenth century, to jeer, spit and throw stones at. There may not be another King Charles, so tainted he is by what has come to pass. He will become in popular history a royal backstairs lecher, forever sneaking off to see his pinch-faced paramour.

A 97-year-old Queen who stood on the balcony with Winston Churchill on VE Day in 1945 will attend the grand state funeral of this girl. Once a rival for the love of Edward VIII, who likewise fled the monarchy for love, the Queen Mother has seen much come and go. A Europe that was once a chequerboard of kings, an England that once fought for King and Country, that did not lose its hope. An England that came through.

It is an England now in doubt, perhaps, because of this. A government soon to crush the House of Lords may go one step further now. To a suburban monarchy, perhaps, with kings on bicycles with butterfly nets and pipes and queens with shopping trolleys and spectacles and arts degrees.

And so things change. The death of Cinderella, most will say. A baby-minder raised to greatness by her youth and looks and a prince's timing. *It's time. She'll do. Can she handle the pace? We'll see. Does she know the world she is bound for and its labyrinthine ways? She will. She's young. She'll learn.*

And she did learn too. As in Stephen Sondheim's *Into the Woods*, the happy ending was the first act only. There were horrors to come, unimagined by the children who heard the story. The bulimia. The fighting. The self-slashing on the palace stairs. The public adulteries, him and her. The amazing Oscar-standard performance on television. *When there's three in a marriage, it becomes a little crowded . . . I adored him, but he let me down, rather.*

And so it goes. She was for a time the greatest celebrity of England and the Queen and her consort and children and grandchildren cowered in her light. She was what every shopgirl dreamed of being, and wept because the prince chose her instead. She was a chocolate-box lid, a perfume ad, a Mills & Boon cover in the flesh. She was all of us transfigured and made great.

And so things change. The press that fed this fairytale are lepers now.

They followed Cinderella into the dark tunnel and there killed her. The goose is dead, the golden egg is no more. The police are at the gate with their notebooks out. The press may never be as powerful again.

And so it goes. And dreams are what we live by in our lives. The dream that love will last, the pet dog will always be there, the children always little and trusting and wide-eyed. That grandma will be always there. And the little shop on the corner will not close.

And the point of queens and princes are these dreams, the better selves we live by in our thought. The gossip, the weddings, births and illnesses. *The Queen is out of danger and has been delivered by caesarean birth of a son. The nation rejoices. The King is dead, long live the Queen. Ascending the throne at the same age, twenty-five, as Queen Elizabeth I, Her Gracious Majesty Queen Elizabeth II spoke with clear sincerity of her duty.* And the long trumpets play and the costumed aristocracy of England slowly progress down the ancient Abbey aisle, an abbey built by Edward the Confessor a thousand years ago . . . And so it went. Continuity, dignity, integrity, example. But now no more.

For what has happened in these twenty years – no, it can be dated, twenty-seven years, since the Queen allowed the cameras to eavesdrop on her days, the family watching *I Love Lucy* on the television, the family at a barbecue in scarves, the Queen sharply asking her advisers if she could sell Lord's cricket ground – has brought them, in the manner of the serpent of knowledge in the Garden of Eden, into a kind of glittering pornography.

Princes have had mistresses before – Lillie Langtry, famously, and Lady Randolph Churchill attended on the fat and surly Prince of Wales, who was challenged to a duel once by the cuckolded Randolph Churchill, piqued at his wife's behaviour. Kings have had male lovers. Edward II and Gaveston. William III and Arnold Joost Van Keppel, Earl of Albemarle and ancestor (marvellously) of Camilla.

Queens have begotten bastards: Queen Victoria's actual grandfather, famously, was a Jewish tailor attached to the House of Hanover. And this was known. And it was looked on calmly and politely. And from time immemorial people have mocked the sex lives of their rulers. *Homeward we bring your bald conqueror,* his troops would sing of Julius Caesar. *Romans, lock up your wives.*

It has always been known, but it has never before been seen. When a princess, seen from above in a gym suit, exercising on a bike, a look of dreamy stimulated pleasure on her face, was blazed across the world, a wall of privacy was breached. And the last great royal house started to tremble. All bets were off now, and we knew it.

And the money to be made by tireless prurience was millions. You could retire on one photograph of a princess sucking toes. Had Princess Di been a normal divorcee harassed by her ex-husband as she was harassed every day by the paparazzi, she could have put him in gaol.

But no, she was a celebrity, a star, a golden dream. And so new rules applied. And knowing this, and keen for money herself, she manipulated the rules.

Few who have not gone through it know what the ego-rush of celebrity is like. The constant avenue of smiles. The ever-available free food and drink. The handsome flatterers ever dazzled by your wisdom. *The feeling that one is important, and one has an important role.* And then, cold turkey, the end of that feeling, or its cruel interruption. *When no-one's listening to you,* she said, *when you feel no-one's listening to you . . . you have so much pain inside yourself that you try to hurt yourself on the outside because you want help. But it's the wrong help you're asking for. People see it as crying wolf or attention seeking, and they think because you're in the media all the time, you've got enough attention, in inverted commas. But I was actually crying out because I wanted to get better in order to go forward and continue my duty and my role as wife, mother, Princess of Wales. So yes, I did inflict hurt on myself. I didn't like myself. I was ashamed because I couldn't cope with the pressure.*

Poor little Cinderella. Poor gormless randy prince. And so it goes.

But it will not end this week, of course, or next week, or the next, with a nation's red-eyed bafflement and a Hamlet-Prince's grief by a new Ophelia's grave: *Woo't outface me with thy weeping? Woo't eat a crocodile? I'll do it!* For already Hollywood will be moving: *this is great, it's a story of now. Moral – be careful what it is you want most in life, 'cause you just might get it. It's a great conception.* A Star Is Born *with tiaras. Let's MOVE. Elvis won't be in it, baby, this is real money.* And so it always was.

And this, I suppose, is what we call history. Cleopatra was one such vulgar, sensational tale of a princess brought to bloody death by her passions and her luck with men. Caesar cut down while she waited a mile away. Antony who said to her while drunk, *let's rule the world together.* Every now and then there's a story like this and some dull hack like Shakespeare to make money from it by doing it badly.

It will not cease to happen while men hunger for blood and skirts blowing up long, royal legs to a promised land, and women dream of a prince who will rescue them from a life that is less than happy. We all have our sustaining fantasies, they keep us alive and functioning. The big dreams matter, and that's an end of it, although we know they are but dreams.

And so it goes.

September, 1997

Princess Diana 2

Diana's coffin passed the threshold of the ancient Abbey at 11 a.m. precisely and an hour later, at noon precisely, moved with British military exactitude out again, into sunlight and popular legend. In the intervening sixty minutes a hit song was relaunched, the monarchy dealt a mortal blow, a lot of gorgeous choir music exulted to the vaulting naves by boys with angel faces and applause heard in that sacred site of the West for the first time in a thousand years. And an ode to love was read by a Labor Prime Minister with a pop-star face in a voice reminiscent of Larry Olivier impersonating the world's most caring Sunday school teacher and his party thereby assured of government for fifteen years. And ... a handsome young rake, Charles Spencer (who could have got by acclamation the leadership of the Tory Party *or* the Liberal Democrats that morning had he sought it), gave a funeral address as good as Gettysburg, with a moral force that his cousin Winston Spencer Churchill would not have disowned, in curse of the British royal ethic of the stiff upper lip and the pinched lives of the children of the great. And, almost incidentally, a televisual miracle of heard music and roved statuary thrilled to their bones a billion witnesses across the world.

And England changed forever. Bouquet after bouquet thrown at the onward moving hearse in a wave of emotion more like South America than England showed among many lesser things that the Poms were mad as hell and they weren't going to take it any more and the war for their souls between Thatcher's cold punishing fury and Diana's cuddling warmth had been won at last by the ethic of unstinted love, best defined by *The Nostradamus Kid* (and *The Reader's Digest* of April 1955) as fullness of response.

And back in Australia John Howard, who a year ago precisely had refused to meet her lest he thereby offend the Queen, grovel, grovel, was comprehensively doomed. Di's slim pale hand reached out of the grave and seized his windpipe and shook him till bits fell off him and he shrieked like a dying crow. All that he stood for, including mediocre public utterance, shrank in her light to munchkin size, and his party's vote fled away to nothing. A few days later, from a Mosman podium alongside Noel Pearson, I called his Cabinet 'these crab lice on the body politic' and perhaps 300 former voters for him applauded hugely. Pushing my luck, I then called *him* 'this itching haemorrhoid on the body politic' and was even more applauded, though three shocked Mosman matrons frogmarched their choir-singing children towards the exit. And apart from a few decaying monarchist octogenarians on talk radio, John Howard had no friends left, and Kim Beazley an easy run to the Lodge whenever the poll occurs (you have my word).

And so it goes. The cliché, *my God, the Poms really do know how to turn it on, don't they? and at a moment's notice too*, doesn't really cover it, but it says a fair bit. The Dunkirk spirit. The guts of the young men on Goose Green. It maybe helped that they'd been rehearsing the Queen Mother's funeral for fifteen years, with exactly those pans and those dissolves from stone fretwork to choir-singing faces, foolishly heedless in all that time of the great lady's daily diet of that finest of English preservatives Gilbey's Gin. I'm told that most of her staff these days are elderly homosexuals, and it is her wont round seven most nights to say to them down the blower, 'If any of you old queens are still awake, this old Queen would like a gin.'

And so it goes. Another example of this British capacity for turning up unfussed on schedule is the wonderful movie *Brassed Off*, about the narrow survival of a colliery band in the era of Thatcher mine closures. Though the title is dreadful the film is as good as *Chariots of Fire* and, like it, left me sitting on the road and weeping for about twelve minutes. The ordinary *decency* of working-class people (declaring my interest, I am son of a man who was for eight years a Maitland coal miner) and the horror of what happened to them – the break-up of their communities and marriages, the suicidal depressions and alcoholic violence and the loss (yes) of their music – is here shown in a style that mixes Ealing comedy, agitprop and backstage musical. No punch is pulled, not even the miners' own betrayal for severance terms of their cause. *There were 220 mines in Britain when Thatcher came to power. There are twenty now. Discuss.* Pete Postlethwaite, as the band master, gives one of the great performances in English-speaking cinema: a big brown-eyed lizard-like face, expressionless yet saying everything – about, among other things, the undeniable divinity of music, God's consolation for real life, which in 'Jerusalem' and 'Land of Hope and Glory', and 'Danny Boy' gives us back the world that ought to be. See it if you've a mind to. My curse will haunt you into a hell of red-hot worms if you do not.

. . . It's been a terrible couple of weeks, with Jeff Bernard and George Solti and Hans Eysenck and the saintly nun of Calcutta and Jessie Bradman going (and the Don soon, too, if he keeps his word) and also, God help us, Dodi Al Fayed who put up the money for *Chariots of Fire*, that hymn of praise to Jewish chutzpah, and thus risked, Puttnam said at the time, decapitation on the steps of the mosque. 'He principally wants to meet the Queen at the world premiere,' Puttnam explained that year to a gathering of Australian writers, in explanation of Dodi's bizarre investment, 'and he will, he will, he'll meet the Queen.' And so it goes.

September, 1997

Cheryl Kernot

On the bad night of 3 March Cheryl Kernot said with a frozen smile just five words, 'Mary Delahunty is in Parliament', and was widely derided by political journalists as having 'lost it' or 'spat the dummy' or 'shown herself to be too out of control for electoral politics'.

Thirteen years before that Bob Hawke, openly weeping real tears, revealed his daughter was a heroin addict and suffered, by contrast, no political harm. No-one, moreover, said he had 'lost it' or 'spat the dummy' when seven years before that he called a reporter 'a bloody pest' and admitted in interviews to multiple adultery and via his biographer D'Alpuget to being a 'mean drunk' and a 'rat with women'.

He was thought to be a better man for confessing these excesses, and to have brought a pleasing level of truthfulness to politics by airing them.

So, too, these days is Jeff Kennett, by shovelling sand into the camera lenses of the media. And Kim Beazley by weeping on the floor of Parliament over the Stolen Children. And John Howard by storming out of a meeting with Jennie George because a souvenir shop has been trashed by coincidental rioters.

Men, it seems, are permitted to weep in politics now and women are not – men can complain and stamp their feet and shout, but women cannot. Women have to be tougher than that.

If Carmen Lawrence, moreover, evades a moot question of when she first knew a particular fact she can be brought to trial. Peter Reith can evade a similar question – on Dubai – and suffer, it seems, no harm.

Women pay for their sins, you see, and men, quite properly, do not. It is the woman taken in adultery who is stoned to death and her male partner, by ancient custom, let off. It is Cheryl Kernot's sexual history that is damagingly aired – or Pauline Hanson's – while Andrew Peacock's, or Don Dunstan's, or Bob Brown's, is mercifully airbrushed from history. Men deserve this consideration, and women do not.

The media are accustomed to telling only one story about famous women, and it is the story of the Female Meteor. She is here, she is up, she is bright and, whoops, she is gone; and why did she vanish? That is the question. What was her fatal flaw? Carmen Lawrence, Bronwyn Bishop, Sallyanne Atkinson fit this tragic scenario (and Marilyn Monroe and Judy Garland and Princess Di), this narrative arc of quick rise and fast fade, and Cheryl (and Pauline) must be *made* to fit its eternal contours whatever the actual facts. Given the choice, the media will always print the story they prefer.

When Cheryl Kernot's house was knocked down by a truck, a house then containing her little daughter, and she was rushing sleepless into Hobart Airport at dawn, she was asked if she was a bad mother for not being at home on the occasion when her home, predictably, was hit by a truck. She said that kind of question made her wonder if politics was worth it. 'Too volatile for politics', the media said. 'Hasn't got what it takes.'

What the media knew, and did *not* say, was what had happened to her *previous* house. It was burned to the ground by a demented arsonist who, in prison, left Cheryl all his earthly goods in his will and topped himself. The same little daughter was in the house that burned and in the house that was demolished and her mother was rushing back to convince her that this double devastation did not portend anything, our houses are not cursed with destruction, before then rushing back to prove her mettle to the wary, blokey Labor Party in Conference.

Lost it, said the media. Spat the dummy. Just as she had when, having given up $1.4 million (yes, Bill O'Chee's famed figure) in pension for a perhaps noble cause, she allowed herself a moment of open, honest regret at her fool self-sacrifice.

The media are not so merciless with others. Actors, rock singers, novelists, painters, other journos can rage, throw punches, change wives, drink to excess or do drugs, and it is not felt they should lose their jobs or their income.

For politicians, however, there are different rules. They must work eighteen hours a day and not show impatience or exhaustion. They must deal tactfully with all sorts of people and yet be totally honest with all of them. They must not fudge an answer though their survival depends on it. They must be tough and ambitious, yet warm and caring. They must abandon high incomes for decades and work punishing schedules away from home, and not reach out, not ever, for something soft in the night. They must not be arrogant. And they must not be weak. If they are not arrogant, they are said to be weak, to be lacking 'ticker'. If they are not weak, they are said to be arrogant and so undeserving (as were, presumably, Churchill, Menzies, Whitlam, Thatcher, De Gaulle) of the job, the job of *leadership*.

The net result – and it is coming fast – will be I fear the kind of politician who is utterly pre-set and pre-scripted and choreographed, like Tony Blair, whom I have described elsewhere as 'a crisply-spoken hologram'. A person whose niceness, intelligence and steely resolve are all on the autocue and maybe nowhere else. A person with no visible human variability, like Joh's or Jeff's or Neville's or Cheryl's or Winston's or Franklin's or Honest Abe's.

A person as unlikely as Max Headroom, or as prattling and waxen as Peter Reith. A politician trained in Passive Totalitarianism to say only what it is now, today, permissible to hear.

What we need, of course, is not better politicians (look at Bob Hawke's first Cabinet, politicians look pretty good *in retrospect*) but better political journalists – who do not hunt as a pack and tell, at day's end, exactly, repetitively, the same slim story. Political journalists who see the larger context, the policy imperatives, the historical dimension. Who can distinguish the importance of a presidential blowjob and an imminent worldwide financial catastrophe. Who get the proportions right.

But we won't get that, of course. Not from this lot. They are too busy charting the descending arcs of spat dummies and female meteors. Doing again what was done before, again and again and again, by minds equivalently lazy.

There are none so blind, it is well said, as those who will not see. And there are none so vile and contemptible as those who, having seen, will never speak full truth of what they see, or even try to. The Australian political journalist, alas, thus far, this decade, is both.

October, 1998

Helen Demidenko and Carmen Lawrence

In the simultaneous headline-hogging stories of Helen Demidenko and Carmen Lawrence lie tempting parallels. Both are female, famous, honoured and praised in the past and now on trial. Both are accused of lying, and of distorting history. Both have been publicly damned by members of their own families. Both are ambitious, tough and not easy to write off. Both are this week on the ropes.

And yet their probable fates are so different, so palpably and shockingly different, as to raise fundamental questions about the present practice – would call it malpractice – of our democracy. Consider this.

Demidenko lied. She impersonated (allegedly impersonated) someone she was not in order to make seem more true a contentious fiction that stirred up racial hatred, probably, in a country with laws against it. She did this to become famous, and massively succeeded. She is the best-known

24-year-old in the country, probably. She has been found out in her fraud-ulence (alleged fraudulence) this week and . . .

And what?

She will not go to prison, like other frauds. She will not be stripped of her prizes. Her book will not be removed from bookshops. Her earnings from it will not be confiscated. She will not be prevented from writing other books. She will not be prevented from appearing on radio broadcasts, or writing articles in her defence. Her value as a contributor and her fee for occasional journalism and public speaking will probably go up. She will, in short, be publicly derided a little, not effectively — that is, financially — punished at all.

Consider now Carmen Lawrence.

If John Howard is right, what she did was this. She lied — or allegedly lied. She said, like many politicians before her, that she knew less of a cru-cial matter than she did. Caught out, she affirmed her previous falsehood with radiant brazenness. In court — what might be called a Kangaroo Court court — her falsehood was incontestably contradicted and . . .

And what?

She will be deprived of her Cabinet ministry, one in which she has per-formed ably. She may lose at election her parliamentary seat, a seat she won on merit, and possibly gender. She may be deprived of her current income, and her parliamentary pension, due to serving too few years in the House. She will, if a Howard government arrives, be fined hundreds of thousands of dollars for daring to defend herself against the immoderate slanders of her West Australian nemesis. A stinking albatross around her neck, named Penny Easton, will go with her to her grave.

So for the big liar, Demidenko, chuckles and wealth. For the small liar, Lawrence, ignominy and poverty. There is one law, in short, for the ordinary citizen and another for the politician. For the ordinary citizen, rich rewards. For the politician — from one of many causes — sudden death, and after that shame and oblivion.

I am not too keen on this contrast. It shows once again — to me at least — the Australian tendency to concentrate on questions of guilt and never on questions of punishment and what punishment should properly occur.

Certainly Lawrence is guilty (or probably, or possibly). But guilty of what? Of fudging her knowledge of a matter of evidence which unfortunately turned bad? I didn't see the petition, she said in the way that John Howard every week of his life says, I haven't seen the report, or, I didn't see the headline, or, I didn't hear the item, when everyone in the country knows he has. Should she lose her livelihood for doing what he does every week? Her professional standing? Her good name? Her future?

How many of us, when asked something similar, have fudged our answer in the same way? Did you know the boss is having an affair? Well no, I didn't. It's not true, is it? Did you know about that poor girl's abortion? No, I didn't. That's just gossip, isn't it? How many of us, having done that, would expect to be fired for saying it? Yet this is what is happening to Carmen Lawrence.

If crimes of this smallness and punishment of this enormity are going to become the order of our new McCarthyist day we'd better ask now what similar crimes John Howard (say) is guilty of, and how he should be punished. When did he first know, for instance, that Noel Crichton-Browne had been accused of bashing his wife? Nineteen eighty-nine? Nineteen ninety? Did he know it when he was still – for the first time – leader of the party? If not, did he report it to his leader Andrew Peacock? Or his leader John Hewson? Or his leader Alexander Downer? If he didn't, why did he keep this crucial knowledge hidden? What was he afraid of? Why did he subsequently (if it is subsequently) back, and accept in his quadrumvirate of leadership, a man he knew was electoral nitro-glycerine?

Now, should he go to gaol for this? Or should he only lose his position as party leader, for wittingly concealing from public knowledge the evil doings of his fellow party leader? What should be his punishment for this cover-up?

A Royal Commission should look into these important questions, clearly. It should do so for a couple of months, on $100 000 a day. Andrew Peacock should be called to testify, and John Hewson, and Alexander Downer. And Noel Crichton-Browne.

For henceforth, and the Coalition should know this, it is just possible that all bets are off.

November, 1995

Howard and Nixon

If John Howard finds 'boring' a line of questioning that could end in him serving five years in gaol for unlawful conspiracy, he must be easily bored. He would have yawned through Watergate, and snored through World War Two. 'I'm bored, quite frankly' is a better line than 'I am not a crook', I suppose, but the upshot, I bleakly predict, will be very much the same – rumour, revelation, tardy confession, 'smoking gun' headlines, dobbing, shredding, bail, plea bargaining, missing documents, lapses of memory, Senate inquiry, High Court interrogation, whiffs of dismissal, bestselling memoirs, eventual gaolings, a miniseries, and world-wide contempt for our country as great – or nearly as great – as it was for Nixon's America.

Many have noted in private the resemblance between Howard and Nixon but few have done so in public, and none have written up, as I do here, the details.

The stern religious upbringing. The pious commanding mother. The un-fashionable high school. The solemn, nerdish persona. The faithful Dag-woodish marriage to the loyal, unplaintive wife. The early, unexpected political promotion to the top tier of government. The party leadership at forty-six. The first narrow defeat. The loss, at forty-eight, of the party leader-ship. The parallel cries of 'You won't have Nixon to kick around any more' and 'I'd have to be Lazarus with a triple by-pass to think of running for the leadership again'. The determination, meanwhile, to continue schmoozing and scramble back somehow. The resumption of the party leadership at fifty-five. Talk of his remaking – a new Nixon, a new Howard – as a man who has learned a few things along the way, a moderate leader now for all the people. The parallel catchcries of 'bring us together' and 'for all of us'. The attainment of the highest office at fifty-six.

An immediate revelation, thereafter, of the mean and vengeful side. Sack-ings. Vendettas. Blacklists of public servants. The rapid undermining of wel-fare institutions. A war with the young on campuses. A bitter fight with the media. An initial surge in public popularity, then a return of suspicion. Is this the old Nixon after all? A passion for secrecy in all matters. A secret war in Cambodia. A secret revolutionary army (or so it is alleged) in Dubai.

The scenario would admittedly now require a second electoral victory before the Watergate (read Waterfront) scandals and final anguished resig-nation but things, this week, have speeded up, with the secret army revealed ahead of schedule and its oberleutnants, the E. Howard Hunts and Gordon Liddys, already grassing to the papers. We can expect the Judge Sirica and Sam Irvine stages to be over by Christmas and the talk of impeachment (in our case the dismissal of the entire implicated Cabinet by a rueful Governor General) round January and the exalting by Australia Day '99 of the meek and baffled Beazley to the Lodge, the inevitable electoral massacre by mid-March and the gaoling of the guilty parties, only three of them serving ministers, round late May. We might reasonably then expect the emergence of some of them as born-again Christians and the launch of their luminous incarceration memoirs round the lighting of the Olympic torch, by a copi-ously weeping Franca Arena.

The Nixon parallel should probably not be pushed too far, however. Alexander Downer, as an instance, is no Henry Kissinger and Bronwyn Bishop nowhere near as mad as Martha Mitchell, though equally persecuted by her great and powerful acquaintance. Janette Howard is not so dim and stoic as Pat Nixon, nor Tim Fischer so stupid and corrupt (and not, as far as I know, corrupt at all) as Spiro Agnew, though he has, unluckily, the same face. There is no young man in the Howard back room as good-looking or intelligent as John Dean. There was nowhere in the Nixon entourage a biographer as fawning as David Barnett.

What is common in both case studies, however, is the Shakespearian dimension of soured and rancid hubris: in the man impelled to power, like Macbeth, there are always demons that will not let him wield it wisely. His upward struggle has been so bitter and wounding that only waspish malice and sporadic paranoia attend his coronation and foreshortened reign. His victory, unlike Hal's and Keating's, is never sweet; for all it bodes is a life ill-lost for a brief hollow crown and then quick disgrace and aggrieved oblivion – a severed head held up with goggling eyes for history's mockery, but nothing worthwhile or pleasurable. The ill-wrought phrase 'mean-spirited' somehow fits. In both Howard and Nixon there was no larger spirit, only gnawing need.

Nixon, though, it should be said in his mitigation, had many strengths and qualities unremarked in his turgid Australian remake. Many who met him spoke with wonder (some of them to me) of his personal charm, and his Zelig-like ability, shared with many world statesmen, to appear to be the person on earth most like the awestruck listener. All found him formidably intelligent, and able well into his early eighties to chart and commentate on with startling wisdom the tides and eddies of modern history and the impact on it of its leading personalities, many of whom, of course, he knew as friends. No-one doubted the rightness of the informed and passionate over-view that sped his rapprochement with China, nor the beneficent impact of his doctrine of détente. None found him arrogant; and if sometimes under-informed, he was never closed off to new knowledge; all were in some way disarmed by his eagerness to be liked and by his beautiful baritone voice.

Few of his acquaintance speak so warmly of John Howard. Coolness, enclosedness, intellectual impenetrability and tedium of discourse, a curdled Vegemite voice and earnest personality that wearies world leaders, in particular Blair and Clinton, are the usual qualities that spring to their lips. Shirley MacLaine nodded off while he was speaking and many more have wished they could have.

His foreign policy stances, moreover, have unlike Nixon's been mostly disastrous. His pussyfooting round Hanson has made him loathed in Asia. His refusal to sign their civil liberties accord has astonished the European community. His policy on greenhouse gases has made him, in many scientific circles, a pariah. His billions for Suharto have angered the democratic oppo-sitionists of Indonesia. His record on race relations (he made no protest for twenty years against the imprisonment of Nelson Mandela) have made him, to use a current well-worn phrase, an international laughing-stock. Where-soever on the planet he gets to his feet (as a nice phrase now has it) he shrinks to the occasion.

Is Howard *worse* than Nixon then? It seems so, alas, in many respects. He certainly heads the most negative, black-hearted, chaotic, foul-tempered and vengeful government since World War Two, and perhaps since Federation, rewarding life's lottery winners and punishing its losers.

Thank God it has only a few months to run, before the hearings, trials and sentencings begin. I am not a particularly cruel person, but, as with Watergate, I shall enjoy the spectacle.

May, 1997

Kim Beazley

I write this on Friday morning, convinced that Labor will win – its major-ity fourteen to thirty; if over thirty, Reith, Fischer and Howard to lose their seats – and in a mood of gratitude therefore that I know Beazley well, or well enough (among his associates only Mick Young really knew him), and vote for him with pleasure. If the vote goes the other way I will then, I suppose, find faults in him – windiness, kindliness, not enough killer instinct, too many good manners for a profession well described by Yeats as 'weasels fighting in a hole'.

The last time I talked with him at length (in politics length is three minutes), in a burnt-out church in Parramatta on the morning after the debate, we discussed, the way one does, medieval weaponry. The crossbow, he sharply asserted, was nowhere near as effective as the longbow, whose arrow showers were the deadliest artillery till the Big Berthas of World War One. We talked then in detail of Agincourt, the horses caught in the mud and being hacked to pieces by the infantry and how the rain that morning changed history. The way one does.

The next time I was with him was immediately after his launching speech (that stirring anthem of defiant hope so like, at times, the war cry of a battle-maddened elephant), in a small room with his family. 'The best thing you gave me,' he said amiably to his father, 'was a good pair of lungs.'

We've talked at other times of Catholicism, retirement, Hungarians (he married one), Shane Warne, skin cancer, the grammar of cinema, the war in New Guinea, the tendencies of West Australians towards both brave-hearted goodness and the blackest villainy (the Anzacs, he reminds us, were mostly West Australians, and so were the vilest corporate criminals), Curtin and MacArthur, the reputation (a favourite passion) of the Australian soldier in World War One. 'The Germans came eventually to know,' he said, 'that when Australians arrived in opposite trenches, within forty-eight hours they would be attacked.'

In all these conversations, over three years of working for and with him – on three Budget speeches, campaign tactics, odd bits of policy – I was struck, as journalists on his plane have been, by his *openness*, frankness and willing-ness to engage with relative strangers at the highest level of discourse, to bring, like a great teacher, the other mind up to his level, neither hectoring nor lecturing but informing, drawing out, wrestling mightily with the subject at hand. He believes, I suspect (it might come from Moral Rearmament, or elsewhere), that every human soul has a right to be treated equally, talked to as a sentient, intelligent equal, and is therefore a nightmare to his minders, who can't get him away from conversations with people in supermarkets he's suddenly brow-to-brow with. He has the eager questingness of a teen-ager and the information bank of what he could have been, an Oxford don.

A Rhodes scholar, he has one other thing in common, he says, with Bill Clinton, and that was playing second row in football for his Oxford college. Like a powerful Oxford Union debater (on his feet, speaking from the heart without notes and at length, he is in this country second only to Noel Pearson), or like a good army general, I suppose, he believes in rules, rules of engagement.

You do not, for instance, attack your opponent personally, or unfairly, however effective the barb. You do not pretend an emotion (as Peter Costello does) that has no *basis* in what you actually feel. You allow yourself to rise up in flames of self-righteousness only when the cause is great, and your opponents are in fact iniquitous. You do not cheat. You do not pretend.

I saw him in tears in the House over the Stolen Children, and immediately afterwards cursing himself – while admitting it was effective politics – for having lost his dignity. Dignity, propriety, tradition, mannerly argument are very important to him. He could, I believe, be transplanted into the House of Commons of 1948, and stand up beside Nye Bevan and Roy Jenkins as one of its most forensic, impassioned and detailed orators.

He is, yes, cuddly, but he has steel and fire as well; and brain. And a remarkable capacity to engage you on about four levels at once. To tell you great things, and yet mock himself as well, with a sharp, sudden salvo of laughter. Like all great leaders he both excites and relaxes you. You feel, as you do with a slightly feared father, at home with him. Alert, but fond.

Of another big, engaging, hugely laughing polio survivor, Franklin D. Roosevelt, it was correctly said that he had, perhaps, for a President, a second-rate *intellect* but a first-rate *temperament*; and it was the temperament that mattered most. Of Beazley it should, remarkably, be said that he has an intellect that is first-rate and a temperament that is first-rate. But no great anger, and that's a worry.

No-one but this big bonhomous cushion of a man could have held, in its extremis, a thing as bitter and fractious as the Labor Party together. No-one else with his knowledge of his region, nation, party, tribal grouping, proud statehood, historical placement and the spiritual shimmers and practicalities of office could have welded them into such a resurgent force. He is the man best equipped to be Prime Minister since, no, not Menzies, he was lazier. No, not Chifley, he was less eloquent. No, not Curtin, his temperament was panicky and painful. Let's be frank about this. Deakin. Or Neville Wran.

Pray God I am right, and he has made it.

Of course he has.

What a great day for a soiled, sad country. Pray God I am right.

October, 1998

Bob Carr

Bob Carr is a Labor hero now, and his rather ordinary life, I suppose, will take on, like Chifley's, legendary force. The fibro beginnings and swottish boyhood. The day he came in short pants holding an ice-cream cone to join, at fourteen, a train driver's son, the Party. The apprenticeship of fire in the Young Labor movement of Keating, Richo, Laurie Brereton. The academic triumphs at Matraville High and UNSW. Years of thoughtful journalism with Packer and the ABC. The life plan to be, at forty-five, Australia's Foreign Minister. The state seat that was to lead to the federal seat, and then, at thirty-eight, the Environment Ministry. The Labor debacle of 1988, when six potential Premiers lost their seats, and he alone was left standing. His unwilling acceptance of the leadership, and the end of his life plan. The sour but bracing years of Opposition, the near miss of '91, the leadership threats and ugly photos and mocking headlines, the wilderness years of bushwalking, Proust, the uncompleted novel, the parliamentary harassment of the hated enemy. The narrow victory of '95. The uncertain years since then. And then last Saturday night, and the speech that echoed Henry Fonda in *The Grapes of Wrath: wherever there's a poor guy who's lost his job, I'll be there.* A new iconic presence. A new story. The novelist as politician. An Australian Adlai Stevenson, Roy Jenkins, Michael Foot, but one that wins. The intellectual's *via dolorosa*, nose to book, as the horny-handed multitude throw bricks and mock him on his way. But see how the story ends.

I've known Bob for eighteen years now. I've spent a lot of nights with him, at the theatre and over Italian and Chinese meals, and collaborated on speeches with him and talked at length on the phone, but I don't know him well. 'We are intimate,' I would say, 'but not close.' He has, like many politicians, a force-field of humorous reserve around him that seals out intruders, and only a few people – Helena his wife, John McCarthy his old Young Labor comrade, Kris Neill his female Chief of Staff, his fellow diarist Rodney Cavalier, his former minders Bruce Hawker and Graeme Wedderburn, Paul Keating perhaps – can penetrate. He reveals much to us others, in selective flashes of lightning, but not all. He does his nightclub acts, the devilish mimicry, the delightful spontaneous self-mocking heroic soliloquies. But we do not know him.

He wept on the night before the poll in 1995, thinking all was lost, alone in his darkened office among the vain cardboard boxes of press releases of seven years, high above the lights of the city. He wept at the funeral of a young policeman killed off-duty, of a young firefighter with children. Sometimes his famous carapace of cool and tireless and ironic professionalism drops, not often.

He acted quickly and formidably in my presence, for instance, when Franca Arena accused him and others of protecting paedophiles. Within half an hour there was a judge, an inquiry, a set of guidelines, no panic, brilliant lines given on radio, and Franca's eventual doom. He evinces cold fire sometimes when talking of heroin, the drug that killed his brother at twenty-nine, after a year of coma, but deals with the issue justly and objectively. He is not convinced, he says, that supplying free an addictive poison to its pathetic victims would help the world much, but he will hear the arguments. And after heroin what? Crack? Cocaine? White lightning? Why not? Why not?

His voice is the best and most durable in Australian politics. Baritone, classless, inclusive, big enough to command a thousand people without amplification, and pinion interjectors with a subclause; it is bigger somehow than his lean, Clark Kentish frame. It adds to him what I call that quality of 'authoritative tenderness' that woos an audience, a radio audience in particular, and wins elections. A tenderness deepened, perhaps, by the death of a sibling, his childlessness and other thwartings. 'That's a voice I'd kill for,' said Paul Keating simply.

Like many good leaders, Beazley for instance, he both excites and relaxes you. He makes friends across unusual gulfs of belief and culture. Cavalier on the left, Alan Jones on the right esteem him highly, Gore Vidal and Norman Mailer are pen-pals and overseas hosts. He loves America and Europe, and once in a rush caught two acts of *Don Giovanni* on his way from his hotel to Frankfurt Airport, and nearly missed his plane. Nick Greiner once called a by-election in January and thus prevented him seeing *The Madness of George III* on stage in London. 'It was at that point,' he said, 'I determined to destroy him.' If he were not bound up in his unsought destiny as Labor saviour, he would be opera critic of the London *Guardian*, or roving correspondent, like Hitchens, of *Vanity Fair*.

He has an intricate inner life. At one point he told me he was half-convinced there was a parallel universe in which John Fahey was still Premier and he was a fading disc jockey in Queanbeyan. He admires *Idlewild*, a novel in which Jack Kennedy survives his assassination, and Marilyn Monroe survives her suicide, and they meet again in the 1990s, and the world is very different. He is intrigued not only by what happened, and how it happened, but what else might have happened.

He is famously and copiously a reader (Anthony Powell he now ranks higher than Proust, having read both novel-cycles while in office), but more secretly a writer too – of diaries, passionate book reviews (Lincoln and the American Civil War his specialty) and, endlessly, his novel on Young Labor people in 1971. Keating is in it under his own name, vividly and buoyantly evoked, others more disguised. Publishers are tussling for it, but may have to wait.

He bushwalks still, strolls beaches, eats carrots, drinks coffee, has late-night conversations like the student he has never ceased to be. He strives always to find out *what happened*, and the full context of why it happened. The Kennedy White House. Chifley's defeat.

He is loyal and kindly to the most wayward friends. Malcolm MacGregor worked for him, left him, worked for the Liberals, attacked him personally in print, went off the grog, rebefriended him, invited him as Premier to his fortieth birthday party, and Bob came. His staff, the best in political Australia, have worked seven days a week for him since Christmas, as they would, I believe, for no other. He ran, and amazingly won, a campaign of no big promises, standing on his record, *and not criticising the Opposition*. That took some doing.

He stood on a table last Friday night, and thanked his staff in a remarkable, tired, unconfident, self-effacing speech. There were lines on his face, and a searing of his spirit, a cathartic gathering of inner exhaustions that weren't there a year ago. He looked and felt like Chifley, or Dunstan, a Labor hero.

He had become a part of the story, the big story, he had for so long studied. Like an archaeologist time-travelling in his favourite Egyptian dynasty, he had arrived at last, in full focus, in the prime of his intellect and curiosity, a leader, a man for all seasons, at the hub of things. I will watch what he does now, as a friend, an admirer, with interest.

March, 1999

Noel Pearson

The night I first met Noel Pearson was an eventually famous one, at the Mosman RSL when fifty were expected, 500 turned away and 600 admitted, and Noel and Lois O'Donoghue and Aden Ridgeway and I spoke and a school choir sang and the roaring, applauding, uplifted, upstanding middle-class crowd, 70 per cent of them Liberal voters, made us feel, for a time, that the cause of Aboriginal reconciliation was not yet lost and good might yet prevail in these millennial years and all might yet be well.

We were wrong, I suppose; for it all looks pretty hopeless now, but that night, round 10.30, when Noel arrived red-eyed and worn out, having spoken in two other states that day and flown for thousands of miles, and at 10.30 began a speech that lasted nearly an hour with a self-effacing joke ('I used to dream of being a first-grade footballer, until it became clear to me that I had a Mark Ella mind in a Kim Beazley body') and slowly grew into the best oration I had ever heard, better, it seemed, than anything by Lincoln or Churchill or Nye Bevan or Martin Luther King, it all seemed very different. At its end a choir of children sang 'We Are One But We Are Many' and on stage with linked hands, mine with Noel's, we were singing along, and Noel said to me, 'This is a pretty good song, this one. Who wrote it?' I was startled. 'Haven't you heard it before?' I asked. 'No,' he said. 'Should I?' And the puzzle of him deepened.

He was thirty-one then, and had once already retired from the field of blood and honour to become, he said in his contentious valedictory audience on *AM*, an ordinary Melbourne lawyer. He had discussed with Keating a parliamentary seat but had decided against it. He was worn out, buggered, stuffed, and needed a year off maybe to go fishing, commune with his people, have a life. And within six months he was back, looking sicker and sicker, working harder and harder, running on empty, working up to a heart attack, some said, and yet . . .

No-one who hasn't heard Noel speak at full throttle for half an hour or more can imagine what it's like. It's a rolling surge of massive, accumulating righteousness that hypnotises as it swells and beats and summons the lightning, unmans reason, storms the thinking heart. Churchill, Lincoln, Padraic Pearse were capable, with a lot of rewriting, of sentences like the ones that rise unbidden from Noel's weary mouth, and you feel yourself lifting out of the seat and it's a somehow ennobling experience just to *listen*, and you come away altered, and you can't believe mere words can do this to you, and you know at last what leadership is . . . And then, I suppose, in the usual way, if you're like me, you take a few months to forget.

He's an enigma to those who don't know him, and a maddening frustration to those who do. To pin him down to a talk on the phone is hard; to talk face-to-face well nigh impossible. He vanishes every now and then, to deal with family obligations, or Cape York tribal business, or simply to 'go fishin''. Lew Griffiths, who for six years has been chronicling his movements on videotape, often can't find him either. Pearson is unmarried, but has a girlfriend. He works hard as a public figure, braving even Roy and H.G., and scrubbing up well for that audience, but is lately, he told me, despondent, detesting the Howard government and still unbelieving of, astonished at, what they are doing. He sees few silver linings.

I talked to him too of his entering Parliament, where he surely belongs (and where, as I write this, Aden Ridgeway is doing very well indeed), one night outside a hotel where he had spoken brilliantly and fruitlessly to a gathering of drunken, interjecting film producers. It was midnight, and he was pretty weary. The seat of Sydney, centred in Redfern, could, I suggested, be his for the asking. He said sourly, 'No, too soon, mate.' I said, 'Listen, you do not know how late it is. They will probably fucking shoot you, or photograph you in bed with a moose.' He chuckled drily, said, 'A man's gotta do what a man's gotta do', got into his cab and was sound asleep by the time it moved off. I found this simultaneously inspiring and dispiriting. When, a few months later, he went after a seat and they were all locked up, I was pretty gloomy. Perhaps the moment had passed.

One of his favourite memories, he says, was when in 1970 there was a re-enactment in Cape York of Captain Cook's arrival and all the little children, him among them, had to line up on the beach and wave Union Jacks in welcome. 'There was irony in this pantomime,' he says, 'and although I was a child, I picked it up.'

His Lutheran schooling impelled and powered a mastery of grammatical, onrolling English that has already cost, I believe, one politician his career. When he said Alexander Downer, like his grandfather, who helped write the Constitution, was inclined to regard Aborigines as 'so many legally invisible vermin', it was a political uppercut from which Downer never recovered. When he called the Liberals 'racist scum' it helped – I believe, some don't – swell the anti-Liberal vote of thinking people all over Australia. His power with words – they are always unrehearsed, for though he speaks like an angel, he writes like a clerk – are a measure of what can be achieved by the Aboriginal cause. It's not a trivial thought.

All who meet him feel about him a fated end, and a stoicism in him about it. Aboriginal men, on the average, do not go far past fifty, and he is thirty-four now, and aware of it, and perhaps running. Many fear for his health, or foresee the kind of quietus that came for Martin Luther King at the hand of a lone redneck, or something worse, at a similar time in his people's struggle. I fear for him, but what can you do. He is walking down a particular road, and there is no turning.

August, 1999

Joh and Custard at Kingaroy

I

'Tell me, tell me, you young fellers, be frank,' said Sir Joh Bjelke-Petersen to Custard, the rock band, as they posed with him against his ruined peanut thrasher in warm sunlight, all of them having grown up in Queensland in his era, 'did *you* think I was a fascist dictator? Be frank.'

There was an agonised, astounded pause. 'Well . . .' began Matthew.

'It's hard to judge,' said Paul, quickly.

'I mean, maybe history . . .' said David.

Several photos were clicked off. 'Thank you, thank you, thank you,' said Sir Joh each time to Johnno the cameraman.

'I mean, I never . . .' said Big Chief Wahtooti.

'Yes well, when a lot of these television people accuse me of that,' Sir Joh unconcernedly went on, 'accuse me of being a fascist dictator, I used to say to them, well, if I am, I'm a very *nice* one.'

2

Cane fires were burning low on a horizon that was black under a darkening orange twilight – were they cane fires? It seemed the wrong season for them, bushfires perhaps, burn-offs – and as the van, with Big Chief Wah-tooti at the wheel, roared on through the softening dark towards Brisbane, home, the familiar, and the clinking pile of stubbies grew at our feet on the shifting floor, the boys were silent, thinking things over. It had been a strange day.

'I suppose,' I said at last, 'there've been lots of nights like this in the van, on the way to the next gig, lots of conversations. Or avoiding conversation?'

'No, we *embrace* conversation,' David said, 'because it's a couple of hours gone that way. Often the stereo gets cranked up to full bore, with music that only one band member knows, and is trying to educate the rest of us in.'

'We all get pretty angry then,' Danny said, 'because we're all sitting for two hours in the van listening.'

'Yeah, to Bob Dylan or Bruce Springsteen, or Spy Versus Spy.' David looked out at the fires, the black horizon, the blaze of dying sunset. 'This time of day goes quickly, because it's an interesting time of day. The worst time is when it's pitch black and all you've got are the trucks coming toward you and trying to overtake you.'

'How much energy, musical energy, do you lose from the travelling, from just having to get from place to place?'

'I reckon 90 per cent,' David said.

'Especially from Brisbane to Adelaide,' said Paul. 'It's so much driving.'

They spoke of the male bonding thing when they travel together, on and on through the nights of the yarning and drinking, and how it continued into the idleness of hotels, and watching movies after midnight and drinking again and smoking dope, together as usual, as always, and why not, no girls, or hardly any – 'We're not a chicks' kind of band,' observed Danny ruefully – no writing music when they should have been, exhausted, gloomy, travelling on, the bad habits growing. Their view of themselves and their future was somewhere between neutral-optimistic and melancholic: two years after their first recording contract they can see that they might, in five years, David said, be making it big. 'We're in our Hamburg phase,' Paul said, referring to the Beatles' long apprenticeship. 'We're learning.'

The best gigs were still the small ones. With small audiences now and then it all came together musically and you could feel the crackling magic in the air, and you reached up for the unattainable harmony, got one hand on it . . . The worst gig was a few years back, in a Sydney pub, getting paid one schooner each for the night for playing really badly.

But it felt all right, or just about all right, for the rest of this year. They'd be touring soon with their absolute hero, Frank Black ('My absolute ambition on earth,' Dee said, 'is to play on a bill with Frank Black.'), and making a bit of money. Money was much on their minds, along with their profile, especially since the recording company took so much of it away. Not politics much. They were contentedly neutral in politics, which probably meant secretly quarrelsome. Maybe the first apolitical band.

'Why,' I asked, 'did you want to meet, and get photographed with, Sir Joh Bjelke-Petersen?'

David looked at me, assessing with acuity what kind of moron I was. 'Queensland icon with a Queensland band,' he said straightforwardly, 'and we didn't want a sporting figure. Like say Wally Lewis. That felt wrong.'

'What was your impression of him? Of Sir Joh?'

He looked away, and out at the darkening, changing view, the eternal Queensland landscape of Dad and Dave, replaying the odd afternoon behind his eyes.

'Very talkative. Very interesting. And very *personable*.'

3

The last time I'd seen Joh Bjelke-Petersen was on the night of the Queensland election in 1989, in the Tally Room, when thirty-three years of National Party government – Nicklin, Pizzey, Bjelke-Petersen, Ahern, Cooper – nineteen years of them Joh's, had come, astoundingly, shockingly somehow, to an end despite the infamous gerrymander that allowed him one scandalous year to be triumphantly elected by 26 per cent of the vote, and Wayne Goss, the sleek, shrewd, short-back-and-sides young Labor victor, standing maybe five metres away from where Joh was sitting, in a tired assessment proclaimed, 'Tonight marks the end of the Bjelke-Petersen era!' And there were cheers then from the minders and party members and befuddled citizens present, and me, and Joh cracking hardy raised his hand in imperious acknowledgment, as though the cheers were for him. Senile, one of the journos said, he doesn't know what's happened, but I saw the raised hand for the defiant, up-you gesture that it was: I am who I am, and I shall my goodness stay that way. Master of my feet, and captain of their soles. Don't you worry about that.

I spent the rest of that long uplifting night of bemused and fuddled rejoicing, a night of preposterous incident to look back on, like V.E. Day, or the liberation of Paris, or a bucks' night maybe, with the deliciously artful mimic Gerry Connolly, going from bar to nightclub to Labor branch celebration to coffee shop to greasy spoon till dawn, and Gerry performed on request his Bjelke-Petersen version of 'I Did It My Way', climaxing in the quavered utterance, 'Queensland is not a state, it's a condition! And the condition is, you do it my way.' Which as the sun rose by the muggy river and the bacon and eggs arrived, and the Vegemite toast, had Andrew Olle (whom Gerry addressed in Joh's voice throughout as Wally) and Paul Murphy and Quentin Dempster in actual spluttering pain. We all of us knew then, as the sun rose, and the monumental hangovers began to assert themselves, we'd come out of a long absurdist nightmare, one devised perhaps by Lewis Carroll, in which all words and actions were also their opposite, and the nightmare as well was one we looked back to with warmish nostalgia. It was hard entirely to hate Sir Joh and that was a fact: he was both an unforgivable tyrant and a national treasure – a favourite mouldy old feral teddy bear in the attic we returned to in dreams, glad that though the stuffing was protruding out of him and one eyeball hanging from a single thread, he was still there.

4

'What are your relations with Sir Joh like these days, Bob?' David warily asked, suspecting an imminent tapeworm in his gizzard, an Iscariot, a saboteur.

'Indescribable,' I answered cautiously. 'I've never met him.'

We were approaching in warm blond sunlight among parched brown ordinary hills a sign that said No Visitors Except By Appointment, and then a cattle grid and a compound of unremarkable wooden buildings, red-roofed, white-painted Queenslanders with complacent verandahs, an Australian flag on a flagpole over one of them. Not the grand white-pillared equivalent of Tara, the mansion from *Gone with the Wind*, I'd expected. Nothing would be what I'd expected. Queensland is like that. Queensland, as Sir Robert Menzies remarked, is different.

And then as we drove up, looking precisely like himself, or an animated colour-in-book drawing of himself, Joh came sauntering grumpily towards us, in dark glasses and a snappy blue suit, out of what looked like a large dog kennel. His overwhelming resemblance to himself – to his younger self, it seemed, his skin clear, his gait effortless, his handshake firm – was astonishing somehow. The bewitching I knew, I had been warned, the eerie charm, the hypnotism, had begun.

5

It had been a long drive – punctuated near-fatally by a swerving, screeching, narrowly averted pile-up on a crowded freeway when Paul at the wheel had by desperate hysterical executive action saved us all from premature extinction ('Here lies Ellis and Custard,' I imagined the tombstone saying, 'the rest is silence.') and a few stops for soft drinks, petrol, cassette tapes and some abominable curry-flavoured Kingaroy peanuts that had been left over, it seemed from their morbid aroma, from early in the First World War. Much of it was an unending tedium behind a particular horse's arse in a horse van on the flat road forever ahead of us towards an eternally receding vista of high-piled clouds, Queensland clouds, they are like no other, in an egg-blue sky.

Towns with Tolkien names went by: Blackbutt, Yarraman, Fernvale, followed by their burgeoning cemeteries. A rusty little suburb of sorrowful mobile homes. A car in a frontyard with its bonnet bashed in. A brick toilet in the middle of nowhere. A sign saying: Give Us A Go: Ipswich and West Moreton Building Society. Wooden churches, brightly painted, that round Byron Bay would have long since been sold to hippy ceramicists or retired historians, were still aloft and functioning in these masochistic latitudes and weekly praising the Lord; so much like my forties Murwillumbah memories it felt like time travel. The same remembered breath rose up from the wooden towns, a mixed contented atmosphere of warmth, laziness, nepotism, corruption and smugness and frangipani smells, and I felt at home and at ease and simultaneously disgusted. A dam, as big as or was it bigger (there was argument in the peanut-addled back of the van from Chief Wahtooti and the edgy mini-stars) than Sydney Harbour, endlessly lapped at the warm winter sky. I grew tense too. Paul at the wheel, jaded and shamefaced from the near-collision, but doggedly proud to have saved everyone's lives, was growing incrementally gloomy as he neared his native territory – his mother was still living just up the road, a contented hippy she was, a rural atheist fallen among fundamentalists. Fearing a further accident I drew him into soothing conversation.

'What was it like living in Fernvale?'

'Hopeless. Boring. But it's good. I like the country. Though the social life leaves a lot to be desired.'

'Expand.'

'Oh, it's just that I had nothing to do, it was all farm boys getting drunk on the weekend, you know, go down the creek and cause trouble and chase cows around.'

'How did you occupy your time as a kid, when you weren't at school?'

'Playing guitar. Chasing cows around. Collecting firewood and cow manure and lighting fires and fishing and swimming. Lot of farm-kid things,' he added disconsolately. 'All the things that city kids didn't do. The good thing was, we were so close to Brisbane. Only an hour away. Not like we're in the middle of nowhere.'

The kilometres ran under our wheels. A town of beautiful Queensland verandahs. A white-plaster soldier at the far sad end of a wide empty street. I thought of how like *Huckleberry Finn* it all still was up here, in my childhood and his, farm-boy mischief and itching for travel. I thought of Joh living seventeen years in a cow shed before he came out exasperated at forty-one and abruptly married Flo and began with phlegmatic vigour siring descendants: a story out of the last ten centuries, current in Queensland still. I have seen the past, I decided, and it works.

6

The great man under his dark glasses (his eyes were sore from an infection, he explained, and they craved the shade) was slightly uncertain of what in tarnation we were there for. Custard, he'd been shiftily told, was a group of young performers of old-time music, a notable example of private enterprise in the youth of today, in need of a photo for the cover of their album, and while the boys dodged round this crashing defamation of their music – yes, *some* of it's old time, Sir Joh, some of it – he conducted us with the disarming courtesy for which he is justly famed into a smallish cathedral-shaped wooden structure that was his office, with photos up on the wall of him with a lot of famous people, including, in pride of place, Margaret Thatcher and Russ Hinze. There were too few chairs and we all stood awkwardly about while seated at his desk he gave us what amounted to a brief and gracefully persuasive sermon on his political career. This, he asserted in sentences that were entirely grammatical and nothing like the fractured, metaphor-mangling verbosity of popular caricature, was wrecked by Mike Ahern, the deputy who, the sly young pup, during a five-day period when Joh was overseas, arranged the Fitzgerald Inquiry into Police Corruption behind his back, and its tentacles in due course encircled and politically smothered Joh. He spoke with good humour of his periods in gaol and under house arrest, and under persistent humiliating media harassment, and the bankrupting fortune his legal defence cost him (reducing him perhaps to occasionally posing with rock bands, for instance, for smallish fees), but then with something more like bitterness of the money made by Tony Fitzgerald from his persecution. 'Three hundred and fifty dollars an hour,' he said. 'As long,' he added aggrievedly, 'as he liked to work each day. So he made $1.4 million in the two years he was there. I was a member of Parliament for forty-one years continuously,' he went on, his familiar Kirk-Douglas-whacked-with-a-crowbar countenance agleam with Old Testament self-righteousness now, 'and I was a minister for five years, and I was Premier for just on twenty years, and I never made a million dollars in superannuation in all that time. But he did. In just one year. Sitting up there, throwing stuff at you. He made $1.4 million in just two years. They tipped me up, and held me upside down, and found nothing, and made a lot of money.'

This was persuasive. His eyes, unveiled in the shade of the office, were large and heavy-lidded and blue, and delicately appealed for our sympathy and got it. Quickly we were being drawn into his world, and with a jovial magnetism more like that of a man in his forties he lassoed us with his logic and hog-tied us to his dreams. Tasmania, he insisted, should secede when Keating's republic comes and be a tax haven like Hong Kong, incidentally free then of all Australia's preposterous foreign debt. Businesses will flock there. From all over the world. Every speech he makes on the subject 'goes like a rocket. It's an ideal place, I say, water all round it, makes it easier. And it's beautiful, it's attractive, it's got mountains, and snow, and skiing, and lakes and rivers galore, ports and airports, and it's all there. Why pay a billion and a half dollars in tax to Canberra and get only a billion back? I could run Tasmania by phone from here in Kingaroy, and give you a better deal than *that*.'

Custard laughed. The charm of the man, the directness, a man sixty years their senior, was so *involving*. The Joh-for-Canberra push of recent years seemed so much more imaginable now. He was a kind of comic wizard, like Merlin in *The Once and Future King*, a shaman-clown. The famous blarney was getting through.

WHAT WERE WE DOING HERE? AND WHY NOW DID WE SO DEARLY WANT TO STAY?

7

The trip back through the dark towards Brisbane amid the clinking stubbies and the growing disquiet erupted into factious argument now and then. Marihuana should be legalised. No, it shouldn't, it makes you paranoid. Well, it shouldn't be penalised. We should live in Sydney, near our recording company. No we shouldn't. We gain by being a Queensland band. Yeah, in front of all those tiny audiences. Maybe we should do nothing at all for three months, then pretend we've just come back from Nashville where we've been this roaring success. No-one will know any different. No-one ever checks. The bastards. Custard was clearly troubled by what had washed over them that afternoon. So much of what he said had made sense.

8

'That's Charlie,' said Joh, indicating the huge formidable black bull behind a fence. 'He's an old bull now. John used to ride on his back when he was a boy. Yes, he's an old bull, Charlie is, coming to the end of his career.' A mild surge of laughter glinted in his corrugated voice. 'I suggested to John we should maybe eat Charlie for last Christmas dinner but he wouldn't hear of it. Very upset he was too. Understandably I suppose, because they're old mates. But the time comes, you know, the time comes.'

Johnno, the photographer, had at long last persuaded Joh out of his enclosed pulpit and into the surrounding vegetation such as it was, and had posed him beside his famous peanut thrasher with all of us. Now a wreck, and returned to him in that condition free of charge by the man who bought it from him thirty years ago, it was his own invention, and it filled him with nostalgia. Lovingly elucidating its long-defunct innards, he described what levers went what way and how the sorely punished peanuts coped. He posed against it proudly, and every time the camera clicked he said thank you. He was almost absurdly polite and kindly (though we never scored a cup of tea from him, now I come to think of it, or a pumpkin scone) and generous with his time, which we were hogging. He had maybe a year left, maybe five, and here we were hogging it.

'Got *visitors* have you, Joh?' said Flo as she lumbered by, in her caught-you-at-the-cookie-jar thin familiar tone of voice. John Bjelke-Petersen went by in a muck sweat, working like a dog. He wasn't sure John should go into politics, Joh said, he was so much help about the place.

He talked with abiding wonder about the genius of his fellow inventors, Ford and Edison. I realised then with a sort of a jolt that his mind, his young mind, was formed in their immediate after-glow. He was of that generation, born when the world was fluid still and the century still declaring itself. He *remembered* the First World War. And here he was among us, agog with the future still. It was hard not to admire him, fascism, ratbaggery and all.

9

In the van, as the lights of Brisbane swam through the frangipani darkness towards us, Custard began to brood on failure. Fashions had changed three times this year already, they said, and would their album, their first, coincide correctly with the new upheaval in October? They were going on *Denton* and *Hey Hey* and *Live and Sweaty* but was this enough? Did they *look* any good as well as sounding terrific? And where, you bastard, they added, turning on me, is the movie you promised to write about us, like *A Hard Day's Night*? Empty stubbies of Four-X and cider and my decimated hip flask of Johnny Walker lay at the root, I decided, of their bellicose enquiry. It'll happen, I mumbled, don't worry, trust me. Don't you worry about that. We agreed to meet on their tour in Perth, when I got back from Eritrea, with one leg blown off by land mines. Do in-depth research. Drink together a bit. They were unconvinced. And what if it fails? they wanted to know. What then? (What then? said Plato's ghost, somewhere over the Brisbane River. What then?)

'After music, at thirty, there's always road crew. Bitterness dash road crew,' said Matthew, chuckling bitterly. 'Where are you now, musician? Where do you hope to be? Bitter dash road crew.'

'If you walk in, though, and give the road crew a joint or a six-pack,' said Paul, 'you've won them for the whole tour then. They're happy. That's how easy it is.'

'Also you've got to swear a lot,' said David, 'and talk about girls in a very bad way. Road crew, that's the future.'

The neon lights were nearing now, the muggy river. The bridges. Parliament House. 'The great thing about Joh,' said David, 'is he didn't *give* a fuck.'

10

'And against everybody's considered advice I gaoled another thousand demonstrators,' Joh concluded in uproarious triumph, 'for blocking the Friday traffic! And a day later I won the election with an *increased majority*!'

Custard against their better judgement laughed uproariously too, laughing along with his victory. The magic was working now. We would have followed him anywhere. Through an acre of juicy cowpats, anywhere.

He nodded to a young black frizzy man going by in a muck sweat. 'Nice young feller that,' he said. 'Friend of John's. Forget his name. Very handy about the place.'

He unnerved us then with quiet remembered hints of the demon socialism, which he sometimes half believed in. He and his mother always fed the swaggies that came to the door in the Depression, he said, and gave them work when they could. Poor fellers, miles from their families, it wasn't their fault moneychangers got it wrong. The trick is to tell the moneychangers how to do it right. Do away with all taxes! All but those for the bare essentials! Let the spirit of man roam free.

I observed with wonder his manifest happiness, a man who lived in a cow shed until he was forty and so knew where he stood and what for, and had never drunk anything stronger in his life than, probably, jasmine tea. A saint, perhaps. A Saint of Misrule.

God had been kind to him, he confided when I remarked on his rude good health. His secret was to chop logs every morning for the wood stoves in the various dwellings on the property and not overeat. His hard work in his youth, clearing the land of its dense vegetation, its old-growth forests ('So many trees,' he said, 'you could scarcely walk between them.'), had stood him in good stead. He bore the health of his early sacrifice.

This sacrifice, however, and that of his father, building up a difficult property to a point where it was prospering even in Depression times, had led him incidentally into politics. His father died, and the Death Duty people immediately turned up. 'They came in, they started in the kitchen,' he said, still stung by the memory, 'with notebooks, they pulled out all the spoons, and the knives, and the forks, they wrote it all down, they put their own value on them. I argued about a desk I'd bought; it was mine, not Father's. "Where's your receipt, young man?" they said. "I haven't got one," I said, "I just . . . bought it." "That's your bad luck," they said. And I had to pay death duties on that. And then, my goodness, Mother died as well, and it happened again. They came back – and this was in the Depression – and took a whole lot more. Every other spoon and fork that was left. And there was nothing, absolutely nothing I could do about it. Not then. Death duties. It was the first thing I did away with when I came to power. People shouldn't be burgled like that, in the middle of their grief. It's not right.'

He took us on a tour of the farm, hills and trees and paddocks he had known and cleared and ploughed for sixty years. His sacred sites. His dreaming. You saw how it added up. Possession. Duty. Continuance. Family. Very seductive, it was. I tried to keep in my mind the police brutality, the moonlight state, the laws against *serving* homosexuals in Queensland bars, the bulldozers by night on the lovely hotel. But it was hard to do. All I could see was a sweet and quirky old man among his memories, fresh as paint and brimming with hope and possibility.

He steered us slowly back to the van, posing with us for a few last shots in his dark glasses, like a sullen mafia don among his beaming acolytes, once unknowingly with a bag of marihuana held above his head. I said a little crustily later I wasn't sure what that proved, except that old men don't very often look over their shoulder any more. He evinced a little puzzlement at what my role in the juggernaut was, enquiring gently how I liked the travelling from place to place in the back of a truck at my age. I was writing an article, I said. Ah, he said, quite right. He complimented the lads on their courage, advising always to take the risks, the way you are now, get up early, get there before the other fellow, continue in your excellent career of old-time music, don't care too much for rules and regulations in an increasingly policed and preposterous world. Why, a man was sued for a million dollars only the other day, for sexual harassment, for looking at a young woman's breasts when he was talking to her. In America. Imagine that. Ridiculous.

His greatest experience, he said, as he stood by the van and Johnno took some final landscapes before we left, was meeting the men, Armstrong, Aldrin and Collins, who'd been first on the moon. He looked up at night at the moon and tried to imagine them there and he couldn't. He said this to Armstrong, who said he couldn't imagine it either. Did it really happen, he was always wondering, or was it just a . . . nightmare? He spoke of looking at the universe through the great telescope 'in that place south of Canberra, at galaxy after galaxy, every one with billions of stars. You see right down on the southern horizon, there's a bright cluster there, they've known about it for a long time, and they estimate there's about five million planets in that one bright cluster. Five million of them. And it's about 10 000 light years away. And that's an enormous distance. And with every big new telescope they build they find another galaxy. With billions of planets there. There's no end to them, they go on and on.

'It's remarkable isn't it, how it all goes together, God's creation. Those sorts of things just don't happen. And Aldrin looked down at the earth, you know, from the moon, and he quoted from the eighth verse of the eighth chapter of Psalms, "When I consider the heavens, the work of Thy fingers, the moon, the stars, and what you have created, what is man then, that Thou art mindful of him?"'

It was a good note to end on, and as in the slanting afternoon light we drove away up the track and watched him recede as he attentively, watchfully, saw us out of his consciousness, I felt a pang at the possibility that I might never see or talk to him again, beyond morality, a kind of Prospero, or Puck, or Feste, impossible to hate, impossible not to laugh with.

The boys posed for Johnno in a peanut field up the road (Joh had long since ceased to grow them, avocados now, keeping up with the times) and ate some dirty raw peanuts from the ground. I kept imagining Joh coming over the horizon crying, 'Peanut thieves! Peanut thieves!' and blamming away with a double-bore shotgun, but this too was only a caricature. The true man was elsewhere, in a special peculiar dreaming reserved for the jocular protestant saints.

July, 1994

Francis James

Francis James was a man of opalescent complexity and my great friend in the last years of his life. His wisdom, good cheer and capacity to inspire with his love of life and learning – history, flying, politics, gardening, grammar, music and international intrigue – were exceeded only by his kindness. His advice and example, his hospitality and wit, his bonhomie and shrewdness, his marvellous, regal, piss-taking voice, and his cork-like buoyancy in the face of adversity – temporary blindness, starvation, torture and four-year incarceration – added up to a healing spring to which I would always have recourse when I was down and from which I would always come away exhilarated. His final illness, much of which I witnessed, and his death – the day before spent with me – hit me as hard as it did the hundreds of his other intimate friends, as hard as the death of my father and the loss through fire of my house and all my family photos.

So when I heard a film was to be made about him by two men who had never met him, I was pretty annoyed, not least because it was a film that I – or Chris Masters or Geoff Burton or Paul Murphy or Stephen Ramsey or David Flatman or Stuart Littlemore, all of whom were seasoned documentary makers who knew him when he was alive – might better have made.

At Joyce James's behest (they had winningly told her, in commencing negotiations with her, that they didn't need her and could make it without her) I withdrew my co-operation, as had Gough Whitlam and many others close to Francis's family. I did so in some gloom, because I knew the offending duo well. I liked them and had worked with each with some success in the past.

They made it anyway. I saw it on Friday and was very surprised. For instead of a lump-witted exposé of a fatuous poseur or a dodgy double agent, what they gave me, and gave posterity, was a fair glimpse of the man on most of his radiant levels. The charmer. The dreamer. The adventurer. The historical expert. The heat-seeking Edwardian Englishman. The informed Liberal conscience of ignorant Australia. The latter-day court jester. The conman, caught out. All that was missing perhaps was the churchman. And the good friend.

Lewis Fitzgerald, the writer-director, shows considerable mettle, breadth and guile as a director and a biographer. Slyly choosing as his model the brain-washing scene from the great Frankenheimer spy film *The Manchurian Candidate*, he interweaves enacted scenes of interrogation and lonely imprisonment with re-told remembrances from those few James contemporaries that dared cross Joyce's picket line. All are seen at a distance, in their big cluttered libraries and drawing rooms, in their extreme old age (John Douglas Pringle, improbably alive, mellifluously impersonates the shrivelled corpse of Lenin sitting up in his catafalque), and so add to the overall ambience of dwindling pallid mystery.

The camerawork in the enacted scenes (fire and flood and memory wash through the lonely, dripping prison cell; Francis palely, luminously beams as remembered symphonies drench the soundtrack) is very good, the performance and writing less so. One yearns for the authentic Jamesian cadence of the portly golden utterance in the dialogue. Unfortunately for Fitzgerald, in the real, recorded interview one gets it. And though John Derum is fine in physical appearance, with his lizard-lidded bug eyes, milk-bottle shoulders and silent-movie overacting, he is vocally disappointing.

All the witnesses that were spoken to came to much the same conclusion. That he was indeed a liar, but never yielded to his own outrageous embroideries. That he was a romantic of the T.E. Lawrence kind and for such a man the mere, dull world was not enough; it needed sub-editing. That all he untruthfully asserted caused little harm to anyone but a few flummoxed editors (And who cares about them?) and he gave much pleasure to others with his hearty stories. That if he was a spy, he was the most vividly up-front one in history and therefore pretty inept. That no school or structure could hold him. That he could charm the birds from the trees.

This is all fair enough, I suppose. But the verdict fails to note how China changed him. One morning after being roughly led away to what he believed would be his execution, he promised the Almighty, he told me, that if he ever got out of this fix, he would strive to be a good man, perform deeds of kindness and serve the world. And he kept that vow, as all of his acquaintance would attest.

He became as well, in born-again contrast to his former self, a tetchy custodian of Truth, checking and triple-checking in libraries and archives all that was yet in doubt. He conceived with me and Paul Murphy the notion of *Media Watch*, which Littlemore later, cheekily, did instead. It should have been Francis, Mr Valiant-for-Truth, every Monday night at nine-twenty. He would have been magnificent.

Derum did get one thing dead right, which was his puckishness, his Robin Goodfellow side, his mocking watchfulness, as though he had lately come from a distant planet and like a good zoologist was taking note with distaste of the human species: what fools these mortals be.

A goodish film all in all. Well worth a long look. Not a patch on the one I would have made of course, but, ah well. It brought things flooding back to me. I knew Francis for thirty years, and I miss him. As Arthur Miller paid to Willy Loman, another brave dreamer, attention should be paid to such a man.

August, 1994

Pauline Hanson

I was in Queensland for ten days of its election and, as always, predicted in writing (on a grubby pad countersigned by one Sir James Killen) the result within three seats – forty-eight seats to Labor, I said, and seven to One Nation. It was a pretty scary night, in the quietest Tally Room I can remember, with everyone moving up and down before the big board in restless unbelief, till Pauline Hanson arrived very early and stayed late, in a palegold spotlight with a jostling swarm of paparazzi, like Kim Novak at a Hollywood premiere, to gloat and prattle and raise her strange yellow devil-cat eyes while everyone looked at her with a kind of erotic, stirred revulsion: how could this dread improbability be happening?

A few things should be said.

One is the obvious, that seven of the One Nation seats were won with National and Liberal preferences, and these preferences will never so slavishly go to One Nation again.

You have my word on that.

The next thing to be said is, the result that night had very little to do with racism. A poll ten days before showed Aboriginal-bludging and Asian-swamping questions important to only one in ten of One Nation voters, who like everyone else listed unemployment, health, the breakdown of rural services, the ending of rural communities and the break-up of families as the top concerns. One in ten of One Nation voters is 2.5 per cent of Queensland, the usual number of racist obsessives. The usual suspects. That number hasn't changed.

It had almost nothing to do with race. However it is interpreted by the CNN reporters, and however 'sexy' the race issue continues to be to the journalists who follow after Hanson, sniffing around her like dogs, they are missing the point. And so is John Howard if he believes he can call an election on Wik and win it on Hanson preferences.

What the vote was about was a revolt against Economic Correctness, and against the fool prevailing belief that less and less Australian industries with less and less Australians working in them for less and less wages and longer and longer hours and more and more sackees leaving more and more home towns and more and more grieving families to travel further and further kilometres to an unknown life destination in possibly crime is *good for Australia*. It's a vote against the belief that a further profit in annual billions for a board of directors already rich as Croesus or Corrigan justifies the destruction overnight of tens of thousands of ordinary human lives and families, and the belief that this destruction in turn is good for Australia.

John Howard says he knows how vulnerable people are feeling in these times of economic change. He does not. For they are feeling as vulnerable as a man who has already had his arm torn off by a lion, and sits in the corner holding his bleeding stump and waiting for the lion to finish eating and come for him again. This is something more than vulnerability. It is injury, and shock, and rage. And he does not know the carnage that is waiting for him if he calls an election. And he will be surprised.

In the South Australian election of last year, which I also worked on, there was an 18 per cent vote for the Democrats, in the week before

Kernot defected. This is a figure very like the 23 per cent that in Queensland preferred One Nation. The reason I believe is the same. It is universal and growing and inevitable now, and cannot be bought off by the glass beads of GST and the Telstra sale and the repeated oafish assertion that all the economic indicators are good and the freeing up of trade will bring more jobs when everyone's experience (in the banks, in the privatised utilities, in the corner stores) is that it brings less jobs, less jobs everywhere.

There is a further big thing that should perhaps be said, and it's this.

Like Christianity, One Nation has a savage half and a civilising, merciful half. In Christianity the savage half expresses itself in the burning of heretics, the humiliation of adulteresses, the exorcising of epileptics for devil possession, the slaughter of heathen indigenes, the burying of suicides in unhallowed ground, and so on. And the merciful civilising half is expressed in the belief that the needy must be succoured, the sick healed, the dying comforted, the prisoner visited, the forgiven sinner enfolded in everlasting arms. In One Nation the savage half is obvious, and to do with guns and Aborigines and cutting off Robyn Nevin's money and hanging and castration and putting Asians back on the boat and sending them home.

But the merciful half is also there. The belief that families matter, and neighbourhoods, and towns, and the predictability of our life on earth and the hope of our children for good and better times. And this is the part that, on the whole, is being voted for in a world where the cargo cultism of the major parties has brought only fractured lives, injustice, wife-beating, divorce and drunken misery. This is why people want One Nation's solutions. And why, therefore, their solutions are not all wrong.

You heard me.

For the tariff barriers will go up again, whatever the sado-monetarist academics and the purblind gnomes of Canberra now say. And Australia will not be an outcast and a pariah when that happens. Any more than it became an outcast and a pariah when we said our greenhouse emissions were going up, not down. Funny that. It is amazing what our trading partners will put up with when they have to. The tariff barriers of Japan. Of the EU. Of the USA. The criminal greed of Suharto and Marcos. The Mafia economy and 900 per cent inflation of modern Russia. The fatwah on Salman Rushdie. The Israeli H-bomb. The Pakistani H-bomb. The lethal injections in the gaols of America. The beheadings of Saudi Arabia. The deaths in custody of black adolescent Australians. The murderous wickedness of the tobacco multinationals. East Timor. Tiananmen Square.

It is a fantasy that we have no other choice but to go the way the world is going. It is a greater fantasy that we can survive as a democracy without that choice. The true Nut Religionists are the Economically Correct brigade, the compulsive privatising Thatcherites, crying *efficient and competitive, efficient and competitive*, as ordinary humanity goes to hell. And it is One Nation that, however neurotically and woundedly and waywardly, is asking the actual questions that the next election winner must answer, and answer well, and soon.

June, 1998

Garfield Barwick

Gar Barwick is dead: it's a strange thought. For many in the Labor Party over much of its history he was like The Ghost Who Walks – eternal, unflinching, always approaching greyly through fog to do them ill. On a mission of God down the ages to do them down.

He helped wreck Chifley with his argument before the Privy Council in London against Bank Nationalisation – in a long and torpid joust with Evatt through an English summer so hot that two of the judges died. The result, a greedy armada of marauding overseas banks, now sacking their human employees and charging their craven customers fortunes to even talk to them, is something we well might think of in the imminent years of Australia's financial ruin. A single government bank would never have allowed that, and Barwick was its destroyer.

He gravely wounded Evatt with his argument before the High Court in favour of a Communist Party Dissolution Bill. This is a bill that allowed two ministers to call you a communist if they didn't like you and put you in gaol and confiscate your property. Evatt won that one and so prevented Australia from becoming a McCarthyist nightmare of random denunciations and shattered careers. But Barwick got his revenge. He argued before the Petrov Royal Commission that Evatt had harboured communist spies in his office and tempted Evatt into behaving so untidily and hysterically (he was thrown out of the inquiry, then re-entered yelping hoarsely and was thrown out again) that it ended his credibility and his largely brilliant career. Evatt's pitiable, disorderly behaviour in those months, unleashed by his nemesis Barwick, spurred in turn the Labor Split and kept the Labor Party from office – and, with it, a vast measure of social mercy like Medicare, child-care, free access to universities and so on – for eighteen years.

And, of course, he advised the cowardly Jack Kerr that he could sack, if he wanted to, Gough Whitlam, and do so suddenly, without warning. Thus aborting perhaps forever the noble experiment of Rooseveltian welfarism in a country sorely in need of it. Kerr would not have done it if Barwick, then Chief Justice of the High Court, had said he oughtn't, and of course he said he should.

These are considerable villainies, and they touch the cusp of evil. Many good lives were made miserable by Barwick's well-paid espousal of McCarthyist persecution; careers were truncated and shrunken by the loss of the Whitlam era and people howled for lack of Medicare. Australia is a much more shrivelled place because of Barwick and his arid, repetitive mediocrity and punishing vengefulness and its present government is his testimony and his legacy, and John Howard his spiritual heir.

I hate him deeply. I lived near him for twenty years – he was down the road in Careel Bay – and couldn't bear to look at him when he went by in the street.

It wasn't because he left the working class without a backward look and went to work in the big end of town and there made his Big Quid arguing the rights of the big corporations against the lower orders, and never took a brief for something he believed in without money attached to it. It wasn't because when he was on his feet or at his bench in the High Court or addressing the House he was boring, earnest and remorseless and repetitive as John Howard and never added a phrase to the language that anyone remembered. It wasn't just that when he was Chief Justice he improperly arrogated to himself decisions over matters he was keen on, or companies he had shares in – decisions that should have gone to the full bench. It wasn't just that when he was Chief Justice he wasted a nation's fortune constructing by Canberra's lakeside in the dimensions of his ego what became known as Gar's Mahal.

It wasn't just that he warned that if Whitlam got in, the Jews would take over. It wasn't just that he advised the rich, and advised them publicly, to avoid tax whenever they could. It wasn't just that he was 'the poisonous dwarf' and 'truculent runt' of legend, the latter Whitlam's phrase, a mix of avarice, class ache, altitude envy and personal malice. It was a fair bit more than that.

A lawyer takes briefs and argues them, that's what he does. A judge makes judgments according to precedent and conscience, that's what he does. Barwick did something worse than this.

He did it in 1960, when he was Attorney General. He drafted a Crimes Act whose purpose was to find and punish traitors. By his definition traitors were those who disagreed with government foreign policy and said so, who sent medical supplies to countries which might or might not in the future be at war with our allies – not us, our allies – and people whose 'known character' was likely to make them suspectable of sabotage and espionage. Espionage now covered, in his view, information sent openly to countries with which we were not yet at war, and might never be.

He copped, in short, the whole Cold War vocabulary and its diseased fantasy that Russia was about to atomic-bomb and conquer and enslave America and the West; and in pursuit of this lunacy he proposed to turn Australia into a fascist hellhole, with show trials of left-wing suspects who were then invited to name names or do seven years in gaol. Had he become Prime Minister, and he very nearly did, he would have done this – to amiable, fair-go, freedom-of-conscience Australia. Imagine that. Union protest, public alarm and a towering parliamentary speech from Whitlam ended his aim of turning his country into an on-going inquisition with himself as its Torquemada, but he kept it in mind.

And on Whitlam, as on so many others, he had his revenge.

In the times I saw his unprepossessing figure pottering about in Careel Bay I thought of confronting him and abusing him, the way one might, but couldn't summon the energy to argue with a dour and venal, power-corrupted, tunnel-visioned sadist and martinet. Life was too short. Not his life, as it turned out.

Of B.A. Santamaria, Francis James once said, 'It's a curious anomaly, Robert, is it not, that a good man can do evil.' With Garfield Barwick there was no such contradiction. For there was not much good in him, and little human kindness, and he served his rotten masters to the end.

July, 1997

Les Murray

Funny how things move round. A week ago any informed person would have said that Les Murray had come close to crossing some shadow line, and his status was now in peril. He was, they would have said, an icon impaired, a national treasure in turnaround, another tall poppy awaiting the scythe; sad, very sad, but inevitable really.

Then the rescuing cavalry came, as they did last week for Bullimore, and now Les, with his T.S. Eliot Award, is back on his bluegum Parnassus, our favourite marsupial once more while a glad nation lifts its voice in a single hymn of rejoicing for a local boy (oh yes) made good in the Great World where it matters, and the carpers and critics are swimming like mad and clumsily scrambling back on board for the Town Hall ceremonials, the miniseries, the study chart, the legend. How different is Overseas, where achievement it seems still counts and not mere wayward opinion, the achievement from one who has written three or four poems as good as 'Prufrock' or 'Easter 1916' or 'The Whitsun Weddings', how different from here, where a crude cartoon replaces everybody well known and no fraction of human depth or contradiction is ever (or so it seems) acknowledged or explored.

I've known Les well for thirty-seven years now – as room-mate, fellow student and fellow traveller in Europe, Australia and impoverished, questing, troubled youth. He was my Best Man and in some seasons, not all, my best friend and one whose conversation (Johnsonian, Shavian, Chestertonian, Falstaffian) I thirstily sought as a healing fountain of unstinted kindness when I was down. We've slept on each other's grubby floors in many cities, eaten and starved together in many streets and forgiven each other astonishing philosophical differences as friends in the old days used to. Last week, as a fair test of his enduring affection, my dog nearly killed his beloved chook Patrick White, and he would, I think, have forgiven that too. And though a lot is written about him, there is little I wholly recognise as Les.

He speaks (for instance) about eighteen languages, including German, all the Scandinavians, Italian, Afrikaans, Indonesian, Gaelic and some Aboriginal dialects he has helped retrieve from oblivion. He tells Aboriginal legends like a tribal elder – last week, to my children, how the Southern Cross came to be: it's a local Taree warrior and his two wives, who ascended into the heavens after particular local adventures from a particular rock on the coast. He goes in his mind into legends, seizing their poetic truth, as others go with equal fervour into grand opera, and into religions too. 'A religion is a long poem,' he would say, 'a poem is a short religion.'

But he has other interests than poetry and theology and salacious gossip and weird coincidence and the lifelong sagas of old acquaintance, the coming Republic, the flag, the oath of allegiance, the North Coast white-trash peasantry he calls his tribe, and the trendy evils wrought on the human mind by Radio National. He can, for instance, identify by silhouette every plane that ever flew and chart on paper the course of most land battles ever fought. He can quote verbatim great speeches of the American Civil War and can identify by sight most war medals ever struck, and still regrets, I think, his rejection, due to vast flat feet, by the RAAF when he was seventeen. He plays passable cricket and, by my witness, dreadful golf. He excels in poolrooms and libraries, adores yum cha and routinely graces with delicate, uproarious conversation the houses of old friends. His loyalty to friends and his patience with those of his acquaintance now mortally sick or mentally

173

ill is widely known, and touches in my view the hem of earthly saint-hood.

He is a converted Catholic and yet stood proud in the little free Pres-byterian chookhouse on its grassy meadow (no organ, no piano and one strong male voice leading the singing) for his father Cecil's funeral in 1985, proud of the dirt-farming faith of his forefathers and the harsh, true-hearted Christendom in which he was raised. He has picked his grave site and visits it, settling into the thought of his earthly destination.

And he is a kind of socialist I think, at least as far as writers go. 'No Melbourne Cup racehorse,' he famously once said, 'is ever expected to pull a dung cart by night to earn its food.' He is also a defender of his hard-yakkering relatives, the wretched of the earth (*when I was a boy we were all so poor we could scarce afford a roof to our mouths*), and their moods and greeds and sorrows, including the latest mood on immigration. He believes like them, and he may be right, that the heirs of Gallipoli are being slowly, cruelly excluded from the country they have graced and defended with their suffering, excluded by purblind urban élites, and in one of his greater poems, 'Where Will We Hold Australia?', he passionately argues this. It is probably no more contentious a thought than asking if white Americans should be allowed unlimited immigration into Bali, or if Bali should be culturally pro-tected, but of course it was taken wrong, its worried complexities airbrushed into ignorant, jingoistic simplicities. 'Pauline Hanson,' he said with acerbity yesterday, 'has been lately getting wrong these last four months what I've been getting right for years.'

He hated the proposed Australia Card and all its related Orwellian tyr-annies, and would have gone to gaol to fight it. He is a loyal and loving husband of a remarkable wife. He believes in animals as kindred souls. Some of his poems attempt a language for different species. He is suspicious of publishers and denounces them, generically, as 'air hostesses in training', and academics who make more teaching his poems than he does writing them.

He grew up very lonely on a remote farm, an only child tormented by the recurring promise of a sibling and then silence after miscarriages, mis-carriages caused, he at last found out, by the butchering surgical instruments that brought him into the world, something he thinks his parents blamed him for. Tormented, too, by the death of his mother when he was eleven and Cecil's decision thereafter never to attempt a happiness he could not share with her. He was persecuted in the usual joyless, unanswerable way for his fatness (a depressive breakdown was lately triggered by meeting again in Taree an unforgotten female schoolfellow who mocked him waspishly for it way back then), his inability at sport, his fear that Cecil also, like his mother, might somehow one night not come home. *Father, come home soon. Come home alive.* He found in books and in wandered hillsides and animal friends and inward conversation in those sad years his partial salvation.

He used to half jokingly call himself 'the spiritual wing of the Country Party', but the famous Labor Party test, *if you've never had holes in your shoes, you don't know what it's like,* is one he passed *cum laude* with flapping soles and soaking socks and he has voted, I know, both ways in his time, and has no quarrel with the government subsidy of the weak and suffering. He was seriously poor for all of his youth (meat-pie poor, one-singlet poor) and except for a few years when he was John Gorton's translator he has lived on the border of mincemeat-and-spag down most of his days. He lives still in two prefabricated shacks on a forty-acre property he neared bankruptcy buying for nostalgic, family reasons. He has cows on agistment and dogs and a horse and walks by the old creek learning the language of birds, and he loves old Hollywood movies when he can see them, Bogart, Mitchum, Tracy, and pines in his isolation for SBS and its blissful profusion of tongues.

He had paid his dues in short, *language worships and forgives everyone by whom it lives,* and so has Val, who supported him in the bad years, teaching school, and he merits more considered and thoughtful attention than the vulgar Al Capp cartoonisation that in recent journalism has been his lot. In my forthcoming book, *Goodbye Jerusalem,* I wrote, as a friend, in spirited defence of him when he, last year, was down. Others have been less considerate, more fairweather in their thankfulness, waiting till his fearsome brush with death to give him niggard praise, which they withdrew days after. He deserved more, and deserved better than these forgetful snipers and Vicars of Bray. But we are a shallow twitchy nation these days (relaxed and comfortable, deny, deny) and undeserving, I sadly suspect, of one now in the Pantheon who as greatly speaks for us as Larkin did for England or Cormac McCarthy does for America. We should be so lucky.

There were helicopters on his lawn on Wednesday morning and the agisted cows were sniffing their wheels and chewing their safety belts, and things have changed, I guess, for Les. But it might have been very different, tragic even. We should, I think, be a little more careful in our sneering. We might get suddenly caught by history, looking foolish.

January, 1997

James McAuley

The shadow of the Cold War ever lengthens down the century, and Gerard Henderson of the soft remorseful Right and Donald Horne of the soft self-mocking Left are quarrelling still in 1999 over who in the McCarthyist fifties was politically wise and who was mentally unstable – this time over the costive, cantankerous cadaver of James McAuley, the poet, professor, pianist, atheist, Catholic convert, western suburbs boy made good, wartime insider, friend of New Guinea, foe of world communism, CIA-paid *Quadrant* editor, screamer in the night. There was a shadowy thin man in a stovepipe hat in the corner of his every bedroom, waiting for him to die. The screaming made him a poor house-guest in most suburbs, and a famously dreadful room-mate.

His biographer, Cassandra Pybus, did not know him, and neither did I. Her book, however, wonderfully evokes the pre-war Sydney University revues (with Jim on piano composing and singing blasphemous ditties) and rival waspish newspapers (Whitlam at *Hermes* versus Horne at *honi soit*) and the all-night coffee-fuelled raves about the shape of the universe and the secret, risky acts of student sex (oft ending in botched abortions) whose last fine, careless fag-end I witnessed in the latter fifties and early sixties.

She gets well, too, how it was in the dodgy wartime quangos, in particular the one confected by the drunk, erratic perpetual student Alf Conlon (he studied medicine for decades, but never passed it) out of a distant acquaintance with Curtin and a need to save his mates, McAuley and John Kerr among them, from active service, but not, alas, from the long, sly, lazy afternoon that resulted in Ern Malley and the shame lifelong of poor Max Harris. Out of this, and much boredom in teaching and writing reports, McAuley had a good safe war – seeing, at his own insistence, battlefront bloodshed only once, in New Guinea, and killing, perhaps, to his horror, a man or two, a fact that changed his life.

He pursued religion, significantly, after that, joining Mother Church in 1952, and came back again and again, as a wiser and wiser and ever more paternal colonial advisor, to New Guinea (did he have a male black lover there? Pybus hints, but cannot know), his twin post-war passions eventually commingling in his obsession with one Mother Marie Thérèse of Papua, a saintly woman already dead who in her lifetime was much harassed by the Devil. 'He took the form of a gorilla,' her disciple Archbishop de Boismenu alleged, 'and tried to strangle her.' He also pushed her out of portholes and held her underwater, electrified her bed, and sent squads of loud chittering monkeys to suffocate her and tear at her with claws, and under the pretext of letting her rest a while, attempted to seduce her, but he was usually gone by midnight – having no doubt a number of other, similar calls to make in the neighbourhood.

That McAuley believed this nonsense (and why shouldn't he? – a Catholic believes in the Devil, and a Devil who is an active agent in the world of men) does not, as Henderson in his defence of him asserts, prove Stalin was not a bad man, and that Jim was not right to think so, but it puts in some psychological context his belief that communism was an ultimate Evil, and that his old quadrangle acquaintance Whitlam, the Fabian socialist, was a knowing and active handmaiden of Satan.

Catholicism looks sillier and sillier these days (do we eat Christ's living flesh each Sunday? should we?) and those who convert to it – Newman, Wilde, Waugh, Graham Greene, Les Murray – more and more psychologically suspect.

And other things about McAuley – his rejection of an academic post in London, his long tepid stay in Tasmania, lording it over the provincials, his tightening circles of male mateship, his unusual fondness for the *Epic of Gilgamesh*, which Pybus rightly alleges was the world's first male-bonding road movie, his involvement as a Redfern church organist with the drab mascaraed relics of the fugitive Bishop Leadbetter, his playful friendship with Harold Stewart, depressive co-author with Jim of Ern Malley, his reverence for God's spy Santamaria, his laziness as *Quadrant* editor, his frequent, late bursts of womanising, his nightmares, devil fantasias and repeated recitations, even in his last weeks, of Shakespeare's envenomed sonnet on lust – bespeak a man ill at ease with his place in the world (a back-block suburban boy forever a-bluster on campus?) and seeking a better world to strut in. It is as a campus figure that he fares best in this book, ever kindly and available to students, conducting tutorials down to his dying weeks. A good man fallen among Groupers, perhaps, and dark angels. Perhaps not.

The book suffers a good deal, I think, from its late date of composition. Horne is clearly a big information source, and Santamaria, and Peter Coleman and the ill-used girlfriend of his student days, Joan Fraser, and their contributions are pretty illuminating, but too many of his intimates are dead, and one yearns for a line or two from Alf Conlon, or Bert Evatt, or John Kerr. I would give a lot to see film of him at the piano in a student revue, or lecturing in Hobart in his middle age. Such living memorials are cheaply possible now but the subjects, of course, are less interesting.

One returns with frustration to an unfinished quest for the source of so many of his mysterious lines.

When nightmare breathes upon the mind
As on a glass and peers behind
With mad and watchful eyes, malevolently;

When in the sexual night descended
The spirit quivers undefended
At the quick of human mystery;

When a woman's hair is a bush of pain
And the heart is a blind man in the rain
That nightlong sings of what it cannot see.

'Gnostic Prelude'

But of course these things are inaccessible to us now, and they always will be.

From my late teens onward I have been able to recite much McAuley from memory, but on revisiting him in my fifties I find him a little over-burnished, a little drained of blood, a little self-censored, in the end, of the sometimes beastly impulses that fed the torrent that gave his verse, or should have given it, emotional, erectile, passionate force. With similar cultural constraints Ken Slessor did better, I think, with the mere English language and its rhyming cul-de-sacs, and Doug Stewart and Alec Hope and R.D. Fitzgerald. At the heart of Jim's aroused and fanatical ideological hatreds and wars with the Devil and loathing of his fleshly self, perhaps, is this fear that he is not quite good enough as a poet or, like Hemingway, has lost his talent to some pursuing demon or in some sad Faustian pact with God for his soul's salvation.

He could have done better, and more, or lived longer, or left the church in disgust (he might have, he really might have), and been now like the once fierce Hornes and Whitlams grown gracefully old, a benign figure in the nineties, lording it sweetly over the fleeting century, a wise and kind and fairly talented, and uncontroversially respected, man.

August, 1999

Dame Pattie Menzies

In her last years Dame Pattie Menzies was to many, but not all, Australians a figure somewhere between the Queen Mother and Dame Vera Lynn, a link with former glories and simpler times. Well into her nineties, her ability to address vast audiences without notes and beguile awed visitors with her disarming table-talk prolonged and sweetened the Menzies legend even as, historically, it fell into disrepute. Last week, as a measure of her eminence, an affectionate nation farewelled her in the first state funeral ever given a Prime Ministerial wife.

Born in 1899 the daughter of a professional politician, and married from 1920 to 1978 to the longest-serving Prime Minister since Pitt the Younger, Pattie Maie Leckie was a woman of her time, her class, her country and her husband's arduous calling.

Ever at his side, in later years with an arsenal of pills and medicaments that she forced through his mountainous reluctance, she was a constant caring presence, ever anxious for his revival. She it was who persuaded him of the possibility of his resurrection, after what seemed like his political extinction in 1941, in a party-room revolt. 'Leave me alone,' he famously cried from the back benches, 'it is a dreadful experience to be exhumed.' She it also was who cautioned him against the long trip to war-torn England that occasioned the coup, a visit during which he busily fantasised replacing Winston Churchill as British Prime Minister, and took steps to do so. A wiser political head than he, a better judge of character, a fiercer hater, a more efficient deflater of reputation, she was also marvellously able to smooth in the aftermath of quarrels those feathers his famed arrogance – and considerable drunken spleen – had ruffled.

It was her example at his side during his most surprising achievement, the forced creation, out of bickering political dregs and splinters, of the shrewdly misnamed Liberal Party after electoral debacle in 1943 and its achievement of power with a mighty majority in 1949, that set the style of the subsequent party organisation, a determined flurry of middle-aged ladies in blue rinses running social evenings with an iron will and slowly, efficiently, over coffee, cake and a match-making waltz or two mustering the numbers for their lords and masters, the men.

A woman of her time, Dame Pattie kept chooks in the backyard of

Yarralumla, the Prime Minister's lodge, and at least once with soap and brush scrubbed its wooden floors herself. An expert driver, she served as well in those days before white Commonwealth cars as her husband's lifelong chauffeur. She gracefully coped with his astonishing alcoholic intake (three full bottles of Houghton's white burgundy with every evening meal, preceded by several sunset martinis), his twenty-stone girth, his cultural philistinism (he never read a new book after 1941, though he annually re-read Shakespeare, much of it aloud) and his noisy afternoons round the broadcasted football and the barbecue. The marriage survived at least one major infidelity (with the wife of a newspaper proprietor who editorially thereafter advocated a vote for Labor), the serious injury in a trivial backyard incident of a young son who was thereby intellectually impaired, and her husband's frequent public protestations of love for Her Majesty the Queen.

She was patient, and loyal, and played her part. At his side (a gentler Lady Macbeth, some said, for the Rexona Age) she presided over the period of Australian McCarthyism, the attempted introduction of a police state (in which any two Cabinet ministers could at will declare any citizen a communist, and then at will imprison him), narrowly defeated in a referendum; the barbarisation of the Australian broadcast media; the blinkered protectionism that eventually wrecked the Australian economy; the death by slow starvation of much of its vigorous culture; and the soured emigration of its finer talents to England. It was a period, too, of that suburban banality – monarchist, conformist, quietly racist, Protestant, sun-drenched, smiling, timid lawnmowers on Sunday mornings, the last grim, unbelieving years of church membership and supposedly virgin brides – that enflamed the rage of both Barry Humphries and Patrick White, an age when everything was possible and little worthwhile came to pass, an age that erupted into rock'n'roll and psychedelia and sexual experiment and set a generational gulf that was never bridged. Dame Pattie was the grand role model of this ladylike brave-face hypocrisy, a woman of her time who spoke no evil, kept smiling and thought of England.

In Menzies' final, wheelchair-burdened years after his massive stroke, she was virtually his prisoner. 'I can't go out,' she whispered harshly to a visiting publisher. 'He won't let me leave the house.' Freed by his death, she became in his absence an icon in her own right, a lingering fount of hope for her husband's fractious party in its long decline. Her years of dedicated social work and charitable organising were sincere and, in a local way, effective. She was a good woman, and liked by all who knew her.

For many Australian women she provided a sustaining fantasy of what a woman's life should be: helpmeet, solace, friend, hostess. It was not her fault to be born when she was. It was in her nature to play her part with loyal and determined energy. History will judge her husband, while probably forgiving her. The flags are flying at half mast over Canberra this week, and she will be missed.

September, 1995

Brian Harradine

A note

Brian Harradine was always trouble. As long ago as 1968 (that fabled year) Gough Whitlam resigned the party leadership and recontested it in defence of him – the ruckus thus lost Labor its chance of government, some say, in 1969 – against the Cairnsite Left.

Expelled in 1972, he achieved against improbable odds in 1976 that Independent Tasmanian Senate seat he has held ever since. A Catholic, a trade union man, a family values campaigner, a rusted-on Tasmanian, he has been a yearly nuisance to governments Right and Left exacting benison ruthlessly for decades in return for his vote. None can predict the elaborate twists and writhings of his conscience. His face, exactly like de Valera's, hides a mind as tormented, multi-layered and bruised of conscience as that great, self-succouring patriot and trimmer.

Yesterday in a near empty Senate, looking exactly like a mouldy, true-hearted Disney mouse, or a Capra town clerk in some unwritten saga of municipal repentance, he said no to the GST and so brought undone the life, works and thinking of John Howard, a man he admires, and the talismanic reform he has touted for thirty years. He apologised in a personal phone call before he did so. And then, in that wavery Irish Catholic voice of his, somewhere between Santamaria, Billy McMahon and Sandy Stone, he let rip.

'The true test of a civilised society,' he said, 'is how it treats its most vulnerable.' His voice went up a notch. 'The question that I have to ask myself is whether I am going to be a party to imposing an impersonal, indiscriminate tax on my children, my grandchildren and their children for generations to come. I cannot.' He added with a touch of wounded humour that his name would no doubt be mud, but it had been mud before and would be, he had no doubt, mud again. A great parliamentary moment, all said who were not there, and I was absent, too, and I agree.

I met him only once, in a Canberra Chinese restaurant on the day he betrayed the hopes of the Aborigines he danced with on Parliament Hill. He came towards me saying, 'I've always wanted to meet you. I always thought you a force for the greater Catholic good.'

Or words to that effect. I gulped, then rallied.

'I've heard,' I said, 'you sit up late most nights watching *A Man for All Seasons* and pumping iron.'

He looked amused. 'Something like that,' he said.

'I suppose,' I said, gathering boldness, 'I must come under your definition of Sodom and Gomorrah because I did the Full Monty.'

'It wasn't my definition,' he said sharply. 'It was Richard Alston's. I would not be so vulgar.'

I asked him how he could do that to the Aborigines. 'I didn't,' he said. 'Look at the small print. They've got what they want, in the small print.'

I believe he believed that. An interesting man, in a time when most policy formulation is done by bland men studying focus groups, a conscience of his intricacy and guile, a capacity for moral guilt like his, a willingness to measure issues against divine formulations and immortal longings and the history of his tribe, is an absorbing, quiet spectacle, an anomaly to treasure. I believe him good (though as Francis James remarked of Santamaria, a good man who can do evil) and wish him many jovial grandchildren and Christmases to come.

May, 1999

The Dead Kennedys

Four plane crashes now, only three of them fatal – for Joe Junior in 1944, John Junior yesterday and Kathleen in 1948. The fourth, in 1964, broke Teddy's back, and his recovery, like Jack's survival of many spine operations and two Final Unctions, was a minor miracle. An assassination attempt in 1960 when a gun a few metres from Jack's face was snatched from the gunman's hand. Two successful assassinations, one on the day Bobby saved his son David from drowning. The coincidence deeply depressed David, who overdosed on heroin at twenty-nine. A stillbirth to Jackie in 1956 and the death of a son, Patrick, three days old, in 1963. The death in a plane crash in 1973 of Jackie's stepson Alexander, whose father Aristotle Onassis then said she had the 'evil eye'. A death in a game of touch football in mountain snow of Bobby's son Michael, at thirty-nine. A case of bone cancer for Patrick, Teddy's son, which lost him a leg at twelve. The alcoholism of his wife Joan. The dementia of his sister Rosemary, made mad by one of the world's first prefrontal lobotomies. The Addison's disease of Jack (a condition resembling AIDS), whose experimental amphetamine treatment by the White House quack, 'Dr Feelgood', may well have unsettled and inflamed his mind. A massive stroke for the patriarch, Joe Senior, that saw him speechlessly watching the murders of two of his sons on television. Three runs for President by three brothers, one successful. Two for Vice-President, by Jack in 1956 and brother-in-law Sargent Shriver in 1972, both unsuccessful.

Two cases of suspected murder, of Marilyn Monroe in 1962 and Mary Jo Kopechne in 1969, both almost certainly unfounded. One case of rape, more likely. Mafia links to old Joe's bootlegging fortune, links that made it seem to some that the Mob had had Jack hit when Bobby, as Attorney General, went after Joe's accomplice, Frank Costello, thus demonstrating ingratitude. A girl shared with Sam Giancana, the mobster who ensured, perhaps, Jack's election with forged votes in Chicago.

Lots of other girls. Marilyn, Grace Kelly, Audrey Hepburn – whom Jack would have wed had she not been Protestant – Angie Dickinson, Marlene Dietrich, the secretaries Fiddle and Faddle that Jack would romp with in the White House pool. Old Joe's First Honourable Mistress, Gloria Swanson, indulged like royalty in her special suite at Hyannisport. Jackie's affairs while Jack was alive with Bobby, Leonard Bernstein and Mike Nichols, and her netting after Bobby's death of the world's richest man, Onassis, allowed in his marital contract sexual access only twice a year. Her stated purpose, prescient as it turned out, was to keep her children in Europe, 'safe from America'.

Jackie's enduring world celebrity, though she gave no interviews for thirty years. Rose, who saw it all, and managed much of it, and died at 104. And John-John, who saluted his father's coffin as a little boy on his third birthday and might have had his job by acclamation had he not died yesterday, at thirty-eight.

What does this Kennedy curse-and-legend add up to, this bright, brash mix of Irish popish piety, clan loyalty, big teeth, touch football, drug abuse, alcoholism, immortal oratory, spin-doctoring, Harvard elitism, Cold War populism, hectic fornication, left-wing grandstanding and pulp celebrity such as the world has never seen? Celebrity recorded by a million times more words in this half century than, in his lifetime, Jesus Christ? Not too much, perhaps. A lot, maybe.

Some of it is the world's memory of the extended families that are no more, who are always there for you, and caring for you, in your extremity of sickness and personal trouble. Some of it is the world of royal princedoms that so many Cinderellas dreamed of marrying into, and so many Monica Lewinskys dreamed of touching, however briefly, in the night.

Some of it is plain spin-doctoring, by the century's masters in that field. The word 'charisma', for instance, was exhumed from the ancient Greek to describe the Kennedys. It had no modern currency before them. The cult of youth-in-politics was invented too, to justify a man who may not have had long to live, and the slogan 'vigour' to cloak his chronic illness. The TV debate was invented for him, and the backstage political documentary. Some of it was the best speechwriting – by Sorensen, Goodwin, Schlesinger, Galbraith – of the century. Some of it was the luck of the Kennedys' film star looks and the arrival of the medium, television, that altered politics into something more like game shows or celebrity interviews. Some of it was Joe's belief that a family is a partnership down the centuries whose purpose is an enduring brand name, a name that has clout. He certainly succeeded in creating that.

Some of it is our need to have others live our lives more glamorously, and more dramatically, for us, to go through sickness, crisis, romance, despair and triumph more grandly, more poetically, more powerfully, than we do. The need for heroes includes, as a rule, the need for the heroes' deaths.

But much of the Kennedy story, I fear, is about Irishness, and Boston–American Irishness. The piety, boozing, deal-making, vote-rigging, skirt-chasing, rule-bending, devil-may-care audacity of purpose, and the singing, as Jack, Bobby and Teddy did in trio more than once, of 'Those Wedding Bells Are Breaking Up That Old Gang of Mine' in the bar that never closes on a snowy winter's night.

Many Catholic Irish families of Belfast have lost as many sons and brothers as violently as the Kennedys. Many last century were hanged or hunted down or flogged or starved to death. Once you see what the Irish have put up with, and hoped for, and dreamed of, and lost forever and sung of, you will understand more clearly this grand soap opera, ending now with the century, that has so absorbed the world.

July, 1999

Don Dunstan

I rang last Monday morning to check with Don on the filming of the first part of our documentary, on 7 and 8 February. He would walk, I hoped, round some of his favourite saved buildings, cook a meal, have a Last Supper with friends, or a Don's Last Party, play on the grand piano the Liszt and Schubert pieces that would be our sole soundtrack, dig his garden, revisit his restaurant, Don's Table, read some favourite poetry in that famous golden Tennysonian voice, reflect, perhaps, on sexual McCarthyism in the age of AIDS, and Lewinsky, curse Hinch, denounce with his dark angelic fury the Quislings that have sold Australia's economy to the crazy animal whims of the free market, remember Adele, add his particular stoic grace to an unbeliever's death . . .

And then he came on the phone in the hospital ward. His voice had worsened, and had that blurry, thick-tongued imprecision you get with a dentist's injection. I can't do it, he said. I can't be heard like this. I said it might get better. He said he knew it wouldn't.

'I'm in the home stretch, old mate,' he said. 'I'm truly sorry.'

I realised then this was maybe our last conversation. I told him I loved him very much, and gloomily added, 'I'd normally say Godspeed but it's the wrong theology. And,' I added, 'the wrong velocity.'

A pause, no laughter; then:

'That it is. See you, mate.'

'See you, Don.'

I then kicked the wall for a while, and drank, and cursed, and pined, the way you do, for the most significant Australian since Chifley, since Federation perhaps, the man whose political brilliance hacked out the path that Whitlam followed, and to some extent took credit for. And I went feeling foul and frail to Jim McClelland's memorial service in Sydney Town Hall, where Whitlam and Killen with much inner grief told of the adjacent deaths of Jim Cope, Cleaver Bunton and our vivid Brisbane friend Brian Sweeney, and the final stages of the fading from life of Neville Bonner and King Hussein, who survived, I think, twenty-two assassination attempts but not, like Don, the mutiny in the blood that was cancer. That was an enemy with bite. No-one noted much the enormities of this week, so enraptured were they with Mark Taylor quitting, and Monica testifying, and the entire IOC in unison murmuring that drugs in sport were okay.

On Thursday Mike Rann, the South Australian State Labor leader, rang to say Don could see us both on Saturday morning, but his breathing wasn't good and he had tubes sticking out of him, and we had perhaps about an hour. That would have to do, I decided, and booked my ticket, wondering what you say apart from thanks for the memory to such a man at such a time. Mike cursed himself for having donated, like the good citizen he was, all his Dunstan tapes and photos to the Constitutional Museum, which the present Liberal government, of course (like the pharaohs who defaced and hacked to rubble the monuments of their predecessors), closed down. Where were the tapes and photos now? He didn't know.

Mike came to work for Don in 1977, and in one intense period, sitting up each night till 4 a.m., wrote five major speeches for him in a week. Don, he explains, was not only the architect of policy change in the Labor Party but also the initiating Prospero (a role that in his old age he might have played well) of its tardy professionalism. He *invented* the press release, the testing by poll of policy (you do not *change* party policy, he said, after testing it, you work out how to sell it better), and the then novel notion that you have to win the *second* election, and the third, and the fourth, and entrench yourself in order to get things done. Nine years before Wran, seventeen years before Hawke, twenty-two years before Goss, twenty-four years before Keating, he was leading a moribund party and a somnolent country (and a state in theological rigor mortis) in ways that, after ferocious intellectual quarrel with himself, he had decided were best. Aboriginal equality. Female equality. The inevitability of the multiculture. The actuality of democracy. The possibility of Australia (even South Australia) leading, not following, in the arts. Shadow Minister Chris Schact (in a sorrowing five-hour conversation at Bridie O'Reilly's in Sydney) remembered him at a Norwood branch meeting telling a dumbstruck audience that an Australian film industry could start in South Australia. In 1974 it did, with *Picnic at Hanging Rock*, then *Storm Boy*, then *Breaker Morant*.

So, too, did the flashier, shallower things – the sidewalk cafes, the art gallery wine-tastings, the poetry recitations to accompanying orchestra among lions at the zoo. The heady trail of international celebrities – Yevtushenko, Rushdie, Burgess, Vidal, Nureyev, Gratowski, Arundhati Roy – that year by year raised Adelaide's Festival of the Arts to parity with Edinburgh's, an ultimate Good Time you would remember all your life.

But it's important, Mike added, not to lose the real Dunstan under the glamorous honeymoon icing of his era. This was a man who, in Parliament since 1953 (while Churchill and Stalin were still in power), pursued a vision of social equity and union rights and worker participation and architectural sacred sites and minority equality and cultural independence and ungerry-mandered representative government (he *lost* the 1968 election with 54 per cent of the vote), and a skilful humanistic balance between government intervention and personal initiative – between individual incentive and cautious bureaucracy – that had few echoes anywhere; in the Palme years of Sweden, perhaps, or the New Deal thirties of F.D. Roosevelt, perhaps; or the first two years of Harold Wilson, or Gough Whitlam. This was no mere flashy magazine editor slumming, for a time, in electoral politics. This was no dilettante in pink shorts. This was twenty-six years of hard slog in the branches, in the Caucus, in party committees and national conferences, turning round things as basic as the White Australia Policy. This was a man who paid, as they say, his party dues. Who worked in his retirement, unlike some, for his party's good. Who just about *invented* Aboriginal Land Rights, and certainly invented Meals on Wheels. Who in 1957 was in Cyprus bargaining for the release of Archbishop Makarios. This was a man who changed his country, not singlehandedly but by years of persuasive discussion, and changed it, with a persistent, eloquent selflessness, for the good. If any have cause to doubt this, let them speak now, or forever, etc.

Mike was in Sydney on Friday at lunch with Bob Carr, and suddenly got word that Don, after an agitated Thursday night, was in a coma now with only a dimly flickering pulse. He left the restaurant, rang me, rushed for the airport, was caught in traffic, missed the plane. I agreed to come down anyway, the way you do. I was up at 4 a.m. and write this now exhausted, remembering, cursing, giving interviews, writing, drinking, not happy. So many remembrances now lost, of a great – or minor – Renaissance prince.

There was a farewell occasion at which he movingly, wonderfully spoke, in December; unrecorded. There were dinners with friends in his last autumnal journeys to Sydney and Melbourne; unrecorded. And the promised film, too late, unmade. And a slow trawl now through the footage not yet destroyed by those in fear of his legend, those who went after him in life, whose enmity, he said, was a constant source of comfort to him.

Like many public men of charm and magnetism, his private life was uneasy. He was shy and uncommunicative at parties, and even in his restaurant (goat on toast, fine wines), where most nights he was waiter, he was stiff and timid with customers who loved him. He was betrayed more often than most politicians are – by lovers, staff members, ministers, old friends – or he thought he was. He would nurse a wound long years and not reveal it. He felt, as the nights drew in and the tumours bloomed and spread, a little unregarded, a bit let down, forgotten even. He saw the dismantling of his radiant Athens, his Felicia, by double-dealing dwarves and was not content.

And in his last years, as in his first, he was torn between his love of the Labor Party and his dismay at what had become of it. He detested (and in his obituary interview with Negus said he detested) the mindless factionalism which was now but a squabble, dogs over rotting meat, 'for the spoils of defeat'. He hated the Hawke–Keating lurch toward Global Economics that, however it was bandaided, in the end meant only surrender to foreign, uncaring boardrooms of our national Self, our society, our destiny. He was not at one with the Muscular Cowardice of these millennial times. He believed in a better world. He was the kind of man of whom his fellow Fabian G.B. Shaw once said, 'Some men see things as they are and ask why. I dream of things that never were and ask why not?'

Don was a why-not kind of man. He was a doer in a world of postponers. A maestro of the possible. A leader. A hero of that better polity he saw in his last days shrinking from the world.

One of his favourite quotes, and he read it magnificently, was, unsurprisingly for an old St Peter's College man, from Tennyson.

We are not now that strength which in old days
Moved earth and heaven; that which we are, we are –
One equal temper of heroic hearts,
Made weak by time and fate, but strong in will
To strive, to seek, to find and not to yield.

Vale, Don Dunstan. Godspeed.

February, 1999

BOOK FIVE

Broadcast News

The Late John Hewson

Anyone looking for the literary equivalent of the late John Hewson should probably start in *David Copperfield* with Uriah Heep – 'I used to be 'umble, Master Copperfield, but now I own a Fewwawi' – and then perhaps go deeper into Russian literature, into Gogol perhaps, the lonely sad thin government clerk with the bright new overcoat that is abruptly stolen from him at a party thrown to celebrate its purchase, who turns up at the office in his old tatty overcoat looking grubbier and sadder than ever, or one of Chekhov's rusty dreamers, Astrov perhaps, possessed he believes of the final future truth but no-one will listen any more.

I say the late Dr Hewson because he is, alas, after this last fortnight now no more, an irrecoverable, discarded Pinocchio on history's dust heap, who never quite got to be a real boy, with weeds growing on his posthumously lengthening nose. Strange how the press awardeth charisma and taketh it away. As charismatic now as a wire coathanger, as fearsome as a rabid curlew, as wise and majestic in his daily utterance as a suddenly gelded greyhound, as suddenly yesterday's man as Max Gillies, that ex-parrot, or his glove puppet Bob Hawke. John Hewson, this afterthought, this brief angry asterisk beneath our national history, deserves perhaps a little analysis before he goes forever into the bottom drawer.

Into such minds as his, I think, especially those reared like mine in fundamentalist religions, there soon inevitably descends the doctrine of predestination. The good doctor knew he was fated for führership, and his mere marriage, his lisp, the public mockery of his Ferrari, the *Woman's Day* inquiry into his divorce, the improving trade figures, the dickhead candidate for Wills, his luckless kissing of the poisoned hem of Her Majesty the Queen, are all only his earthly trials, you see, his herculean labours, his pilgrim burdens on his upward passage into glory foredoomed and written down in the book of fate before the beginning of the world. This divine sense of history has made him incapable of reacting sensibly in the present and he looks more and more like a stumbling dill, pratfalling like John Cleese around the china shop of his arid theology with the holy grail of the GST glowing under his shirt. Roads and railways and electrical grids, yes, you can have 'em and it won't cost a penny more, not a penny more, because our GST, you see, hereinafter known as our magic puddin', has endless powers of manufacturing more and more money and everybody can have a little bit. Pretty soon fate will be telling him to burn his abacus and invent a new, trick currency based on beads or seashells or Ferrari hubcaps and with this instead he can prove he was foredoomed to save the world.

This dim drongo, this thin Antipodean Yeltsin with inflation avalanching at his back, this Jerry Lewis doppelgänger pie-fighting with the ingredients of numeracy against all the civilities of man, might seem harshly used by this broadcast. But by pitting himself and his pocket calculator and his mean dreams against our nation's health and education and culture, the broad sunburnt kindly civilisation we have rather come to like, and, worse, against our ABC, he has brought it on himself. Perhaps when he next feels predestined, he might feel predestined to do a little thinking first.

April, 1991

Thatcher's Children

In the current climactic three-way British political contest between Jerusalem, Babylon and Toad Hall, repeatedly interrupted by Bob Hawke popping up out of manholes saying 'happy birthday' and 'bloody awful' and 'too close to call' and 'when I was up at Oxford' and 'I'm not a betting man but . . .' in the mingled manner of Paul Hogan and Kermit the Frog, disrupting peaceful country pubs and standing on tiptoe beside Big Ben, and even further dismaying the already harried party leaders with his breezy, fawning pre-vision of their own imminent ruin and fatheaded elder statesmanship about a week from now, only one thing really matters and that is the memory of Thatcherism, an appalling doctrine which like Moby Dick rears up whitely in the dark of the mind, chewing the lifeboats of socialism and spitting out the poor, a doctrine frightening in its animal force and arithmetical purity, sado-monetarism, as Denis Healey called it, which has affected the civility of England like nothing since the Black Plague. (Thatcher voice) Bring out your dead, ding ding. Get on your bike, ding ding. Don't be a Moaning Minnie, starve like a man, ding ding. There is no such thing as society, ding ding. There are only families. Get yourself a cardboard box, ding ding, and busk.

Margaret Hilda Roberts Thatcher, a baseborn Lincolnshire coquette who swived her way upmarket into oil millions, replacing in Denis's silken sheets the *initial* Margaret Thatcher and casting her into outer darkness, poor old thing, and thereafter as a lifelong kept woman rightly felt everyone else should work hard for a living to redress the national balance, especially those in the North who, unlike herself, have not taken the oral pledge and improved their accents on the Henry Higgins plan into a scorching asexual whisper like her own, and therefore showed themselves to be not only poor but undeserving and expendable. The wasteland in the North and the short-lived capitalist Disneyland in the South restored the primacy of the Kingdom of Mercia – Saxon conquerors over Celtic peasantry – for the first time since the eighth century and exalted the greed-is-good gang, stockbrokers, property developers, green belt moneylenders, Oxbridge remittance men and supermarket Gradgrinds, into a self-righteous dominance unimaginable in Christian times. The nudge-nudge wink-wink say-no-more say-no-more can-I-sell-you-a-watch brigade who are in the end Thatcher's people, football hooligans of the spirit whose brutish rise, along with the wrecking of the BBC, the National Gallery, the National Theatre, the National Health, British Rail ding ding and British good humour, has been her sole achievement, and it is against these monsters, thank God, the numbers at long last are stacked. John Major may deny his incubus and tardily try to dilute her manifest cruelty, but she is there behind his shoulder with fangs dripping, and it is against this – too late perhaps for British civilisation – however much he tries to play on our natural human fear of redheads and the Welsh, that the British at last are voting. I predict an outright Labour majority of eighteen seats, or maybe as low as sixteen. Oh clouds unfold.

May, 1991

The Rodney King Riots

America the Beautyless erotically and apocalyptically unveiled itself in the Hollywood holocaust of last week in the usual, recognisable American way of murder, arson, mayhem, fascism by jury, upmarket looting and pillaging, or power-shopping as I suppose it must be currently called, casual slaughter, federal hypocrisy, presidential spinelessness and crocodile tears, race, lies and videotape, and all the out-winging vultures of Darwinian capitalism at long last coming home to roost among the uprearing flames of the angel city where dreams, if you wish upon a star, come true. It couldn't have happened to a nicer town, where on any morning you see dignified old black men rooting in garbage cans for food while in a white stretch-limousine Warren Beatty glides by with twin blondes going down on him simultaneously to a nation's applause, a town built on greed, plastic surgery, toothcaps, Mafia money, historical ignorance, cultural barbarism, the wisdom of Bob Hope, the singing voice of Shirley Temple, the Piltdown economics of Ronald Reagan, the spiritual leadership of Shirley MacLaine, the moral courage of Sylvester Stallone, the philosophical rectitude of Mel Gibson blamming away and, oh Christ, American salesmanship, the belief that harsh reality can be squeezed by sheer force of talking into a beautiful dream and all the ruin and starvation and blood and sorrow and the lost black children of the streets can be hidden away under a huge, outgoing, tooth-capped charismatic smile and a song from Harry Connick Jnr about the love that heals all. I used to have a great anti-Hollywood curse, which was God speed the San Andreas Fault, but maybe what has happened is even better, with the fires of class vengeance everywhere and blustering hypocrisy exposed everywhere for what it is, and the greed, and the dream of Lincoln of a land united a sorry sham, and Roosevelt a fading Tinkerbell, remote, irretrievable, the panto-mime theatre now silent, the curtain down. The American system, which massively declares that 93 per cent of its populace are failures because they are not millionaires and then arms that 93 per cent with handguns, has declared itself.

That American system that routinely evicts from hospital the fatally ill when they cannot pay the $6000 a day to stay there has declared itself. That American system that regards all government-subsidised education as a com-munist plot and the employment on slave wages of illegal wetback immi-grants as economically shrewd and the child prostitution of its Spanish colonies as free-market economics. That American system that holds the million-dollar note to be self-evident and nothing else, and the human being only an incidental and disposable means to the getting of that million-dollar note. That American system that believes all human beings to be replaceable, like their noses and teeth and motor cars and livers and hearts and wives, has declared itself and may itself be replaced in the end by wandering mobs of Afghan-style robber barons and murderers. It couldn't happen to a nicer country or a nicer town with Bobby Kennedy's blood on its hands. Kennedy offered the last slim hope of American civility and inter-racial communion.

America's extremities of wealth and poverty, and its cruelty and its rubbing the nose of its helpless poor into its helpless poverty, is unparalleled in recent recorded history. That system, whose logical end is the heroin trade or armed and murderous anarchy or an unofficial return to black slavery, may well have achieved its end. Burn, baby, burn.

May, 1991

Ross Perot

The current American presidential frontrunner H. Ross Perot, a dead ringer for Grumpy out of *Snow White and the Seven Dwarfs* in both altitude and physiognomy, clearly understands the need in a largely illiterate country for any presidential candidate to resemble closely a character out of American childhood film or comic-book myth, even as John F. Kennedy closely resembled Archie and his wife resembled Veronica, and Lyndon Johnson resembled Wyle E. Coyote out of *The Roadrunner*, Bobby Kennedy resembled Bugs Bunny, Richard and Pat Nixon, Dagwood and Blondie, Jimmy and Roslyn Carter, Trixie and Dixie, and Ronald Reagan, in a stroke of genius, Ronald Reagan, a character he had shrewdly and artfully and laboriously confected in a hundred childhood Saturday matinees of three generations of his neckless addled voters.

Americans, you see, have very small brains, and any new addition to their dream-life confuses them, as the unexpected five-foot Greek nerd Michael Dukakis proved, and only the very familiar excites them, as the relentless career of Madonna, a straightforward peroxide-blonde compilation of Harlow, Monroe and Mae West, in yearly mammiferous tedium likewise proves. Under normal circumstances Governor Clinton's wet, boyish Van Johnson and George Bush's avuncular, bourgeois Robert Young out of *Father Knows Best* might command the inside track in the great race of the world, but H. Ross Perot, prefiguring as he does a Federal Cabinet composed of Sneezy, Happy, Dopey, Sleepy, Doc and so on, together with a political philosophy you can whistle, *hey ho, hey ho, it's off to work we go*, and overlarding it with dim race memories of perky little Harry Truman giving them hell and simple-hearted Mr Smith making it in Washington, is tapping deeper veins of caramel sentimentality in heartland America, the which caramel sentimentality is the prime fuel of this most ruthless and culturally carnivorous nation since the Romans.

But of course it ain't over yet. Evidence may yet come to light that

H. Ross Perot once ate quiche or wore lipstick or lace corsets or was seen playing dominos in the park with Lee Harvey Oswald or strip poker in a motel with Lady Bird Johnson or changed the spelling of his surname, reducing it down from Perotonitis or something, or once kept for three weeks on his staff a female black masseuse who had in fact graduated in Marxist studies from the Sorbonne in the same year as Pol Pot, or any other of those tiny anomalies that the Republican Party Dirty Tricks department relentlessly inflates into campaign issues, like Gary Hart misremembering his age and his post-marital promiscuity, *oh my gawsh*, and Michael Dukakis undergoing treatment for depression after the suicide of his brother, or Ed Muskie after weeks of sleepless campaign exhaustion bursting into tears over an insult to his wife. Good Presidents all of them had they been put on, alterers for the better of a greedy, bloodthirsty and decaying planet, and such tiny weevils of rumour pumped up into strangling pythons of campaign scandal by cruel and wicked men may well bring this happy questing dwarf undone, as they have so many others. Or on the other hand the countervailing rumours behind George Bush's widely unknown and maybe fictional admission to Bethesda Hospital after he was unexpectedly mugged while waiting outside his mistress's Georgetown apartment at midnight for his minders to pick him up might well bring him undone, if anyone is foolish enough to broadcast this anywhere in the world and thus annoy the vengeful CIA, his *alma mater*, into pre-emptive assassination by machine gun in the radio studio in mid-transmission, or one rumour of Governor Clinton and cocaine, or Governor and Mrs Clinton and premarital sex.

What is going on here? Is this a proper political prelude to what is effectively world government? Is this the way world superpower leaders should be chosen by those 42 per cent of eligible Americans still crazy enough to venture out at night into the gang-warring streets to vote for them? No, no, no way. The United States of America is an experiment which has failed, and it should, in short, be burned to the ground and the ashes sown with salt. I hope I make myself clear. Failing that, God speed the San Andreas Fault.

June, 1992

Hewson and Reith

I'm pretty pleased I have to admit that my once imperious glove puppet Dr Hewson is now behaving as I have long wished, helter-skeltering hither and yon, falling over his feet, exuding panic, self-pity, paranoia, imprecision, stark innumeracy, incipient BO and all the masterful charisma of a fridge magnet, attacking like a hydrophobic duck the Americans, the Japanese, the Europeans, the multiculturals, the migrants, the capitalists, the workers, the sugar-sotted Queensland Nationals, the tariff-glutted Victorian Liberals, the neo-Keynesian pump-priming New South Wales Liberals, the molly-coddled corporate pirates, the feather-bedded union heavies, the Big Australian, the small farmer, Malcolm Fraser, the truck owners, the local car manufacturers – he doesn't need to buy Australian-made any more, once his new zero tariff brings down the cost of his next imported Ferrari by eight thousand dollars – the old, the young, the unemployed, the wearers of crutches and false teeth, appealing for succour to the farcically tottering Major government, writing tut-tut letters to the wrong president, unveiling his ghastly upper legs in front of nauseated football crowds, wrapping himself in the flag, singing 'I'll never walk alone' in the shower, abusing Malcolm Fraser, the Australian dollar, the pro-communist *Sydney Morning Herald* and his own house-builder from any passing soapbox, repeatedly and querulously asserting on television that he is not and never was a feral abacus, what a lovely phrase, loudly and rambunctiously in the classic British manner contemplating the disfranchisement of all who do not own property because of their untidy front lawns, shrivelling rapidly down to a three-inch midget with a tiny raised fist and a threatening stammer. Yes, that's the way I want to remember him. This, well, let's hear the litany ... This hyperactive bobby pin, this sado-monetarist dill, this Harvard fundamentalist prig, this ferret up the trousers of decent civilisation, this antipodean Dan Quayle.

Dr Hewson, I believe, and his accompanying crony and fellow–lurching Blue Meanie, Peter Reith, a sneer and a pair of glasses in search of a face, a malicious rage in the Darwinian universe in search of an innocent victim, this Peter Sellers routine without the acting talent, this Inspector Clouseau forever falling with finger upraised down the unexpected manhole. The two of them, I believe, are so ideological zealous that *they* believe that wearing clothes in the Antarctic is cheating, for this is protection, you see, and protection is wrong the way the chloroform is wrong, and condoms and fluoride and umbrellas, anything that interferes with man's essential duty of suffering the chill winds of reality and thus earning his Toorak mansion and his golf buggy. It is suffering that purifies, like AIDS and toothache purifies. *Ve haf vays of making you pure.* Dr Hewson who for eleven years went to a government-subsidised and protected school, for six years went to a government-subsidised and protected university, for five years had on the Prime Minister's advisory staff a government-subsidised and protected job and for five more years as a member of Parliament had a government-subsidised and protected job, plus cheap lunches, is, after thirty-three years of government protection from the winds that blow through real life, extremely adamant that nobody *else* gets government subsidy or government protection from anything – like ill health or ill luck or old age or job loss or poor parenting or runs on sterling. Because look at the mess that government swaddling lifelong has made of him.

Well, there might be something in it, I suppose. The man is certainly a whimpering wreck, divorced, derided, confronted everywhere with emptying rooms, pitiably begging from the other side of the glass, like Scrooge at Christmas, to be admitted to a human race that increasingly regards him with a kind of puzzled horror. Like Pinocchio he wants to be a real boy, and it's not working, and in a week's time he'll be behind – as I predicted – in all the polls and cursed on the hustings by even Kennett, his loathsome doppelgänger, as his hope sinks too, and John Howard will move to replace him, and at that point I will ask you to remember that on Thursday 23 August I said his fate was already sealed, and I was right.

Some people have accused me of being unduly harsh on the dim, innumerate Dr Hewson, and if there is truth in this it is because I understand him so well. I too was a lapsed fundamentalist uni droob who tardily came to alcohol when I was all of twenty-four, *like him*, and thereafter believed myself, *like him*, to be the predestined guardian of the great simplicities that govern mankind. One simple, cruel and sloganeering deity thus replacing another – the Lord Jehovah out, the haloed abacus in – but unlike him I found out in my mid-thirties that the world is trickier than that and no embracing formula will ever suffice to explain and control what happens. The doctor has yet to learn this, to the extreme annoyance of his multiplying post-rationalist neo-protectionist adversaries, but he possibly, no, probably will, on election night, when it is all too late.

August, 1992

The Lure of Statistics

The figures out yesterday show the number of people in jobs in Australia, a paltry 7.5 million, had not changed since late 1991. This, the expert commentators said, was cause for dismay, although the number of Australians in full-time work had gone up, which was encouraging, because the unemployment rate was stuck at around 10.7 per cent of those currently seeking work, stuck, that is, until more people started seeking work, at which time the unemployment figures would go up again, and the thing most likely to make more people seek work was the news that there was more work around, which led to the paradox of the unemployment rate and the employment rate both going up at the same time, which is what they usually do, the expert commentators said, as well they might, since they could be out of a job if there was no cause for dismay. Their employment in fact depended on dismay, and they needed the work.

It's a paradox all right, especially when you realise those extra numbers thus encouraged to seek work by there being more work around include schoolboys seeking part-time work as paperboys, and schoolgirls seeking part-time work as babysitters, and housewives seeking part-time work as exotic dancers or ceramic potters or writers for *A Country Practice*, the idea that they must do more with their lives having abruptly arrived in their minds via Ray Martin's *Midday Show*. Both figures go up at the same time: employed and unemployed, rubbery as hell.

Things were much better, we were told, in May 1953, when the number of people in work was not 7.5 million but 2.132 million. This is a better figure, we are told. It is a better figure because then only 2.183 million were seeking work out of a total population of not 16.7 million, as it is now, but 6.8 million, as it was then. Well, is it a better figure? The number of people in work today is 44.9 per cent of the total population. The number of people in work then was 32.8 per cent of the total population. How can this lower figure be a better figure than the higher figure? When there are 12 per cent *more* people in work now than there were then?

Well, of course it's a better figure. Less people in percentage terms were *seeking* work then, and all but 2.7 per cent had got it. That makes it a better figure, a 7 per cent better figure. And why weren't they seeking work? Well, housewives knew their place then, didn't they. And the baby boom was on, and so there were more people under the age of ten, which meant there were less people under the age of twenty seeking work, because there were more people currently being babies. And girls, by marrying early, got out of the workforce sooner, and by having more children stayed out of it longer, probably forever, not only out of the workforce, but out of the unemployment figures, which is what counts, or what the expert commentators count, because they need the work.

Let me repeat what I just said. In May 1953, when the number of people in work was 32.8 per cent of the population, there was less *un*employment than there was in May 1993, when the number of people in work was 44.9 per cent of the population, when there was more unemployment. In fact the unemployment rate then was one quarter of what it is now. What a golden age. The figures are even more exciting when you realise there were people in work then who hadn't even sought work, like the buffeted six-year-old sons of Italian greengrocers, who, more exciting still, weren't even being paid. And there were more farmers' wives then because there were more farmers, who, though they worked like dogs fourteen hours a day, weren't even listed as employed or unemployed.

Now I'm not saying that, even with 12 per cent more people in work now than there were then, we are necessarily better off. I mean, house prices for one thing are two and a half times, as a percentage of average earnings, more than they were then, and interest rates now are three and a half times what they were then, and the price of petrol is five times what it was then, and we use more electricity on our microwaves and CDs and VHSs and hot-water systems and guitar amplifiers and personal vibrators. They sat up under forty-watt lamps playing Scrabble and had a shared bath twice a week, or they did up where I was in May 1953, which is why I'm filthy but a great speller. We had simpler needs then. We made our own entertainment.

But what I am saying is – pay attention – what I am saying is that all figures thus lamented over should be treated with deep suspicion until you've worked out, which is pretty hard, precisely what they mean. There are lies, Harry Truman used to say over and over, damned lies and statistics. And these, to be frank, have been some of them.

Damned lies especially in this case, because I just made *all* of these figures up out of a vague race memory of what they should be, and you wouldn't have known, would you? You would never have known. Beware of experts bearing statistics, I say. They might be as irresponsible as me. No, they're much more irresponsible in fact because the broad thrust of my figures, you'll find when you look them up, is quite correct. More people proportionally are in work now than there were then – it's in the Mitchell Library – and they've been keeping that from you for years, because they thrive on dismay and rumour and panic, you see; panic especially sustains them, panic is their meat and drink, and they need the work, you see, there's not that much work about. I mean, look at yesterday's unemployment figures.

June, 1993

The North Shore Liberals

On Sydney's leafy mortgage-fardled, Ferrari-strewn royal and royalist North Shore, what looks like a political machine-gun massacre has lately taken place where Smiles for tax, Greiner for technical corruption plus five o'clock shadow, Moore for loyal friendship plus whingeing monotone, Hazzard for being culpably nice to rich old grieving widows and crying poor while swimming Scrooge McDuck–like through his money, and Collins for press leaks and lack of inches and starving lawyers, and Metherell certainly for hubris and hairdo beyond the call of self-delusion, fell or will fall like Flanders poppies or English gentlemen within mere weeks and will be closely and imitatively followed, alas in dimwit kamikaze fashion, by the crude Ballina social climber Michael Yabsley, not currently of the North Shore but, significantly, the blow-in local member of nervous nouveau Vaucluse, whose manure mouth and murderous curses and rabid pratfalls down most media trapdoors in the last four days have brought such innocent pleasure to us all, up to and before that is his abject forced apology on Tuesday night to his gorgeous icy nemesis Clover Moore, Beatrice to his Dante. Why does she so despise him? She will pay.

Out of all this now, these casual slaughters, accidental tragedies, Dickensian cycles of inheritance and retribution, weeping, bone-pointing courtroom forgetfulness, Humpty-Dumpty bandaid repair jobs and noble speeches before the guillotine, the question must arise: why are the Liberals like this? Why do they fly so high and haughty and fall so grossly into the effluent? Can there be a reason? Why are they so balefully outraged if the three vote now and then against them? Why do they shout out leprous vengeance on their parliamentary saviours as, Malvolio-like, they limp cross-gartered into laughable oblivion time after time, time after time, Kennett and Gorton and Fraser and Menzies and Hughes and Dowd and Brown and Smiles wriggling on a pin and shaking their tiny fists in righteous bafflement at their eviction from the control room of earthly power, time after time. Why are they *like* this? It must be that they think they are not as other men and that power of necessity accrues to a higher and purer species to which they belong, and never descends on a lower, more bestial species resident on the south shore which they are predestined by a kind of northern line divinity, Pymble-born, Wahroonga-schooled, Harvard-polished and Friedman-steeled, to rule, with firm compassion and Christian strictness, of course, with birch and rugger-tough and bridge-and-sodomy-sharpened worldly unsentimental benevolence, but nonetheless to rule. So the laws that govern this lesser, more beastly species do not, of course, and must not apply to them, the higher, more godlike ones.

Men who believe that 'human' is itself defined by the possession of a tennis court, an accountant, a golf cart and a cocktail shaker and who think they are in fact empowered by their superior genetic origins and scholastic training to do things the beasts must not, like trade in public service positions and parliamentary seats, conceal hidden millions of income while touting for Legal Aid, flog off old schools and legendary showgrounds to balance drop-sical, innumerate and lurk-filled budgets and kick-backs to mates, green-light old dormitory intimates to slaughter the environment and bulldoze the heritage to rubble on a subtle nod and a knowing wink and a school tie.

For they are a proud, green, leafy-bordered, golf-carting and opera-going élite, a ruling class above the law and beyond our ken whose high castle walls are unbreachable, unscalable by us the lesser breeds, the lower orders, the beasts, who cannot begin to understand the higher cause of money in its purest, more acquisitive sense, and power shared with some courtly joshing and ribbing and chivvying among establishment equals. We poor, petty non-events, we Neanderthal hold-overs with our outmoded pre-Fried-manite belief in society and mercy and love and heart and joy in however profitless artistic achievement, who are looked on by them, the golf-carting Ferrari-polishing baronial classes, as, well, a kind of joke at which they laugh behind their decorous hands. And it is this, this blinkered eye, this narrow band of thought, this tunnel view, this mean heart, this thin soul, this racked self-pitying ignorance of the teeming world, that is the reason why the Liberals and all who voyage with them do not get it, and never will, and so will not prevail. For a proud man who believes himself predestined is never vigilant and so always quickly falls, and the more vulgar, earthier, less cock-sure creatures of even the National Country Party, like even Wal Murray himself, will always survive them. This is why the Liberals are stupid, self-pitying, laughable and doomed, and I thank our Neanderthal God for that.

June, 1992

The Return of Slavery

Comparing Dr Hewson's proposed sado-monetarist neo-Dickensian economic miracle of the youth wage – three dollars an hour and all the pride you can swallow for four racked years, plus a twenty-first birthday key to nine months' anticlimax and then suicide row – with slavery, as some fool commentators have done, is pretty hard on slavery I think, which in its golden age in antebellum Alabama at least gave one sufficient food, nocturnal shelter and morning transport to one's place of work free of charge. Under Dr Hewson's new draconian mathematics of desperate social division and personal humiliation you will be able to afford any two of the above, food, shelter, transport, but not the third, lest you lose arithmetical concentration, let alone any of life's little pleasures like a night out at the pictures or an hour and a half in the dentist's chair. Slavery also, unlike the good doctor, offered lifelong continuity of workplace companionship, continuity of address and extended family groupings and ample opportunities for community singing on the job in the green cotton-dotted hills of old Alabama. It seems like only yesterday.

The firmly smacking doctor, like his lovelorn salivating predecessor Malvolio, will not stand for any of this. You have to stay silent, divided, alone, insecure, on the move, scared, rattled, self-doubting, self-hating, near-suicidal and broke, the way he was in his pimpled youth as a lapsed Baptist university nerd, eagerly sniffing out the post-Christian cosmos and the post-Friedman fiscal mysteries and trying, apparently in vain, on his first wife's donated wages, some say, to learn to add. None of these cushy slave conditions for you. You're here to suffer in silence, create wealth for your natural masters, to spend on Fewwawis, gawages full of Fewwawis, that's how it opewates. It's perfectly clear. How dare you ask, young Master Twist, for more.

His toughly rational world system, however – it used to be called barbarism – does have in common with traditional American slavery the supreme employer's enshrined inalienable right to sexually interfere with his female underlings and fire them if they resist. For henceforth under Gradgrind Hewsonism probably any teenage female so harassed who then quits her job in a petticoat-rumpled dudgeon will probably, under Hewsonism, bear-pit capitalist Hewsonism, not then be allowed back on the dole, and so must choose to yield instead to the new unstated doctrine of come across or starve under this, the harasser's mandate, that is also playfully known as free enterprise bargaining.

I used in my foolishness to think that all of the above innumerate political and sociological stupidity was only a by-product of the dimly smirking Dr Hewson's boyishly charming inability to add or to foresee the inevitable economic consequences of his pure, dry, hard, proactively cannibalistic doctrines, raising prices for instance whilst simultaneously lowering salaries or, in other words, in two fell swoops abolishing the customer, but now I think it must go deeper than that, into a kind of leashed cruelty in his nature, one common to most serving Liberals, I think, who to the amateur anthropologist are a very odd lot indeed. When you see what in boarding schools the Liberals do to their own children, I used jokingly to say, you mustn't be surprised at what they plan to do to yours, and when you see, I now unjokingly add, what Dr Hewson at Christmas did to his own children, you must not be surprised at the senseless barbarism with which he threatens all of yours. For children after all in the Pymble capitalist cosmology to which Dr Hewson was a keen, late, fundamentalist convert are only expendable, deniable, reprogrammable adhesions to a true man's jungle will to conquer, smash, take over, asset-strip, sack, sell, rationalise and move on. Inconvenient encumbrances to be moved like draught pieces round the boarding schools and ski lodges and drug clinics and remedial American accountancy courses of this smog-fardled planet and seen only when unavoidable at weddings, family bankruptcy, the readings of disputed wills and maybe Christmas, though the good doctor plainly differs on this.

I used to imagine Dr Hewson as an insipidly handsome Dorian Gray whose decaying portrait up in the cobwebbed attic was eerily turning day by day and brushstroke by brushstroke into the ghastly face of Jeff Kennett. But today, this week, I realise I was wrong and the portrait in the Hewson attic, in the wing he is currently refusing to pay for, is that of Ebenezer Scrooge, the enemy of Christmas, the starver of waifs, the torturer of employees, the masterful monetarist captain of cotton mills in which infants work fourteen hours a day and drop dead at age twelve. Human kindness, bah humbug. Neighbourly concern, a job you like, bah humbug. And bah humbug, too, to the right to look round for other work and experiment with your destiny that used to be a human right, replaced last Saturday week with a human rate that is *half* of what it was, half human. Hewsonism – the taste of the latterly medieval, beast-flogged century to come. I thank the kindly God of Dickens and Roosevelt and Whitlam and Saint Vincent de Paul that this miserable thin man is bound soon to be put politically out of his misery – very soon.

July, 1992

Election Eve, 1993

A broadcast (in the manner of Mr W. Churchill)

It was a long year ago I spoke to you first on this wavelength of the then assumedly invincible Hewson plague and I counselled hope, assuring the many who had already almost surrendered alas in their hearts to what they feared was the inevitable that the dread virus of Ferrari barbarism, so fatal in Britain and New Zealand, might yet be stilled, and our decent Australian civilisation preserved against the monetarist buffetings of the straiteners and the punishers who would enslave our workforce and bind our souls to a set of numbers and flog us into service of their avarice and their sadism and their greed like the braying mules in Pinocchio who once were little boys. A long year ago I stood alone and spoke alone, with only Paul Keating in distant echo of my trumpet call. And the word spread, and from that dim genesis last March the light of our promised salvation reached its glad beams nationwide. This week victory was in sight. Tonight it is uncertain. Some say the moment, with yesterday's figures, has passed. It may be so. I hope, I pray and on the whole, grasping the larger hope, I believe that this vile infection of our national genius for kindly solutions will be expunged, and by tomorrow night, with a majority of five to thirteen – most probably nine – the crisis will be over, the boil lanced, the spreading cancer arrested, the day saved.

But if it does not turn out that way and darkness henceforth enshrouds our civility and our cheery hearts, and we again in its shadow revert to the wolf and the jackal and the shark and the leech that this late-blooming Thatcheristic viciousness would have us be, and Hewson, its wetly jogging prophet, would make us into. If we become again, as in other centuries and countries, but weasels fighting in a hole – no sisterhood, no brotherhood, no neighbourhood, no number other than one, no person other than me – and compulsory voting is, as threatened, abolished and election campaigns reduced to a week, and unions emasculated, and schools reduced to engines of profit for mindless philistine profiteers, and health services run on the noble principle of your money or your life, and boss and worker, as in olden times, again at each other's throats, and Kakadu mined, and the Daintree logged, and the Hawkesbury dead and rank and stinking, we shall in that stark hour of tyranny have learned a lesson too late, as did those foolish democratic Germans who believed that Hitler could be housetrained. The lesson is one of eternal vigilance – the price of liberty – of discerning tyranny when it threatens, and moving fast.

It is possible that I shall not speak to you again, since I am on the list, and satire and thought are unwelcome under Coalition broadcast guidelines, unless it is in some secret meeting of the democratic underground in a Bondi sewer or similar. If that is the case, and this is indeed my last such broadcast under the sort of democratic freedom for which till now we have shown, I fear, too little gratitude by half, I thank you for your attention and bid you sincerely . . . take care.

March, 1993

Election Aftermath, 1993

A broadcast (in the manner of Mr W. Churchill)

How sweet it is. Now that it is over, and the dread hour of our nation's utmost peril has passed and what last week seemed the onrolling wave of the future is this week but an ex-parrot in the ashcan of history, and we all, all of us who cared, with satisfaction watch the Liberal Party wash like a sackful of fighting rats over Niagara into the dark and boiling abyss and forgetful spume of time, leaderless, rudderless, aimless, futureless, crashed and splintered, doomed for a decade or more to roam like Lear through the elements howling and spread round blame and vengeance until the bleeding stops and their destiny is accepted as another nut religion at the frayed margin of human thought, like Scientology or voodoo or the Branch Davidian, another superseded species like the dodo or the orc or the giant wombat that the great god Darwin has judged and found unfit to survive. Now that it is clear that the Liberal Party only ever aberrantly gained and held power in Australia on the strength of those linked forgeries, the Red Menace and the Yellow Peril and the downward thrust of China and the migrant threat to employment and the imminence of nuclear conflict and the vital importance of the American alliance and the whiff of socio-political chaos that came with the Whitlam sacking, and never *once* achieved office with a policy that won on its merits, only ever a scare, now that it is clear, in a week when all but one of the State Liberal governments would, if tested, lose office and not regain it in our time, that the Liberal Party will probably soon be as extinct as the DLP, and the Labor Party in Rooseveltian consensus will overwhelm the coming century, it is appropriate, I think, to turn our sated thoughts elsewhere, to the Australian journalists who got it all so wrong.

What a pack of grovelling sycophantic mortgage-preserving rat finks they were. *Now* we know they always hated Hewson and believed his policies innumerate, his personality neurotic and divisive and his philosophy a branch-line of tyranny, but when this information was needed, *before* the election, it was withheld. They weren't there to ensure their country's good, or even to refer to it, only to pick the winner and grovel before his imminence like flowers flung before the advancing chariot of imperial Caesar, hailing his beastly simplicities as the shape of the inevitable future and not as the thing which they knew they were, which was the spirit of the jackal striving to return, with its slave wages for youth, its free market for health, its auctioning off to the lowest bidder for immediate incineration of all the advantages gained in a century by those who work with their hands, and with what incompetence they picked the winner despite the always *uncertain* polls of *undecided* voters in record numbers. They didn't matter, because no government, they said in that baseless, ebullient, lazy, vigorous manner they substituted for actual researched thought, no government had ever survived 11 per cent unemployment. No government. Ever.

Well, Roosevelt's government in 1936 did. Joe Lyons' government in 1934 and 1937 and Menzies' government in 1940 did. Baldwin's in Britain in 1935 did. Mackenzie King's in Canada in 1934 and 1938 did. Forbes' in New Zealand in 1932 did, and Savage's in 1938 did. And that was when unemployment was 25 or 30 per cent. Thatcher's in 1987 did, Major's in 1992 did. The majority of English-speaking governments in fact when so placed, in an unemployment haemorrhage, fared pretty well. One admittedly didn't: Malcolm Fraser's, possibly because he also achieved 11 per cent inflation, a Dismissal-traumatised electorate and a drought. So the pundits had, in short, based their whole premise of Liberal invincibility on a confidently asserted, unresearched untruth in defiance of what the voters through the polls were actually saying, polls in which the 18- to 24-year-olds – in short the unemployed *themselves* – were voting Labor by 50 to 37 per cent. *Hey hey hey, what a big surprise.* And now, unrepentant, they are tormenting the Caesar that once they hailed, analysing his failure in the same shrewd, no-nonsense cadences that so recently predicted his victory. If they can so confidently ignore an undecided vote of 15 per cent, an undecided vote that plainly, if you think about it, last election voted Labor, and then not ask the inevitable question: what will these ex-Labor voters, given this turbulent campaign, do now? Tiptoe home to Labor or vote for disruptive social change? If they can get things as obvious as a million undecided voters wrong, how good are they? How good in particular is Paul Lyneham, with his winning snickers and penetrating stares, soused on camera in some opinions, and cruel to the brink of giggling, Caligula dementia, when he especially is so wrong and yet so smart-arsed and determinedly protective, it seemed to me, of his mortgage and his Kingswood under an imminent Liberal government which he jeeringly predicted night after night just in case. And how good are they all, all the windy little sphincters, having consistently predicted a certain Liberal victory since 1986?

Backstage at Bankstown on election night with Keating and the true believers and the astonishment and the champagne, I felt for the first time politically useful and not just politically attentive, having with these eccentric broadcasts tempted the loathsome, bewigged, adulterous Hewson to intemperance, dimwittedness and deep unease. Pray God the feeling comes again. John Howard, the Liberal Party's answer to Ronnie Corbett, will win the leadership by three votes on Tuesday – as if it matters. I thank you.

March, 1993

The Liberal Party's Future

The once great Liberal Party has altered in its posture from that of the bully to that of the coward in a mere two weeks, a long time in politics, all of which reminds one, if one has a memory as long as mine, of Winston Churchill's judgment of the Germans: 'The Hun is always either at your throat or at your feet.' It was, I assess, a foolish day these pin-striped and arse-corked Malvolios, these uptight, punishing, cocktail-shaking and golf-carting foes of human dignity and human pleasure and democratic civility, took on the ABC and the multiculture and the young and the sick and the gay and the wives and mothers and the night nurses and the fast-fooders and the tourist trade and the non-drivers and the childless and the renters and the churches and the Japanese and the sugar-producers and, most of all, Bryan Brown. And even in this past week Hewson's best man at his most recent marriage, Michael Baum, that toxic Jiminy Cricket for whom there should be an urgent insecticide, has begun to say so. Ah yes. But one mustn't gloat, or even vengefully call Hewson a man mugged by reality, who'll do anything and say anything to retain the party leadership. Ah no, we must be careful, for a good democracy depends, it is true, very true, on a sound Opposition, and the Liberal Party Opposition is now in need of policies. May I suggest a few.

Atomic bomb Maralinga and warn the illiterates living there of the coming holocaust by dropping *leaflets*. Go to war in Vietnam on a forged invitation in order to stop Red China invading Australia and raping and enslaving its people. Choose young teenagers, otherwise unwilling to die in Vietnam, by pulling their birthdays out of a hat. Once you get them to Vietnam, spray them with Agent Orange. Outlaw the Communist Party and gaol its membership, defining as its membership anyone that two conferring Cabinet ministers declare is a communist. Confiscate all their worldly goods. Try to stop the building of the Sydney Opera House because it is a waste of public money. If you are unable to do this, make sure it is finished fast and cheaply. Fire the architect. Pull down Sydney and build half-empty skyscrapers everywhere. When this causes too much traffic on the bridge, try to stop the building of a harbour tunnel. Discontinue the midnight Manly ferry because it is a waste of public money. Stop all trains with sleeping compartments in those that go to tourist destinations like the Gold Coast. Abolish dining cars on trains. Make sure people now travel overnight on hundreds of buses down narrow highways, buses that could crash; keep them off the safe railways at all costs; deprive them of sleep.

Sack teachers and sell schools. Build prisons and employ police. Make sure no-one in prison gets any time off for good behaviour. Make sure they behave badly always, especially when they get out. Give everyone in the country who wants one the right to purchase a gun. Make sure that all gun-owners can, if they wish, be insane. Mine Kakadu. Log the Daintree. Dam the Franklin. Mine and process uranium. Pulverise forests. Sell the consequent woodchips cheap to Japan, and buy them back dear. Make sure all sexually harassing employers can fire female employees who do not agree to their terms. Call this enterprise bargaining. Pay night nurses no more than day nurses, thus ensuring that hospitals lack staff at night and more of the sick thus die.

These are classic Liberal Party policies that have worked before, and won elections before, and they should be tried again. I mean, the Liberal Party is about what *works*, isn't it? And these *worked*, didn't they? I mean, what else do they have to offer? What else have they ever offered? It's a friendly question. I thank you.

April, 1993

Truth in America

Like many others I am intrigued and revolted by America – God speed the San Andreas fault, I say still – not least because of its attitude in politics and journalism and jurisprudence to the historical truth of what is and is not so. At Ranch Apocalypse in Waco, Texas, for instance, the FBI, we are told, has now backed away from its original assertion that they saw David Koresh's disciples lighting fires all over the compound and heard them shooting thóse who tried to escape the subsequent holocaust, now that the newsreel film and the medical evidence have shown different.

Backed away? Does this mean someone will be charged with perjury and sent to gaol for twelve years? Of course not. It was just something that was tried on in the usual hyperbolic lying and smiling American way, like the many Elvis sightings, or the Kennedys' murder of Marilyn Monroe, or like President Clinton's recent astonishing public assertion that the Waco inferno was nothing more than a lot of religious fanatics murdering themselves. Will he be charged with breaching, as he most certainly did, the laws of sub judice in order to influence improperly the jury verdict in subsequent law cases, some of which carry a penalty of electrocution, and himself sent to gaol for seven years? Of course not. He was just trying it on.

In the Woody Allen custody case it has been established that Woody Allen may *not* have molested sexually his seven-year-old adopted daughter Dylan and that the videotape in which she alleged he did was repeatedly edited and her testimony probably contrived and prompted and coached by someone off-screen. Does this mean Mia Farrow will go to gaol for con-cocting perjured evidence of a heinous crime, conviction for which would almost certainly result in Woody Allen being beaten to death in prison? Of course not. She was just trying it on in the American way, as every American has a God-given right under bullshit capitalism to do, whatever the cost to another human soul.

This loss of the truth – and a sense for the need for the truth – in America is a result in part of a school system that emphasises the craft of salesmanship above all else, and a social and financial system that rewards little else other than salesmanship, enhancing oneself, putting up a good pitch, trying it on, a system that can make millions on the stock market out of the rumour that President Bush has just died after chundering on the Japanese Prime Minister, or that President Gorbachev has just been seriously wounded in his Crimea dacha, or that Pan Am is bankrupt, has no incentive to be any other way.

There is money in lying, big, big bucks, and pulp magazines that confidently assert Marilyn had Elvis's love child on Mars have close parallels in finance and law and politics and publishing. *My client has agreed in return for $7 million not to say in court that you molested your daughter . . . Although it was you that actually murdered Sharon Tate by stabbing her repeatedly to death, we will let you go free if you now agree to testify in court that Charlie Manson told you to . . . If you can put in a paragraph where John Lennon has a homosexual affair with Brian Epstein, this could be worth $10 million in world-wide sales. Now are you convinced he did not have this homosexual affair? . . . Danny Kaye and Larry Olivier, that smells like a million dollars . . . I've got a great idea, let's put J. Edgar Hoover in a dress . . . If we can start up a rumour that aspirin cures AIDS and run that rumour through the New York stock exchange for only one day . . .*

The worry of it is that genuine efforts to find the truth and print it, like Oliver Stone's film *JFK*, are now tarred with the same salacious brush that lately painted Hillary Clinton's cheerful fat consort as more sexually avid than Murphy's bull, as if it was even medically possible that one who roots all night and runs America all day could jog two miles each morning and still be overweight, and all condemned in the perceptive public mind to the same unvarying, disgusted unbelief.

So history is lost, and we begin not to know what *happened* when we need to. Under Christianity it was believed that a lie told under oath in court lost the liar his immortal soul, and there is a lot of truth in this, for if all that is known of ourselves by history are the lies we have told each other for money, momentary bursts of money, what can we, or our descendants, know in the end of what happened, and, lacking that knowledge, what are we worth?

We have truly lost our souls. A man on oath, said my old Lismore school-mate St Thomas More, is holding himself in his hands like water, and if he once but spreads his fingers he may never hope to find himself again. The truth, I think, *should* get in the way of a good story. It is essential.

April, 1993

An *Irish* Peyton Place

This broadcast is from Ireland, where this week at long last condoms were in Parliament declared to be not a contraceptive at all, at all, but a shield against AIDS, and so made legally available to everyone, don't you see, including five-year-olds. The responsible minister, Brendan Howlan, said he did not 'envisage the vending machines in schools, but mostly in lavatories and other places of entertainment'. I am as a startled traveller less pleased by this legislation than I might be since it will mean at the end of the day, I think, less Irish in the world, and less of that particular hypnotic kindness, and welcoming sympathy, and strength of heart, and gift of language beautifully spoken which touches up each word as it goes by, as the London Elizabethans did in times agone, treating speech as a kind of carnal delight and human contact as a privilege. There should not be less of this in the world but more.

The Irish have got so many things right in the way of breadth of culture and beauty of landscape and talkbalk radio and lack of snobbery and courtesy of discourse and freedom from burglary and from most known crime, apart from blowing up the English, that one wonders why they have not been studied as a social model by a wondering world. This of course is how we Australians were sixty years ago – I have seen the past and it works, Murwillumbah 1922, I'd put it, and it's looking great – and is a measure of how much we here cast away for metropolitan noise and Freudian unease and American hype and that vilest modern carcinoma, salesmanship, which, with its lies and money haemorrhage, eats all affordable happiness away.

So many Australian names go by: Lynch the stonemason, Daly the real estate agent, Chifley the veterinarian, that I am now considering a vivid novel set in a nonexistent small town in County Kerry where Paul Keating the ardent mercer is rivalled in his love for Carmen Lawrence, the principled milkmaid, by John Kerin the stern farmer, Neville Wran the well-heeled pub owner, and Jeff Kennett the IRA gunman on the run; their blighted love is urged on by Joan Kirner the kindly nun, Susan Ryan the life-wounded librarian and Ros Kelly the scarlet woman, and frowned on by Tom Uren the peat farmer, Rex Connor the stonemason, and Jim McClelland the drunken mayor; and Bronwyn Bishop, the mother superior, in the course of the story's contortions, crosses the path of Laurie Brereton the bookie's runner, Graham Richardson the bookie and Gerry Hand the fraught horse trainer and John Button the sly jockey, whose horse by a nose preserves their ancestral stone cottage from the rival property developers Jim Killen and Lionel Bowen and even from the curse of the spoiled priest, Brian Burke. Paul Kelly, Paul Murphy and Peter Collins do walk-ons as revolutionary theorists, Bob Carr as a dog trainer, and Fred Daly, Lionel Murphy, Frank Thring and Vince Gair as tinkers. Two good priests, John Bannon and Bill Hayden, and a shrewd barmaid, Kate Fitzpatrick, save the day.

The great thing about it is not only its genetic plausibility – this is what they might have been had their ancestors stayed home – but also the fact that you don't have to describe the characters, they are all already so vividly there, which makes you think how far-flung from our true destinies we in colonies are, and makes you pine for home.

May, 1993

Mabo

The Mabo case opened this week a cauldron of maggots that will wriggle all over republican Australia till the millennium's end and probably beyond. It has done so by merely raising the obvious, that six million (was it?) black people were here before we were, and by merely raising the question of what happened to them and to their seed, even unto the eighth and ninth generation of rape and poisoning and glaucoma and dirt and suicide and cheap sherry, and children severed from their mothers in suckling infancy and brought up in Panania in the way that they should go, and atomic radiation and long despair. And what moreover do we owe them for the loss of their earth and their heaven, their Genesis and their Revelation, their dreaming, for what in our pioneering ignorance we took from them, their totality, their all, and by merely stating our preferred question, *what do we owe them?* – real estate, with these five thousand niggling provisos – we have shown how shallow and venal and contemptible our white Western thinking is, and how little we understand.

It is like awarding the surviving relatives of the six million Jews that

Hitlerism slaughtered by gas and bullets a square metre each of the Black
Forest and declaring the blood guilt thus redeemed. It is like awarding the
surviving shattered relatives of the two million (was it?) slaughtered in the
killing fields of Pol Pot a postcard picture each of the Angkor Wat and declaring the murderous debt repaid. And these are not unreasonable comparisons when all over the placid paddocks of our conquered continent are our
killing fields, the poisoned waterholes ploughed under waving wheat and
lowing cows and nibbling sheep. It is why we whites will never be truly
comfortable here, since our forefathers' murderous ignorance then in the
light of our guilty knowledge now is no excuse. When we see the enormity
of what since our arrival has come to pass and the impossibility of repairing
or restoring what was so senselessly burnt and bludgeoned away, when
brindle relatives now trace their connection back to the same Irish rapist in
1869, and their ever-lightening skin to the gin-jockeys of the drunken, guf-
fawing generations of bored country teenagers, what can be restored, ever,
of what was once there?

I accompanied the Maralinga Royal Commission round the outback in
one of the great unfolding illuminations of my life in the all too portentous
year of 1984 – ignorance is strength, Big Brother does not err – and each
day watched amazed the grey bent head of Jim McClelland hearing distressed
under gum trees and tarpaulins and blue blazing skies the story of a people
unexpectedly atomic-bombed by another people unwilling even to apologise
for their haughty mistake, or to clean up their radio-active mess, on the
grounds that they had before then dropped warning leaflets down on tribal
people who could not read, excusing thus the black oily mist and the blindness and the coughing and the deaths of an unconsulted people whose homeland, whose country, whose earth, had been thus violated. And I asked in
my mind two things. One was: has ever racism taken a more dramatic form,
to deny the *existence* of a people at whom you are aiming nuclear weapons?
And the other was: has there ever been a people more blithe and jocular
and forgiving and mild as the Australian Aborigines? They plant no bombs
in public places. They take no hostages. They hijack no aeroplanes. They
machine-gun no magistrates on courthouse steps. They hang no Cabinet
ministers from the Harbour Bridge. They have every cause, they have every
right, but they do not.

They attend their funerals and make their jokes and drink their solace and
hold no grudges. The great sadness, of course, is that, in accordance with
our view of them, they are now exterminating themselves, with every white
wife taken, with every grey blanket knotted and tied round a teenage neck
in an outback cell, with every glue pot sniffed, they are yielding to the
hateful verdict of the British: *terra nullius*, they were never here.

Soon, too soon, the gene pool will be whitewashed, and a particular raw
genius will be gone from the world, and no restoration of barren desert

acreage with demeaning strings attached will alter that, I fear. We have a blood guilt on us, and it should be spoken, and a cenotaph built to the Aboriginal dead in this great war for the land, their mother. Like a repressed memory of childhood incest, it should be brought into the light for our nation's health, if we can call it a nation, if we dare call it a nation. How dare we?

June, 1993

Land Rights

Mabo persists, an expanding virus daily tempting fascism out of the rural cesspits, where it has long lain dormant, and out of suburban embitterment and sexual grief and career frustration, and on to John Laws' radio show.

Tim Fischer's all too characteristic assertion to the gaping primates of his hog-slaughtering party on the weekend that the Aboriginals should lose their land because they failed in five or six thousand years to invent the wheel, much as did Herr Fischer's German ancestors likewise fail to invent in their long Black Forest years the circular saw, has some interesting resonances to it, I think.

I could argue, for instance, with equal moral force that all white Queenslanders should lose their farms and quarter-acre blocks because they didn't have high school education till 1945, and, not knowing Shakespeare, therefore they are inherently undeserving of land according to the new arbitrary Ellis rule of thumb. Or that all white Tasmanians should lose their land because oral sex is still illegal there, and, not knowing fellatio or cunnilingus, they are irredeemably underinformed and beyond redemption. Or that the inability of all white Australians to track wild animals through dense bushland, or to catch cricket balls left-handed, or to unerringly dig in deserts for water, or to transmit thoughts from mind to mind, or simultaneously inhale and exhale while playing the didgeridoo, proves they are insufficiently evolved and therefore, by definition, expendable.

The idea, moreover, that Aborigines should lose their land because they sometimes drink alcohol to excess is fascinating. It could with equal dementia be argued that John Elliott should be hanged, drawn and quartered because he once manufactured beer and sold it in barrels. Saying Aborigines should lose their land because they didn't *use* it in a particular way that we can imagine, which is the received Lang Hancock and redneck Darwinian gospel, is like saying you should lose yours because you put a swimming pool in it instead of growing tomatoes. It is like saying the English should be deprived of England because for three thousand years they mined coal and burnt it instead of developing solar and hydro-electric power. It is like saying the white New Zealanders should be deprived of New Zealand because their forefathers exterminated the moa and with it a valuable tourist attraction, the undeserving bastards, or saying that the white North Americans should be deprived of North America because they wiped out the buffalo and with it a valuable export in the form of cutlets to the Hindus, who can't eat cow because of their religion but are crazy about buffalo, something the North Americans should have thought of at the time and didn't. Reprehensibly failed to think of it.

It's pretty easy, in short, to hold any culture guilty of not using land in the proper way. But to confiscate that land therefore is quite a step. Aborigines certainly have a lot of answer for. They exterminated the great wombat, they skinned, roasted and ate koalas, they knocked out teenagers' teeth without anaesthetic, they mutilated their penises in the interests of contraception, they failed to develop an adequate wine-growing industry in the Adelaide Hills and the Hunter Valley, and most reprehensibly they failed to dig a channel from the Great Australian Bight that would have replenished the inland sea, where they could have built tourist hotels and varoomed about in catamarans and hovercrafts, the idle shiftless bastards.

They failed most culpably, moreover, to upgrade the boomerang into an *Apollo* space shuttle in five thousand culpable years, and for this they stand condemned. But should they lose their earth for this, their birthright, their mother, the womb they immemorially inhabit and worship? And should they lose it to us, whose only claim to it is that we with poisoned wells and smoking firearms conquered it, murdering millions of them, old women, mothers and babies, murdering them down to a tiny democratic minority of only 200 000, and took it from them, slaughtering its forests and native animals and concreting its wetlands and letting loose on its ecology our clever imports of cane toads and rabbits and feral cats, and Bonds and Holmes à Courts and Strassers and Abels and Conrad Blacks? In what way do we mass murderers deserve it more than the murderees?

The true argument, that we were the strongest and the strong prevail, was never, of course, in these hypocrite decades plainly uttered. We assumed our divinely sanctioned rule, by right of conquest, of blood and gunpowder, poison and gold. But of course it is not in the Coalition's nature to tell the historical truth. They never have, and why should they start now, preferring pompous and poisonous historical fiction always, as did their Nazi predecessors with their 'Protocols of the Elders of Zion'. May they come to as sticky an end. But I fear they may not, I fear this black McCarthyism will work, and there is a great and murderous tumult to come.

June, 1993

Bloomsday

I took part this week in Bloomsday, the ritual recitation of James Joyce's great unreadable word-glutted novel *Ulysses* by certain elders of the tribe, Paul Murphy, Tom Keneally, Jim McClelland, Bob Carr, John Derum, Linda Cropper, and such camp-followers like myself of the Dublin diaspora as cannot let a 16 June go by without a Guinness or two and an Irish stew and a spiritual toe in the water of that immortal torrent of life in its glory and banality one morning and one afternoon and one night in Dublin of 1904. And I reflected as the day stumbled on – the queues more unpunctual, the dead-flat Aussie voices fraying in the deeps and doldrums and grammatical bogs of the Malory pastiche and the urinous midnight drunken totterings of Leopold Bloom in that glad morning of his cuckolding, so near and so long ago, and the Australian Opera and *Technicolour Dreamcoat* cast members and Ignatius Jones through a megaphone singing clear and high as the morning star 'Love's Old Sweet Song', 'The Harp That Once Through Tara's Halls', 'The Croppy Boy', 'The Last Rose of Summer', before the verbal tumbril resumed its lumbering pilgrimage toward the final fatal coital *yes* of Molly Bloom – that this was what civilisation meant, the passing on, the passing on of information, mere information, down the generations, information tedious and dreamscapes inscrutable and loves and wishes and follies and limericks and eructations to states unborn in accents yet unknown, the glimmering trivia of long knowledge that by transfusion flows in successive human veins, and comes to be called a culture, world literature, that which we share.

And this is why, I further reflected in that state public library before those state opera singers and the Arts Council-funded Patrick Healey of Dublin, whose ever-brimming voice engirdles the planet as no other in our time, among those state-paid academics, writers and actors and politicians, why I am a socialist still, and believe that no coition between market forces can ever engender a BBC or a Bolshoi Ballet or a National Gallery, and why I hold it a shame that James Joyce throughout life had to beg his friends for his daily crust of bread, as he birthed this gift of enormous life that, a thousand smuggled censorship court hearings later, we now imbibe, since Joyce and his even grubbier contemporary Henry Lawson deserved better than this, the literary equivalent of singing behind an upturned hat for a frugal supper of mockery and middle-class pity the songs that would define their race. This is why I am a socialist still, and believe the Royal Shakespeare Company and the Australian Opera and the Adelaide Festival to be greater than the sum of their box-office bottom lines, and believe with Frank Crean that with taxes we buy civilisation, that passing on of the radiances within us. And with every diminishment of tax we lose a little of it, a spur line, an old school, a travelling library, a local kindergarten, a Meals on Wheels, and as in Kennett's Victoria anarchy follows on that loss, the displaced schoolkids with flick knives fighting for a patch of cramped schoolyard, the hospitals evicting the dying for want of beds, the foreclosed mortgages of the lately jobless pitching families into the street, and the soul of the people shrinking for want of the bloodstream to the heart that is, or was once, their culture, their dreaming. This is why I am a socialist still, and believe that no unleashing of the greed of the rich is any substitute for these conjoined memories that define us and make us calm and proud, that no dropped crumb from the table of Christopher Skase will ever give us a Shakespeare or a Joyce, but the old dreary socialist order might, tax-fed, snob-fuelled, civilised, proud, unreconstructedly Whitlamite, a nation on the march and not just on the make.

If our taxes went up 10 per cent, much that we now mourn might be restored, including a lot of jobs, and the oxygen that feeds our nation's heartbeat might no longer asthmatically gasp toward its extinction. This is why I am a socialist still, and in this Bloomsweek recommend civilisation in place of the sado-monetarist barbarism that daily gnaws at the foundations of our remembered human gladness and will not let it be.

June, 1993

Bombing of Baghdad, Taxes

There isn't much that should be said about the latest rocket bombing of downtown Baghdad, and its attendant midnight slaughter of a famous female painter and her family in the incineration of her ultimate watercolours because, in an adjacent building, it is said, certain sinister officials, all of whom survived because they were unexpectedly not at work at midnight, once discussed, it is said, the murder of President Bush, and then didn't do it, all of which Bill Clinton felt good about – much as you or I might bomb, for instance, to smithereens the National Gallery in Canberra, and burn to cinders and ashes its Sidney Nolans and Albert Tuckers, because in an adjacent building certain sinister officials of the Treasury once discussed with Paul Keating the imposition of a GST, and then didn't do it. And then say that *we* felt good about it.

No, there isn't much that should be said beyond the insipid reflection that American foreign policy is, and after fifty years remains, as racist as it ever was, choosing as its bombing targets only the blacks, the Hispanics and the oriental heathens, not the pale-skinned Bosnian Serbs who are actually killing people, but only the swarthier Arab infidels who are thinking about it, and, oh yes, the Somalis, who are black as your hat. Curious that.

In fifty years of Cold War, not one Russian citizen was ever a bomb target, though literally millions of Chinese, Koreans, Vietnamese, Cambodians, Lebanese, Iranians, Iraquis, Grenadians, Panamanians, Angolans, Nicaraguans and Cubans were, and not one white South African. Curious that. So it goes, and so it goes.

In other news, Professor Fitzgerald in his contentious report this week lent force and strength to what I long have held, to wit, that we are not, and for years have not been, taxed enough. For tax is what keeps a nation going, I long have held, providing its art galleries and ABCs and orchestras and Medicare and sewerage and universities, and up till now its Qantas and Commonwealth Bank, and toll-free highways and soccer stadiums and Meals on Wheels and Telstra. Lack of tax is what runs these down, or sees them sold off for pittances to usurers and scrooges who strip and fillet them in profit's pointless name, throwing out of work their loyal employees, and onto the streets their grieving families, families that, while ever tax lasted, had had security lifelong, and food and warmth and a roof, good things now gone as the economy shrivels in market freedom's lousy pointless name, as any fool can see.

For any fool knows well what vampire economists like Friedman and Thatcher and Hewson, and mutton-pated pundits like Max and Peter Walsh, have long, too long, forgot, that the untaxed rich cannot be trusted to spend the money at home, preferring in Disneyland and Paris and Gstaad and Aspen and Tahiti and Tiffany's and Harrod's to spend the money that last year as tax sustained, for instance, a public servant grade 2 at the Water Board year round, fiddling with paperclips year round at his superfluous tenth-floor desk, and splashing with his children along Bondi Beach at weekends, and buying them fairy floss and helium balloons. Any fool knows well that however superfluous that public servant is, it is better that he be in work, and his children fed and secure, and his wife uncrazed by domestic calculation, even if his work is redundant and paid for out of the straining public purse, when the alternative is that purse being spent by Christopher Skase on a beachside mansion in Spain, which is the true result of lowering tax and pruning back the public service and freeing the market up for foreign bankers.

Any fool can see that a man no longer employed, and earning thirty thousand *less* than he earned last year, is a greater drain on the public purse than the tax, spread over millions of taxpayers, that it cost last year to keep him in work, and any fool knows well that the dislocated violent children of high schools closed and sold to save tax dollars, and the dislocated frightened nurses no longer at work in the hospitals closed and sold, and the fearful lonely old people no longer brought Meals on Wheels to save tax dollars, and the infants locked out of pre-schools closed and sold to save tax dollars, and the post offices closed, and the rail lines discontinued in efficiency's name, and the bus crashes caused by the rail lines discontinued and closed in efficiency's name, and the devastated men in their fifties no longer in work, are all in all, at day and century's end, a social cost too great for the money so saved in tax fore-gone and spent by Skase and Elliott and Bond in foreign ports on Van Goghs and Maseratis and champagne, as any fool can see.

Pray God the fools are heard, and the wisely monkeying Walshes shouted down before all that is worth having and worth keeping is lost. With taxes you buy civilisation, it was long ago said, and it is clear today – as the unemployed skinheads trade in drugs and guns and fascist rhetoric on the mean and meaner streets and in the murderous infected alleys of the filthy decaying cities of the West for want of the jobs that the tax dollars saved by the Walshes might have bought them, along with their spiritual sal-vation – it is clear that without taxes you inherit barbarity, the whirlwind, the moral void, the hell on earth for which there is now no absolution. I beg the government not to bring taxes down again. The cost, the cost thereof, is too great.

June, 1993

Liberal Tendencies

In the same week as a Coalition government in New South Wales abolished Happy Time, a Coalition Opposition in Queensland proposed a Coalition merger into one cheery kamikaze bomber crew singing 'God Save Queen Squidgy' and 'Watch Out Below', and a former Coalition leader in Canberra cast doubt on the Coalition leadership's ability to lead a small child up a luminous yellow line to an outdoor toilet, and Bronwyn Bishop said with a smirk that she had no leadership ambitions, and Ken Aldred, clearing his throat, tried to impose a frail consciousness of his surname onto a nation still unable to spell it, and Tony Packard tried to convince an over-attentive Manly doctor that the crime with which President Nixon all but achieved impeachment, to wit, electronically bugging the discourse of the unknowing, was a misdemeanour too trivial to bother with, though Nixon's name is blackened worldwide in the similitude of incarnate evil for all time because of it. Yes, ah yes.

In this ordinary run-of-the-mill disaster of a Coalition week, one like many another, my once but no longer famed glove puppet John Hewson, looking fit and well and only four feet shorter than the leering bitter dwarf of election night, fearlessly and frankly averred that the Coalition had a future and he was it, and that the Prime Minister, moreover, had gone missing and could anyone tell him where he was because he needed to avoid him whenever possible and sit quietly in a corner relearning his $3\times$ table and drubbing his lips. My sympathy for my fellow fundamentalist apostate Hewson, as is well known from the book I wrote about him, is very great, in particular because of his unfortunate innumeracy and emotional deafness, but for the Coalition parties I'm afraid it is less so. Not that the subject is of any great interest any more because they have no future, but their doom, their doom I say, is of their own contriving. I mean, abolishing Happy Time and bugging Kingswood customers and spending taxpayers' money on trans-European orgies of morning prayer in what shall hereinafter be known as the Packard-Pickard-Pickering-Peacock syndrome: *let me stuff it up for you.*

In all of these examples, the born-to-rule tendencies of the Liberals are made plain to us lesser earthlings of the south shore and the outer suburbs, as is the oil-rag-smelling multicultural heresy which Dr Hewson shrewdly labelled a mistake. We are not meant to matter and our right to vote is a rectifiable anomaly easily cured by, well, the abolition of by-elections in the case of Kennett or the decompulsifying of voting by the government fiat in the case of Coalition policy, closely followed by, I guess, as in England's case, the holding of elections on a Thursday before 6 p.m. so only the self-employed and the idle rich can make it to a booth, or, as in Greiner's case, with voting rules so elaborate – tick this ballot number, that one, but not both, fill out boxes one to eighty-four – that the elderly and uneducated are routinely, as in 1991, disenfranchised. That the Coalition have not, though they do not know it, legitimately won federal power since 1949. The '51, '54, '55 and '58 victories were won on Red scares and the growing lunacy of Dr Evatt; 1961 on a hundred aberrant communist preferences; 1963 – a shoo-in for Labor – on the coincidental unnerving assassination a week before of President Kennedy; 1966 on the manifest necessity of our participation in Vietnam lest the advancing Yellow Peril take Cape York and thereafter, enslaving all Australia, rape its women and fill them with slant-eyed, chopstick-wielding foetuses; 1969 by a vote which numerically Labor won; 1975 by the Whitlam sacking; 1977 by the Whitlam sacking; 1980 by a death duty scare, the rumour of a boom and nervy lisp of Bill Hayden; and that's it.

Never by policy, and never by force of truthful argument, have they done it, even with parliamentarians as talented as Howard and Peacock at their head. So a lack of policy – save that of closing hospitals, and charging road tolls, and sacking teachers and selling schools and abolishing learning, and gaoling Chamberlains, and confirming convicted buggers in our mother of parliaments, and abolishing Happy Time, and selling the Easter Showground, and banning condoms in prisons full of AIDS, and adopting after Mabo race-relations policies far in political arrears of those of the long-time ruling tyranny of South Africa, a lack of the kind of policy, in short, that rewards and uplifts and nourishes a nation, rather than scalding and straitening and punishing it – is at the heart of their impending doom, which I do not grieve. And no fiddling with mere leadership will avert it, least of all the retaining of John Hewson or the elevation of Bronwyn Bishop or Peter Reith, however artfully they re-order their respective thinning hair, none of whom in political terms would know if a Bondi tram were up them till the bell rang. No, nor Michael Kroger either, who would require something more of the dimension of the Southern Aurora to achieve the same realisation. You have to be a bit like that to join the Liberal Party of course, and they, alas, did, and they are among the best of them. By God, you should see the others.

July, 1993

Sexual McCarthyism

I was interested to hear it said on the Terry Lane show this week that a lot of social workers are currently in a quandary because of the numbers of young teenage children in their charge who regard what has happened to them not so much as traumatic sexual abuse as an interesting learning experience.

You are scarred for life! the social workers cried. *Emotionally crippled, you hear?*

Rubbish, the children replied, *it was heaps of fun, he was a nice man, sure beats dominoes.*

This raises, I think, for the first time in these broadcasts the difficult matter of sex, and how differently it is looked on by different eyes and ages and ideologies. A baby girl of nine months having her nappy changed by a male relative may regard any passing digital contact as par for the course. Her six-year-old sister playing doctor under the house with the five-year-old boy next door may regard it, correctly, as something kids do. Her ten-year-old cousin, dwindling under the hot caress of a Justice of the Supreme Court, is supposed by contrast to regard it as a fate worse than death. Well, that might be right sometimes, I suppose, especially if the assailant is one's father or one's uncle and the contact is frequent, unsought and threatening and compulsory and inescapable and penetration takes place, impregnation, abortion and so on, but we must be careful, I think, in these matters of degree. A lot of routine deflorations in the back seats of Holden Kingswoods do a lot worse psychological harm, and nobody goes to gaol, or should. A lot of wedding nights are a trauma from which life-long some women never recover, and yet their husbands are not clapped in irons on the second day of the honeymoon, nor should they be. If psychological harm is the true measure of it, as it should be, then examination results, rejection from the hockey team, the death of pets, teenage abortion, the first experience of oral sex through a bursting condom and the obscene catcalls of carloads of young passing hoons should be gaoling offences, and yet are not, and must not be.

Among all these things, unwanted sex is a difficult category, I think, a hard ask, and its definitions vary. What some regard as sexual harassment in the office, others regard as courtship. Many a happy marriage, it was wisely and lately said, was begun with a clumsy, unsought grope at the water cooler.

Who at the office Christmas party has not strayed? Should all of us then be locked up on Boxing Day for what abruptly ensued in the filing room between surprised and aroused but only half-consenting adults?

I worry how sexual abuse and sexual harassment have become, in the absence of the communist menace or nuclear attack, the great devils of our time, the motiveless root of all evil, the great Satan, as omnipresent as they are incurable. I worry about the truth. I worry about the tactical uses of these issues. I worry how Mia Farrow, for instance, like many women, plainly manufactured evidence of sexual abuse by Woody Allen, yet did not, when it was rejected by the judge, go to gaol for perjury. It is too easy a bogey, this malicious labelling of uncertain, spontaneous human response with the name of unforgivable sin. Was Humphrey Bogart's first carnal attempt at age forty-four on Lauren Bacall, then aged eighteen, sexual abuse? Why not? Was it then a good thing? Why? How can he be forgiven and Woody Allen not? Are you sure?

It is hard enough being on earth without having our ordinary fleshly humanity thus policed. If Woody Allen was denied sexual consent by Mia Farrow for two years, as he was, and responded, as he did, by sniffing carnally around the nearest adult female in his admittedly family group, it should perhaps result in partial forgiveness instead of a worldwide boycott, as some proposed, of his work, and seven years, as Mia Farrow proposed, in Alcatraz beating off sodomites and serial killers and CNN reporters, who deserve our understanding too, I guess. Sex is a difficult thing, a wounding thing, a troubling thing, at times – with AIDS, a lethal thing – but not an outrage, whomever it is offered by. It is not going to be stopped by headlines or legislation or Ita Buttrose or Bronwyn Bishop or ABC broadcasts on Saturday. In Elizabethan England, an era of lethal syphilis and almost certain pregnancy, it still went promiscuously, abundantly on, as it will now, and henceforth, whatever the sterile sisterhood says. A little mercy is required, a little dropping rain, a little knowledge, a little forgiveness, a little less government in the wayward bedrooms of the nation.

July, 1993

Gaol

There was yesterday in Israel a man called Demanjuk, long thought to be Ivan the Terrible of Treblinka, declared innocent because he wasn't Ivan the Terrible at all, just someone else. And this was a great relief to the government and people of Israel because they don't have capital punishment, you see, except for war criminals, and a hanged Ivan the Terrible might have aroused those people who want to bring back the rope in general, and embarrassed Israel's liberal image of itself, because Israel usually has no capital punishment, you see. Has no capital punishment? Tell it to the orphaned children fleeing under bombardment in Lebanon tonight, paying in blood and trauma for their neighbours' unproven sins. Tell it to the patriots of Gaza and the Golan Heights dying daily on the wire of concentration camps and slum settlements for the idea of an Arab Palestine. No capital punishment? Oh no. Just a lot of random death. Capital punishment is of course a horror but in the end it is only death, and death comes to us all in many ways.

I'm not sure the young black man who hangs himself in a prison cell in Longreach or Alice Springs has died a better death, despairing of himself and Australia and the universe, than one hanged by someone else. I'm not sure some raped young man in Long Bay, dying achingly of AIDS contracted while serving a short sentence for car theft, dies better either. Because it is not just in the literal sense of death by AIDS, or death by bludgeoning or skewering or a cut throat with a broken light bulb, that a prison sentence, however short, is so often the sentence of death. Because these days it is almost always a kind of death to go to gaol at all.

You do not get a job if you have been to gaol in these recession years. You do not easily keep the wife you had, or get access to your children. You are not automatically shouted drinks or made welcome in the old neighbourhood or in your parents' home. You might acquire another name and work in a mining camp in the north-west maybe, but that is also a kind of death, even if you do not bring with you the seeds of HIV or heroin addiction, a death you carry with you that will have its day.

To go to gaol is to die, probably. For what then should you be sent to gaol, with that spiritual or physical certainty before you? For being black and drunk and fighting mad in Redfern? For holding up a petrol station for the cash you need for heroin? For selling crack in schoolyards to improve your income level in a depressed free market economy? For date rape? For fiddling the books by computer for money to put on a horse? For child abuse? For availing oneself of an under-age brothel in Bangkok? For stealing a car, for evading parking fines, for resisting arrest, for swearing while drunk at a man in blue?

None of these things seem to me to be deserving of the death that mostly gaol is. Gaol itself, when you think about it, when you visit it, when you speak to its graduates, seems such a barbarity. Womanless, fearful, foul-smelling, menacing and paranoia-inducing at every turn, it takes from you the bulk of your twenties or your thirties and cuts the thread that is your life and delivers you nowhere. Gaol itself is an inconceivable obscenity, even before the AIDS and the heroin and the death by beating and the pack-rape in the prison corridor comes into it, and yet we are building gaols, and privatising them, and calling for truth in sentencing, and longer sentences, hard labour, an end to weekend passes-out with a girl. How dare we?

How dare we so arrogate to ourselves the fate of another human soul, whatever he has done? Any system of fine or surtax or community service or conjugal visit, any system even of being tortured all afternoon with a dentist's drill and then sent home, is better than this legislated hell, this death, this death in life, this dying after torture in dishonour and self-hate. The prison system of this country, the engine of black genocide and social Darwinism and unadmitted surburban sadism, should be burned to the ground. You see if I am right.

July, 1993

Civilisation

One may measure the strength of a culture, if one is of a mind to, by all those who are sufficiently trusting of their fellow citizens to know they are in no danger and the conversation will be agreeable, by which I mean hitchhikers. In Ireland, where I now am, there are hundreds of thousands of them, old men in waistcoats and watch-chains, off to visit a distant sister, young prim girls in an ankle-length skirts off to a jazz festival, nine-year-old boys off to see a schoolmate on the other side of town, all of them cheerfully and wittily ready to share their life and opinions and prejudices and prayers with any passing motorist, and to wryly and patiently hear out his. And he in turn will know he is in no danger from them of either assault or kidnapping or psychological strain, and what a miracle that is.

Another measure of a culture's strength, I believe, is in its art galleries. In the National Gallery in Dublin the Rembrandts and Monets and Rodins have no glass or plastic in front of them, standing nakedly open to both admiring gaze and, if it happens, vandalistic assault. But there will be no assault, no ink thrown, or ripping knives, or hammers battering marble noses, because the people can be trusted to know art is good, and culture a universal, never-drying well, and no harm should come to it.

Another measure is song and how much of it takes place in pubs and cafes and schools and churches and private houses, spontaneous joyous evidence that minute by minute the soul of the singer is being cured of its ache, song being the great consolation we have as a species for dying, the way we make it acceptable and sweet and grand.

This too is known in Ireland, where the happiness measure is greater than in any country I have visited, though I suspect some Caribbean islands rival it and some less fraught parts of Central Africa. Happiness. What a strange thing to say of a country steeped in medieval superstitions still, and contraceptive perturbation still, a chronically disastrous balance of payments, a sinking currency and an unemployment rate nearing 30 per cent. Happiness, visible, palpable everywhere. Can our measures be wrong and theirs right? Can a five-bedroom house with a water view be less important than we think? Are the things we care about in fact wrong? Can beauty of landscape and sensible clarity in architecture and modesty of life-purpose and good manners and richness of speech be more important than a flash car and jewellery and a million dollar mortgage and a private school education? It could.

There is something else as well, of course, which is not fashionable to mention. There is a uniculture, a monoculture. They all come from the one place, they are all part of the one big story, as the somewhat Irish Paul Keating lately said of Labor Party members. They share the same heroes and the same hope of a sweet engulfing national destiny. They know who to barrack for in sport and music and what they should be proud of. No multiculturalising of Ireland could improve it, no infusion of Palestinian shopkeepers or Vietnamese restaurateurs or PLO army sergeants or Californian Scientologists or plastic surgeons. It is what it is, the distillation of three thousand years of clear, self-knowing selfhood, a perfect capsule of oneness and genetic unanimity, one of the few such miracles on this earth. All who call for a multiculture, believing it like the free market to be the cure for all things, should look to America where all is multi, and ethnic and racial murder is ever on the streets, and then look to Ireland where all is one.

Identity means a great deal. Humans require for happiness, Robert Ardrey said, identity, stimulation and security, in that order, and we are fools to so rashly fritter identity away on the stupid theory that all casseroles are good, that clitorectomising Mohammedans inserted into the Aboriginal communities of Western Australia would do those communities good, that middle-western Americans permitted to migrate on ten dollar fares into the mountains of Bali would give that over-traditional country the exogamous boost it needs, that Jews and Arabs in Palestine will eventually settle down.

Some things should be left as they are, and most things, alas, are not. There is nothing to be done about it, of course, in a world already muddy with cultural confusion, but to look with mourning on Ireland and the Ukraine and the Caribbean and the few un-interbred Aboriginal poleis on the islands above Darwin for what the world once had, and lost.

August, 1993

Europe

Travelling in Europe, a pleasurable tyranny, leaves one's Antipodean self-esteem lower than it was before. All around one, man's magnificence, triumphal mural after triumphal monument, asks of the grimy pilgrim, *what have you done lately, knucklehead? Painted any Sistine Chapels? Designed any Moscow Undergrounds? You dim, random swarm of swamp genes, how dare you pass this way, even once.* Faced with the Chartres Cathedral, or even the Trevi Fountain, one's pride in Aboriginal rock paintings, or even Sidney Nolan, frankly fades. There is an obviousness about European art – Christ Risen, Aurelius By Battle Uplifted – that makes pale the edgy soulfulness of us colonial come-latelies. *Why not just get on with it?* it seems to be crying out. Oscar and *who*? The Tree of *what*? For me this underlines the Australian problem, of being a huge country that borders on nowhere. France feels more French because the bordering Italians, Germans and Spaniards are comparable but different, and of course inferior, as the French know. My God, we lack a space shuttle and a Buckingham Palace both. How can we hope to compete? Let us not even try. Let us grovel instead before the conquering lords of capitalism and hope they throw the odd chewed bone our way – a Mitsubishi factory, a McDonald's franchise, a local licence to market foreign cheese and import mangos and bananas – so we quickly forget, as colonies do, what else we might uniquely have made here and sold to the world. Five more Opera Houses, an AIDS cure, a sun-fuelled electric battery, an edible saltbush, a singing oyster, a foul-mouthed Shakespeare-reciting white cockatoo, a Judy Davis broadcast theatre, an underwater Great Barrier Reef gambling casino, and Strop and Hoges' nightclub. We decline, as colonies do, into imitative sycophancy, lie-back-and-enjoy-it capitulation to what we then see as the inevitable, our economic and cultural death, which is a pity.

What is clear from what makes Europe run, the palaces, cathedrals, galleries, gigantic statuary and vast fountained squares that tourists flood through, each of which would have been blasted in its time as a waste of public money by the Hewsons, Kennetts, Greiners and Peter Walshes of their medieval day, is that only through profligate squandering on artistic indulgence and local pride is a country's economy assured. It is only Windsor Castle, not the cost-efficient South London gasworks, that people come to see. The Statue of Liberty, not the New York drainage system; the Sydney Opera House, not the Enmore Town Hall.

Standing this very day under Michelangelo's David, one among the ten million people every year who spend ten dollars each to stand and gaze up at its gigantic casual tenderness, plus twenty more dollars on the postcards and guidebooks, and two hundred more on the hotels, it became clear to me that the sole engine of modern economics *is* this tourist-drawing artistic indulgence, and if Australia does not swiftly provide itself with eight or ten more Opera Houses or Adelaide Festivals or Sydney Dance Companies or Kakadu National Parks or Crocodile Dundees doing back flips on water skis, it will go to the wall. Nothing else so durably earns money as this artistic indulgence unless, like the Grand Canyon or Niagara Falls, it is its equivalent in landscape or national waterworks. Britain without its Royal Shakespeare Company and National Theatre and Buckingham Palace and National Gallery and their international outrider, the BBC, would be bankrupt, and so will we be soon, like Lithuania or Somalia or Upper Volta or Tierra del Fuego, all of which have sewage farms that are the model of economic privatised efficiency and would bring tears of pleasure to poor deluded Nick Greiner's eyes. We in Australia had better get on with it soon, with something that *really* counts in dollar terms, like a Bayreuth Ring Cycle, or go under.

August, 1993

Hewson's Ruin, Fred's Funeral and Joh's Jury

If ever proof were given of the importance of lighting and make-up and lapel design and colour control and script and wakefulness in the visual media it was by *The* (ha!) *Great Debate.* Keating, sallow, raisin-eyed, waxen, faltering and shifty in a sharp suit at such odds with the turpid background that I immediately suspected the purblind studio director of designing Parliament House, was further harassed by the compositions, which made his head marginally smaller than Hewson's and Hewson's blue decisive crazy eyes and broadly jutting Kirk Douglas jaw impressive and dominant and almost agreeably demonic. Things known to every third-rate camera person are continuing mysteries, it seems, to the Gore Hill apparatchik-in-charge-of-unwitting-assassinations or whatever his or her current job description is and he or she should enrol in a film school weekend course urgently, and learn basics, if he or she hasn't already and taken Liberal Party coin.

I've known Keating in a small, ships-passing way for sixteen years and like him for his hopeful unschooled feisty combative brightness and his gang-banger's relationship with our mother tongue and his Labor heart and, while simultaneously detesting his ideologically adulterous ten-year fling in the eighties with the Gekkos and the trickledowners and his needless car-boot sale of much of Australia to the grossest foreign bidders, I wish him well since I believe him in the end to be a flawed good man with some brimming, foul-mouthed promise of hope, albeit one fallen among bankers, and much unlike Bob Hawke, whose heart and mind are made of gilded plasticine. And to see him so reduced by mere lighting and make-up was a great pain to me, not least because my fortunes hang on his government's good will.

That the ABC should so erode its earthly saviour in his hour of trial is, unfortunately, no surprise to me. The capacity for suicide of that riesling-sodden nest of castrates is infinite and subtle, every day a little death, a tactical retreat, every hour a tiny crumbling sell-out to the barbarous dark that, like the great Nothing in *The Never Ending Story,* may soon engulf us all. May all responsible be locked in a lift all night with Frank Crook and a pint of Diet Coke.

It was in this gloomy mood I went the following day to Fred Hollows' funeral with Tracey Ellison and Paul Murphy and my son Jack and his lifelong holiday companion Ben Hollows and most of Australia's living legends and national treasures and also-rans, and the common multitudes taught to love him as I with regret and closer knowledge could not, and during its clangorous, moving tribal enormities, 'The Lord's My Shepherd', 'Song of Joy', conceived a poem in Larkin style called 'Small Talk at State Funerals'.

I looked around the high-reaching pillars, and heard the choir, and numbered the famed faces as they sat and patiently listened as Frank Hardy railed at their Marxist shortcomings and Fred in his coffin did not move, and felt that this was one of those vast enclosing moments by which an era is defined, a moment that should be carved in bas-relief on a pharaoh's tomb. Whitlam, Hawke and Hewson in the one short pew. Two rows in front of Hewson, Keating, and between them Leo McLeay, the cause of the trouble. Carr and Fahey, Schacht and Loosely, Uren and Chaney, Keneally and Bryan Brown. Fred's brother high on the rostrum saying God Bless Fred. I thought of the funeral of Edward VII and all of the crowned heads of Europe celebrating an era soon to pass. It was good to be there, in a good seat, drinking in the heaven-supplicating architecture and the music and the printing (and the singing) of the legend, and moved enough to refrain from asking Gaby Hollows to tell the cameras Fred would have voted Labor.

I went out, gave radio interviews, missed Keating, turned my back on Bob Hawke, handshook Whitlam and went and drank Guinness alone. The days grow short when you reach September. Once when the communion wine and the Eucharist came round I murmured to Tracey, 'Another fine mess you've got me into, Stanley', and the whole pew broke up. You've got to laugh, as Fred did till the end, but death's a serious business I've decided, and there's a lot of it about.

Joh's Jury was astonishing and confronting evidence of our great fresh-hearted Australian dislike of bullshit and political rhetoric, and our willingness to face unpleasant human truths (it's hard to imagine for instance parallel dramatisations of Iran–Contra or the contaminated blood scandal in Paris), and of such historic and political force as to be (as were *Platoon* and *Wall Street*) a bit difficult to judge as mere art. The clear and energetic performances, good writing, great research, shapely hectic direction and moral force did not however erase an impression of journalism dressed up as high drama (this of course may be a new Australian genre, a very Australian one), and the gross tonnage of Joh-shaped plasticine on the Dudley Mooreish face of Gerry Connolly proved a poor and slightly droidish substitute for, say, casting Frank Wilson, a dead ringer, and copping, if need be, a worse mimicry of that unique and stately peasant voice. These few niggles, however, are but fleas on a charging rhinoceros of national righteousness that altered, I believe, our entire history and killed off at last, thank God, the National Party, and a special Oscar should be struck in its praise.

March, 1993

The Monarchy Thus Far

This week, on the White House lawn, we heard that marvellous deep and grieving voice of Yitzhak Rabin, conqueror himself of Gaza and master twice in these long hard years of the armies of Israel, in a speech of biblical force – *Oh Jonathan, thou wert slain in thine high places* – and Shakespearian intensity – *tomorrow and tomorrow and tomorrow* – speak of the stains of battle and the eyes of those bereaved of their sons by these long years of strife, eyes he could no longer meet as the coffins descended and the women and the old men wept for shame of the history of which he was so long a part, as warrior and general and commander of needless regiments of darkness, and heard him then cry out, *Enough of blood and tears! Enough!* It was tempting perhaps for those of us who watched and listened and shimmered with the moment to think, At last, here is an end, at length some promised good, an end to sacrifice and the ceaseless reaping of the whirlwind of the children of Esau and Jacob, an end to the bloody self-lacerating spirit of Masada and a time to gather into the barn, as Ecclesiastes recommended in this, the appropriate season, the meagre autumn harvest at last, and sleep at last a long sleep of exhausted calm.

But we have seen such resolutions before, and such happy endings, such handshakes and such pleasing words, and we should be wary, I think, of immediate inordinate rejoicing, for we rejoiced even so when the Berlin Wall came down and the Soviet empire was sundered and the Cold War vanished in a moment, in the blinking of an eye. And what have we now, in the wake of that high day of universal peace: the tottering economies of Europe, the stuttering machine guns of Sarajevo ethnically cleansing the night of human impurities, and the stealthy armies of Georgia moving ever by night, and Lithuania bankrupt, and the Baltic states a shambles, the Moslem republics in bloody *jihad*, and the once calm streets of Moscow a nightly chaos of armed and warring mafiosi, armed with pistols bought from destitute army officers financially ruined by Yeltsin's Great Leap Forward into 2000 per cent inflation, and families freezing on the streets. For hell, as our grandmothers used to say, is paved with good intentions.

Seventy per cent of Russians want the Soviet Union back now, and no wonder. Free hospitals, a certain roof, an assured job, streets at midnight free

of brigands, the best live theatre, ballet, circuses, parklands and urban transport on the planet, along with Gorbachev-free speech and fine black bread
and pickled garlic and red champagne and endless romantic good fellowship
and disorderly cheer. Limitless free education for the young and generous
pensions for the old now seem, in view of the corrupt and murderous stand-
over capitalism that followed, along with bubonic plague and AIDS and civil
war, an ill-lost paradise and golden age of egalitarian peace. So we flirt with
change in this new world, I think, I really think, at our peril, as even the ten
thousand blacks that have died in South Africa since the release of Nelson
Mandela have in their last crazed seconds found, as the burning tyres about
their necks have seared out their eyes, and they screamed and screamed: Is
this the looked-for end? Is this the promised good?

I worry as well, as a matter of fact, about our Australian republic, and
wonder if such nose-thumbing change is also a mistake, and if in the imminent popularly elected presidency of Derryn Hinch, or Bruce Ruxton, or
Geraldine Doogue, or Gary Foley, or, aargh, John Laws, or Malcolm Turnbull, with reserve powers to sack governments and deploy armies and declare
war, we will have our promised good, our looked-for end. Maybe in the
simple genetic *in*justice of impotent royalty across the water, we have all
that we need *if* elective majesty has such terrors in it, like Ronald Reagan,
and Adolf Hitler, and Margaret Thatcher, and Idi Amin Dada, and Lee Kuan
Yew. Monarchy as a system has done no harm that I can see to Holland or
Sweden or Norway or Denmark or Canada, these best and fairest societies
in human history, and its removal has done much harm to most of Africa,
or this is what I believe.

It is worth a thought at any rate. We must watch out for change, I think,
enormous declarative icon-smashing change, for once the door is opened,
what winds that then would blow may take the house away.

September, 1993

Boris Yeltsin and John Kerr

The famous Olympic victory, which I alone with signal prescience utterly
failed to foresee, provides proof at any rate of Ellis's thirteenth law, lately
composed beneath the soaring wonders of Michelangelo's Sistine Chapel,

that since most national economies depend on tourism, and all tourism in turn depends on government-subsidised acts of wasteful extravagance and prodigal expenditure of taxpayers' money, like the Opera House or the Statue of Liberty or the Albert Hall, all economy therefore should be based on conspicuous waste, and any reduction in government expenditure on, for instance, sleeper trains will only hurt the overall economy it was supposed to save, and economic rationalism therefore, from this Olympic perspective, is even more idiotic than it seemed before.

To other matters. Like all who have gone there for more than an hour or two, I am a lover of Russia. And like most who have once drunk in its rare sweet savours, I am a lover, too, and a fellow traveller of the Gorbachev spring, and like all who care about humanity tonight, and abhor chaos and blood and blundering tyranny, I am appalled by what is transpiring. As autumn descends on that loveliest of parkland cultures, and the guns are oiled, and the tank treads rasped into battle readiness, and the heaven-probing nuclear warheads, aiming God knows where – Siberia perhaps, Georgia – await the signal to fire from the button in Boris Yeltsin's briefcase, and the shriek and growl of secret police are heard once more beneath the onion domes, and the impotent protesters gather by torchlight again in the square (the Russian people, Solzhenitsyn said, are a rabble in search of a whip) tonight, holding the whip hand high above that curiously timid and pious people, its latest Ivan roars out the latest superstition of the free market, the economical alternative that the polls this week democratically judged to be even worse than communism, and threatens with bloody extinction all in his way.

And the Americans, with their usual gift for backing history's viler losers – Stalin they long called Uncle Joe, Khrushchev they always execrated – have mistaken this cruel buffoon, because of his fashionable capitalistic prattle, for a courageous democrat, rewarding his each act of putsch and ballot-stuffing and constitution-breaching and media seizure with bouquets and billions and hymns of praise, much as they would Bill Clinton if he sacked Congress, ruled by decree and tried to institute Marxism overnight. For make no mistake, what is happening in that mighty city is the usual police-state birthing process wherein the people reject the disastrous policies of a foolish demagogue, and the foolish demagogue then brings in the army to punish them for their perception, and soon elections are cancelled and Opposition leaders are under torture, and billions in aid will make its way from America to this, the latest anti-communist crook and strong man.

It has nothing to do with democracy and everything to do, I fear, with the death gasps of economic rationalism, which, having for ten years laid waste the known world like some strange dark virus that simultaneously numbs the brain while emptying the wallet, is at last in Lithuania and Poland

and Russia being found out and correctly strangled in its crib. The only mystery is why any shred of belief persists any more in the free market – perhaps it should be called the slave market – that has brought all these cruel wonders to pass, in the child brothels of Bangkok, and the living skeletons of Somalia, and the stilled factories of Scotland and the dole-numbed streets of Blacktown and Brixton and the Bronx, a belief that is clutched at with all the dimwitted fervour of fundamentalist faith.

Well, faith is the substance of things hoped for, St Paul said, the evidence of things not seen, and in the ferocious faith which gleams tonight in the long dull fleshy face of Boris Yeltsin – Big Brother, we love Big Brother – freedom is slavery, ignorance is strength, Big Brother was always with us, Big Brother is forever, and as the tanks prepare to roll, and the towers of democracy crumble in fleeting moonlight, and the button in the briefcase awaits its apocalyptic destiny, and the leaves blow, and the snow settles, we can see the substance of the horror of rich and poor and freedom lost that unless resisted may yet destroy us all.

I want you to imagine tonight, if you will, that it is 1975 again, and Sir John Kerr has just prorogued Parliament, as he did then, giving as his reason, as he did then, Parliament's unwillingness to enact necessary legislation, and therefore calling fresh elections. I want you further to imagine that Parliament, as in fact nearly happened, refuses to be prorogued, and continues to sit, and appeals to the Queen to overrule Sir John Kerr's decision, as in fact it did. I ask you then to imagine that the Queen does overrule his decision, legally empowering the democratically elected Prime Minister and his duly constituted Cabinet to go about their business and their lawful occasions. I ask you now to imagine that Sir John Kerr unlawfully decides to use his reserve powers, and calls out the army, and with it surrounds Parliament House, cutting off its electricity, telephones and water, and preventing food from being delivered to its canteen, putting barbed wire around it and ordering it with loud hailers to come out, to abolish itself, because he is now unilaterally inventing a new constitution under which its successor will be elected, a constitution, incidentally, giving greater powers to himself.

I want you to imagine Parliament resists, declaring correctly that this assault on itself is illegal and proposing to defend itself with gunfire if necessary. I want you then to imagine that a battle ensues with tanks and mortars and the defending rifle-fire of the duly elected members of the House of Representatives and the Senate, the building on fire and guerilla bands of loyal public servants attacking the crack army troops from behind. I want you to imagine that several army units defect to the side of the lawfully elected government and the slaughter increases. Soon, after a long murderous day and night with a hundred duly elected members of Parliament dead, Jim Cairns, Clyde Cameron, Kim Beazley, Fred Daly, and three hundred assorted others, drink waiters, *Hansard* typists, wounded, Gough Whitlam, the Prime Minister, and Frank Crean, the deputy Prime Minister, come out with their hands on their heads. They are then taken to prison and charged with treason, the Labor Party abolished and prevented from contesting the new election held under a new constitution that gives all power to Sir John Kerr; the *Sydney Morning Herald*, the *Australian*, the *National Times* all gagged; and all television required to play triumphal music under Kerr's every utterance.

Well, this is precisely the equivalent historically of what happened *this* week in Russia, and with, moreover, the warm approval of it by not only the Americans – that can be easily understood – but of the present Labor government of Australia, whose current Prime Minister, Paul Keating, was himself in 1975, along with Gough Whitlam, sacked as Minister for Minerals and Energy by Sir John Kerr. The stated reason for approving this constitutional atrocity, correctly declared unlawful by Russia's own equivalent of the Queen, the Constitutional Court, was that Russia's own Sir John Kerr lookalike, Boris Yeltsin, favours economic rationalism and will have it by God, or by hook or by crook, in the face of which manifest necessity all democracy should of course now cease. Economic rationalism, whose basic tenet is that, if you have a choice between taxing foreigners and taxing Australians, you should tax Australians, or if you have a choice between taxing foreign products and putting Australians out of work, you should put Australians out of work. It is of course a policy that is manifestly insane, and the Russians know it, having, with a 1000 per cent inflation rate and massive unemployment, found it out the hard way, very quickly, and are rightly resisting it, and armies are being called out to enforce it.

Economic rationalism is dying the world over, but like a wounded tiger it is now at its most dangerous, the massed armaments of Wall Street are after humankind, trying to staunch their mathematical humiliation with buckets of blood and more blood, and smouldering democracies everywhere, and we should resist them as heroically as did Rutskoy and Uzbelatov and like them try to prevail, for the battle is now joined and the outcome uncertain. Keep the scarlet banner high. It stands for humankind.

September, 1993

BOOK SIX

Metropolitan Distractions

Bob Mitchum Recalled

We celebrated Bob Mitchum's life and achievements at the Papillon restaurant with appropriate reverence, Dick Hall bringing a bottle of genuine home-town ketchup in memory of the great man's famous appearance clad only in that condiment at a fancy dress party to which he declared he was a hot dog, and Al Clark bringing a rare CD of Mitchum vigorously singing certain calypso standards, 'Momma Looka Boo Boo' and others, in what can only be described as a manly baritone yelp. The management having amazingly, or so they said, no CD-player, I lurched out into the street and bought one, leaving less cash than it cost and my passport with a kindly perspiring young Italian in an electrical shop, and ringing my staggered agent Rose Creswell, who was furious not to have been invited, for more money. This money for long hours failed to arrive while my credibility dwindled and much good red was consumed and the bill mounted and Mitchum's macho shriek and attendant bongos dismayed the surrounding unbopping clientele, some of them heirs to old money.

Richard Brennan was there (of course) and Ross Matthews and Michael Thornhill and Errol Sullivan and the agelessly desirable Penne Hackforth-Jones and Maggie Fink. And Barry Parrish, who spent most of the afternoon sitting bolt upright and sleeping profoundly after reciting a good deal of Alfred Lord Tennyson, whose birthday Mitchum shared. The food was stupendous and the decor (high Jamesian ceilings, unpretentious chairs and plain tablecloths in the style of twenties Manhattan) so beguiling that we proclaimed it the new Algonquin, and to that end begged of the largely fearless management a big round table (I offered to buy one, but that proved unnecessary) and planned a regular lunch of contentious affable people there once a month. My money arrived round 4.30 and I was able both to pay my share of the stupendous bill and to retrieve my passport from the young man in the electrical store who fell to his knees and wept on my hand, and to drift off up York Street serenely bearing an armful of ghetto blaster and reflecting that life can be good in even one's fifties given old acquaintance, alcohol and a notional cause for drinking it. Mankind's great recurrent question, as I have often said, is where's the party, and its eternal consuming task the confection of a moral excuse for having one. In Ireland it is simpler, and one merely turns up at the pub and begins the singing early, the theological contention round eight and the fist fights at nine-thirty.

For life is joyous, comrades, as John Hepworth's recorded voice remarked at his funeral, and it's brief, too, as the extinguishment of the lovely, leggy Princess Di so shockingly showed. It was interesting, I thought, to see how little her infamous love life mattered in the stunned hours after her ending (during two of which I was obliged by the *Courier Mail* to write fifteen hundred words) and how much her good works did, in a strangely resonant further parallel with Evita that should set Andrew Lloyd Webber thinking, if that's the right word for what Andrew does. People don't mind wayward sexual behaviour at all any more, I think. They understand how it happens, if the night is right and the moon is full and the ocean calm, and the peekaboo prurience of the Murdoch and post-Murdoch press (what I called in my piece 'a sort of glittering pornography') more a careful marketing construct than an actual customer need. No-one cares much any more if Blanche and Bob do it three times a week, or not, and I surely doubt they ever did.

. . . Al Clark ran into Blanche on the sidewalk on his way to our second round table Papillon lunch and would have invited her along but for his premonition that she would dash a good deal of costly claret in my face, and we abused him roundly for his British reticence, for it might have been fun. Rose was invited this time and tardily, amazingly, sent her regrets, so till Catriona Hughes turned up looking amused and feisty at four ('I quite like your *Herald* column,' she said, 'but why do they print it under a picture of Brian Johns?'), the only female present was Alexandra Long who wrote (with Algonquin brilliance) *Thank God He Met Lizzie* and responded gamely when we suggested she and Cherie Nolan should now pose nude together as a career move matching Samantha Lang's glamorous strapless forties cleavage in the Saturday colour supplement. 'I'd do it,' she said, 'but Cherie would never *speak* to me again.'

The day was long and memorable and it all escapes me now, though I do recall turning up fairly fortified at the Thurless for several Guinnesses at six to discuss our pub drama *Fred Daly Tonight* and accusing a mortified young man there of being a Liberal and storming out and falling into a taxi and sleeping like a corpse, in a hotel I thought a better alternative on the whole to driving thirty miles home. Thank God I am habitually abstemious or this way of life could prove tempting. In the Northern Beaches it's all hot Horlicks and to bed at nine with an improving book and walking the dogs and writing fucking literature.

Life is joyous, comrades, and very brief. Pray God we all make Mitchum's eighty-first. Mamma looka booboo and out.

September, 1997

Ken Branagh

Ken Branagh had had another lousy fortnight (L.A., London, Paris and Sydney in nine groggy days) and his smile when I met him (cocktails, Greater Union, jet lag, a harbourside roof) was a tad forced. He was nice to me nonetheless, pleased that my ten-year-old son had liked *Henry V* and full of cautious praise for its author, an Englishman of a certain local repute. And he is an unexpected pleasure to look at, a beautiful man, like a Michelangelo archangel in designer stubble.

He came and he went, having survived without imploding intimate dialogues that began, 'Did you find our projection facilities to your satisfaction, er, Kenneth?' and was later seen on a film set in deep fraternal colloquy with Dennis Whitburn, the dread fate of many unwarned blow-ins who thereafter learn fast.

I'd like to have said a bit more to him (though less, of course, than Dennis), like, mind how you go, have a nice life, don't *care* too much, keep working on the stage. He's a stupendous talent of possibly Wellesian portent and the barracuda pool he's just dived into is deeply anxious that he be power-munched down to his wishbone with vigour and swiftness and his spreading bloodstains flushed away lest his chromosomes prove infectious.

This is a quaint and torrid way of saying that *Mary Shelley's Frankenstein* is a good film (though that's not the point) and if Jane Campion, say, had been its writer-director it would have been hailed as a masterpiece of resuscitated nineteenth-century femino-Gothic sensibility (which it is) by fools too frightened to say aught else, and any faults it might *seem* to have are those of Mary Shelley, and how well and how tactfully Ms Campion has worked around them.

But they're not saying any of that, no way, because the word is out and the fix is in – and Branagh is in the cross-hairs of an industry that is always gangsterly and murderous in the face of many-tentacled talent, as Von Stroheim, Chaplin, Renoir, Preston Sturges, Welles and, lately, Woody Allen found. These arty bastards, you see, who write *and* direct *and* act, all at Academy Award level, put honest tradesmen like us and Ray Stark out of work. Because they can do *everything* they don't need anyone to *mediate* and the true trade of Hollywood is not making things but *mediating*, mediating between septumless brain-dead egomaniacs and Caligula, their agent. In such a crazed metropolis a mild-mannered, punctual, economical, profit-making and Oscar-smelling Proteus like Branagh is as welcome as a breeze from Three Mile Island. He has to be stopped. He will be. *If this film works he may be fucking unstoppable!*

So the word went out, *Frankenstein* is a turkey, pass it on. He has to be stopped! *Frankenstein* DOA, *Frankenstein* neck deep in doo-doo, so the millions who therefore never see it will believe that's what it is. That's how it works. Fashions are confidently declared and the film journalists leap like a chorus line into appropriate, sneering posture, ta-daa. And competing homoerotic rubbish like *Interview with the Vampire* minces past without a dissenting murmur because, well, it comes from the system, doesn't it, and Branagh is not part of the *system*, and he must be bloodily expunged.

It's just possible he was set up, the way Puttnam was, Sir Puttnam sorry (hello David), to slaughter himself and, expiring, bleed all over a canvas far too titanic for a mere puny Englishman, as Puttnam with Columbia and later Hugh Hudson with *Revolution* did, but it's also (yes) possible he (yes) misjudged the public mood for patched faces and ripped hearts held high above the butchered bosoms of brides on wedding nights of the full moon and for this, maybe, he should be chidden but not for accurately making *Mary Shelley's Frankenstein* which was what he set out to do and then with tireless British precision and Irish brio did. Casting Helena Bonham Carter as the aforesaid mutilee was a needlessly Brit-fond foolishness perhaps when a young Pfeiffer or a Meg Ryan maybe was more the go (in horror movies, for preference, butcher blondes), but this is not the point. The point is that a company town that exalted *Reds*, and *Rocky*, and *L.A. Story*, and *Dances with Wolves* because their actor-managers were their own dull kind of tap-dancing mover and shaker, and cast out Chaplin, Von Stroheim, Welles and Allen and Sturges because they appeared arty and mutinous and self-willed and, well, talented, is not a town whose judgements we should cretinously mimic, ever. Just see the movie and yourself decide, okay? The foremost talent of the English-speaking cinema may not have absolutely stuffed up, you never know. You never know.

It's too late now I guess. What sheep you are entirely.

February, 1995

Stanley Kubrick

Stanley Kubrick was a titan of world cinema who lived in mysterious reclusiveness for thirty-six years in England, never even visiting Europe, and worked for years on several masterpieces, like his *Napoleon* (in which Napoleon spent the eve of Waterloo doing accounts), a film he somehow never made. The few films he did make, like *2001*, *Dr Strangelove* and *Eyes Wide Shut*, we should be very thankful for.

Or that is the story we were told these thirty years while the much-hyped *A Clockwork Orange*, *Barry Lyndon*, *The Shining* and *Full Metal Jacket* came out and were each found to be curiously disappointing. Their reputations waned while his grew ever more huge, his enigmatic secrecy and compulsive procrastination feeding our need for an unseen magus, a maestro pondering his next big costly surprise. If he wasn't that, if he wasn't some sort of Oracle, some sort of guru, what was he?

A pretentious overrated neurotic fraud, perhaps? A talented youngster who grew old and lost it, perhaps?

Heaven forbid.

A good deal of the truth of it, I suspect, was that he made sufficient money out of *Lolita* (*How did they ever make a movie out of Lolita?* the poster asked, and the answer is, by ageing her up to sixteen) to permit him never to work again, and his life thereafter became, like the last years of Howard Hughes, a flattered and fairly crazy self-indulgence.

For Kubrick wasn't all that well in his mind. He feared flying – so much so that he shot his Vietnam film, *Full Metal Jacket*, in the London Gas Works, an atmosphere so unlike the Mekong Delta as to puzzle everybody and to ensure its commercial failure. I've heard rumours (a crew member told me) that he had large pictures around his walls of humans having sex with animals. He was so secretive he concealed from his chosen writer Frederic Raphael (who wrote *Darling* and *The Glittering Prizes* and *After the War*) the name of the author of the novel he was to adapt into *Eyes Wide Shut*, though wily Freddy guessed it early: Arthur Schnitzler. And he was so self-absorbed that he crossed out most of his last collaborator's famously witty dialogue lest it shift attention (as did the jokes of *Strangelove*) from himself. This was a Stanley Kubrick film, after all, and in Stanley Kubrick credit battles he took no prisoners.

Anthony Burgess suffered much the same authorial gazumping when his brilliant futuristic and linguistic adventure *A Clockwork Orange* – whose rights he sold out early, when he was broke, for seven hundred pounds – was adapted by Kubrick and he was neither paid a penny more nor invited to the premiere and had, he said, 'to queue up round the block, like everybody else, to see it'. For this was *Stanley Kubrick's A Clockwork Orange*, the posters said so, and that was that. And when it inspired some copycat killings, it was Stanley Kubrick who took it off the screens of England, the way one would. And Anthony Burgess took the rap.

Seen now, it's pretty dreadful – lots of speeded-up running-and-jumping and nude fornication, a central sadistic rape, involving scissors over nipples while Beethoven plays, which turns the stomach with its prurience, and ham-fisted punchline, hoodlums becoming coppers, that is obvious a mile off. Yet the poster, a cruel young face with one false eyelash (*A little of the old ultra violence*), is an enduring work of popular art, like its predecessor, a stone hand with a vertical sword (*This is the year of Spartacus*) and, of course, the young face behind asteroid-reflecting plexiglass (*2001 – Take the trip*).

Kubrick's first job was as a stills photographer of advertisements in glossy magazines, and he learned important skills in that medium, and useful rules of thumb. Big, simple compositions in two dimensions only. An image that is a single arresting idea. In the earth–moon–sun image of *2001*, I am told, the sun was a pin-hole and the whole set-up the size of a dollar coin, but it looked enormous, cosmic, engulfing, on the screen. A great single arresting idea with Zarathustra at its back. How could it fail?

The process work of *2001*, of course (it was arduously achieved by the English technicians from *Dr Who*), changed cinema history, but the film's long climax fizzles. The central dull astronaut, Keir Dullea, battles HAL, the mutinous homicidal computer, narrowly defeats him, has a cosmic acid trip through all of space and time, grows old in an unexpected white mansion at the end of the universe, grows young again, becomes again a foetus and is, yes, rebirthed in a mighty image, embryo against the Milky Way, as the first star-child of the universe. Any honest response to that film – especially now – involves a vast sense of anticlimax, a feeling of *What? What did he say? Run that past me again?* 'On the surface he looks deep,' as Mungo Macallum once said of another person, 'but deep down he's really rather shallow.'

So too, I fear, is *Full Metal Jacket*. The first half, involving a brutal black sarmajor who is played by a real sarmajor, involves a lot of blustery shallow amateur acting that is pretty wearisome before he is fragged just before interval, and some mad scenes that are eye-rolling lip-licking nonsense. There is eye-rolling and lip-licking in *The Shining* too, which wrecks its initial impelling onrushing credibility. No madman, however mad, even Jack Nicholson when mad, behaves like that. It's another Stanley Kubrick indulgence, and it shouldn't be there. He is forgiven things no other director could survive. Why is this?

One reason I suppose is his films are always more like film *packaging* and the packaging is brilliant. Another is his adroit ability to seem to be the first in a particular field – adult space drama, paedophile romance, nuclear-war black farce – though the book authors Arthur C. Clarke, Vladimir Nabokov and Peter George were by definition there before him and, in the case of Nabokov at least, did the work much better than he. If there is a flatter, more vapid adaptation of a world masterpiece than Kubrick's *Lolita*, with Peter Sellers repeatedly arriving in different disguises, I would like to see it; no I wouldn't. Though the poster of course (heart-shaped sunglasses, a young girl's face, a lollypop), the *packaging*, as always, is marvellous.

Peter Sellers also arrives in different disguises in *Dr Strangelove* (as US President, crazed ex-Nazi adviser, and stuffy English officer Mandrake), I don't know why, perhaps because Sellers liked to do that, and Kubrick takes credit for inventing a form of comedy, now seen every week in *The Simpsons* – madman in charge of nuclear installations, much dark laughter as the world's end nears – that in fact had been around for years, in *Mad* Magazine, the Goons, and *The Sid Caesar Show*. It is *very well done*, Sellers' Dr Strangelove and George C. Scott's General Buck Turgidson being particularly memorable, and is one of Kubrick's three assured artistic successes, bad back-projection and all, and survives, like the others (*The Killing* and *Paths of Glory*), the test of time.

Spartacus is mostly brilliant too (Kubrick, with characteristic perversity, first repudiated it but then seriously worsened it with his director's cut) in especially its now classic slave-breakout sequence, though it's gravely distorted by the Jean Simmons character Varinia – a hard-bitten gladiators' whore who becomes when pregnant a kind of giggling suburban housewife – and the final intercutting of Spartacus's brutal crucifixion and her attempted seduction with wine and melons by the lovesick Roman dictator Laurence Olivier.

So *The Killing*, a racehorse assassination flick; *Paths of Glory*, a good strong pacifist war movie (blameless soldiers on trial for cowardice are defended in court by, alas, Kirk Douglas and thus get the firing squad); and *Dr Strangelove*, a nuclear-war black farce, are pretty well it, really. Are these enough to make him a world immortal? Maybe.

But not if you look at *Strangelove* beside *Fail Safe*, a nuclear-war-room suspense film made the same year; and *Paths of Glory* beside, say, *King and Country*, about the trial of a deserter from World War One, made seven years later. And *A Clockwork Orange* beside *Taxi Driver*. And *Full Metal Jacket* beside *Platoon*. And *2001* beside Tarkovsky's magnificent space parable *Solaris*. He dwindles and dwindles again.

He dwindles too if you look at his work beside that of another dwarfish

Jewish New York auteur, born a few blocks away, Woody Allen, who made *Play It Again, Sam, Bananas, Everything You Always Wanted to Know About Sex, Sleeper, Love and Death, Annie Hall, Interiors, Manhattan, Stardust Memories, A Midsummer Night's Sex Comedy, Zelig, Broadway Danny Rose, The Purple Rose of Cairo, Hannah and Her Sisters, September, Radio Days, Another Woman, Crimes and Misdemeanors, Alice, Husbands and Wives, Shadows and Fog, Manhattan Murder Mystery, Bullets Over Broadway, Don't Drink the Water, Mighty Aphrodite, Everyone Says I Love You, Deconstructing Harry* and *Celebrity* and played good clarinet every Monday night while Kubrick was locked up in his English mansion thinking mighty thoughts, and occasionally coming out to make (not always) a goose of himself. Or Sidney Lumet, also small, ill-tempered, Jewish and a New Yorker, who made *12 Angry Men, Long Day's Journey Into Night, The Fugitive Kind, The Hill, The Pawnbroker, The Group, Murder on the Orient Express, The Anderson Tapes, The Seagull, Serpico, Bye Bye Braverman, Equus, The Wiz, Just Tell Me What You Want, Prince of the City, The Verdict, Deathtrap, Daniel, Garbo Talks, The Morning After, Power, Running on Empty, Family Business, Q&A, Close to Eden, Stranger Among Us, Guilty as Sin, Night Falls on Manhattan, Critical Care* and *Gloria* in a career exactly as long thus far as Stanley's.

I may be wrong of course, and *Eyes Wide Shut* may be terrific. But I predict it will be brilliant in parts, gross in parts, disorderly, dismaying, confusing, a bit pretentious, unexpectedly shallow sometimes, and a bit long. See if this is so.

Stanley Kubrick is an unclothed emperor, discuss. A neurotic middlebrow dressed up as something larger, discuss. A man whose greatest talent lay in public relations, not cinema; trailers, not films. Discuss. History will tell.

July, 1999

Eyes Wide Shut

I saw *Eyes Wide Shut* at last, on, yes, the opening day, in the cinema complex of my home town after a pool game with my son Jack and his mate Liam and a schooner of Kilkenny at Maggie Moore's, and spent every alternate thirty seconds asleep through the last ninety minutes of it, and found it, as I feared I would, a mixed bag of the great, the beautiful, the dull, the pointless, the arousing, the aggravating, the tiresome and, oh yes, the amateur. But I wouldn't know, I was mostly asleep I guess, or, if awake, pretty overjoyed to see vast golden hectares of Kidman's epidermis or her straining nipples under her negligee and Tom Cruise looking *ugly* in every shot (a pleasing surprise) as he grinned at yet another gorgeous woman mad for his tiny body. But mostly I was angry that Kubrick never learned, or soon forgot, the rudiments of screenwriting.

These can be learned in a couple of hours, and a dill, though not the mighty Stanley, can master them in a weekend. They include not writing scenes where the hero goes down a corridor, knocks, waits, greets the man who opens it by name, comes in, takes his coat off, agrees he would like a drink, considers what among a number of differing options that particular drink might be, decides, and after a dilatory amiable preamble nominates the drink to the patient friend, and waits for the drink to arrive, and takes it, and sips it, *without simultaneously doing, or feeling, or signalling, or encoding more interesting things* than a capacity to walk upright without farting or a taste for unwatered scotch. And not having dialogue so free of all personal quirk, and individual rhythm, and not having a pattern of speech so pasteurised, and blow-waved, and ethnically cleansed, that the characters sound like droids, or the dead-souled astronauts of *2001* or *The Thunderbirds*. And not assuming that you are the first man on earth to have pondered adulterous temptation, or feminine lust, or the radiant prettiness of Christmas, and that other writers have not been there before you, like, say, the author of Genesis, and Chaucer and Tolstoy and Flaubert and Nabokov, and that fronting up like some sort of sexual pioneer on the basis of this is like walking onto the stage of the London Palladium and, after a trumpet fanfare and a drum roll and a blaze of rainbow spotlights, reciting at long last the alphabet, and awaiting applause.

There is a scene, for Christ's sake, where a Much Older Man with grey sideburns and a caressing foreign accent and a number of Come-wiz-me-to-the-kasbah lines of oily foreplay is dancing with the splishily drunk Nicole and arousing her with smooth talk and she is saying, 'But I'm a married woman!', a scene that Mills & Boon would have knocked back as pitiably old-fashioned. There are a great number of scenes in which a goofily grinning Candide-like Tom Cruise (he is supposed to be a Manhattan society doctor) is about to be (I suppose) groped, held down and fellated by this or that gorgeous woman with nothing better to do with her weekend, when his mobile phone luckily rings and his marriage is saved, hallelujah, once again. There is a scene in which he finds that a gorgeous downtown hooker he nearly fucked has HIV, a condition he, a doctor, had never dreamed could happen in the city of New York in the decade of the nineties. Silly sausage.

And so on. It's beautifully shot and framed and the black and white images of Nicole being mounted by other men in Tom's daydreams rank high as single chapters in the story of the century's tasteful pornography, and her soliloquy (self-written, I am told) about being multitudinously fucked by the entire US navy and laughing over their heaving shoulders at her husband; and the restless, onrushing camera, swooping and gliding and circling, are always impressive as cinema, as moment, as image, as trailer, or trailer-to-be, but content, *content*, has to live up to glamorous presentation, and it just plain doesn't.

It's a story that was written and is therefore properly set in the more hypocritical 1930s, before Hefner and Oprah and Portnoy and Jong and Greer let billions of us know that lust was okay, and when masked flagellant secret societies flourished in Old Vienna, and some homosexual cross-dressing sub-groups of the emerging sadistic Nazis – and the minute Kubrick chose to update it (and most stories should never be updated, they belong where they are set), his cause, and the story's viability, was lost. This is Kubrick's *Piano*, a glowing, pompous, endless Nothing that the fearful middle-brows of movie reviewing cringe before; that shows, at last, for all the world to see, that the emperor (like his leading lady) has no clothes.

At the Byron Bay Writers' Festival, whence I then repaired, I saw again *Praise*, a much better film. It too concerns itself with sex, and sexual excess, and carnal obsession, but every frame of it is believable, and funny, and tender, and sad, and wonderfully written and superbly acted by performers who know their characters. As the central ravenous nymphomaniac Cynthia, who is fat and bossy, with an always inflamed or bleeding skin condition, and who jumps on top of her man twice a day and bounces up and down moaning, and curses when he comes too soon, Sacha Horler is as good as Judy Davis in *Winter of Our Dreams* or Shelley Winters in *A Place in the Sun*, both attractive and repellent. And you watch her wilfully, stupidly, throw away her only possible, distantly possible, chance of happiness (on a farm among his haughty, hostile family), and get pregnant, and *submit* to the abortion, and agree to call it quits when she might, if she chose, have stayed and worn him down – you watch with a sort of dazed wonderment, as you might observe your Macedonian grandparents or a pair of performing seals. As her dim and sluggish lover, Peter Fenton is pretty much as good as she, a scaly young man on the dole who drinks too much and yields to most of what life *incidentally* offers him (including heroin, hopelessness and a shabby hotel where the neighbours shout and throw things all through the night) yet also knows what he can't put up with life-long. Which is her, poor kid. You feel for both of them, laugh at them as you would at pet animals, but you can't help them, though you want to. You can only watch, and shake your head.

Superbly shot, much of it in one grubby room, which somehow suggests all of Brisbane without showing it, by our greatest lighting cameraman, Dion

Beebe, and directed with unobtrusive genius by the lapsed New Yorker John Curran (who had the good sense to cast the undersigned as a gelded bloodhound in *Down, Rusty Down* and thereby amaze the world), it benefits greatly from the script penned by the novel's author, who knew the story's essence by heart and so was able to tell it swiftly. With a voiceover narrative of course: the shortest cut there is to audience intimacy. It's not *quite* as good as *The Year My Voice Broke*, but it's in the league, one of the best fifteen Australian films, I gingerly suggest, yet made; a film that is, unlike most made here, entirely without flaws.

Kubrick, had he cared to look and listen, might have learned a lot from his upstate neighbour, or those other New Yorkers, Lumet, Allen, Mazursky and Scorsese, who got up early and did the work, but he was too far up himself to notice, and in so following his secret heart he blew himself out of the water, and all his posterity too. It couldn't have happened to a prouder, more dead-hearted fraud and on the whole I'm glad it did, and the myth is now exploded, and washing away in the rain.

Obediently yours.

August, 1999

Lindsay Anderson

'Goodbye,' said Lindsay Anderson, offering me his hand on a Palm Beach verandah. 'Try not to be bitter.'

. . . I'm getting tired of death. The night before I read of Lindsay's passing, my 87-year-old friend Bill Cormack was rushed to hospital with restricted breathing. He was a drover in the twenties and a greyhound trainer and S.P. bookie and public servant thereafter. His kitchen-table orations on God and politics and his command of Australian slang ('A closed mouth catches no elephants.' 'There's no pockets in a shroud.' 'Stingy? He'd skin a louse for its hide.') were some of the small rewards of life that on my visits home to Lismore I looked forward to. I sat with Phyl, his wife, while she surveyed an empty house and thought of her future. They were married in 1942. He's in the same hospital as my mother, Elsie, but in a different ward and neither of them can walk any more so they can't visit each other and have a yarn. They're the best of friends and go back forty years.

I write a lot of obituaries now. I'm flattered to be asked but I don't like it much. I've been sounded out on doing two biographies – Leonard Teale and Francis James – but I haven't the time. I'll be dead soon myself. And daily I am diminished, as the poet said, with the passing of others and the tolling of the bell. 'See you at the next one,' said John Clayton at Johnny Ewart's cremation, a strangely buoyant gig. And at each one there is regret at things not said to the living man that are now past saying. Like, you're a good actor. And, you lit up a great, dark corner of my life.

My contacts with Lindsay Anderson were few but I adored him, of course. I watched his open rehearsals of *The Changing Room* in 1971 on the stage of the Royal Court in youthful wonderment. How he turned a series of foul-mouthed quarrels between sometimes bollocky working-class footballers in a grimy dressing shed into a vision splendid of upward striving and sorrowing humankind worthy of Michelangelo beats me, but he did it. It was a mighty theatrical experience in the end, but how improbable he seemed as its creator, with his stuffy Cheltenham College voice and his precise, declarative, effeminate movements, his schoolmasterly hauteur. I suppose he enjoyed pushing the naked young men round the stage, taking them by the elbow and telling them how to stand, but who cares any more. Only the Office of Sexual Harassment, which needs the work I suppose. We all need the work, and we do what we can.

He was always very tactful in private, in that royal, piss-taking ruling-class way. Alex Buzo (whom he awesomely called 'Alexander') introduced me to him as the co-author of the famous *The Legend of King O'Malley*. He looked both alert and foxed and eventually said, 'Ye-es, we're very *provincial* in London, we hear so little of what's going on in the *real world*.' And when some thirteen years later I asked him had he read Peter Carey's novel *Bliss* and why he'd decided not to direct the film of it, he said, 'Well, it's more like *three* novels really, isn't it?' His restraint, the things he left unsaid, were a great part of his charisma, which for a tiny little queeny martinet was pretty large. Happily his marvellous farewell-note film *Is That All There Is?* gets a lot of this magnetic mischief, which was somewhere between Puck and Iago.

He was less tactful in his public utterances. His lecture in the State Theatre on the foolishness of post-structuralist criticism had a good few feral academics hissing, I remember, and in one case actually spitting. His public defences of *If . . .* and the campus riots it caused, or presaged, saw him widely condemned in England as a dangerous young left-wing radical. He was then forty-eight. His call to arms of a politically committed cinema, in the first edition of *Sight and Sound*, which he founded, was similarly greeted. He was then, I suppose, thirty-four. Too old even then for the typecasting. The next year he won his only Oscar, for *The Station*, one of the first poetic documentaries of ordinary life. In this, as in all things, he was a pioneer.

All that he did – his incisive monographs, his championing of Ford and Ganz, his co-founding with Richardson and Reisz of Woodfall, his mischievously leftist episodes of *Robin Hood*, his co-invention with Godard of Brechtian cinema, his occasional acting (Who has now forgotten his speech, 'as my eye moves down these names', to the honour roll of the dead in *Chariots of Fire?*), his luminous use of the nonagenarian Lillian Gish as the *sturdier* sister of Bette Davis in *The Whales of August,* his attack on Thatcherite England in *Britannia Hospital* – declares him as that rarest of human creatures, the cinematic equivalent of a man of letters. An example for some to follow perhaps, those of us who can spell.

'Try not to be bitter.' We were talking about *Newsfront,* of course, a mere thirteen years after its making, on James Ricketson's verandah among cheeping lorikeets in warm Australian light. He liked the film, he said, apart from 'all that silly stuff at the end about brother pinching brother's girl', the stuff I was proudest of.

Try not to be bitter. And try not, as Ralph Richardson said so effectively in *O Lucky Man,* to die like a dog. Lindsay didn't, I'm sure. I hope his death had the dignity he gave to the suicides Jill Bennett and Rachel Roberts, his dear old friends, as he spread, in the coda of his final film, their ashes on the Thames and Alan Price sang the title song, 'Is That All There Is?'. Lindsay was the best of England, and in his veins was mixed the literary blood of Malory and Bunyan, of Swift and Pope, of Waugh and Priestley and Orwell and Larkin, and the many godchildren of its theatrical revival, Wesker, Brenton, Storey, Bond and Hare. And Brecht, of course, and Marx, whose revolution was brought to its focus in the British Museum Reading Room, a dread and holy English place. It is those that most truly hate England, and with great cause, or have a lover's quarrel with her till the end, as Lindsay did, that England loves best in the aftertime, and rightly so. He is among her best, though his life's work, like Larkin's and Orwell's, proved slim. He will be sorely missed.

September, 1994

Star Quality

After the underglamorous AFI Awards (Holden, Dingo, Harmer, Thring, a waft of Ottos, a smirk of Keatings, a sad wracked wraith of John Paul Young) I am at 4 a.m. brought in view of five simultaneous margaritas by the blazingly baby-faced Russell Crowe and begin to wonder, amid the licked salt and the shotten breeze and the brain damage, Is this chirpy juvenile a superstar now? Is Tara Morice (palely loitering now, a miffed Cinderella, out on the marble stairway)? Will she be when *Ballroom* grosses $100 million? How does it work? Does Russell's Brando-standard performance in a film that storms the planet make him bankable or is that option currently closed by the same insensate process that once exalted Bryan Brown after eight star vehicles that all lost money? And the insubstantial Mel Gibson after two noisy successes in which he served as a special effect? Is Lisa Harrow now the presiding Bette Davisish bitch goddess whom we should all now flatter? How fares the wind for Jack Thompson at fifty? How many immanent Mirandas, Taras and Kerrys cancel out a Judy? The perspiring numerologists of Hoyts and Roadshow need to know. No doubt they will seek American advice, then again sweeten future flops with the still underpraised Charlie Schlatter, whose hour is surely at hand. Gawsh darn, that ol' American know-how sure sets the planet right, look at happy bigamous oligarchic heretic-beheading Kuwait, gawsh darn; and how lucky we all are down here down under that one of our own girls wed the great Tom Cruise.

The Prime Minister, overwrought and steadfastly grinning amid Bill Hunter's bearhug, warily thanks me for the feral abacus, whose potent reiteration, not least by the lipdrubbing Dr Hewson, has put Labor in this week's poll thirty seats ahead. I feel gratefully tempted to reveal his almighty, headkicking own best Hewson line ('The man's a wimp, I bet he steps out of the shower to piss.') but decide against it in the interests of the common weal.

I peruse his shrewd, saturnine, mid-Michelangelo, pale Hibernian visage and wonder what other destiny he probably dodged by gatecrashing Parliament early. Deputy manager of the Regent Hotel probably, after a swift rise from cornflake waiter in a mere thirty years. How improbable, I muse, is stardom of any sort, and how little it all means. Garry McDonald is a big star: discuss. Leo McKern is a star. John Button. Danny De Vito. Paul (gasp) Mercurio. Edward G. Robinson. Jeff (gasp) Kennett. I ask you.

Stars as a rule are made, not born, by correct casting of good actors (and there are thousands) in films that succeed and stars, as a rule, are easier to create than haggle for. Had any one of the four films John Walton was great in succeeded he might have usurped Jack Thompson's husky imperium by now and be knocking back, not accepting, the roles I write him, as Brownie annually does, rightly or wrongly. Stardom is a dud theory anyway, as those great money earners *ET*, *Star Wars* and *Home Alone* and those great money losers *Ishtar*, *The Missouri Breaks* and *Dick Tracy* prove, and brings only grief, expense, purblind miscasting and that silly mixture of hubris and venal fawning that brings us all undone.

Frankie J. sings in his Elvis mode 'Viva Las Vegas' better than the original. God, how happy we all are, down here, down under, unhelped, alone.

Yankee, go home.

November, 1992

Asleep at Question Time, Awake at SPAA

I awoke, and to my horror the entire Federal Opposition was baring its crooked fangs in uproars of laughter and pointing at me and slapping its tailored knees and shouting, 'He's fallen asleep! He's fallen asleep in his own joke!'

It was as nightmarish a waking vision as I've ever had and as Mia Farrow once memorably shrieked, in I think the Devil's embrace, it was no dream. I had nodded off in Question Time, and snored I think, while seated in the House of Representatives in a green padded chair alongside the government back benches, and the subsequent uproar delayed for about two minutes the second half of a thoughtful, perceptive answer by Michael Lee. He later on walked past me, squeezed my arm and said, 'I forgive you', in a voice as heavy and frigid as a Russian glacier. I saw him four times in the next five days – at airports, in parking lots, in public toilets, and each time he said, 'I've completely forgotten it', and smiled with full lips in that unnerving way he has, like one who in a Donald O'Connor movie is about to burst into song.

The Labor Right has long memories I reckon, and when he's Prime Minister I'll be pulled out of my retirement home and put in the stocks, with the word Snoozy hung about my neck and mud pies given free to passing schoolboys.

Worst about the experience were the bitter contorted features and derisive whoops of John Howard who is currently on a mission from God to do me harm. 'That's a Bob Ellis line!' he shouts at random, his bridgework bulging. 'That's a Bob Ellis line! He's fallen asleep!' He does it on public transport, everywhere. What an appalling little tick. I'm half inclined to stand against him and bring him to ruin. My ten-year-old son told me a joke last night. Knock knock. Who's there? Howard. Howard who? Howard I know, I'm only a mindless monster.

I decided on the grounds of crashing poverty not to go to the Screen Producers Association conference this year. Two thousand dollars, a return airfare to Galway, to hear foreign drongos say 'let's face it', and 'bums on seats'. Then I saw the guest list: Michael Lee, John Howard and my furry friend Sir David Puttnam, who dislikes me more than the others, I think, for taking two years instead of six months to write *The Nostradamus Kid* while his credibility with Warners waned. So I had to go, I decided: this much misery was irresistible.

So I did, driving down for my first time on a day of major flooding and running out of petrol outside Albury and drenching my one suit with the spare jerry can and searching the many roads, avenues and streets called Queen in Carlton and Melbourne before discovering the Carlton Radisson in Albert Park and being forbidden entrance because I reeked of petrol and might have been planning a fiery suicide during Sir David's opening address.

I eventually got in, claiming to be the famous Bob Ellis (a figure increasingly remote from me, clearly a man of calm and wisdom and influence and not the reeking wreck asnore in the third row) and am currently as this organ goes prematurely to press leering at the dentally augmented Sir David across a bowl of summer fruit. He seems also, like the serene Mr Lee beside him, to have forgiven me.

I hope this does not apply to John Howard.

I plan to ask him tomorrow (I look forward to his yelp when I stand up) if he is now sorry, and grovellingly apologetic, for having as Treasurer put in 10BA the insensate proviso that each film must be finished by 30 June – which meant everybody was shooting in October–November and competing for the same lighting cameraman whose prices therefore tripled and with them the budgets of all Australian films which now cost three times what they ought, thus necessitating presales to foreigners and a star system we cannot afford and all the misery, in short, in the world. All the John Howard misery. It's a John Howard of an industry, if I may adapt the old John Clarke line, therefore, still.

What a ghastly little fuckwit he is entirely, with all the droning self-righteousness of the truly mediocre, like an unwelcome brother-in-law at a

Christmas dinner forever sounding off on his favourite subject while the pudding cools. He supported, successively, the atomic bombing of Australia, the atomic bombing of the Pacific, conscripting kids to fight under Agent Orange in Vietnam, the abolition of Medicare, and the invention of 10BA. But he's learnt his lesson. Oh yes. He's a new John Howard. New, fresh. A fresh new alternative to a tired government. That's him. Over there. The ugly little bloke third to the left.

Thank God he will lose his seat in a Labor landslide. Things could be much, much worse. I pitched successfully to Sir David and am seeing him at ten, over coffee. Watch this space.

November, 1995

Bronwyn Bishop, Angel Baby

Once more I sauntered in and assumed my usual place in the House of Representatives and once more my thunderstruck local member Bronwyn Bishop quickly left the chamber and twenty minutes later quickly returned in a different dress.

I am curious about this socio-political phenomenon, which has happened thrice now, and what it means. One theory that has gripped my fellow staff members is that she sees me and wets herself, but there may be subtler explanations. One is that like Norma Desmond in *Sunset Boulevard*, whom in general demeanour she closely resembles ('Tell Mr De Mille I am ready for my close-up.'), she feels the ageing film star's restless need to change costume six or seven times a day and so divert attention from the sags and wrinkles, and Question Time, when the nation is presumably watching, is one of those times, and my presence in the chamber is a coincidence unconnected with this daily routine of erotic display.

Another is that she is attempting to seduce me and thus erase me as a political rival with her subsequent account on ABC television, in the manner of Princess Di, of my lumbering, slow, hydraulic technique; but I give this little credence because she knows that so placed I could under the Australian constitution demand equal time, and so provoked, feel free of gallantry.

They are a peculiar bunch, Alexander Downer especially, who close-up looks like nothing so much as his own soft toy spin-off.

John Howard came to the Screen Producers Association conference and droningly addressed it, using the dread pronunciation 'fillum' and, while saying nothing exceptional (he informed us, usefully, that Australia had made the first feature-length film while we all slapped our foreheads in amazement and said things like 'wow'), somehow drained all light from the universe and all joy from the world and, shrinking and shrivelling under our dismayed gaze like a raisin in the sun, radiated meanness, negativity and plaintive misery that knew no end. He looked like someone running, with fading hope, for the office of deputy headmaster of Warialda Primary School on a policy of hourly public canings and wondering why the entire kindergarten was against him. He eventually agreed to answer two questions only, but such was the mass of his negative personality that no-one could think of a second. What an awful little man.

What he's most like, someone said, is a schoolboy in a school cap sitting with clenched knuckles outside the headmaster's office, knowing he'll eventually get the cane.

. . . My habit of crashing into Michael Lee three times a day in all the cities of the continent continues. Most recently was in Canberra at night as he hurtled off to see *Angel Baby* in Parliament House, in some trepidation of its rumoured content. I said it was an initially uproarious but eventually tragic narrative of two schizophrenics in love and attempting to have a baby while off their medication and he'd adore it, and his face fell. I look forward to his abashed and sorrowing demeanour in Question Time tomorrow while he fights the impulse to stand on tiptoe and squawk like a seagull. He is, I think, a perhaps over-impressionable young man and I fear for him.

It's an astonishing piece of Australian cinema, one of our best. In description it sounds like just another of the my-God-isn't-Melbourne-awful-and-why-don't-I-have-the-courage-to-hitchhike-all-the-way-to-Surfers-Paradise-and-find-happiness genre that Film Victoria so favours in its funding, but it's more than that. It draws the audience into the characters' billowing mania, making us, too, believe that what they hope for (a normal life, in a flat, with a baby, and a normal job, and a wage, and a lot of joyous rooting) is against all the objective evidence truly possible, and devastating us too when their inevitable clinical depression crashes down on their heads, completing the medical cycle and wrecking their lives. The final image is as great in its content and pleasing as any in world cinema, and Jackie Mc-Kenzie's performance the best by an Australian female since Judy Davis's doleful druggie hooker in *Winter of Our Dreams*. Like all great cinema it takes us to another place, and accustoms us to alien territory, in this case the world of the mad.

It shows, too, how sensible it is to have a writer/director rather than the other sort. A writer/director will not miscast, because he (or, of course, she) has seen the film already. He'll not misjudge the tuning of the dialogue, because he's heard the film already. She'll not do flashy shots that divert us from the narrative, because she has no emotional need to. He'll stick with the film and its core of meaning right through the post-production (that worst of times), because he has toward it the constancy of a lover, and not, like the 'job' director, the fleetingness of a ship-board root. She won't say stuff it, and walk out. The other sort will, or may. The writer/director knows intimately the film he or she is making, and that's a big help. Many 'job' directors at the rough cut stage are still finding out.

It sounds pretty obvious, I know, but for twenty years the opposite view prevailed, in spite of the work of Duigan and Cox and Schepisi, and there were seminars all the time entitled: Australian Film: the script is the problem: discuss. And all that time, of course, the script, and the writer, were the solution. What a criminal waste of wonderful years. We get to Jerusalem only by inches, and that's a fact.

November, 1995

Shine, Life, What I Have Written, Love Serenade

Scott Hicks' film *Shine* buffets and disturbs the senses in (I suppose) a most un-Australian way. Emotion is not kept at arm's length nor story minimised. You go down a whitewater rafting journey of the heart through exile, madness and Rachmaninov-led purgation and out the other side.

Oedipal in its shape and flavour, it most resembles *Fear Strikes Out*, a remarkable fifties biopic of a young man driven to baseball stardom and madness by his unrelenting father, with Tony Perkins and Karl Malden in the bruising central roles. With casting no less impactful, *Shine* tells of a career in music that first enlarges and then smashes two egos, father and son, for whom music is never a soothing unguent but an Olympic field of torture.

They are, unsurprisingly, Jewish and the father (a masterful portrayal of bullying love by Armin Müller-Stahl) a concentration camp survivor with the contradictory dual purpose of exalting his son's talent and keeping him in Perth. This leads to a breach between them, when the son accepts a

257

scholarship in London, that is bitter and massive and never healed. Madness follows, a splintered career and a partial recovery and, in later years, a kind of dotty local celebrity.

Never, I think, has parental obsession been better shown – nor the curse of talent in a field where talent must be not only genius but also lucky (he is narrowly beaten for a crucial scholarship by Roger Woodward) to even survive.

Noah Taylor – fourteen again – adds his remarkable qualities (he is himself a considerable musician) of luminous transparency and ferocious tender focus to an already powerful chemistry, and in scenes with Sir John Gielgud (at ninety more than a legend, something like a visiting divinity) and Googie Withers he is not outclassed. As his older incarnation, vagrant, fey and bibble-babbling Geoffrey Rush is equally remarkable (though I suspect over-celebrated for his genial-halfwit party trick, as was Tom Hanks for *Forrest Gump*) in his rickety climb back into life. A staggering overall achievement anyway (we all have had, for at least fifteen minutes, that father), one bound to make its mark internationally.

Life, by Lawrence Johnston – the title a bit of a come-down after *Eternity*, his previous world masterpiece – is set in a brightly coloured modern prison among HIV sufferers and is hard to describe. It has some of the qualities of Eugene O'Neill's *The Iceman Cometh* and *The Long Voyage Home*, and involves an optimistic inmate (David Tredennick) keen to bodybuild, survive, and rejoin his wife, and a gruff, ill-tempered one (John Brumpton, who also wrote the script), and a startling degree of male tenderness that is loving but unerotic – plus several fathoms of longing heterosexual flashback that is very erotic indeed.

It's a fine film, radiantly populated (Brumpton's long convict face, some-where between that of Bisley and that of Brown, is transfixingly iconic and race-memorious), but with a feeling of contrivance about it (the prison walls are made, inaccurately, of glass so we can see more Life going on) that robs it – perhaps – of the hope of high international esteem.

High international esteem, by contrast, may fall in heaps on *What I Have Written* (director John Hughes, writer John A. Scott), a very well-made cheap film, but the more discerning among us will judge it a load of old rope. In typical Cox-led Nabokov-on-the-Yarra fashion it propounds the myth that Melbourne is thronged with sensitive world-travelled folk on independent incomes (*Man of Flowers, My First Wife, Proof*) whose torpid Edwardian marriages (ah my dear, the boredom of Venice, the ennui of Paris, those dreary hotel corridors at the Ritz) are poisoned with thoughts of (shock horror) adultery, the very *thought* of which is an entire betrayal of womankind (if a man had lusted in his heart, etcetera) and deserving, by God, of the torments of hell.

The plot is this. Christopher, a fortyish novelist (Steve Jacobs), suffers a massive stroke and while he lies in hospital near death a manuscript by him is revealed to us. It recounts his recent trip to Europe (ah my dear, the impertinent bellhops) with his patient wife Sorel (Angie Milliken) and his introduction at a dinner party (thrown by a frightful, jumped-up Australian poet in Paris) to Frances, the most exciting woman in the world. She doesn't fuck him but for months thereafter bombards his *écritoire* with endless letters from Paris on how much she would like to and in what exotic positions and costumes. This paragon of far-flung perversion is played by, no, not Ruth Cracknell, as one might reasonably expect, but Gillian Jones – a difficult call but, like the song the sirens sang and that name Achilles used when he dwelt among women, not beyond all conjecture.

The manuscript is then revealed, and the dying man's obsession with this distant Jezebel, to Sorel by his envious university colleague Jeremy (Jacek Komen), who loves her. She is aghast. Can this be true? Or is it only – that's it! – a novel he is writing! Jeremy, the bastard, shows her proof, in the form of actual letters from the unrevealed nymphomaniac, in her handwriting.

OH MY GOD IT IS TRUE. She rails at her spouse, the drooling vegetable, for his mental infidelity and he promptly dies. But then it turns out that the letters, perhaps, were written, perhaps, by . . . no, I won't spoil it for you.

All this wittering mullock might of course be acceptable if placed – with the aid of tongs – in Tolstoy's Moscow or Flaubert's Paris, among the quills and candles and fans of the nineteenth-century la haute bourgeoisie, but in Jeff Kennett's Melbourne, among the sort of rancid academics that wifeswap in their sleep, it arouses crazed giggles early that don't stop. Dion Beebe's images, however, are a continuing visual ravishment and much of the direction, if occasionally portentous, is excellent.

Love Serenade by Shirley Barrett is flawless, delightful, constantly surprising and always itself, and its acclaim at Cannes was well earned. It deals, as everyone now knows, with a pair of lovelorn country-town sisters and their neighbour, the new, pretentious disc jockey from faraway Brisbane – a scrotum-featured golden-throated narcissistic prater of Desiderata and muser on life's follies and a rat with women. Because he is a celebrity, and mysteriously and solemnly inert (and may, on certain evidence, be a fish), they forgive him everything and seek, in turn, to marry him until . . . see it to find out.

Of the four main performances (the fourth is George, a heroically nudist Chinese cook), all of them really good, Miranda Otto is probably the best as the awkward younger (and virgin) sister Dimity, the one felt by the town to be a bit . . . off. She convinces you, amazingly, of her plainness, inexperience, youth and scrambled brain with a series of soft yelps and leery stares that are real and sad and winning. As the disc jockey, George Shevtsov is a lean and lugubrious compendium of sixties womanising bullshit and drug-dimmed self-satisfaction fit to rouse the guilt in even me.

A fine film, if inexplicably made for $3.8 million dollars. Eight hundred thousand, the budget (I hear) of *Life*, would be more the go. The actors, all up, would have got no more than $120 000. What happened, in a four-hander shot mainly in ordinary rooms, to the rest?

July, 1996

Oscar, John Brown and the Unsinkable

Like the Merchant–Ivory films, *Titanic*, *Wilde* and *Mrs Brown* are about the overdressed classes, and keeping stiff the upper lip while the heart breaks in silence. They share a style of costume and deal with true events and actual people, those that ran the gauntlet of the paparazzi (already active) of the day. They have all done well at the box office, and there are reasons for this.

One is that, like *Romeo and Juliet* (and the one-line pitch for *Titanic* was, apparently, 'Romeo and Juliet on the *Titanic*'), the stories are already well known, and the characters in some part of our tribe's memory: Oscar being witty in the dock, the sad old Queen in crowblack mourning for Albert, the brave ship's band on the tilting deck playing 'Nearer My God To Thee'. In all three stories is a Mona Lisa – or Princess Di – enigma: what was he (she) really like? What did he (she) do or say in the hour of death?

In all, too, is the charm of distance, but near distance: a time close enough to feel with, to find again a morality we half remember. 'All theatre audiences,' the late Julius Caesar is said to have said, 'repossess, in the dark, the simpler moral standards of fifty years before they were born.' Thus in *Titanic* the poor boy's discomfort at the rich man's table moves us yet, and John Brown's ferocious bodyguard-love for his moody Queen, and Wilde's absurd and suicidal protective devotion to Bosie, in ways the world may not imagine a hundred years from now – when the movies, I suppose, will be about the ill-used Camilla Parker-Bowles (my mooted title: *Tampon and Squidgy*) or the rush to impeachment by mad prudes of saintly President Bill for prodding the tonsils of eager office bimbos, the way one does. We go with the stories because we can imagine our grandfather (or grandmother) somewhere in them. If the past is another country where all is differently done, it is also a country we like to visit (like Ireland or New Zealand), for that same reason; for its always pleasing mixture of the familiar and the strange.

In all three films are great performances, Fry as the soft-eyed playful Oscar and Dench as the frumpy sullen Queen, so good and clear it is hard to think they are not the actual people, and David Warner as the perfect, sinister, smoke-grey conscienceless manservant, the eighties troubleshooter in preview, as the Empire's old money sinks in an icy sea. All (including, surprisingly, *Titanic*) boast slim sweet thoughtful scripts and lavish crockery and wallpaper and sentiments – sentiments nicely contrasted, in *Titanic*, with the foul-mouthed greedy technobabble of today. One, *Mrs Brown*, is too much like a telemovie – drab and dark and ablur with murky close-ups – but the one-line pitch (did the monarch twiddle the gillie's willy or did the kilt stay firmly down?) so appealing that old women in coachloads daily dodder chumbling upstairs to catch what is perhaps no more than a royal roll in the haggis (or do I mean the heather?) with rough trade. As the eponymous phlegmatic moonlight shagger, Billy Connolly wondrously doffs his long-worn mask of a Sassenach hoon-for-all-pub-brawls to play with dignity, searing quietude and hairy hidden depths a role clearly meant for Sean Connery, who I imagine cost too much; and the great stage actor Tony Sher gives (I think that is the proper verb) a Disraeli of depth and guile and immemorial bitter sorrows, and rings, and ringlets, and fingers to the lips, that seems likewise to be the man himself – or Tony's screen audition for Shylock, perhaps, a performance of howls and sobs and brimstone I alas have seen. A pity the director is a visual moron, but you can't have everything. A pity, too, they cut the shagging scenes, by royal command I suppose, for the drama sorely needs them, and the film seems less portentous, and pretty pointless without them.

While *Titanic* is afloat, the grandly costumed and promenading and ball-going patrician class of Europe and America show now and then what lies beneath the costuming: the ruling-class rite, for instance, of the consummated betrothal in adjoining staterooms ('I have a headache,' pleads Winslet in vain, when Zane seeks to plant his imperial flag before the banns), and the accustomed flesh-market of daughters to wealthy suitors when poor dear Mother's family coffers abruptly run dry; the animal attraction to roistering Left Bank nude portraitists of spirited but corseted rich girls on the wavering cusp of loveless wedlock, and so on; the *complexity*, in short, of life, and its compromising venal shoddiness enhances the social truth of the uptilting leviathan, and the screaming, and the freezing, and the music playing.

Wilde too (superbly directed by Brian Gilbert) boasts delicate depths undramatised till now. Oscar the truant heterosexual, for instance, the doting but ofttimes absent father of little sons, heterosexual in practice (and besotted in his youth by several women, including Lillie Langtry) till expertly bedded and brought out by shy Robbie Ross at thirty; husband very much and loving, in his way, of all-forgiving Constance till her death, son very much of Speranza, romantic firebrand Irish rebel (here played with feverishly smiling fervour by, of course, Vanessa Redgrave), and of Sir William Wilde, medical genius brought likewise low by a public humbling in the dock, Fry's Oscar is a *gentle* poseur whose arrogance (like Whitlam's) is also a playful pose; and a very young man, we sometimes forget, whose career, like John Lennon's, was ashes at forty, and whose rocket of celebrity took eight years, no more, to plunge into shame.

And Queensberry, the sexually dysfunctional proud atheist and fellow icon-smasher, is seen in depth too: as large a rebel himself as Wilde or Speranza, but racked with grief at the suicide of one sodomite son (past boyfriend of the new Prime Minister) and fearful of further bloodstain on the family crest. And Bosie, the mad, bad, beautiful, vengeful bitch of a boy (fierily impersoned with tigerish grey-green eyes by the lovely Jude Law), narcissistic, spoiled and shrieking shamelessly for more money, more; not Oscar's lover (or not for long) but his roving accomplice in copulative polygamy, cruising the Soho streets beside him, in what seems now a very modern way, sharing rent-boys and gleefully watching with blazing eyes the Grand Panjandrum huffing and puffing to his adipose completion. Most remarkable perhaps is Michael Sheen, whose Robbie Ross is that most uncommon figure (in cinema if not in life), the decent, kindly, loyal, big-toothed, worried little queen. The sex scenes, though brief, as alluringly evoke the lush nineties decadence (all red-gold windowlight and spread-eagled bronze bodies and gold wallpaper and silken sheets) of that over-painted Underworld as do Aubrey Beardsley's elegant, lewd line drawings. It's a fine film, in short, based precisely on the late, great Richard Ellmann's wonderful book, the best one-volume biography I've read, and full of actual dialogue (Wilde evicting Queensberry from his house in Tite Street, in Wilde's exact words, and so on), and though a bit rushed at the finish (the imprisonment is too short, and the last sad dwindling to shabby beggary in Paris omitted altogether), the classic dramatic work, I would guess, on the subject – by Julian Mitchell, a lovely writer of, among much else, *Another Country*.

Peter Carey lately said that the past is a kind of science fiction we invent as much as discover, according to its usefulness to us in our time. So it is no accident that now, when widowhoods last longer than ever before, and homosexuals wear once more a leper's bell, and the Western world's below-decks huddled masses grow in number and clamber gasping up for air, that these three films have found big audiences. For the past will always offer more, whatever the Australian Film Commission hirelings tell us, and whenever we go there truly (as in *Breaker Morant, My Brilliant Career, Shine, Flirting, Newsfront, An Angel at My Table*), both praise and big money flow to the brave, true traveller in time. The past is a bigger canvas than the present, with more years to it and more issues, and interesting people to choose from. We should go there more often, and look around.

February, 1998

Rats in the Ranks

A day later I rang Chris Noonan and he, like me, had been thinking of little else. It was a film, he agreed, that got up with you when you left the cinema and followed you home; it sat by the bed while you struggled for sleep and looked at you searchingly with one hand on its knee; it was one of the best films, we both averred, we had seen in the past ten years.

It was *Rats in the Ranks* of course, the stupendously patient Connollys' ill-titled chronicle of the contest for Mayor of Leichhardt in 1994, already a ferocious talking point on its opening night when we saw it, alongside its alert, unsettled lead actors – diminished and humanised and smaller, it seemed, in the foyer – and we went to a bash with them afterwards, a few blocks down the street in Glebe; a talking point among people uncertain of why they were impressed.

Some thought it amazing such folk would so nakedly expose their own Machiavellian duplicity, as they repeatedly regrouped and went back on solemn oaths and slagged each other's character so poisonously on film. Others thought it amazing that the stars defamed would not have attempted legally to abort its opening night or censor its more rancorous contents. How could working politicians, they wondered in sympathetic anguish, be so careless of their political future? (This latter group were then flabbergasted to hear that the Labor Party proposed to screen the film at fundraisers.)

Others, like Sydney's Lord Mayor Frank Sartor (completely recovered, unlike me, from our eight-hour night on the family grappa a year ago), were handsomely unfazed. It had been exactly like that with him, he said, not knowing till the last minute whose votes had actually changed, and whether the weeks of schmoozing had worked. It was for this very reason, he said, he had importuned Bob Carr to change the system to one of direct election by the mere ignorant populace. Working with fratricidal shifting caucuses of three was just too fucking hard.

Some, like Trevor Snape, one of the unveiled participants, found it a little shallow. Those weeks were not entirely consumed, he said, with jostling for personal aggrandisement and catharsis. They were also putting in long hours on benevolent committees, assessing and allaying the woes of our constituents, writing reports and tending their families. There were a million other stories in the naked municipality. This was just one of them.

All, however, had in their ruminations missed the cause, I think, of the film's popularity, which is race memory, Australian race memory at the least. These were people we already knew – Auntie Min and Flash Harry, Mervyn the gawky swot and Edna the phlegmatic washerwoman, Frank the sly old lag, and the enflamed, moustachioed, hubristic stevedore Jim – from the Anglo-Celtic village all we pre-1915 immigrants sailed from and now in remembrance yearn for. They need no introduction because we know them so well already – Kate Butler, all tough durable wrinkles and conscienceful dignity, who believes it's her turn to be Mayor; Evan Jones, the sardonic, spade-faced Labor stalwart nearing ninety who has seen it all; Neil McIndoe, a driven, red-mustachioed equivalent of Yosemite Sam, who is feeling lucky and wins the draw from the hat; Trevor Snape, the conscience-wrung young Labor schnook, all spectacles, elbows and indecision; Kate Harding, well over a hundred, who still pines dreamily for chains of office; and Larry Hand.

Larry I'd call a remarkable creation if he were merely a work of art. As a real person he pulls off the hard double of being both quite astonishing and very familiar – and much more troublingly likeable than the 'low-rent version of Francis Urquhart from *House of Cards*' that Phillip Adams so warmly hailed him as, to Larry's visible pleasure, on opening night.

He looks like a dark-eyed Gene Hackman and acts like, well, a handsomer Richard III, grinning with radiant ruefulness every time it seems (once more) certain he can't arm-twist the needed numbers to his faltering cause. At once dauntless and stoic, unflappable, mock-heroic and matey, quietly contemptuous too of his own dull, tugging powerlust, he behaves throughout with such admirable, gallant shiftiness (assuring telephoned reporters this is off the record mate, while the cameras ceaselessly roll) that I yearned by film's end to run him for Mayor of the Universe, were that position vacant, and write his mighty inauguration speech. He'd win in a walk, of course, so thoroughly, archetypally, unrepentantly, intergalactically is he the thing itself, Political Man, deftly offering you a crumbly cigar. He was there beside the campfires of the Euphrates Basin in the earliest times, massaging the numbers; he is here, in Leichhardt, now.

The Connollys get all this with a breathtaking minimality, at one time holding an unchanged four-shot for six or eight minutes, knowing the observed human tussle was enough, and subtly underplaying the marvel-lous time-worn cityscape of white municipal clock tower, mouldy council chambers and gloomy tenement rooms, while using a dramatic structure based, if I'm not mistaken, on *High Noon*.

This is great anthropology, great political history, and, with its ballad-like singleness of purpose (do not foresake me, oh my numbers), with its ticking-clock chapter headings and occasional shafts of unsettling music, something very close to great cinema. It speaks well of the Australian character that we accept these flawed and clawing, woundable and vengeful human souls as our fellow creatures without self-righteousness or undue mockery, much as we once in times agone copped the womanising of Bob Hawke and the fallen trousers of his majestic predecessor – with amusement, but no moral squint. This is a decent humanistic forgiving society, unafraid (as in *Joh's Jury*, and *Blue Murder*, and *Labor in Power*) to advertise its stumbling gauche-ries and low cunning, and to laugh at them with unjudgmental fondness, and it makes you sometimes, as in this film, glad to be alive.

October, 1996

Kernot, Mike Rann, Von Stauffenberg and Patsy Cline

Cheryl Kernot was on the phone for half an hour last April, telling me how much she had loved my book and how – six degrees of separation – it had reminded her of her own house burning down and her Maitland and New-castle working-class childhood and her dad the Miners' Union organiser and the Labor movement for which, after Keating's end, she now felt much pained and quickened nostalgia. I barely knew her, and was touched by the lucid intimacy of her discourse and the voice – clear, insistent, sweet – that put me in mind of Doris Day's self-chosen nickname, Susie Creamcheese. But I didn't twig, of course, what it foreboded, an electoral realignment that would shaft (perhaps) the Liberal Party forever, though I claim my usual inch or two of credit for changing world history, the way one does. 'Watch October closely' were the last words of my *Herald* column in August and

how right (as usual) I was – and how wrong, by God, because I also predicted a sudden Howard-in-panic election. And so it goes.

I felt right again however when being embraced and kissed on national
television by Mike Rann, the impudently grinning near-winner in South
Australia to whom I predicted a 10.2 per cent swing (it was 9.6) after Labor's
pollsters, with their usual prescience, reckoned he would make no gains and
probably lose seats – the same innumerates who in 1983 told Keating he had
no chance. I assume they're not actually *working* for the CIA but their advice
would not be very different if they were. For a moron could see, but not
they, that a serving Premier who closely resembled a contract player for
Hammer Films (a vampire this week, a human earthworm the next) would
perhaps fare ill against an Opposition leader who combined the charms of
Jack Kennedy and Mickey Rooney with a splash perhaps of Tony Blair and
Tommy Steele and was moreover the best *counter-punching* political intelligence I'd yet seen at work; I babysat him through the Big Debate and was
much pleased by his mischievous deftness: 'Think of the kids, John, think
of the future of the kids,' he would say with a deadly pleading smile. His
only fault, if fault it be in Adelaide, was to yarn long hours in the Tandoori
House over excellent local wine in the campaign's last week and expertly
mimic Dunstan and Hawke (in eye-rolling pursuit of postgraduate bimbos)
and tell great backroom stories that had us helpless with laughter in those
very hours when others, Bobby Kennedy for one, would have been on the
phone past midnight threatening ward heelers with de-selection and sending
in goons to smash up the shops of relevant community leaders. *Beware*, I
said, *the Von Stauffenberg syndrome of premature celebration. Let's have another
drink*, he said, and lost by two seats. He never expected to win, of course,
none of them did, being Labor Party true believers and therefore fucking
masochists. Many of them are female and wear crew-cuts and boiler suits
and at one celebration were even singing 'The Internationale'.

The Australian Film Institute, meanwhile, is proving as fatheaded as
Labor's pollsters in its vote on this year's best. *Doing Time for Patsy Cline*
(good title, bad film) is sumptuously shot and deftly acted but so addled in
its form and so mysterious in its accumulating story that no *normal* audience
can suffer its narrative shallows and structural black holes for very long, and
it is important, I think, to honour (with some exceptions) only those films
that please that audience, or somewhat please them, lest, like *Proof*, they
scare them out of the Australian cinema altogether. 'If *that's* the best Australian film this year,' aggrieved old suburban men and women were saying
after *Proof*, 'I don't want to see any more.' *Thank God He Met Lizzie* (bad
title, good film – title as bad, I told the devastated lady scenarist, as calling
the prominent Siamese musical *The King and Her*) is by contrast a seductive
masterwork (the best Australian dialogue and the best Australian female performance yet and the horniest love comedy) and one bound to be liked by

the ordinary audience if they ever get to see it, but, unlike *Patsy*, it has few nominations, perhaps because it's in sometimes blurry 16-mill and it doesn't *look* as classy, though its emotional effect, in sorrow and joy and sensuality, is overwhelming. *Kiss or Kill* is a deserved nominee in all its categories (in particular editing) but *The Well* is that glummest of hybrids a flawless abomination. Nothing in it is wrong, the acting is superb, and its Look – Ingmar Bergman 1967 I'd put it, portentous, exquisite, mesmeric, confronting and pointless as *Piss Christ* – is beyond all carping and cavil. But it *wants* to be a 28-minute student film (two characters, a single setting, a mystery, a punchline) and that's what it should be. But it's a big arrogant feature film instead, about forty-two hours long, a mountainside *Piano* bristling with dog-eared Freudian symbols and bereft of actual drama, blue-filtered throughout in honour, perhaps, of *Blue Hills*, which was also set in Cooma, and audiences are already hurling themselves out of aeroplanes over the Himalayas to be free of it; and I know by Christ how they feel.

And what about *Idiot Box*, you bungling tools, which is superb?

And *True Love and Chaos*, which is at the very least fucking excellent? I hope the vote count was honest, or I don't in a way. For if it was, we now need random intelligence tests at the door of the Chauvel. Directorial self-confidence is not all that makes a film good, as Paul Cox yearly proves.

It's an ability to hold and please a wider audience than one's duffle-coated peers. *Kiss* and *Lizzie* do this (and so in another context do Cheryl and Mike), and it's time, I think, that the closed onanistic circle of *Cahier* crazies caught up.

November, 1997

Hanson, Capra, Newsfront, *Noyce*

I missed nearly all of the film festival because of the Queensland election, God forgive me, and I feel now like a man lobotomised by a rusty butter knife – because all that fresh, abundant feast of life which each year illumined and sweetened my existence and seared my ageing and mildewed spirit with wisdom and forgiveness was foully thieved from me by two mediocre scumbags called Howard and Borbidge, who will pay, by Christ, you mark my words, for my grief and inconvenience; disgrace and oblivion for both of them I here forfend, however much they sniff and slurp round Pauline, yelping and whingeing for a way back in.

Election night in the quietest Tally Room I can remember, with all about me (Killen, Antony Green, Mackerras, Ross Fitzgerald) moving up and down before the big board. Restless and dumbstruck by our riven nation's Future Shock, I was afforded, however, a scene that fitfully stirred my drowsy screenwriter's heart. Labor by 10.15 had (probably) forty-four seats, but for government needed forty-five, so they tried from their fraught war room to ring the mysterious Independent who had won with Labor preferences the seat of Nicklin (a grumpy local councillor, they were told, a sworn foe of One Nation, a bit of a Greenie, a bit of a Tory, a bit of a Dogpatch eccentric, maybe) and find out if he was prepared for the nation's sake to tip them the wink . . . and they couldn't get him to the phone. He'd gone fishing.

I immediately saw this as Frank Capra might have – with Jimmy Stewart fly-fishing in dawn mist and melancholically perusing his Pocket Longfellow whilst Gary Gray and Mike Kaiser clambered sweating up the mossy bank in their stained tuxedos, babbling frantically of the mighty part he now could play in his country's future, and him unmoved, and unpleased at the inter-ruption, and turning a page and saying, 'L-let me read t'you what *Lawngfeller* had t's-say . . . It's in here sh-somewhere . . .'

And so on. A film I did see at the festival, Capra's *Meet John Doe*, was interestingly prescient of the current Hansonmania (ordinary jobless fellow whose lines are written for him by Stanwyck, the feisty girl reporter, be-comes the reluctant spearhead of a non-political mass-hysterical movement preaching neighbourly helpfulness that is then *taken over* by a devious captain of industry who seeks – and in the Fascist cause, by God – the American Presidency and a New World Order) and showed, from 1941, how human matters don't change too much, and showed that the predicament we are now in (loss of neighbourhood, loss therefore of self) has been seen on the planet before, and a system built on the greed of the few is not a democratic system and cannot stand.

It also showed how wrong the experts are about what a good screenplay is made of. Many of the scenes are five and six minutes long, each one a small and delicate playlet that stands on its own. There are speeches three pages long, four or five of them, uninterrupted and rhetorical. There are maybe forty-three major characters (in the sense of characters vividly realised, that you will clearly remember in late old age) and new, engaging characters still arriving as the Christmas death hour tolls and Long John Willoughby (Gary Cooper) ascends the Town Hall clock to kill himself on schedule. It showed too that black-and-white is the only narrative medium that actually does the work of narrating well. You know straight away from the faces what the people are like. You look at the faces, and not the surrounds or the costuming. You can watch five or six faces in the one composition at the one time, and see everything that is happening within each one. Most importantly, being unlike life, it feels like fiction – or legend – and you accept more readily what is on the screen as the tale you are in, the given reality that will do for now.

Meet John Doe was Paul Burns' choice as the last film he would show as Festival Director in part because it *was* in black-and-white; it was a proper, measured and moving climax to a glorious, clear-headed, bald-headed and sensible regime. Few have given, like Paul, so much joy in so much depth to so many duffle-coated fools for so long on this earth. His wise and pleasurable programming has, as they say, immeasurably enriched our lives.

Except, that is, on Wednesday of the first week, when it damn near ruined mine. I flew down from Brisbane for the day to take part, with Noyce and Elfick and a dozen talkative scullions, in the twentieth anniversary screening-plus-punch-up of *Newsfront*, which Paul was touting as our very own *Citizen Kane* (disputatious multiple auteurs, questionable, shifting credits, the glory, mendacity and spleen of a vexed Australian classic already fading to pink in rusty cans on a junk heap in Guatemala), and found to my horror (a) that I'd been quoted vilely bagging Noyce as an ungrateful no-talent bum who was dead lucky to have met me and (b) that Noyce was beside the baggage carousel smiling at me. I said I'd been misquoted and he with joviality said he was absolutely certain I *hadn't* been and we shared a cab to town and we sorted out the casting of *The Quiet American* and we made it up, or sort of made it up. Enemies, I famously once said (it's in the Macquarie Dictionary, and therefore probably immortal), are people you haven't seen for a while.

What I *actually* said, for what it's worth, believing a telephone interview on the Les Murray film had ceased and the rest was mere additional, passing chat and off the record, was that Noyce was an interesting mixed bag – great at casting, and at inspiring, with his crude, crashing energy, great performances out of both actors and crew; indecisive on script; glitched and paralytic sometimes on set, yet able triumphantly to edit his way out of considerable trouble; auteur of perhaps the most suspenseful sequence in recent cinema, in *Clear and Present Danger*, involving rooftop assassins and a motorcade; an unreliable chooser of projects (*Newsfront* yes, *Sliver* no, *The Saint* no); visually undistinguished yet a master of montage and music placement and the dramatic sculpting of a single scene, and so on. I certainly did add waspishly that he'd looked right through me (jet-lagged? martinis?) when last we met, and yes, he owed me everything because *Newsfront* made him and *Heatwave* would have done for him, but it was in the context of all the rest and was moreover playfully said, but that of course was all that was quoted (Mad Dog Ellis Lashes Out Again) – by Big Bad Bryce Corbett of *Page Thirteen*, a plausible media tapeworm of a doubtless common kind whose every vapid question is a secretly planted landmine of later explosive misinterpretation and whose nose I will break at our next encounter (Mad Dog Ellis Loses It), or at least speak uncivilly to. Needless to say, he wrote nothing about the Murray film at all, why would he? And so it goes.

Sorry, Noyce; sorry. We each by now know people worse than each other, and should bind henceforth to ourselves with hoops of steel such friends as we had once in better times, when the world was young, or younger, and still had lingering flecks of that Whitlam glow.

I'm truly sorry.

And so it goes.

June, 1998

Tasmania, Bacon, Beazley and Woody

In Tasmania that last week before the election I felt I had somehow never lived anywhere else and that this was the Good Place from which I was an exile, and I wanted to be home – in the sandstone town by the water with coffee houses and bookshops and the markets on the cobblestones and the moral arguments in the Irish pubs and the stone stairways and the friendships as friendships ought to be and the weather hurrying through the sky over hills and mountains and upsloping farms and green meadows and houses of white wood under horse-tail clouds as Tolkien might have seen them in his mind. This was life in its right *proportions*, with nature and architecture and humankind and its dreaming in orderly tranquillity and not at war.

I talked, of course, with Jim Bacon about a film industry there – a *Bally-kissangel* or a *Hamish Macbeth* and a *Storm Boy* and an Imax and processing studios and sound stages and free ferries and money from a certain Beazley government – and he was very friendly and glad my presence ensured his victory as Carr and Blair and Rann and Beattie thankfully found, and my prediction of 14-2-9 was, as ever, about right. I had a good time and made friends I mean to keep as high in my heart as family members, Bob Brown among them, a great man I suspect, and Margaret Scott and the remarkable Richard Flanagan and the admirable Duncan Kerr and Peter Hay and Mike Foley and Jack Tilley, who is like a Conrad character, and his great friend Isabel, the tawny nude violinist (beloved but, in Truffaut fashion, not attained), and Julie the future senator who looks like Vanessa Redgrave at twenty and in a red spangled miniskirt danced with long legs the victory night away and life, oh yes, was sweet and fading and a southern Camelot gleaming and fleeting and the moon rising and the clouds rushing and Honey Bacon, former croupier, standing amazed as First Lady in the same building with an armful of bouquets, and so it goes.

. . . On the campaign trail today, which afforded Beazley an opportunity to appear in a shower cap in a milk factory (asked in its canteen what he wanted, he ordered a short black and then, after aghast spin-doctoring, a flat white), I arrived late, just as the Leader's car was driving away. He ordered it stopped, got out, embraced me laughing and, while cameras recorded, said he'd left instructions with the security men that I be shot, as my faxed jokes were lowering the tone of his Big Picture, and drove on. He grows more homicidally mysterious by the day, like all big generous men approaching power, I suppose. The Caligula Syndrome. Where's my horse? Let's make him a Senator! There's Ellis. Shoot him! Ho ho.

Interesting, too, how politicians mostly race for power against some physical imperfection: Blair, Beattie, Bacon, Keating, Kinnock against onrushing baldness (Thatcher, reportedly, too), Clinton against Southern-fried obesity and Teddy Kennedy against the lurid and pustular decay of his nose. Jack Kennedy, of course, against Addison's disease, which resembles AIDS. Evatt against Alzheimer's disease. Beazley *in just the last two years* is sprouting facial moles; one on his forehead, I told him, transfixes the nation while he speaks with brilliance unheard. I gave him Clearasil; told him to merely paint it on. He took it to the bathroom and came back aghast with his face two-toned and gave it up as a bad job and possibly unmanly. It will cost him, I assess, no more than fifty thousand votes, maybe eight seats, no more. Funny how these things matter. And so it goes.

I saw the Woody Allen documentary *Wild Man Blues* while awaiting the Tasmanian ferry and loved it, of course, not least because he gave such good clarinet (his music nourishes his acting, I suspect, as Norman Kaye's formidable organ-playing nourishes his and, like Robert Mitchum's poetry, Jimmy Stewart's air-force career and watercolours, Mel Gibson's many books on political theory and Graham Blundell's Nobel Prize for physics, it sits beneath his gloopy deadpan expression as an underlying quiet confidence), but mostly because he is exactly like the parts he's played. Fearful of hotel switchboards and plumbing. Cringing under the disapproval of his ninety-year-old Jewish mother. Cravenly polite with admirers. Wilting under the thumb of Soon-Yi. Gloomy about growing old. Steeped in his music and its traditions. Reclusive, self-doubting, melancholy, a tetchy centenarian in the making, I suspect, to judge by his cantankerous father, now ninety-six and getting absent-minded over lunch. And *normal*, very normal, which is why he communicates in a way that sassy ego-trippers like Warren Beatty and Robin Williams and Michael Jackson don't. Mia's view that he is a homosexual paederast climbing nightly in the bedroom windows of four-year-olds in restless quest of Quality Time is pretty unlikely I think. That he should survive such charges is a measure of how good he is, and how beloved, and rightly.

The weather is warming, and Wall Street crashing and Yeltsin trashing the furniture and Costello painting on lips in the mirror and, over Palm Beach, the sun coming gladly up. My country moves, though not with certainty, towards a Beazley imperium, a restored ABC, a Tasmanian cinema, a rapid naval conquest of a Balkanised Indonesia I suppose and better times. But it's not fixed. And all our lives might be immeasurably worse, and worse, and worse, as we jog with trickling flames toward the Olympiad and worldwide contempt and start to drink heavily and wish we lived elsewhere.

And so it goes.

September, 1998

Abbott and Costello, The Pillow Book, Star Wars

Night over Barrenjoey, the lighthouse winking, four o'clock in the morning, a dreary diffident melancholy in my heart. My book, number one on the bestseller list, has been banned (of course) on the orders of Abbott and Costello, that humourless comedy team, and their lawyers Laurel, Hardy, Curly and Mo, and the eight thousand I won't make this week, and the eight thousand I won't make next week, and the house to replace the one burnt down I won't complete this year – all weigh heavy on my pocket calculator and my soul. I get calls most days from people who already see the book as the Labor Party's New Testament ('I thought the story was over, but I know now it's only a chapter.'), or a disorderly masterpiece, or a good read, but this matters less than it might (believe me, Virginia) when you're broke and looking at thirty years of research and six months of ill-paid aftermidnight scribbling now, as they say, in turnaround. Ah well. So it goes. I want to pick up the new kitchen table at Baltic Pine workshop but my wife won't let me.

So I've been to the pictures. *The Pillow Book* was no fucking consolation. I left soon after the inscribed smooth skin of the lover of the author (female) and the publisher (male) was flayed off the back of his gorgeous corpse and a further gormless young wet naked man was being berated ('You have ruined a masterpiece!') for standing out in rain that washed the text from his body, after liking a lot of it but not being in the mood for its principal theme, the burning and drowning of masterpieces; but also detesting Greenaway's decadence (and it is nothing less, and Roman in its cannibalistic salacity) and admiring his delicate painterly power of composition, superimposition and pastiche with equal vigour and sorrow. His films, I told him to his face in a television interview, are 'a series of perfectly executed postcards dipped in vomit' and he was very annoyed; but they are, and good on him I suppose, but I wish he'd go away.

Star Wars, a restored (and lengthened) masterpiece, was more to my taste. I saw it with two little boys, and found it both good and bad in ways I hadn't remembered. A lot of the acting in the early parts was pretty crook (Darth Vader huffing and puffing, the extras all jolly-good-sir, Christopher Lee a sinister nonentity) and the golden robot C-3PO in his witterings round the sandhills tried the patience. Luke Skywalker (Mark Hamill), amazingly, didn't appear until fifteen minutes in and it wasn't until Alec Guinness arrived like the prophet Elijah out of a sandstorm, acting very well indeed, that the whole thing climbed into earnest credibility; and though it wasn't always good thereafter (the frontier-pub-with-monsters sequence was as amateur in its make-up and costuming as Halloween Night in Newport), and Han Solo (Harrison Ford) didn't arrive till *forty-five* minutes in, both film and ship took off into hyperspace and became the experience one remembered.

Although the dialogue is never much better than comic strip ('We're doomed! We'll never save the princess now!'), the layered structure is brave and masterly. A tedious length of time is expended by Alec Guinness in what looks like a concrete Mexican cabana explaining to Hamill the vexed history of the Jedi Knights and the concept of the Force, and it was right there, probably, that the long-shamed studio executive got up and rejected the entire completed film without further ado. But the scene is *necessary* (we oldies used to call such things the exposition scene, and they used to take up ten minutes of even James Bond films) and adds by its contrast to the impact of the later action sequences and by its content to the shocking revelation ('I *am* your father!') of the second chapter. The whole film has a kind of honest vivacity and gung-ho heartiness to it because, I suspect, its writer was its director (for the last and only time) and he enjoyed the technical challenges and forgave himself the bad bits where his later hacks cursed and drank and cut their way through the technological thicket wishing they were dead. The deft piss-taking rivalship of Luke and Solo for the love of the spirited, mocking Princess Leia (Carrie Fisher) was Lucas's alone, the Lucas of *American Graffiti*, and a lot harder to imagine than you might think. The additions were not many but included Jabba the Hutt, a kind of mafioso turd slug, asserting with big brown dripping eyes his loving patience with Han Solo while threatening him with imminent massacre if he does not pay his debt – an hommage, I guess, to Lucas's friend Coppola, both pleasing and revolting to watch, in the way that such things are.

And so on. So it goes. My friend Al Clark has pointed out that it was *Star Wars*, however, that changed everything, and changed it pretty much for the worse. Whereas before it little honourable films like *Five Easy Pieces* were made by the studios for, say, $4 million and were thought successes if they made $10 million, *Star Wars* proved you could make $500 million (and this was back when that was a lot of money), so the little films weren't made much any more and *Superman*, *Batman* and *ET* were and the stars' fees climbed and climbed and the meganightmare, abating somewhat lately, followed for twenty years. It was time ill lost on what were essentially chapters in the history of publicity and marketing and not film-making (though the first two Indiana Jones films were excellent in their own right and led to the overwhelming semi-masterwork *Schindler's List*) and money ill spent by, and on, those actors' agents who then took over the studios and made films essentially as deals (Zeffirelli and Gibson have the same agent, so let's make *Hamlet* with them both) and the devil Marketing overwhelmed cinema itself and it's a pity.

Star Wars therefore has a lot to answer for, Al says. Like *The Wasteland* it's both a great work of art and a bad influence. And so it goes.

April, 1997

Jonathan Hardy, Actor

O.J. Simpson said no, the bastard, to the $70 million I perhaps overgenerously offered him to play Othello opposite Nicole Kidman as Desdemona and Yahoo Serious as Iago (direction myself, producer Greg Coote, music silverchair) plus a share in the profits from the blood-spouting soft toys – on the specious grounds, the bastard, that he judged it 'a cynical casting exercise'. You can't please anyone these days. You offer international content, high culture, erotic miscegenation, immortal suspense and youth appeal and all you get is criticism. I should probably open a bookshop in North Byron Bay and forget show business altogether. I'm not as young as I was.

It's been a brum week overall. My close friends Ken Branagh and Emma Thompson broke up, and so did their star-crossed equivalents Kym Wilson and Jeremy Sims (my erstwhile Palm Beach neighbours), mere days before their triumphant opening night of *Rosencrantz and Guildenstern Are Dead*.

I went to this in the company of the Premier who explained the jokes to me. Derived from the intermittent entrances in *Hamlet* of Shakespeare's nervous understudies for Abbott and Costello – or Downer and Costello perhaps – its theme, the Premier patiently explained, is that you barely have time to discover which gig you are in and which role you should be playing before you are in your grave. Peter Collins, for instance, on weekends believes he is an admiral, the Premier said, and Phillip Adams that he is both the father of his country and an ancient Egyptian corpse. Reality is eluding both of them and neither of them is young.

How true this is, I thought that night as I packed my bags and flew south to serve Kim Beazley and my country by composing coarse descriptions of John Howard. (Yesterday's feather duster. Like a dead match on a window sill, dreaming it once was fire.) I mean, I wanted to be a Seventh Day Adventist parson once. And a fighter pilot in the coming World War against the Commies. And David McNicoll's son-in-law. And the next Orson Welles. Lord, Lord, we know who we are, as the late Ophelia of Denmark noted before she topped herself, but we know not what we may be.

Of course, this is all that Shakespeare is ever up to and it was shrewd of Stoppard to have picked it up. We are assigned a role to which we are unsuited, and we fearfully attempt to play it and come unstuck. Brutus, the philosopher, is a poor demagogue and generalissimo. Hamlet, the anarchic student, a poor assassin and palace revolutionary. Coriolanus, the good army general, a poor grassroots politician. Viola, a girl, a poor boy. Bottom, an adequate knockabout busker, a poor consort to the Queen of the Fairies. And so on. O.J. Simpson, a charismatic and stirring grid-iron player but an ill-tempered cuckold. John Howard, I suppose, an adequate suburban solicitor but a poor national saviour.

Give us this day our daily mask, as Jeremy as Guildenstern said on the night that established him as the next Bell or Branagh. Or even Welles perhaps, the irreverent young pup.

Or the next Jonathan Hardy.

Hardy dominated the show of course, as the actor-manager of the players who do *The Murder of Gonzago* so tellingly at Hamlet's behest before being cast out unpaid and slung into the castle cesspool. Gilbraltar-still and wearily sonorous, self-regretful and self-mocking, he seemed a thousand years old, a wandering Jew of the acting profession who has seen it all and found no human perversion, in spotlight or darkness, tavern yard or palace ballroom, that any longer surprises him. His mesmerising pallid stillness and lordly ursine corpulence (the product not of self-indulgence but of his second, more dodgy heart transplant) and the smallest trickle of real blood from his high and haughty nose gave an eerie monumentality to his presence that put one in mind of Ralph Richardson in his formidable age or Frank Thring on his fourteenth rough riesling, and made one feel privileged, that opening night, to be his witness.

Or made me feel that, anyway. Hardy is that Australian commonplace, an undercelebrated great man. Teacher, director, singer, screenwriter (and Oscar nominee for *Breaker Morant*), playwright, mime, enthuser (and for his first burl at Shakespeare, Jeremy's voice coach), aficionado of Duende and brilliant conversationalist, he has come with genius out of so many manholes, tap dancing and waving a straw hat, that he is barely known at all. And attention, serious attention should be paid to such a man. This week, on stage in his artistic prime, and serene as the world's last autumn, and impressive as Big Ben, important and radiant, he can be seen.

Observe him if you can, oh ye of little resonance, and learn from him, and from Jeremy, while you're up, and his amazing team.

And go out more often, all of you. History is happening all around, you bastards, and you are looking away.

August, 1991

The Boys

Little that we know – or imagine we know – of the fibro suburbs and the chronically jobless or the lure of drink or the wordless despair of working-class lives without aim or fulfilment or flavour or destination will prepare us for the fierce and punishing impact – like the smash of a heavy spanner to the bridge of the nose – of *The Boys*, a film by Gordon Graham, Stephen Sewell, Rowan Woods, Robert Connolly and John Maynard that derives from events that led to the pack-rape, stabbing and ghastly decapitation of the nurse and sometime beauty queen Anita Cobby, by three sourhearted brothers with time on their hands and a grudge or two against the universe. For it is, as in Mike Leigh's films, the thing itself; you think *this is how it must have been*.

Gordon Graham wrote the play about ten years ago, and I saw it at the time. Much has changed, but precious little of its bruised and desolate heart. The essential conundrum, how could something as basic and unremarkable and potentially admirable as *brotherly fellow-feeling* lead to such an end, baits and mocks us as before. It's a film that goes home with you and sits by your bed looking at you accusingly when you turn off the light, and is down in the kitchen with you in the morning, smirking over the Cornflakes.

At the film's beginning, Brett Sprague returns home from a year in the slammer to find his grimy-fibro family in disorder. His younger brother Stevie has a teenage girlfriend, Nola, up the duff and living in. His older brother Glenn has moved out with his girlfriend Jackie, and his mother Sandra (shades of *Hamlet*) has taken up with Abo, a Maori drifter. His own girlfriend Michelle, moreover, treats him with a mixture of sexual energy and ball-busting scorn.

Like the late Prince of Denmark, Brett is displeased by the changes in his once ordered kingdom. He is, we gather, a control freak – a bit like (perhaps) Paul Keating, whose background, verbal skills and contemptuous know-it-all curve of the mouth he probably shares. He wants things back the way they were. He wants, moreover, some level of homicidal revenge on the bottleshop owner (the always marvellous Peter Hehir) who not only put him in gaol but sliced his belly with a carving knife.

As played by David Wenham, Brett's mixture of suppuration, scar tissue, tenderness, flammable menace, beer-sucking silence, lazy arrogance and bloodymindedness adds up to the best and deepest and fullest etching of such a man on film since, I guess, M. Brando in *A Streetcar Named Desire*. As in all great characters in world drama (Hamlet, Uncle Vanya, Willy Loman, Jimmy Porter) you are seeing him, although he is very familiar, up there for the first time. Every move he makes is both unexpected and, within his toey tempestuous character, inevitable. The scene where, caught short with unwelcome impotence and fiddling fruitlessly in his trousers, he reacts to Michelle's taunt 'You took it up the arse, didn't you?' with murderous roaring violence, is one of the most frightening (and understandable from both perspectives) I've seen.

As Michelle the ever-surprising Toni Collette is feisty, horny, contemptuous, foul-mouthed and unrecognisable; and *working class* to her painted fingertips. So too is Lyn Curran as Sandra, the weary life-worn mum: nothing human surprises her any more, nothing promised brings her hope; a fearful grimy forgiveness of expected evil is all her lot; a collaboration with the worst. As Glenn and Stevie, the sons who follow, like wary disciples, Brett's lordly hunger for sacrificial blood, John Polson (the smarter, more salvageable one) and Anthony Hayes (the dumber, more passive and wreckable one) add volumes of doomed goodness to the tragedy. If only, we feel, they had lived by a *beach*, and so been able each morning to wrestle the battering surf, or cleanse their egos on a bucking windsurfer, to booze less and gripe less, and get the dirty water off their chests with athletic challenge and the odd guitar solo, none of it would have happened, not the worst of it anyway. Anna Lise as the fearful dim pregnant Nola is equally good, and near definitive, and as Jackie, the spiky restless fiancée begging Glenn to break with his toxic brothers and drive off down the road with her, Jeanette Cronin, long a favourite actress of mine, communicates more than most Oscar laureates and has us in tears.

I'm sure its long rehearsals helped, and its testing pre-history as a play in several versions. The young director Rowan Woods has, however, maddeningly achieved a kind of lasting masterpiece yet failed his primary audience *by omitting the murder itself*, or any *hint* of the murder (a few frantic blurred freeze-frames were all that was needed), and smugly awaiting the critics' echoing applause in the empty cinema – depending on the local audience's pre-knowledge of the Cobby pack-rape and decapitation (it will not be as widely remembered in, say, Somalia) to fill the maddening silence at the end. He is a towering fool to do this, and he or his masters should fix it. They would do as well to leave the murder out of *Othello*, having worked up so gravely and tenderly to it, for the good and solid reason that the rape-murder failed in *Blackrock*. So, you morons, did the film.

It is nonetheless (and I may be wrong in my surly caveat) our film of the year – one that like *Angel Baby* opens up to us a moral universe, and a chapter of the battered heart, that we did not believe could ever engage our sympathies. See it just for the performances, if you need a reason, Wenham's and Polson's in particular, as the Lucifer and Gabriel of Australia's wounded underworld. See it fast. It may be gone very soon.

March, 1998

Bastards from the Bush 1

We started filming this week at long last in Sydney, then Yass, then Canberra, in a painter's studio, a schoolroom, a poolroom, a pub, a street corner, a garish pink convertible, a lakeside park, a suburban footpath, and the office in Parliament House of Kim Beazley, a documentary about me and Les Murray cast in the shape of a road film, Rosencrantz and Guildenstern in roisterous voyage to the end of the night, down tracks winding back to Gundagais and Jerusalems long left but unforgotten, discuss. The director Geoff Burton and I began our first, uncompleted film on Les in 1967 – some landscape shots, a quarrel on location, a postponement, no money for stock, a thirty-year delay – and this will have to do instead, I guess; in the long run we are all dead, discuss, and this will have to do.

Les was less controversial back then, and not yet, as now, world famous; not my Best Man yet nor the fierce combative campaigner for literary grants, the Republic, a new Australian flag and the whitetrash North Coast peasantry he long has brandished as his tribe and kin; not yet the narrow survivor, as he is of late, of a liver abscess, a coma, a weekend of national prayer, an immediate Russian spy scandal, a manageable case of diabetes and a Black Dog of depression he wrote a bleak little book about. Yet he still seems a lot like Les to me: his girth was slimmer in 1959 when I met him first but his buoyancy, his erudition, his vivid ribaldry and witch's cackle are much the same. I told him I planned to turn him into a soft toy: you pull a string and it cackles just like Les. He negotiated, quickly, for his percentage, cackling the while.

Life has a way of rounding itself out into a pleasing shape and in the next two years I am to work, in a number of happy coincidences, with most of my warmest and best-loved old acquaintance: with Storry Walton on a NIDA book and Geoff Barnes (met also in 1959) on the Murray film and Norman Kaye and Andy Lloyd-James on a film about the Stolen Children,

and Freudenberg and Evan Williams on *The Backroom Shakespeare* and Denny
Lawrence and Chris Neal and John Derum and Des Davis (known since
1956) on our long-wrought musical *Neon Street*, and with Richard Brennan
and Al Clark and Maggie Fink, if you can call it work, on our Round Table
shortlist and Mungo MacCallum on our travelling pundit extravaganza and
Gerry Connolly (if he rings me back) on a stage revue and Paul Cox on a
brainless Hollywood epic and sharing Byron Bay digs in the fifty-third of
our mateship with Leyland Minter (Wayland Gibson of *The Nostradamus
Kid*), and Murray and Burton, of course, and Jack my son and Annie my
better three-quarters, and all of it in sum is like a last bright, sad, glib round-
up of my life (though Michael Boddy is not on the list as yet, nor Stephen
Ramsey, both sorely missed) before we all of us begin that final garrulous
limping dawdle into the grave. *Ask not*, as the other Willy neatly says, *where
man's glory most begins and ends, But only say of me, I had such friends.*

And so it goes, and goes. Murray of the living means, perhaps, the most
of the mates. We did a sequence where he and I drink whisky and stumble
fatly about on Parliament's steps in afternoon light, and the dialogue went
as follows.

Ellis: This is a terrible day, Murray. (*waves newspaper, doomfully*) April 8th, 1998. Even
as we speak, Aboriginal land rights are being abolished, just up the hill. (*sits, drinking
whisky*) At midnight men came ashore with dogs on chains to end a hundred years
of union progress. And on top of this *Tammy Wynette is eight hours dead*! Our greatest,
most eloquent ally in the noble cause of female subjugation . . .

Murray: (*comfortably*) There, there, Robert . . .

Ellis: (*overlapping*) . . . And what are you going to do about it?

Murray: I'll do something, I'll do something, but not until they give me my just
recognition . . .

Ellis: You'll get your just recognition! I shall make you Poet Laureate!

Murray: I don't want to be Poet Laureate.

Ellis: (*shaking head*) The man is insatiable.

Murray: (*buoyantly*) Bloke said to me the other day, 'Australia is being sold off to
foreigners.' And I thought about it, and I shook my head and said, 'Poor fellows!
Poor fellows!'

You get the drift. I was near forgetting how nice it is to be off again on a
gonzo shoot in a big pink silly car (fear and loathing on the road to Gundagai), in perpetual transit from town to town and stuff-up to stuff-up, in
vehicles that won't start or get lost or have their keys untimely locked in
their boot, or to lie awake in grimy hotels while black dogs distantly bay or
closely pant and whinge, or bellicose coppers chase burglars down the corridor just outside, or to implore in vain with waved fish the curlews to come
back, come back, for the panorama lakeside silhouette that is unrepeatable

and beautiful and yearningly imagined thereafter, or to watch Kim Beazley's moistening minder point once again to his watch and cover his eyes while his jovial boss chats breezily on with Murray well into the second hour, beweeping Gettysburg and Gallipoli and the Australian fighting man, or to eat Chinese and drink too much and shout of contraception's evils to a blameless adjacent female and curse the heavens and the economic fashion and life's brevity and drink some more. If there are better ways to make a living, please ring me with the information, reverse charges, at any hour.

April, 1998

Bastards from the Bush 2

Our stock is being held up on the wharves by demonstrating unionists and I'm being asked to tell my friend Bob Carr to get it released as part of his dramatic intervention in the current civil war. Les Murray is refusing to go up in a hot-air balloon and so am I if it's Thursday, my unlucky day, and our featured actor Noel Pearson is not returning my calls, possibly because we're out of mobile range, or it might be something else, like he currently loathes Les, the infamous redneck, or he's gone fishing. A drenching rain is gratifying the farmers of Bunyah but washing out precious days of the shoot before Murray leaves the country on May the second. My son Jack drove up to join us last night through pelting rain then tumbling fog in pitch darkness before his radio eerily ceased, in what my dad, the commercial traveller, used to call the Bulahdelah Effect – a sort of Twilight Zone all travellers enter in that hellhole's environs, and for a time he drove on through a kind of Hammer Film miasma, believing he was already dead. A bureaucrat is refusing to let Murray re-enact his boyhood sufferings at the hands of the giggling prickteasers of Taree High but says we can do it outside the gate. We wait until he goes home for the day and climb the fence. Our meal last night in The Little Snail in Forster was excellent, with everyone passing up the escargots for the local oysters, which the maître d' disarmingly swears no longer give you hepatitis. Murray and Izzard, the producer, are quarrelling over the authentic locations of the Sacred Relics and drinking too much, I think, in view of Murray's diabetes. He says we can film him injecting himself through his dirty trouser leg and happily rolling his eyes, but he may change his mind when he sobers up, if he lives.

It's a film shoot like many another – by which I mean, I suppose, an experience unlike any other in life – and very specific to itself, like a particular invasion by moonlight of a particular ominous coastline in a particular local war – unrepeatable, wondrous, terrifying. It's what you live in for a while, like a crushing bout of influenza, and then you live somewhere else, avoiding all contact with your fellow-sufferers, lest, as of war, you remember too much.

As always with documentaries there seems to be adequate footage for a ten-hour miniseries but somehow insufficient zingers for the brisk and shallow fifty minutes the broadcaster probably requires. A dinner conversation with Les and Val, his wife, and his autistic son Alexander (whose every fraught utterance is like a message translated through five intervening codes and languages), you could run for an hour on its own, pretty well uncut, as you likewise could our pungent and festering duologues on the Deity. We're talking now about the CD-ROM, the archival interviews and a sequel two-parter where he shows me Scotland and I show him Ireland and the coffee-table book and the audio-cassettes and the soft toy spinoffs; but life may well be too short, Master Shallow, and that's a fact; the film was after all a reaction to Murray nearly dying, and Ray Alchin died last week, the usual unexpected massive heart attack, at my age, and so it goes.

My other contemporary, John Howard, is not, as I write this, looking too healthy either. *It doesn't require a meeting*, he said last night. *All it requires is the Leader of the Opposition to tell his mates in the union to obey the law of the land. Because we all of us must obey the law. In the meantime we're sticking with Patrick, however many court cases it takes to prove they didn't break the law, as they're now being accused of doing, by the law courts, who are wrong.* What a creepy little contradictory fellow. I've noticed lately that his most common sentence formulation begins with the words *I have never tried to hide the fact that* – or *No-one could accuse me of concealing my intention to* – or *I've never tried to deceive the Australian public about my plans for the waterfront*, or whatever. This probably means, if one follows basic Freud, that most of his existence is an aching preoccupation with what he can hide, or fudge, or retrospectively deny having said, or blame Cheryl Kernot or Beazley for: *It's not my fault, it's nothing to do with me, I'm only the Prime Minister.* Now and then it catches up with him, as when he said a year back, 'I *did* say no student would be worse off, and no student *will* be worse off. I didn't say no *future* student would be worse off.' It's easy to imagine him as the class sneak in primary school in short pants and a constant fury of confected prepubescent self-righteousness: *It wasn't me that told on you, I bet it was him. Now look, I've got these new cigarette cards, and this broken yo-yo, going cheap, going cheap.*

But I digress: I'm turning of late into a political bore and I can't help it.

I think democracy matters, and it does. Or it used to anyway.

Denise Hunter, our editor, says the part where Les and I shout filthy poems from a speeding convertible is the sequence thus far of most interest, and we should, as a rule, omit all Latin puns. Ah well. A fight on the Newcastle with grappling hooks might do the trick, with a background male chorus of tattooed wharfies singing 'Arise Ye Workers from Your Slumbers', and throwing molotov cocktails. Or perhaps a nude wrestling scene: male brotherhood, Murray, male brotherhood. We live in interesting times.

April, 1998

Playing Brendan Behan 1

The run-through was a disaster and afterwards I, the lead actor, behaved badly. The director was at fault, I raged, for rushing us through it, and the lighting man for blinding me, and the set designer for near crippling me, and the fucking *playwright*, whose knowledge, I said, of sexual love and conjugal foreplay was just about as deft and graceful as my tap dancing.

The actual problem, that I remembered only a third of my lines and uttered those with hoarse incompetence and grew increasingly tense and bloodyminded as the evening tottered onward, was plain to everyone sitting nervously afterwards in the mouldy echoing Mission Theatre in downtown Newcastle, and that included me.

The short-term memory of the mid-aged whisky sipper, sneered the tiny devil in my mind, *the stage fright of Larry Olivier, once he was fifty-three.* The lifelong nightmare of myself and others of being on stage in a play whose text is unknown to you and suddenly discerning that you've got no trousers on. I stormed out of the theatre, drove to Sydney and the next day in the Premier's Office (my day job) informed the State Treasurer in a crisp fax that he was a fucking fool. I slopped my chicken laksa at the Chifley Centre, and that night woke up with the symptoms of a stroke, or possibly chicken laksa.

These are the bitter fruits of returning to the stage after twenty-five years in a role longer than Hamlet that involves activities – singing, dancing, eight-minute monologues and the smoking of cigars – I've not before attempted even in private.

I'm losing money, eating badly, sleeping in a bedroom somewhat smaller than the bed and I'm having a terrific time. I understand now why acting is addictive, and how it consumes you, and becomes your creed and anthem and *raison d'être*. Let me explain.

It lets your steam out. Aggressions built up over years can be expelled, got rid of, in a single well-crafted rage against the universe. Griefs that else might turn cancerous are healed, removed, made silent, purged, no more. Like two hours in a gym (or so I'm reliably informed) it leaves you a better citizen, well-mannered to the point of catatonia, and smiling at perfect strangers in the street.

This doesn't feel like me at all.

It puts you in among a group of people that soon becomes your family. The friendship, the level of instant intimacy, the unstinted forgiving loyalty and constant helpfulness happens nowhere else, with the possible exception of an Irish pub. The tendency of leading actors to fall in love with their leading ladies, root like rabbits and come to their senses on closing night is now perfectly understandable to me though in my case I'm sure she'd respond forcefully, with a well-practised working-class right cross. This intimacy is retrievable in later life, I believe, and its price is above rubies. *Dahling! how've you been?* It means something, just like Anzac Day, or Newcastle-earthquake-night reunions.

The popular belief that actors are dumb because they don't make money fails to account for the things they have that are better than money.

One of them is this marvellous mixture of choicelessness and explored variety. You have to say the lines, but you can say them in so many ways. You never leave your body, but the voice you have can be one of many. You can go to corners of yourself without harm (in my case drunken self-pity) that explored in such depth in real life would bring you to ruin. You can live another life (in my case Brendan Behan's) that in some way illuminates and parallels your own.

You can try things on, ways of being charming, ways of behaving repulsively, that real life will not permit you. In one scene I am required to sodomise a shop dummy. In another to sing 'Down by the Salley Gardens' in a clear and pleasing lyric tenor. In another to imitate King Kong. Those who know me will not find these things in my previous repertoire. This will change. I am told by the (female) director that I have a lovely smile of some seductiveness, and I should use it. This is a staggering discovery for one who for the past two decades has rarely smiled at all, believing it the silent equivalent of a bare-faced lie.

There are other things I am learning from my overweight Dublin alcoholic doppelgänger that come as entirely new conceptions. One of them is foreplay. That was a joke. Another is Irish mock heroism, the belief and simultaneous disbelief in the worth of romantic bravery. Another is *bad* jokes told in such a way that the laughs come nonetheless, from that extraordinary Irish quality that is known as charm, but in fact is a whole lot more. Another one is what it's like to be in the culture of the IRA – moonlit, angry, constant, unfulfilled – and how it hunts you down through life and never lets your aching conscience rest.

And so on. All in all, a worthwhile gig. I've come to love Newcastle too and its unpretentious working-class directness and cultural ferocity of purpose. Here they act for nothing at a standard as good as anywhere, and they love the work. I approach opening night with a mixture of stark fear, growing shame and a curious conviction as I lie abed in my cupboard exhausted and purged that it's good to be alive.

September, 1995

Playing Brendan Behan 2

The play closed after, for Newcastle, record audiences, or record audiences for a non-musical, and my reputation as an actor, hitherto nonexistent, was much enhanced, and my Irish accent complimented even by Dubliners. An IRA member played the fiddle unbidden in the front row to the final song and several Novocastrians, not altogether unhinged, came back three times. 'A rich and engaging performance,' said the local critic and Steve J. Spears with his usual mixture of irony and malice wrote, 'Bob Ellis is God!' in the theatre visitors' book, and I was widely celebrated and bought Guinness and much interviewed. The usual question – *how much was I like Brendan Behan?* – I regularly scotched with my police record of eighteen years' commuting to Palm Beach without a single culpable breathalysation and my happy family life but I was never believed. All journalism these days is the superimposition of cartoon figures on reality and they had me tabbed.

I suppose they assumed I drank on stage. I did once, when the froth on the prop Guinness vanished and the genuine article was substituted. I took one sip and blew the entire first act out of my mind. I called for humiliating prompts throughout it and by the second act was sober and angry enough to be impressive and so survived, God help me, the opening night, but every performance thereafter I drank on stage only coffee topped with whipped cream, and carrot juice backstage at interval. My performances varied. Some nights I was hoarse but adequate, others sonorous but dull. A couple of nights I was (I was told) Oscar standard, funny, moving, profound, and the rest of it. And so it goes.

The good nights always coincided with attendant episodes of enough sleep and, I am sorry to say, red meat, carrot juice and chastity. On those nights I felt I was driving the play like a trusty old car and it was not driving me. I felt I could range within it the way one would on honeymoon within a wife: great pleasure, great sharing, complete security.

I can see now why views of the same play are so different. Each night is a special, unrepeatable dream and the telepathic expectation of the audience and its response then renders it great or mediocre. It is all very strange, dreaming to order as Ralph Richardson called it, and something very like magic is always involved. It is no wonder actors are always superstitious, or why they never willingly abandon their trade.

It also explains why (say) John Gaden, who is never off stage, is always so calm in real life and why Marlon Brando, who has been off-stage for forty-seven years, is always furious. Theatre's footlit purgation becomes a psychological need which if denied can drive the sufferer mad. My twenty-eight-year sabbatical from live acting could be seen by unkind persons in the same light I suppose. I understand there is an actual medical state called Limelight Deprivation Syndrome. Usually fathered on ex-politicians like Hawke or Richo, it fits like a glove ex-actors too, ex-actors like Ronald Reagan, Cary Grant, Greta Garbo, George Whaley, Gough Whitlam and me.

Not too ex I hope. I spent today on the floor of the House of Representatives eyeballing an alarmed Bronwyn Bishop who got up and fled. This was upon landing a part-time job with Kim Beazley – approved last night by the full Cabinet in a mood, Kim said, of some levity. It was agreeable, I suppose, to be parachuting into Australian history at a time of flux and crisis, but I'd rather have had two more weeks playing Brendan, I think, in a good town among relatives, old teachers and good new friends.

The play is coming to Sydney, maybe. The wonderful cast is tetchy now over rates of pay and floors to doss on. The dates are uncomfortable, and bad news if there's a snap election. I shouted at the female director while leaving the wrap party. Her husband the author is in a swither of frantic ambition and interceding between us. I've been nominated for an Aria, whatever that may be, for the best rock-clip of 1994, which I directed one long night in Hyde Park. I'm writing a one-man show with Victor Emeljanow, another live white male, on the subject of George Eliot, a dead white female, and directing a miniseries written by my wife on the subject, ominously, of divorce. I'm enjoying Bob Carr's deadpan rendition of my Demidenko jokes. I'd like to direct a film of *The First Stone* but I think Garner hates me. And a film of *Idlewild* in which Jack Kennedy and Marilyn Monroe are still alive and in their seventies and assassins are coming to get them.

So it goes. I try to tell my son Jack, a star of the cancelled series *Echo Point*, that it's all part of life's rich pageant, and there is much to do, and many years ahead. He won't believe me. His oratorio, *The Long Green Shore*, named after his godfather's posthumous book, a book about World War Two, proceeds at a turbulent pace, with loud chords and crashes from his adjacent music room, lest he perish ere it's done. He is sixteen years and nine months old.

There's no business like it.

October, 1995

Playing Brendan Behan 3

Much like the curse of *Macbeth*, I was tardily told, and a chill clutched at my heart, all actors believe as an article of faith in a curse on the Bondi Pavilion, and in the subsequent week the evidence mounted.

Lightning storms bedevilled my opening soliloquy. A chair crumbled to splinters under me in the seventh minute of the first act. A smoothly doffed shoe would not, somehow, go back on. An old Olivetti stage typewriter jammed. A musical keyboard wheezily ceased in mid-performance. A crucial hip flask (crucial to the play, that is) went missing in the second act, and I had to leave the stage betimes to seek it, and was heard hoarsely shrieking at the mortified female director behind the backcloth while on stage two trapped duettists sang an Irish dirge in rising panic, doubting my return.

In the second act on some nights an adjacent loudspeaker admonished potential litterers of the beach, on others a big band played Glenn Miller favourites over tender moments of the drama. A coin that I in Newcastle nightly tossed the full width of the stage to be caught with ease by Tim Richards had him in Bondi nightly humiliated and crawling among the footlights and babbling improvisations. On the day of the opening performance the two young actor–musicians Jonathan and Phil drove off to Coogee for a late siesta, and on the way back their aged limousine repeatedly broke down. They in anguish abandoned it in Bondi Junction and sprinted down the long hill, arriving two minutes after curtain-up time and further traumatised their fellow actors (the undersigned among them) by exhaustedly and violently chundering in the hall. My throat in response seized up, I took a swift nip of Gilbey's gin to loosen it and thirty seconds after the belated curtain-up forgot my lines, then visibly panicked and the *Herald* critic, a tall and surly crosspatch who is on my list, then panned the play and forty of my close friends dishonoured their ticket bookings with paltry excuses, the Premier among them.

So it goes. Nonetheless it was much applauded by those that came, including the Prime Ministerial adviser Shamus Dawes – a man, surprisingly, of Irish lineage; Chris Haywood, John Clayton, George Whaley, Richard Brennan, Hayden Keenan, Stephen Ramsey, Norman Kaye, the famous bookseller Nicholas Pounder who came twice, the producer Andrena Finlay who though nine months' pregnant came twice, a letter-writing Brendan fan who saw it twice in Newcastle and once in Bondi – and, at long last, the *Sun Herald* critic Pamela Payne. *Priscilla's* producer Al Clark, who made a film once with the drunk and dying Richard Burton, wrote of it: 'A fearlessly physical performance, full of rage and playfulness, that brings gravity to slapstick and a puncturing absurdity to catastrophe in a revelatory tightrope walk.'

Though too late, probably. The time, I fear, is out of joint for all of us portly renaissance men from the island of the day before yesterday (Max Cullen the painter, sculptor, poet, cartoonist, playwright, actor, director, mimic, jazz singer, TV reporter and tap dancer will I know agree) and no-one believes any more you can do two things fairly deftly let alone five. Ustinov? We'll let you know. If Mr Welles is still drunk in the foyer please throw him down the stairs.

Let it rest, perturbed spirit, and the angry ghost of the Bondi Pavilion (Who is it I wonder? Thring? Meillon? Hal Lashwood? Spencer the Garbage Man?) do its worst. I was privileged anyway to work with Kate and Brian and Tim and Julie and Phil and Jonathan and Carl and Felicity and Terry, Terry especially, strong, intent and ferociously focused and gifted people who in a better civilisation would have a significant future of sorts, their names up in lights, their faces on a silver screen.

It was good as well to stand out on the verandah over the murmurous neon-stippled water and drink margaritas and Guinness with good and tested friends while the junk-sculpted dragon by the surf breathed fire and the young folk swam nude and the Melanesian hand-drums played and to look across at the moonlit cubist Cezanne perfection of Bondi peninsula where in the unchanged Raffles Hotel, Les Murray and I shared digs and our landlord Abe Saffron talked mildly over breakfast Cornflakes of ordinary things, once, in a distant galaxy long, long ago; and to remember too John Hargreaves who once on a bus to Canberra said gently to me after a speech, 'Well, you're a performer now,' and me thinking maybe at last I was.

Memories are made of this, and they must be hunted down. They are all we know on earth, and all we need to know.

February, 1995

The Roots of Talent

A debate

I am abashed, Madam Chair, at our rare good fortune, and the contrasting misery of our largely blameless though morally contemptible opponents, who have to argue an unsustainable proposition of such rank absurdity I weep for them. For if, Madam Chair, the two years of piano lessons that Mozart had before he composed 'Twinkle Twinkle Little Star' at the age of four were irrelevant to this titanic achievement, if his avaricious father had not set him on a course of music from the hour he had begun to totter about the parlour in his nappy, their argument is, if he had not even had access to a piano, he would still have somehow composed great music anyway, as our opponents' argument would have it. And if Shakespeare, their argument is, poor benighted fools, if Shakespeare had not, alone among his siblings, been taught to read and to write, he would have written stage plays anyway, far from London, in his father's Stratford butcher's shop after hours, never having seen a play of the London kind in his entire life. And if Dickens had not learned shorthand he would still have written as much, and as vividly and freshly, and still died as young.

Going a little further they are here, in fact, alleging, poor fools, that if Picasso had been born in Alice Springs and had lived his entire life in Broken Hill he would have done the exact same paintings and been the exact same rage of Paris and the drinking friend of Cocteau and Stravinsky that he was. They are arguing that Dostoevsky without his gambling debts would have written as much and as fast and as melancholically. That Byron, in a society that tolerated bisexuality, incest, club feet, Harrovians and feminine rhyming, would have been harassed and scalded into writing as bitchily and vengefully as he did. That if Oscar Wilde had not gone to Trinity

289

and Oxford and Greece and Paris and Brighton and the Cafe Royale and Reading Gaol, had he not met and bonked Robbie Ross at the early age of thirty and Bosie a little later, had he stayed in Dublin and worked in the front office as the receptionist for his father, the oculist, and occasionally reviewed a book, with hand on heart, for the *Catholic Times*, or taken holy orders and become a priest in Inniskillen, he *still* would have written *The Importance of Being Earnest* and *The Picture of Dorian Gray* and *The Ballad of Reading Gaol*, or he would have been able to imagine all that anyway, he was born that good, and that particular, that genetically foredoomed to be, divinely, Oscar.

Birth I believe is not good enough, Madam Chair. It takes a little more. It takes a culture, a setting and a local church and a school and a family, a bereavement or a dreadful childhood hurt as a rule – Art is not born in you, Les Murray once said, it is grafted in you through a wound – and an agent and a sympathetic publisher and above all, or in most cases, a rich first wife. Hemingway had a rich first wife, and Scott Fitzgerald, and T.S. Eliot, and D.H. Lawrence and W.B. Yeats and G.B. Shaw, and a time in youth to experiment and slowly fashion over scotch and ice and martinis in appropriate Parisian cafes and Manhattan round tables and Key West bars the style and content they would later brag of as unaidedly their own. No loyal toast is drunk, no monument erected, no fanfare sounded to the rich first wives of our literary giants to whom the century owes so much, nor, I suggest, to the rich first mistresses of this fecund century, all three of them, Ottoline, Anaïs and Antonia, with Diane Keaton coming up on the inside. It was a great distress, I know, to my old friend Clive James when he propositioned Lady Antonia Fraser, now Pinter, and she said, 'No thank you, I only sleep with the first eleven', but she was correctly doing her duty and thinking of England, and the annual queue of her lovers for the Booker Prize.

Behind every great artist, Madam Chair, there is a multitude of stimulation and influence and rare inviting windows of opportunity – a pen, an easel, a pipe organ, a schoolteacher, a pertinent round of applause in early youth, a piece of advice, only connect, avoid the adverb, from another artist; in the case of John Mortimer and Gore Vidal, a blind progenitor to whom in boyhood they read great verse aloud. This is what strokes and goads and what makes an artist. It is no accident Virginia Woolf married a publisher, that Manning Clark listened week after week to his father the preacher, that W.B. Yeats was for forty years enflamed by the beauty of Maude Gonne, or rather it is an accident that *makes* an artist, from the materials at hand.

My team, whose names escape me, will further redundantly argue our case and with a growing sense of anticlimax gather up the necessary points for our unstoppable victory. I grieve for our opponents, Madam Chair, but there is nought to do but pulverise them on the field of honour and shout them alcohol in the following hour of their grief and once more tell them gently, as they sob and bicker in their devastation and in their cups, that artists are made, not born.

March, 1998

Shakespeare in Love

From *Shakespeare in Love* you get – between the boisterous anachronisms – some vivid sense of the sheer *uncertainty* (Black Plague, censorship, duels, arrest, theatre closure, the likely instant bankruptcy of all concerned) in which the great man did his writing.

You sense too that *Romeo and Juliet,* his first big hit, written when he was twenty-nine, was derived from some actual event in his own life, some great thwarted longing for an unattained beloved by cruel fortune lost and always mourned. *Would that I were a glove upon that hand, That I might touch that cheek!* You do not get from this much sense of the Victorian Gentleman image of Shakespeare, chastely at work with his quill in his Blackfriars boarding house, each night writing home a letter to his doting, distant wife.

It seems more roisterous, promiscuous and risky than that, more fuelled with ale, and flighty wives and one-night stands. The contemporary diaries of Simon Forman – astrologer, herbalist, psychologist, necromancer and surgeon, the model for Dr Tench in the film – show a blithe attitude to sex in Elizabethan women, many of whom he himself had stand-up couplings with in his surgery, rapidly, between appointments. Though contraception was unknown and pregnancy likely, they did it anyway, and let the risk of death by clap or jack – as fatal as AIDS then – come and go as it may. It has been through the ages – in bed, park, alley or brothel – a popular pastime, no mistake. It is rarely foregone, even in times of the closest scrutiny, five people in a room, wakeful children, chickens on the bed. The Great Urge will out, that's certain.

Whether Shakespeare was as promiscuous as Forman (who came to some of the Great Hack's opening nights), or as obsessive and true-hearted a lover as Romeo or Hamlet, will never be known. His letters and diaries and play-drafts were burnt in the 1660s by the man who bought his house and needed the room they were in to breed pheasants, the worst act of cultural arson since the ninety lost plays of Sophocles and Lord knows what else were destroyed when Caesar's army unintentionally set alight the Library of Alexandria, and Titus' destruction of Jerusalem burnt much that was written, I guess, of Jesus Christ and his followers.

So Shakespeare, like the mysterious Nazarene rabbi, has become a *tabula rasa*, as to some extent, therefore, has the eye of his beholder. We mould him in our own image, find evidence in his work for Christian belief, agnosticism, spiritualist summoning of dead fathers, love of countryside, love of metropolitan squalor, love of battle, hatred of war, love of revelry, respect for temperance and getting early to bed, whatever. What he was really like, unless the Dark Lady's diaries turn up, will never be known.

How he *wrote*, however, at the rate he did, two and a half plays a year while acting, directing, theatre-managing and with the occasional acrimonious visit to Stratford, is easier to guess.

What he did, I think, was this. He would stay up late, drinking and quarrelling and (possibly) wooing and swiving in stews and alleyways and then *before he slept* would go to his desk and write, without preparation, while his mind was tender and wounded, whatever was there in his head unpurged. *Tomorrow and tomorrow. To be or not to be.* He would then put it in a drawer, and forget about it. Days or weeks later, stone-cold sober, he would begin the writing of a play. It would always be based on *something*, a history, a legend, an Italian novella in translation, or, as in the case of *The Yorkshire Tragedy* or *The Tempest*, a sensational contemporary event, the equivalent of a headline story of the day.

And he would write it like a modern television hack – with exposition ('What news on the Rialto?'), character, motivation, plot points, act breaks and the rest of it. *But when he came to a certain point*, the point where you might, in a Broadway musical, need an aria or a big song number, he would go to his drawer, and pull out one of his drunk night raves, and paste it in. Whatever it was, it would always fit, somehow. Of course it would.

This immediately explains how he was able, unlike any dramatist writing since, to give us both the workaday and ordinary, and the unspoken, nightmarish parts of the lives we lead, the hidden depths, in the same play. It explains why he never lost control. He was as a writer a puritan in the workplace by day, and a demonic reveller by night. He was, like all of us, to double business bound, but he admitted it.

And so he could be a respectable burgher in Stratford, and a tempestuous bar-room roué in London (a reverse of Oscar Wilde's pet formula 'Ernest in town and Jack in the country'), a faithful husband when under the scrutiny of a close provincial (and largely Catholic) township, and a passionate bisexual cruiser in a poxy violent metropolis, where every day might be his last.

I suspect he knew, too, what has only lately become plain to me, that human personality is not a constant, it is *situational*. We are each of us a wandering archipelago of random impulses, and in another place, where the plane lands, or the ship docks or the train pulls in, we are another person. Romeo might have settled down with Rosaline, and met no trouble. Instead, he found himself booked, as it were, into another story (*O I am fortune's fool!*) and played it out to the death. We all do this, and might have done otherwise. And Shakespeare shows us this great truth all the time. Each of his heroes is given a task, to which he is inadequate, and it brings him down into ruin, or the climactic laughter that soon heals all. He is enduringly popular because of this. He shows us how changeable we are, and how readily we can look into his dreams, and go with them.

April, 1999

Assassins

I saw three times in a week the NIDA production of Sondheim's *Assassins* – a work that with grim and blazing jollity celebrates the dark side of the American Dream (it's about most of the deranged young folk that ever took a shot at an American President) – and a certain *déjà vu* enraptured me now and then. It was to the same small theatre, the Parade, now (of course) condemned, that in 1970 I came night after night for *The Legend of King O'Malley*, another play-with-music about America and politics and heroes in gunsights and gods that failed, with another group of NIDA students, who – as it happens – along with authors Michael Boddy and myself, and its director John Bell, and its producer John Clark, revived and relaunched Australian theatre (it is said in the textbooks) into its big and buoyant renaissance.

The actors then were Robyn Nevin, John Paramor, Nick Lathouris, Kate Fitzpatrick, David Cameron, Gillian Jones, Rex Cramphorne, William Yang and Terry O'Brien and, in the subsequent Tasmanian tour, Sandy Gore, Penne Hackforth-Jones and Garry McDonald, and they all had subsequent careers of note, not always in acting – but they weren't any better as a bunch than the astonishing young people full of the joy and bloom of youth and the flaming ambition to do and prevail without limits in a future yet to be that I saw at work this week in the old Parade; and soon, I guess, to be crowding the cattle calls and soap auditions and pizza commercial waiting rooms on what is left of the dole.

For it's a different world now, and the country, as John Wilkes Booth remarks, is not what it was, and I don't like it, with Whitlam-era socialism's ragged remnants – like NIDA, the ABC, the Sydney Theatre Company, the Sydney Dance Company, the now inoperative Meryl Tankard, the mortally squeezed Theatre South and Hunter Valley and New England miracles of thrifty devoted sacrifice and the Adelaide and various writers' festivals – the only bright patches in a fulminating cloud of cannibal barbarism that is devouring our best and finest in arithmetic's name and spewing them into the void.

I'm not that intelligent (my paupered family will testify to this), and it's only lately become clear what makes me happiest. It is live performance: the spectacle now, in the flesh, in the present tense, of the performer's vivid struggle with the work that encoils and impels him, and his awareness of us who are watching. And it's this that gives most human beings most of their joy on earth I think – at school concerts, choir recitals, folk festivals, Moomba and Easter parades and Pamplona bull runs and nights in Rio and the Gay and Lesbian Mardi Gras – so Howardism, of course, must wipe it out, since too much happiness in others is hard for Howard and Reith and Alston to bear: read Alston's letters to the ABC, oh my fellow citizens, and weep for Edens lost.

I was happy and happy again at *Assassins*, which had twelve performances and is no more. I dragged along Bob Carr to see it, blinking through his jet lag, and he loved it and met and lauded the actors, and he's been unpleasingly singing the songs in the office ever since. And I guess he doesn't have the money as yet to do the obvious, and build theatre complexes around resident repertory companies in Queanbeyan, Bathurst, Armidale, Parkes and Byron Bay, but when Beazley gets in this November 21 maybe he will, or they will.

Ah, what's the use. That is heaven's part, our part, as Willy Yeats rightly reckoned, to murmur name upon name, as a mother names her child, when sleep at last has come on limbs that had run wild. Peter Knowles as John Hinckley, drab and soiled and brow-beaten, singing to an image of Jodie Foster how he will prove worthy of her love. Maryanne McCormack as Squeaky Fromme, with more brimming mad energy than Jennifer Hagan and Beatrice Lillie and Barbra Streisand put together, extolling Charles Manson as the Son of God. Ben Graetz, Mick Dodson's nephew, as Czolgosz, who shot McKinley, cursing his life, on six cents an hour, in the burning, scarring heat of the bottle factory and wooing Andrea Wallis's mysterious, coquettish, romantic, deluded, radiant Emma Goldman. Matt Newton, Bert's son, as Charlie Guiteau who shot Garfield, in a performance of demonic, smiling mischief (the pale grey eyes and thin moustache of the music-hall villain and the Puckish vaudeville dance steps of the Music Man) worthy of Donald Sinden or Robert Preston, putting the noose around his neck and singing of his pleasure in the Lord. Myles Pollard as Sam Byck, who planned to crash a jumbo jet into the White House but was shot before he got the plane off the ground, in a performance as good as De Niro in *The King of Comedy*, railing to a cassette recorder advice to Leonard Bernstein on how to write better songs. Jeremy Brennan as Giuseppe Zangara who shot at Roosevelt because his stomach was troubling him and dies in a blaze of defiance on the electric chair, and Ana Below as Sarah Jane Moore, bothered and chaotic and useless with firearms, who couldn't hit Orson Welles, she said, if he was sitting in her lap, who shot her dog by mistake and brought her little son along to watch her shoot Gerald Ford, and missed. And Sam Worthington as Lee Harvey Oswald, a beset and moody urban yokel uncertain whether to shoot himself, his wife or the President that morning and moved by a local coincidence to change history.

And Morgan O'Neill, gloomy, fraught and Mephistophelian, as John Wilkes Booth and his ghost, an actor brooding over bad reviews and the wreck of his beloved South, who almost has us convinced that Lincoln, who killed his country, also deserved to die – until, in his penultimate line, he calls Lincoln a 'nigger lover' and our minds change. And Douglas Blakie, lean and confronting, with a voice as clear and seizing as all cruelty, as the Luciferish Balladeer. And Benhur Helwende, in a remarkable cameo, as a dysfunctional infant in maniacal need of an icecream.

It was, for what it's worth, and not that it matters any more, a wonderful show, arrestingly directed by Tony Knight, and musicked by only two pianos, and designed superbly (a *Cheers* bar at the end of the universe where the killers booze and commiserate, a big pink car that comes on with Sam Byck in it and Frank on the radio singing 'I Did It My Way') by Peter Cooke, not that it matters. It's over now unless somebody, John Derum perhaps, Des Davis perhaps, cares to pick it up in the months ahead. But they didn't see it, so how would they know.

I saw it, and drank in all that it meant about our current ethic of Success that is souring and mocking and maddening us all (if you are not Murdoch or Madonna or Mandela or Mandelson or Millken forget it, go blow your brains out, you're nothing, get off the earth) and grieved that I will not see it again. Grieved too, as I told Matt Newton, that I will not live to see all his performances – if, of course, he gets his chance, his day in the limelight, and why should he, since excellence is no argument in this Rationalist world any more. And I'm thinking about things now, and sifting the speech I am to write for Geoffrey Rush to give at the Arts Labor launch. It could be good. It ought to be. There is so much to say.

Lord, give me the strength. And God help us now.

July, 1998

Len Teale

That week Ellis was beginning film scenarios on the boy Bradman and the dying man Fred Hollows and was therefore in the mood, he supposed, though congruently sick at heart, for the thronged eucalyptine obsequies for Leonard Teale, another Australian legend and his latest friend to suddenly die, and for a ceremony rich with war medals, fraternal tribute, remembered kindness, recited Lawson and the rest of it, in the high-windowed cathedral beside the Town Hall, but not, somehow, though he should have expected it, for the smiling television image hung high on a sandstone pillar of a dim bishop warmly asserting that though he did not personally know the deceased he was nonetheless confident he was now rejoicing in heaven, a reward outclassing, mark you, any earthly Logie or even Oscar, and presumably harmonising with Banjo and Henry in a bebopping angel choir. This kind of vigilant moron, decided Ellis, added another terror to death and my corpse at any rate must not fall into his clutches.

Backstage in wavering shadow as, at the Glen Street Theatre, Ellis's bushfire benefit concert proceeded, Len Teale, small and frail and pensive, his face unassertively but recognisably royal, with fingertips to his downcast chin, listened as Jill Perryman sang 'Someone To Watch Over Me'. 'How many hours of our life,' Ellis murmured to him, 'are spent here quietly like this in the dark, waiting to go on?'

'It's a good feeling,' Len said. 'There are always good acts to follow, things to learn.'

They sat quietly in the shadows then discussed Surprise, Surprise, *the situation comedy Ellis after the by-election would write for him. A wise career move, said Len, one that might see him out.*

On stage Barry Humphries again ignited those immemorial human puppets,

Les, Edna, Sandy, that the obsequious gladdy-trembling audience greeted again as family, as rich relations come again on a visit, and left them at curtain fall in that shimmering state of glow and sadness that in Stratford afflicts the fans of Shakespeare. As always poop, snot and intimate aperture puns, and donger-waving and sprays of spittle cohabited with a kind of autumnal jingoist cry of the genes, a heartsore plumbing of memorial chords that went beyond mere Anglo-Oz nostalgia, an incantation of brand names and shopfronts and street signs that seemed to Ellis, moved now in Len's wake as never before, especially by Sandy, his sere and yellow Master Shallow, as an attempt at national resurrection. There were, said Sandy, better days. In Humphries, as in Len, and Frank Hardy, and Manning Clark and, yes, Fred Hollows, the old Australia radiated its laconic benevolence but in few now living: Les Murray perhaps, Hugh Lunn, Barry Oakley, John Williamson. It would die with them, and with Ellis, probably soon.

Braving the moment, Ellis told Liz Teale of Peter Sellers' funeral – how, amid coincidental peals of thunder and lightning flashes, the bemused parson eventually said the deceased had asked that a certain piece of music be played as his body was committed to the flames, and as the coffin moved a hired big band burst into 'In The Mood'. Liz laughed uproariously, and Neville Teale too, who in the cathedral had reduced the audience to tears with the reading, in a voice that was so like Len's, of Lawson's 'Bush Undertaker', about an inarticulate stockman trying to find the words to farewell his mate. How well the bereaved behave, thought Ellis, looking around at the jovial gathering in Len's Castlecrag home, in the hour of their worst extremity. He kissed Liz and left, still oddly dry-eyed, unable to imagine a world without Len. He was like the gnarled familiar gum tree in everyone's backyard, always hiding its secrets, always good to see. Always there.

Gabi showed Ellis around Fred Hollows' home – the room he held court in while dying, the workshop where through his last years he lovingly crafted chairs and tables whose use would outlive him, the photos in thousands pasted everywhere of his last adventure, saving the world from blindness against the clock. His little girls ran busily round the big house, jumping and shrieking. One of them still cried herself to sleep, said Gabi, asking *where's my daddy gone?* Ellis afterwards mused on death's odd orderings. Frank Hardy outlived Fred, his great mate, by six months, Len Teale survived Johnny Ewart by two, Johnny Willie Fennell by a year. Ayrton Senna outlived by two days John Smith. Harold Wilson is alive. Jackie Kennedy survived Dick Nixon by a month. Rose Kennedy, 102, is still alive, and her son Joe Junior fifty years dead. Don Bradman has outlived Len Teale. John Gielgud, now ninety and full of mischief, made news as Hamlet in 1928, and River Phoenix is dead. We do not know how long we have and that's a fact, or when the curtain may suddenly fall.

Once again Ellis fluffed the line. Around him on the Homicide *set of 1965 the impatience was becoming audible. Across the desk from him Len Teale said, 'It's all right. Take it gently. You'll get there.' What a kind man, thought Ellis. Not at all the man I expected.*

Remembering it, twenty-nine years later, while driving home from Castle-crag, Ellis finally cried.

May, 1994

BOOK SEVEN
At the Barricades

My Country, My Shame

Speech at Bondi

These are terrible days in the story of our country. All that so lately seemed obvious – the family, mateship, good fellowship, ordinary neighbourly decency, the right to organise as workers, a fair go – is under attack and under question. We are losing daily and hourly the final critical battle for Australia's good name in the world. We are becoming ashamed, when overseas, to admit we are Australian, as good white liberal South Africans and Rhodesians were in the sixties ashamed of their birthright. We have become in the world's eyes, or very nearly become, just another white-trash provincial sub-racist post-colonial backwater of small-town hoons and drive-by shootings and McDonald's and Supersavers and casual street violence and prison suicides and drugs – and we are seen as having a perverse and rancorous pride, somehow, in our littleness of mind.

Australia wasn't always like this, or so we were told. It was once the place where victims of tyranny came for a happy ending – where there was space and opportunity and money if you worked and schools for your children and care when you were old, or that was the story. Not any more. We have been downsized, made efficient, and competitive and sad and scared and broke and angry and looking for someone to blame. We have become globalised and corporatised and Thatcherised, which means, as Neil Kinnock once put it, no sisterhood, no brotherhood, no neighbourhood, no number other than one, no person other than me.

But the shame we now feel has always been there, I believe, however hidden under those various euphemisms – cultural cringe, the lucky country, down under – that concealed its actual cause. The shame was always there, because we remembered from history, somehow remembered, the massacres and poisonings and kidnappings and routine slaveries and raping of children on which this mild laconic nation was proudly built. And at the heart of the horror of Howardism – not Hansonism but Howardism – is the anger that gathers like an inflammation round that unadmitted shame. His phrase 'relaxed and comfortable about Australia's past' means, in its essence, 'lest we remember'. For if we did remember, oh my countrymen, oh what then would come of it? Some notion of justice perhaps. Some notion of debt. And that would never do.

Because it does not take much presence of mind to realise that people who have occupied a particular tract of land for 117 000 years before Moses came to Israel have a right to visit it now and then. It does not take much gumption to realise that children torn from their mothers on the basis of their skin colour, and institutionalised with hard labour and forbidden to write to their mothers or meet them or to read their mothers' letters, have a legitimate grievance in law. It does not take much to imagine, as I have lately, over and over, a compound with barbed wire down the middle, with mothers on the one side and crying babies on the other and the mothers able to recognise the individual cries of their individual babies and not being able to get to them and cutting their hands when they tried, suckling babies that were soon all taken away and never seen or held again, or to rate this as grounds for an apology, and a sorry day, and a reconciliation, if that were imaginable, and a monument like the cenotaph to all that was taken and lost and bewept and never given back or held in loving arms. It doesn't take much to imagine that. But it takes a bit to imagine what to do next.

These are terrible days for my country, if I can any more bear to call it mine. I am making a film on the Stolen Children, of course, but what of that. I am writing a book on these and attendant matters, and the horror we are enduring, but what of that. It doesn't feel much like mine any more. It feels like a bloodstained intractable bickering mess, with the graves of the murdered innocent stretching coast to coast and crying out for recognition – of the lives not had, and the loves not found because an all-wise conqueror deemed it best they be ethnically cleansed of not only belief but name and homeland and family. Today is only a small beginning, a footnote on a preface to chapter one if what we must do for all our sakes is to come to pass. Let us do it, but let us do the next thing, and the next. Let us get on with the job. I thank you.

March, 1998

Poisoned Waterholes

A speech to the Mosman RSL

On the matter of poisoned waterholes, I wrote in my book, *Goodbye Jerusalem*, a year ago, of hearing on the radio, out of the past, the voice of Dame Mary Gilmore, telling of going once as a little girl with her mother by horse and sulky to visit a killing ground.

'The waterhole was poisoned,' she said, 'and of course everyone that drank of the water was dead. I recollect my mother saying she wanted to see where they were, and we drove along a little bush track, and by the side of the waterhole there was the father lying dead, the mother beside him, and the baby, about eighteen months or two years old, on his hands and knees dead from drinking the milk of his mother. All through the bush, all around, were dead bodies.'

All around. I went on to say in my book that the Big Lie of our culture was that there weren't many Aborigines here, not really, after 120 000 years of occupation and procreation, not more than a million, really, and so not many killed. In a country the size of China, which had 200 million in 1788, after only 20 000 years of occupation, not so many Aborigines here, and not so many killed. Not the five million Noel Butlin said there were here. No way. Nothing like it. Impossible.

Don't think about it.

Relaxed and comfortable. Put your feet up. Watch the Home Shopping Channel.

Don't think about it.

I *have* thought about it since, and of the time span of Aboriginal occupation here, and the time span of my white tribe's occupation here, of 120 000 years versus two hundred years, a ratio of only 600 to one, which means that if the human habitation of this land had been twenty-four hours, from midnight to midnight, my tribe would have got here at two and a half minutes to midnight.

And yet we have all these rights. And they, miraculously, have none.

And I thought about those babies poisoned by their mother's milk by the infected waterholes and I numbered them in my mind in tens of thousands and tried to conjure up their suckling faces as their lives were extinguished and their traditions, and I went walking by Pittwater with my dogs this morning and I wrote on the back of an envelope this fumbled beginning of a credo, and it is this.

I do not hold that land acquired by the murder of men and children is mine by right of any law that is just, when that land was got in a war that was undeclared and followed by no signed surrender. I do not hold that the Sultan of Brunei, whatever his billions, has rights to that land that are greater than those who have lived and worshipped there since 117 000 years before Moses came to Israel.

I do not hold that the slaughter of children, by land or poisoned mother's milk or ethnic cleansing pogrom, in Rwanda or Yugoslavia or Oodnadatta, is justifiable before any court, reducible in its manifest evil by any repaid amount, or erasable of its horror by any confected apology by any craven politician withering in the glare of the Gallup Polls.

And yet I believe words must be found.

Nor do I hold to the myth of the hard-working white land-owning pioneer, Dad Rudd and his brood of jovial yokels, when so many of them, thousands of them, connived at or committed or covered up in *classic* white-wash the murder of their neighbours, and in any case were involved on a daily basis in the murder of their trusting friends the cows and sheep.

And I am not, by God, too pleased with the pseudo-democratic notion, in this democracy that is only twenty years old, that the half million killed or fatally infected Aborigines, and their four or eight million unborn descendants, and the hundreds of thousands humiliated into alcoholic poisoning or nooses in filthy gaols, have no *right*, just because they are dead, to a vote, or a voice, and no claim on our sympathies as ghosts beyond the grave. I hold that we are involved, and still involved, in their fate, as England is still involved in the Potato Famine of Ireland and the killing there by starvation of half a million children who did no harm.

And the words must be found.

And I am not too pleased myself to have benefited from this carnage, to have a block of land with wondrous water views that other eyes looked out from, 100 000 years before the pharaohs came to Egypt, people who spoke of legends already ancient then, and held corroborees and planned their sacred year.

And I do not hold there is any right of conquest in the modern world, but a right of negotiation, a right to reasoned arbitration, a right to justice or some ghost of it after a trial by a jury of our peers, a right to plead and campaign and publicise, to organise and harass and threaten, and, oh yes, a right to vote. I do not believe Tim Fischer has more right to these rights than I or you, nor his ally the Sultan of Brunei, nor his political fancy woman Pauline Hanson.

And I hold as well that in a hundred years the present colonial occupiers of Chechnya and West Jerusalem and Alice Springs and Wounded Knee will be the pariahs of history and herded in the public mind with the Crusaders and the Nazis and the Ku Klux Klan. Evil in history's eyes is easily known, as easily as we now see the ignorant patronising evil of the present government, those crab lice on the body politic, sucking all decency from its bloodstream and reducing to suppurating sores a once adequate Australian ethic of a fair go, who will not and cannot see what is before them, which is future shame.

And yet words must be found.

And I guess there is in the world no shame that is greater than the murder of children, as happened here in the twenties and thirties and forties and fifties and sixties and seventies, and happened to Lois O'Donoghue, the thieving of their souls.

And I am involved in this shame, because I knew of it, and thought little of it, and did not speak, in fifty years, as I speak now of the moral obscenity that this ignominious Prime Minister has decided is not worth a penny in recompense, or a word of official apology – unlike the billions that have gone to the *private* health funds and the gun owners and the fuel rebate freaks and the removal men that brought him back safe to Kirribilli that he might have more often a water view and the company of his unstolen children and his servants and silver plate and the little continuing shrivelled world of inner Wollstonecraft that is his mind.

And though I am involved, and I am guilty too, I cannot apologise for I have not the authority and the electoral mandate, I can only articulate my shame. My country, my shame.

And words must be found.

For where there be governments, they shall fall, and where there be traditions and religions, they shall wither away. But I hold these things to be self-evident, and also eternal, that all humankind has a *right*, inalienable and unquestionable, to the children they have brought into the world, to see and know and care for them, and a right to the land of their fathers and to their forefathers' faith if they choose to hold it still, and its holy objects and sacred ground that cannot be bought by money or erased by narrow Cabinet majorities or fear of rich and greedy men.

I hold these things to be minimums and I curse the government that does not. And I ask them, even them, to find the words.

For words must be found.

I thank you.

September, 1997

Hansonism

Speech at Manly Corso

In England where I was last week I was asked as an Australian not only about Pauline Hanson and her brain-dead politics of whinge but also if it was true that black land rights were being cancelled this week, and black housing cut by half a billion dollars and the Aboriginal work-for-the-dole scheme cancelled, and Radio Australia starved of its money and the Stolen Children inquiry starved of its money, and if black young men were hanging themselves with knotted blankets in outback gaols and if a boycott threatened our Olympic Games, and if a little black boy was doused in petrol and set alight in Townsville, and if our shillyshallying Prime Minister cried out for nine months not against racism but against political correctness, and gave first his preselection and then his preferences to Pauline Hanson, and if two little Aboriginal boys were sent untried into incarceration for the six weeks of their Christmas holidays for allegedly, and wrongfully, spitting on Pauline Hanson (I am the victim here, she said, I am the victim here), and if Malaysian tourists were assaulted in Surfers Paradise and if Pauline Hanson wrongly said blacks had done it, and if the Prime Minister refused to go to a dinner honouring Victor Chang on the interesting moral ground that a princess was going too. And I said to these English, no, no, that is not my true country, it is only a small minority of bruised and smarting rednecks pining for their guns, and I came home and it was 10 per cent and rising, and 20 per cent in Queensland and rising, and it was my country after all, my country and my shame.

So it seems, or it seems today, that this shrill and ignorant fishwife, this political booby prize, this K-Mart Enoch Powell who would not herself, if put to it, pass her own English language test for entering Australia, this shrieking defender of Australian culture, who would not know the Australian culture of Lawson and Paterson and Streeton and Roberts and Olga Masters and Les Murray and Ronald McKee and Nick Enright and Peter Kenna and Hannie Raison and Jack O'Hagan and John Williamson and Eric Bogle if it came up and bit her, this dysfunctional rejected parent and turbulent and addled multiple divorcee has wished her own emotional chaos on a once fairly peaceful and amiable nation of gentle and dignified minorities and mixed it up in the internationals' minds with the former South Africa and the former Rhodesia and Indonesia in 1965 and Fiji in 1987 and Alabama in 1932 and Mississippi in 1952 and it's a pity.

And this is an era now that will be known soon as the Howard–Hanson era, an era only nine months long and giving birth to such vast and vagrant monsters of the bloodstained mind, such multiplying gremlins as we must stifle soon by some urgent large demonstration of our democratic resolve, by a national strike perhaps, or a great class-action brought by persecuted Chinese people before some international court, or a simple citizen's arrest perhaps, of one in constant criminal breach of her civil and parliamentary obligations, soon, before it is too late.

I am no orator as John Howard is, and I do not have the refined social conscience of Stan Zemanek, and I do not have the power in the land, and over tanks and armies, of the mighty generalissimo Bronwyn Bishop, but in the words of Michael Collins, I do have one power, and that is my refusal, and you have that power too, to say no, this is not my true country, as loudly as you can.

Come home Australia from all this vile American craziness of the dollar first and humanity last. Come home to neighbourhood. Come home to caring, come home to ordinary decency. Come home to your true country. I thank you.

May, 1997

Lorenzo Ervin's Bad Character

I'm on the board of the new Sydney Writers' Week, and I was happy for a while. I had this plan of a big-name short-list – Woody Allen, Ingmar Bergman, Arthur Miller, Lord Jenkins of Hillhead, Norman Mailer and Arthur Schlesinger Junior. Then Lorenzo Ervin was arrested because of his bad character and I realised they all might be too.

For Woody Allen is widely believed to be a paederast. Ingmar Bergman, a three-wives-in-the-bath man from way back, absconded from Sweden and stayed away ten years to evade his income tax. Arthur Miller, a former communist, in the McCarthyist era wrote a play, *The Crucible*, that mocked his government and advocated its overthrow. Norman Mailer stabbed his wife while running for Mayor of New York and while filming *Maidstone* bit off Rip Torn's ear. Arthur Schlesinger, as official Kennedy historian, hid the family's mafia connections and Jack's womanising. And Lord Jenkins, while Harold Wilson's Home Secretary, allowed the publication of *Lady Chatterley's Lover*, a tract that favours heterosexual sodomy.

Men of bad character indeed.

Amanda Vanstone might protest that she would deal with these men on a case-by-case basis but I dare not suggest them now.

Some would say hijacking a plane to Cuba is qualitatively different as a character defect to molesting children, advocating buggery, dodging tax and planning Marxist revolution. But I don't think this government does. These names must be pricked down, along with the Nobel Laureate Arafat, the revisionist historian Irving and Gerry Adams, the hero of his country.

Some bad characters luckily are dead or the visitors' blacklist would be longer. Shamir and Rabin, the Jewish terrorists. Begin, who blew up the King David Hotel, killing scores of English. Robert Mitchum, alumnus of a chain gang, gaoled for drug use. Jimmy Stewart, who as a pilot killed innocent women and children in the terror bombing of Germany. Henry Fonda, two of whose wives suicided. J. Edgar Hoover, the cross-dressing blackmailer and mafia dupe. Lucky for them.

George Bush is alive, of course, once head of a world-wide terrorist organisation called the CIA. Teddy Kennedy, the drunken womaniser suspected of murder. Mike Tyson, the convicted rapist and, like Mailer, earbiter. Tony Blair, lead singer of the grunge band The Ugly Rumours. Nelson Mandela, the bomb-planting saboteur, gaoled for twenty-seven years. Jane Fonda, who flew to Hanoi to give comfort (and possibly weight-loss advice) to her nation's enemies. They must also be pricked down.

. . . There are character grounds, in short, for keeping a lot of people out of the country. Why not those listed above? It's a puzzle.

Supposing you argue that hijacking-and-kidnapping is different, even at the age of nineteen, even while fleeing for your life from the FBI who have gunned down many of your colleagues – behaving like many a freedom fighter in many a modern country, Nicaragua, South Africa. Even though nobody died and you served fourteen years and got an eventual pardon from your fellow terrorist Bush.

Is it hijacking and kidnapping that makes his character different? Or is it his colour? And his colour-heavy message? For if it isn't his colour, and his awareness of it, *what is the good senator afraid he will do here*? Hijack a Qantas 727 to New Zealand and drink all the first-class champagne? Teach Aborigines how to kidnap, throw bombs, make speeches? Why, after behaving well in twenty-two countries, will he suddenly go mad and turn criminal here? I'm sure she can't say.

And I'm also pretty sure she doesn't believe it. All she really wants to do is give a black man a hard time for talking to blacks about black wrongs with eloquence.

Prove that I lie.

Racism is above all other things a product of stupidity. Amanda Vanstone is either a very stupid woman or the mouthpiece of a very stupid Prime Minister – one who daily makes us look like crazy bigots before a baffled world.

Let's test it a little further. Let's ask these morons if they propose to keep O.J. Simpson out, on the grounds of his character. And Michael Jackson, the witness briber. And Muhammad Ali, the draft dodger and Black Muslim separatist. Let's test it out on some *big* black names for a change.

Do it, Amanda. Do it.

July, 1997

A State School Education

A speech to principals and teachers in Dee Why

I am a product of the state school system, of Lismore High in northern New South Wales, in those years, 1954–58, the biggest secondary school in Australia, with fourteen hundred pupils and a first year that went from 1A to 1P and classes with never less that forty-two pupils. In my year and the year ahead of me were Phil Wilkins, the sporting journalist, David Ellyard, the science broadcaster and weatherman, Ken Buttrum, the current head of the Department of Juvenile Justice of New South Wales, Peter Arnison, the former army general in charge of the defence of the land mass of Australia and lately Governor of Queensland, Robert Stitt, the well-known QC, Roy Masters, the famous football coach and journalist, Chris Masters, the *Four Corners* reporter, Leyland Minter, bound soon to win the Nobel Prize for biochemistry, and John Niland, the vice-chancellor of the University of New South Wales – among a formidable army of doctors, nurses, teachers, lawyers and social workers equally deserving, I believe, of honourable fame as any of us.

All of us were saved by Lismore High, in the sense that none of our parents could have then afforded a private school, and the only door through to the larger and wider civilisation that is now our accustomed habitat was the big old red-brick building on the corner of Keen and Magellan streets in downtown Lismore, and its two acres or so of unremarkable playing fields, and certain selfless teachers I am proud to have known. I most of all owe, I believe, the saving of my soul to that school and those teachers, in particular Bill Marwood, who made me love Shakespeare, Bill Maiden, who made me love writing, and Des Davis, now head of Theatre South in Wollongong, who made me love public speaking, a soul saved from the narrow paranoid confines of the Seventh Day Adventist religion in which I was raised, that might have seen me in my life in its offshoot, the Branch Davidian, in the famous fire and shoot-out in Waco, Texas, had it not been for Lismore High and the teachers, and the spelling tests, and the history lessons, and the rote-learned French and Latin and *Golden Treasury* poetry. I now freely honour them all as my saviours, my enlargers out of neurotic flimsiness and into the whole person I *think* I now am.

What does this mean? It means, I think, that Lismore High gave *us* not only the intellectual armaments that made it possible for us to prevail in the great world beyond Lismore, but it also gave *us* a sense of that possibility. There were Aborigines not admitted to that school who therefore had no sense of that possibility, no sense, no hope, of their admissibility to the high-er reaches of our allegedly egalitarian society, who therefore did not attain them, for want of a good state high school, like children of all colours who in generations to come will not attain it for want of a good local state high school, for want of a free education of the highest order. Which means that in the coming generations the Bob Carrs and Michael Kirbys and Mary Gaudrons and Murray Gleesons, the Paul Landas and Phillip Adamses and Peter Thompsons and Greg Pickhavers and John Bells and John Doyles, the Geraldine Doogues and Sue Masters and Olga Masters and Ernie Dingos and Neville Wrans and Bruce Pettys and Bill Leaks and Les Murrays and John Howards will not have the leeway, the room to expand, as artists and craftsmen and performers and citizens and human beings, that their previous incarnations had, and some of them might fall not only by the wayside or down the cracks, but into suicidal despondency, and drug abuse, and lives of crime, and prison, and early death, for want of a good state school like mine, and Michael Kirby's and Roy Masters' and Bob Carr's.

There is a theory about these days that a good state school can be had on the cheap, that less and less funding in some of its areas will not matter, that it can be adequately measured by the cost-effectiveness, that is the *cheapness*, compared with last year, of each graduation, much as you might say that the most *cheaply* built space rocket *of course* will reach the moon as well as the most dearly built space rocket. Do not give heed to those who hold that triumph, triumph in any area of endeavour, can be had on the cheap – that if you make the film *Titanic* for half the 200 million that the current film cost it will do as well at the box office. It will not. It may do very badly indeed. It is precisely as foolish as saying, and the logic is just the same, that studying for one hundred hours for a history exam will get you the same result as studying for two hundred hours.

We must look carefully before we go along with this economic anorexia, I believe, at whom economic rationalism is for. It is not for us. It is not for the wharfies at Patrick soon to be retrenched and probably not paid. It is not for the miners of Cobar still unpaid. It is not for the twenty thousand public servants lately sacked in Canberra from jobs they were doing well. It is not for the pupils of the schools that were sold up by Greiner and Kennett because they were big real-estate earners with handy positions and water views. It was for other people. It was for the screen jockeys and boardroom Caesars who matter.

It was for people who inexplicably do not practise what they preach. Chris Corrigan, for instance, in the week after his sacking of fourteen hundred wharfies for the absurdly high level of their wages – $72 000 some of them, less $27 000 tax for seventy-hour weeks on the night-shift, working Sundays, in physical danger and bitter cold – made out of share movements in those few days $2.1 million, or the average wharfie's average wage for thirty-two years. He made it in less than a week. Chris Corrigan you will not find giving up his next holiday in Switzerland, or his third house, or his next restaurant meal, for the sake of overall company profit. Oh no, sacrifice is for others. Neither will you find him driving a crane on the wharves, or managing a forklift, or sweeping and cleaning, to increase company efficiency. Of course not. Chris Corrigan's work is otherwise. Chris Corrigan is a stevedore. Or he is this week. When he has stripped the assets of Patrick, which was always his plan, and got the generous Australian citizenry to pay $250 million of his debt, he will move on down the road. And so will Kennett. And so will Kemp. And so will John Aquilina. And so did Rodney Cavalier, to his baronial mansion in Bowral, where I used to visit him, when we were friends. And Terry Metherill, in his present happy ending.

You, however, do not have their option, as economic rationalists, of transmuting yourself into something more convenient when your decisions have brought your school to its crisis, to cut your losses when those losses are fifty or sixty or two hundred fragile human beings, who might otherwise have prevailed as Roy Masters and John Niland and Ken Buttrum and I did in the great world, who are now contemplating their first burgled household and their first stolen VCR for the price of their first fix. *They are not expendable*, and you must never walk away from them for any bottom line, whatever the prevailing economic fashion of the day. For fashions change. For thirty years the world economy was run on the thesis of an imminent, likely nuclear war, started accidentally perhaps, between the United States and the

Soviet Union, and billions upon billions were spent, hundreds of billions upon thousands of billions that might otherwise have been spent on public education, arraigning those two great superpowers against this transfixing apocalyptic likelihood, enriching those who might be simply described as Mr Burns beyond the dreams of Midas, and academically impoverishing Lisa Simpson because of that bottom line, because the prevailing fashion was to fight the Reds with the ingredients of Chernobyl to the last nuclear warhead and the last life on earth, lest we all soon suffer the dread fate of the Vietnamese, a fate worse than nuclear war.

Well, the fashion has now altered from better dead than red, to never *in* the red, at any cost, and economic rationalism is upon us, or economic correctness as I call it, with all the fearful force of the Cold War. Economic correctness holds to the belief that anyone who is not a shareholder is as expendable as any soldier on the Somme, and his life and happiness of no *account* and the only thing that has meaning and philosophical significance in the world is the annual increase, preferably in billions, in company profits. Thus Telstra, of blessed memory, posted an annual profit of two billion and celebrated not by giving its workers a bonus or a box of chocolates or a Christmas letter of thanks but by sacking twenty thousand of them, and wrecking or distorting or bitterly harassing the lives of twenty thousand families and the equilibrium of scores of small towns in order that it might be sold at a slightly higher price to foreign shareholders, a higher price in billions that were then quite shrewdly loaned to General Suharto.

I am currently writing a book on economic rationalism called *First Abolish the Customer – One Hundred Arguments Against Economic Rationalism* and I am having difficulty in keeping the number of arguments down to one hundred and one, because the arguments for it are so manifestly incompetent and foolish and probably corrupt.

What is important for you to realise is that you are in the grip of a kind of nut religion, such as was the basis of the arms race and the Cold War, a nut religion which like many nut religions, Scientology for instance, is also a scam. And you, as head-teachers, in the thrall of this nut religion, are offering up unto it human sacrifice, directly contributing to the deaths or the shrivelled lives or the ruined dreams of those *initially* decent young people who are its victims, to satisfy some Torquemada at Moody's or Standard and Poors who has a different definition now of sin and redemption, of sacrifice and salvation, and believes for instance that it is more economically efficient for 80 per cent of Indonesia to starve, or some sado-monetarist in the Kennett government who profoundly believes that money is always better spent in the Crown Casino than in the schoolrooms of the poorer suburbs, schoolrooms currently being turned to rubble as the schools are demolished and the real estate sold up to satisfy the bottom line.

Your bottom line, as teachers, as educators, as educational administrators, cannot, must not, be expressed in figures, for your bottom line is a great phantom convocation of the souls of those whose lives on earth you touch, souls that are saved or cast into outer darkness with a millstone round their neck by your decision to equip, or not, a science laboratory, or close down, or not, a language course, or buy, or not, a particular computer, or cancel, or not, a school play, souls like mine and Roy Masters' and Les Murray's that were better given room to grow than nipped in the bud, or starved of oxygen at birth, souls that, as the souls on the Somme were *not*, however the figures panned out, were *not* expendable, even for the noble cause of making Christopher Corrigan or Christopher Skase or Jeffrey Kennett or Peter Costello a hundred million or so in profit to send on to General Suharto, or on to Doug Moran, or Keith Williams, much more worthy causes. For what shall it profit a man, as penniless Nazarene beggar Jeshua Ben Yusif, also known as a rabbi or teacher, once asked, what shall it *profit* a man if he gain the whole world and lose his own soul? And what shall it profit a man or a woman like you if you gain the long-fought-for bottom line but in its black ink lose the potential of the next Albert Einstein or the next Stephen Hawking or the next Peter Carey or John Williamson or Barry Jones or Jason Lee? I would not be in your shoes for a thousand new shares in Telstra. I do not envy your task. I cannot easily advise on its politics. I do not know how in its thrall you will get through the day, and the night, and the morning after of every coming week for the rest of your lives as you address that question, with fear, and anguish, and conscience. But I ask you to realise what that question is.

May, 1998

Mackellar, 1994

Wheezing, Ellis's car, a rusty, one-eyed, twenty-year-old Volvo, rounded a muddy corner as the rain increased in Warriewood. Up ahead, suddenly, there loomed Bronwyn Bishop's campaign panel van, a modest unostentatious engine of battle chosen, after the hilarious financial scandal of her sacked staff's golden handshakes, to advertise her born-again frugality, and suddenly out of the drenched underpopulated polling booth, the lady herself, under her mouldy red-bearded minder's white umbrella. Ellis tooted his horn. She looked brightly round, and the multidentated hungry grimace, so evocative of Luna Park, melted in descending rain into bilious fury in the instant of recognition. He looked, as he had a year before, into murderous Lady Macbeth eyes that were black pits of immemorial revenge.

'Are you under the illusion you're winning yet?' asked Ian Temby, just three days retired, at the noisy bar of the Hoyts Cinema on the night of The Custodian's *premiere. Ellis, accepting the proffered Heineken, looked at him with puzzlement. 'Yes,' he said. He had never imagined anything else. 'Ah, it gets us all like that,' Temby murmured comfortingly. 'In the second-last week usually. Cheers.' Ellis regarded with sudden blinking misgiving this mild, grey-haired, tin-voiced and arguably saintly inquisitor, Labor candidate for Perth in 1977, another lost Prime Minister perhaps, one inexplicably unelected. It couldn't be, could it? What does he mean, illusion, the prick? I've spent all this MONEY.*

A jostling scrum of television cameras retreated as Ellis, the momentarily conquering hero, bulkily advanced through the clinging drizzle. 'My gut feeling,' he said with portly thoughtfulness, his belly prominent in the shot, 'is there'll be no result tonight. It'll go to preferences, to postal votes, to a re-count and then to court.' The journos nodded sombrely, the *Herald* exit poll in Avalon, sensationally unexpected by all but our mouldy Quixote, suggested he was right. Ellis then, though very tired and feeling a bit like a triumphant El Cid dead and strapped upright on his horse, but victorious nonetheless, strode with the media juggernaut into Narrabeen High and with camera-conscious melancholy voted for himself.

'Your Benefit Concert, sweetness,' said Jane Cameron, Ellis's agent, 'looks like showing a loss.' Ellis sighed and, nibbling on a mint leaf, pondered man's ingratitude. Richo, his charismatic ally and current mate, had chosen, the prick, that very afternoon to resign and everyone stayed home to watch television, and Lex Marinos, Gerry Connolly, Wendy Harmer, Leonard Teale, Phil Scott, Drew Forsythe, Su Cruikshank, Noah Taylor, Terry Serio, Terry Bader, George Washingmachine and the usual suspects bedazzled with their unstinting brilliance an all but empty theatre while a pissed, astonished nation mourned. Ellis, in his widely dreaded but unstoppable sub-Shakespearian oration, beginning 'My fellow monarchists', cursed time's whirligig and its revenges as usual, but the PM *radio program especially, for bumping from its schedule an 'Ellis Gaining' item (it was in the vigorous promo, but not in the actual show) in favour of twenty minutes of manly tears for Richo, the now immortal, unjustly denigrated number cruncher and patriot. Ellis, six years older than Richo, wondered vaguely, as his publicity opportunities shrank and his mortal deadline neared, if he was making his run too late. At his age, he bleakly noted, Shakespeare had two months to live. Neville Wran, his fellow late-starter, hoarsely consoled him in the foyer however, calling the night a good gig nonetheless, one of the best, and*

dawdled anonymously out into Paddington moonlight, a ghost like so many others, his fifteen minutes over, his adrenalin withdrawn.

Despondency hung over Avalon Primary assembly hall, like radiation over doomed Chernobyl. The figures, so good at 7 p.m., with a 19 per cent swing to Ellis in Avalon and Mona Vale (and Bronwyn reportedly in tears and shrieking at her mortified minders), had by nine o'clock gone sour. The Labor wards, astonishingly, had swung the other way. The migrant women, mainly, unable to see through the language difficulty to Bronwyn's true meaning and also believing Ellis guilty as charged (three days before the poll) of the repeated sexual harassment of the Imminent Madonna, had voted as he had always known they would, with their loins. 'It's a two-election campaign, Comrade,' his seventeen-year-old number cruncher from Young Labor, Daniel Jenkyns, the director Michael's son, grumbled consolingly over tepid Carlton Cold. The party soon shrank, reassessing their future life and their relative irritation with Ellis for consuming so much of their valuable youth, and middle age. Bleeding dilettantish wanker, what did he think he was playing at. Bob who?

Ellis woke with a groan at 3 a.m. thinking, Oh my bleeding Jesus Christ. All that MONEY. All that wasted time. A 2 per cent swing, it's not enough. A Hollywood momentum abandoned. How could I have been so DUMB?

He woke up, to his astonishment, a national hero.

To be continued.

March, 1994

Howard Running

Henry Ford had a son that he named, for insufficient reasons, Edsel; Edsel had a son that he more soberly named Henry Ford II, who in a state of unctuous filial piety manufactured a car that he then called the Edsel.

Nobody wanted to buy the Edsel. Something about it, and in many ways it was a good car, gave customers the creeps. At a discount, with a free chocolate cake thrown in, with a Caribbean cruise thrown in, or free twin blondes for four nights no questions asked – they still didn't want to buy it. Thousands of it rusted in Detroit warehouses. Americans thereafter used its name as the code word for an unredeemable dud.

John Howard is the Edsel of Australian politics. Pictured in any setting or suit or light – red-faced in a straw hat under ghost gums, low-angled on a podium in pinstripes, red-eyed and fingerjabbing and shrieking out the dread name 'CARMEN LAWRENCE' in a curdled-Vegemite monotone that *must*, really must, have been invented by Barry Humphries, or greeting with gleaming cheapskate bridgework an effusive paid Chinaman on a city street, or a female interviewer who draws back in unfeigned horror – he resolutely fails to stir the affections or warm the memory or cheer the heart, in an almost archetypal way. He is the retired schoolteacher we never dreamed of looking up and thanking, the unexpectedly tedious dinner guest we never thought of asking back, the vexed and quarrelsome country vicar who decimated Christianity for miles around. He is Misery Guts himself, the snidely whingeing cabbie that makes a traffic jam years longer, the implacable Mormon on the summer lawn, the encyclopaedia salesman one cannot believe is still talking as the constables drag him away.

An Edsel, in short. Unsellable. The car that fell to bits on its first drive round the block. Or Willy Loman, I suppose. He's liked, but he's not . . . well liked. And really unlucky. I write this on the day Jeff Kennett asserted that the Liberals believed the Federal deficit was fifteen billion, and Howard riposted that Kennett, when he said deficit, in fact meant surplus.

Elections, ah elections. They bring out the best in me. The unrepeatable eloquence of the hour of crisis. The gag that alters a nation's fate. The roar of the greasepaint. The smell of the crowd. The joke that is meant for ten minutes only. Like Keating's 'I said I'd toss a coin. I even offered to toss his coin. Someone said, will you toss Andrew Robb's coin, and I said, look, you've got to draw the line somewhere.'

It was good to see the Bronweenies again, chanting 'Labor's got to go! Labor's got to go!' in the same feverish tom-tom unison that cost John Hewson office, as Kim Beazley, laughing, breasted through them like a freed Willy. I recognise one in particular – male, pin-headed, piping voiced, wide as he was tall – who in the Bronwyn Bishop election said to me, 'Stay away from her, you child molester. You're the Mr Bubbles of this campaign and the world shall know it.' His clenched pig face and stately Augustan grammar stayed with me until election day, when I saw him again at a booth. 'Drunk again, Bob!' he shrieked at me charmlessly, unnerving several queued voters from Terrey Hills. 'I remember you!' I shouted back. 'You were much more attractive when you were twelve!' This got no laughs at all and may in fact have dismayed some constituents and lost me some votes, but I was pleased I did it. Some jokes will out. They cannot be contained.

My wife is running against Bronwyn this time (vote against the gremlin in Mackellar; vote against arrogance, its name is Bronwyn Bishop) and feeling both nervous and feisty in a campaign that has already, and shamelessly, contrasted her natural soft blonde hair with the spray-painted meringue that surmounts her implacable adversary, none of whose posters so far are anywhere to be seen. It is sad to see so consummate and so passionate a self-publicist so cravenly hiding her identity from electors she hopes will inadvertently vote Liberal anyway – she who outscored Keating once as preferred Prime Minister, and for six months wore a smile as wide as Luna Park. Poor Norma Desmond. Sad, sad, sad.

It's unwise I know to write in this way of the incoming Minister for the Arts but a man's got to do what a man's got to do.

In this I am in marked contrast to my old friend Mike Brindley, a good screenwriter whose handsome black-whiskered features I descried at Howard's Arts launch when testing the waters. He will be sorry when hauled in manacles before my Committee of Public Safety on 1 April.

Labor, I predict, though I am not sure, by three or five or seven seats. The alternative is unimaginable and therefore, *therefore*, cannot be.

February, 1996

On the Waterfront

It was rainy and wind-swept and late and dark when I came there first, like a movie in black-and-white of an earlier chapter of class war and social mutiny – a fire in a barrel still burning in the rain, and sausages frying under a grey dripping tent and a tea urn and a generator thudding in the dark, a superannuated caravan with a fridge of soft drinks and a wavery TV, posters and graffiti everywhere (SCABS SUCK MAGGOTS OFF), a fair few shouted curses too and weary slogans (MUA, here to stay) and much angry rattling of wire gates, some welding together of gates too, if the truth were known; burly young men, and older men, open-faced and open-hearted and puzzled like the parallel young and older men in *The Full Monty* and *Brassed Off*; this was a war that was worldwide, and Darling Harbour in April '98 in the rain but a skirmish, discuss (the price of work was falling in 1998, and more of the same to the old tune); or was it something bigger?

Sean Chaffer, who looked like a big bulky Boston Kennedy, thirtyish, with wide grey eyes and curly hair, said it wasn't over conditions: he got fifteen dollars an hour and if he worked night overtime, or Sunday overtime, for seventy or eighty hours a week, on the forklift or packing or sweeping when he wasn't on the crane, he made – sure he made – 70 or 72 000 a year, 27 000 of which went on taxes. But the 2.1 million Corrigan reportedly made in share movements in the past few days, he added, was the equivalent of the average wharfie's average wage for thirty-two years. Funny how waterfront efficiency never counted the cost of money ripped off by the central corporate raider, or pushed in tens of thousands at his lawyers, or his security guards, or his dog food, or his cancelled army manoeuvres in the Arab emirates, or his plane fares to Canberra to talk tactics with Reith or Webster or Howard, or his midnight phone calls to his old dad, assuring him he was not the slimeball his brother and sister lately said he was, to broadcast organisations and cheering crowds. No, it was always only the wharfies at fault, moving things too slow, with old rundown cranes, off ships that had to be intricately repacked before they sailed on, with holds half empty, to Brisbane or Townsville – as if the ships would sail out any faster anyway, why would they, when the seamen wanted their shore leave, their two nights in the pubs and nightclubs, catching up with old girlfriends. Not a thing would change from 'waterfront reform' but the wharfies' wages, and the numbers of them (once again, there used to be thirty thousand of them, and there are four thousand now), the numbers of wharfies in regular work. And that was all that was happening.

> What do we want? A more efficient waterfront.
> When do we want it? Now!
>
> – A war cry that did not take on

My little son Tom was beside me and I drove in drenching, lashing rain from Palm Beach to the pickets at Port Botany on Monday 2 May. It was the day the High Court decision was due to come down, after a week of portentous deliberation, at 11.30 and it was Tom's first glimpse of things like this, of men at bitter odds in great and angry numbers and history unfolding and the world changing, and he came to it apprehensive and eager, as if to a football final, bringing schoolbooks in case he got bored. The rain was tremendous, and the electricity failing, and the buffet serving stew, and the police at a respectable murmurous distance, and I was straightway grabbed and given a bull-horn and stood up and made to orate. It was 10.52. The men and women gathered there, in yellow raincoats, under umbrellas, were eager for 'victory'. They had no idea of victory's loopholes; the word was enough.

It hadn't gone well for Corrigan thus far, it was widely thought in the media and now and then said, with the black balaclavas and guard dogs and the pale puff of mace and the midnight commando-style attack (on the night before the Federal Court was to decide if they could be lawfully sacked) of men who were not on strike but at work, in their legal place of work – who weren't, it was tortuously explained by the sombre implacable tedious Corrigan, being *sacked* exactly, or not entirely sacked, but somehow weirdly, miasmically deprived of their right to their tools and their work, work which was now paradoxically being done by others, done in defiance of their duly executed contracts, now somehow in abeyance, inoperative, gazumped, along with the wages owed them; and the two little fearful squealing girls, though headlined as examples of the wharfies' brutish parenting, somehow caused all watching to think that families, and family incomes and school-age victims, and blameless home routines, were now in the firing line of history. Howard's exultant smiles when Reith announced the sackings to a snarling Parliament like a gleeful Blue Meanie from *The Yellow Submarine* didn't go down too well either, and Reith's repeated sweating-and-smirk-ing-and-yapping, sweating-and-smirking-and-yapping about the rorts and scams and workplace inefficiencies of the 'thugs' in the MUA, though no thugs however provoked had gone to gaol yet and all were behaving very mildly considering, seemed crazier and crazier as the nights (and the nightly facedowns on television with Jennie George and the tenacious, hopeful, unflappably energetic, ageing, frayed John Coombs, a member, I decided, of the Bunyan Left of old England, chapel-bred, ferocious, dauntless, sure to life's end he was in the right) went on, and the nation grew, at least for a time, confused.

> *The price of work was falling in 1998*
> *And Peter Reith determined he would seal the workers' fate:*
> *'We will break the wharfies' union, we will do the wharfies down,*
> *And thus we'll please our masters at the big end of the town . . .'*

In the fortnight after the sackings, however, the nation saw an ominous recurring scenario: the wharfies would argue and win their case in a court, and rejoice for the cameras, and toast their victory in lemonade and prepare in wintry dark with astonished joyful hugs and fist-raisings and song to return to work; the Chardonnay Left would celebrate in brasseries the glad and timely restoration of our brotherly democracy *and then before the evening was out* there would come a High Court challenge, and the morning's headlines would note with smug pretended shock the wharfies' last-minute thwarting, a welcome anticlimax just in time for the early edition. Corrigan's dour, mild-mannered but fanatic determination to cede not a millimetre of his pre-set masterplan to spifflicate both his workers' wages and their human rights – nightly presented in such dim, dull, fog-bound cadences it was possible for seconds on end to believe him harmless and his deeds public-spirited – his quenchless Torquemada drive to punish all who crossed him in the face of blows and buffets and public scaldings that would have broken the spirit of even Malcolm Fraser, was for me at long last explained (or perhaps explained) by a big tough red-faced fiftyish man with lumberjack shoulders called John Hill, at the Darling Harbour pickets. 'He came here determined,' he said (or words to that effect), 'to rid the place of idlers and bludgers, and he found a manager bloke who was fond of long lunches – you know, like Mick Young – and he sacked him. And this bloke said all right then, and he waded across the harbour to a job at P&O, and *took with him five shipping contracts*. And then Patrick began to lose money. Or that's what I think.'

The intriguing implication was that the whole catastrophe, born of Corrigan's dimwitted zealotry and organisational incompetence, arose from his pressing need for some fool, some government perhaps, to pay for his redundancies on those wharves he now had to, because of his incompetence, quickly abandon; the action springs (discuss) from a high-placed nong who needs to cover up, a Nixon or Napoleon or Howard who strikes before he himself is struck down, and rapidly arrests and executes his opposition lest he himself be exposed as a fool.

> *Is there aught we hold in common with the greedy parasite*
> *Who would lash us into serfdom, and would crush us with his might?*
> *Is there anything left for us to do but organise and fight?*
> *For the union makes us strong.*
> *Solidarity forever,*
> *Solidarity forever . . .*

Over the Port Botany loudspeakers, now repaired, at 11.30 in the rain, the news was first relayed – five votes to two, then six to one – and the thankful oratory begun (It was never in doubt, was it? No? Bullshit.) before the critical proviso about the company administrators now having the power to pursue a company profit and to act in the interest of the company's creditors was heard or understood. Joy and victory swirled round the wet and roaring crowd, as in a football stadium; this was the story they were in; it was victory; there were no complications; there couldn't be complications. Mick Dolan from the little dais paid tribute to the wives and mothers, for keeping a brave face and putting food on the table, then said, 'And while I had intended not to pay any recognition to the lowest form of life, the lowest form of life on earth, I now say to the scabs out there, you have failed! You backed the wrong horse. We're the victors,' then said Corrigan should shove his proposed new individual contracts where the sun don't shine, right up his clacker.

Dennis Kevins then sang 'Solidarity Forever' unaccompanied in a strong old heartbreaking Celtic voice (I was to speak next, a hard act to follow) and through the eternal melody and the encrusted and long-honoured archaic sentiments and the tears we all were holding back or letting emerge, through the buffeted family feeling and tribal feeling and national feeling that, as on VJ Day, a moment like this must always express, I felt a chill rising. For this indeed was another world now, a world indeed built by the greedy parasite on the blood and bones and lost hope and dead children in the factories and mines, and the unhad children in the clapboard suburbs of the workers down the centuries, to serve his shallow ends with the new machines that were replacing all of us, a world ruled by Moloch and Midas that would not be stayed by song.

In our hands is placed a power greater than their hoarded gold,
Greater than the might of armies magnified
a thousandfold.
We can bring to birth a new world from the ashes of the old
For the union makes us strong . . .

John Coombs turned up, looking exactly like a character played by Stanley Holloway in an Ealing comedy, bouncing about in the happy ending, and in the joy and milling about I begged him now to get all fourteen hundred wharfies to sue for defamation Reith and Howard and Corrigan for $100 000 each, for having called their unremarkable work practices 'the laughing stock of the world', and he said he'd think about it. Then beside him, and Jennie George, and Mick Dolan and Robert Coombs, with Tom beside me fearful the front row would be shot at from behind the wire as it advanced, we marched at the head of the jovial army toward the gates shouting 'MUA here to stay' with increasing tedium and it felt for a time indeed like victory, a victory of sorts. But the rain kept coming down, and doubts were rising, and forces more determined than we knew or could imagine were massing for the final showdown.

Solidarity forever,
Solidarity forever,
Solidarity forever,
For the union makes us strong.

August, 1998

Arts Labor Launch, 1993

A speech for Bryan Brown

Welcome to Artists for Labor, Mr Prime Minister, Mrs Keating, Federal Ministers, party supporters and fellow travellers.

I will begin, as I always do on occasions like this, with a quote from Einstein. 'The satisfaction of physical needs is indeed the indispensable precondition of a satisfactory existence,' Albert Einstein wrote in 1940, 'but in itself it is not enough. In order to be content, men must also have the possibility of developing their intellectual *and artistic* powers to whatever accords with their personal characteristics and abilities.'

'The really valuable thing in the pageant of human life,' he also said, nine years earlier, 'seems to me not the political state, but the creative, sentient individual, the personality; it alone creates the noble and sublime.'

Wise words from a notable man, arguably the Barry Jones of his day, because he puts the point that what we as artists and creative and performing people need most is room for our art to move, and be, and breathe, and grow, and look around itself, and become what it can be.

And the question arises of where, politically, do we find that room, and that breathing space, that freedom? Thirty years ago the answer was clear, it was England, and Europe, and our best talents went there routinely in their thousands, year after year, on the *Orcades*; and twenty years ago I stood on a London stage with Sir John Gielgud – he was talking, I was impersonating a tree, or a fairy, or a sailor, I can't remember which – and watching what he could do better than anyone else in the world, but also thinking, Hey, wait a minute, there are things that we as Australians can do that he can't do, and why don't they let us, and why am I here, being part of something that isn't me, or mine? I was there because the room I needed wasn't here; because of the stifling of the Menzies years it wasn't here, and I was apologising for where I came from, by going there.

But soon that changed, and soon I was back, and part of this great historical Australian excitement, in *Newsfront* and *Stir* and *Breaker Morant* and *Winter of Our Dreams*, and watching *Gallipoli* and *Mad Max* and *My Brilliant Career*, and *Rooted* and *Don's Party* and *How Does Your Garden Grow?*, and in the Nimrod Theatre, defining moments in our historical self-awareness, and the breathing space was here. We were coming to see and know our-selves, grow into ourselves, to give the very age and body of the time his form and pressure, as Shakespeare said in a comparable time of another national awakening.

And this didn't happen just because of Whitlam, but because under Whitlam we found we had the courage to stand up in our own country, and, in our own accent, with our own particular irony and sense of humour, and comradeliness, and reticence and honesty and classlessness, to say this is *us*, g'day, how are we doing, instead of saying *British to the boot heels*, or *I did but see her passing by*, or *a nightingale sang in Berkeley Square*; we in the artistic sense in that era passed through Customs and declared ourselves. We became artists, and an artistic community, in a way that we never were before: we were like a tree of many branches, taking in air, and rain, and earth, and reaching out in different shapes towards the sky.

And why was this? It was because all cinema, all theatrical bodies, all the communion of the visual and the literary arts, are to a great extent political constructs – the BBC, the National Gallery, the National Theatre, the Cana-dian Film Board, Svensk Filmindustrie, without which there'd have been no Ingmar Bergman and little knowledge throughout the world today of Sweden itself. Our performing arts declare our nation and feed its economy as surely as does Hollywood, America's second-largest export earner, declare and feed America. So what politics does for us, as artists, is very deeply our concern. We are more enmeshed in it than many other sorts of people. We have to be.

So we have to choose, as artists, the political construct that best lets us look at our society and how it rules and shapes us, that best lets us ask that society questions about itself, what it adds up to and where it's going, the political construct that lets us look, as *Winter of Our Dreams* did, and *Scales of Justice*, and *Women of the Sun*, at the heart and soul of our country, even if that looking, that search, that quest, isn't for the moment commercial, or politically convenient, or likely to make a quid, and doesn't for the mo-ment show a profit at the box office, because in the end it's a quest that profits us all.

And it's no historical accident that we've been best able to do this under Labor Party governments, since the party of education, of social improve-ment, of race relations and international independence is always the one more interested in a search for truth and self-awareness and less concerned with propping up old myths and self-deceptions, *I did but see her passing by*. And it's no historical accident that it was a Liberal Party government that in the fifties sold our culture out to the American film distributors and the American television bargain-basement junk merchants just as it sold out the Holden car, because the Liberal Party has always been about economic surrender, and the Labor Party always about an economic and national and cultural fight, a fight in the great world to preserve the nation's particular essence, its soul. What shall it profit a man, a condemned Nazarene provincial once asked, if he gain the whole world and lose his own soul? And what shall it profit a society, we might well also ask, and ask here today, if it gets the figures right, and the heart and soul of the society wrong?

The hardest fact that we have to grasp, I think, is that the best things in life are *not* free, just as Einstein sitting with a pencil and a frown for forty-three years was not free or a product of market forces, and, whatever Dr Hewson thinks, these great unfree things cannot be measured on a mere ledger of daily profit and daily loss, things like SBS, the ABC, the National Gallery, the Opera House, the Adelaide Festival, the Sydney Dance Company, the STC, the NTC, Les Murray, Victor Chang, Graham Murphy, Fred Hollows, Joan Sutherland, the local provincial theatre company, the local public library, the day-care centre, the emergency ward. They are not *free* but they are worth*while*, and they are the measure throughout the world of the worth in which we are held, and the cause of people coming here from across the world to praise us for our culture, our art, our freedom to speak, to be what we are. Greed is no basis for a civilisation, love is, and artistic passion, and social mercy, and self-questioning fearlessness and self-mockery, that honest capacity to look into our own heart and chuckle a bit that is Australia's genius and our international pride, formed under Labor governments that let us be.

Some examples of that Australian particularity will be on show this afternoon, a small slice of what we under good government and a good democracy can do.

Dr Hewson thinks a lot about money, and somehow imagines that the getting of money is at the root of all questions, and all endeavour. But it's not. Money wasn't what Fred Hollows, for instance, was about or what he was after, but a search through science and suffering and human kindness and landscape and poetry for the merciful heart of Australia, out of which he could extract the precious ore that would heal the world. Dr Hewson would have discouraged the discoverers of Lorenzo's oil for continuing in a quest that the odds were against: think of the money you'll save, he would have said, mercy costs too much money.

And so do all the good things of life. They are not free, but they are worthwhile, and they are the measure of the worth in which we are held throughout the world, and the cause of people coming here to praise us. Greed for the quid is an insufficient basis for civilisation: there has to be love, and mercy, and artistic passion, and a loud anger, and indulged ego, and lights and music and action and curtain fall and curtain speech and that moment of knowing after a play or a film has finished that your life has enlarged. The thing that can't be calculated on an abacus. The moment of truth.

Paul Keating, from a fibro suburb, a rock band, an industrial apprentice-ship, a political machine, a long apprenticeship of political trauma and despair, has proved one of the great patrons of the arts and the performing arts in Australia, a lover of music, and film, and art, whose money has always been where his mouth is. I'm proud to introduce him.

February, 1993

Arts Labor Launch, 1998

A speech for Geoffrey Rush

We are not here just to show the flag, or to sing sad songs of comfort in the face of certain defeat. This is no mere meeting of the minds of the cappuccino classes of yesteryear in a shared sustaining fantasy of what will never be. For victory is likely now, Labor victory this year or next, and what we here decide and announce will help to shape the soul of the nation, a nation of many colours and tastes and songs of hope, for a decade perhaps, a century perhaps. For in our policy on the arts and letters and music and film lies some large part of our destiny.

I am a child of the Whitlam renaissance, and a proud provincial product of Labor's reasonable dream of a fair go for all who ache to be and do in the limelight, on the silver screen, and in the galleries and orchestras of the world.

I began as a university actor and a clown and a mime, in an era when it suddenly seemed such things were possible as careers in even Queensland, because a brief and quickly broken Labor ceded us that hope. I had three years with the Queensland Theatre Company, and I am back there now and glad to be back, and a year of study in Paris I would never otherwise have dreamed of, on, yes, government monies, a dream of unimaginable rainbows made possible by the Whitlam government and its legacy of patriotic elo-quence and artistic attack. In Paris I learned how Australian I was, and how my masters and models were not Marcel Marceau and Jean-Louis Barrault but George Wallace and Gordon Chater, and Barry Humphries and Graham Kennedy, and I came back re-informed of who and what I was, and where I lived.

Twice, when overseas, I chose to come back to a country I loved. I am back now in a country I love and fear for, and would like to help in some small way to rescue from the gathering, uprising *tsunami* of the north – I refer of course to Ipswich – that would pulverise the best of us to splinters and wash our sweetest and loveliest, most generous and brilliant away.

And this is no pallid threat – where Hanson goes, can Howard be far behind? – no distant murmuration of impotent belligerence and philistine fist-shaking. For One Nation would cut off, and even the artful Oldfield admits this, every penny now spent on the arts by government State and Federal. It's quite a call, oh my fellow citizens, oh my countrymen, you who sometimes go to Opera in the Park and the Byron Bay Blues Festival and your local historical museum or seek a scholarship to NIDA or the Victorian College of the Arts. A call they would no doubt repeat when joining in coalition, as they would, with Howard and Reith and Alston, those closet punishing barbarians who have probably not seen a Sondheim or a Shakespeare, or an evening with Barry Humphries, since they were in high school. A call the Coalition would probably gladly heed, since that priority in One Nation expresses their most secret longing.

I ask you to imagine Australia as it might have been had a party like One Nation gained the influence they now are wielding. No Sydney Theatre Company, no Queensland Theatre Company, no Sydney Dance Theatre, no Film and Television School, no *Breaker Morant*, no *Muriel*, no *Shine*, no NIDA and therefore no place for Mel Gibson to train, no Oscar nominations for Judy Davis, no Tony for Anthony La Paglia, no Oscars for Mel and Jane Campion, no *Piano*, no *Braveheart*, no *L.A. Confidential* with Guy and Russell, no *Neighbours*, no *Home and Away*, no *Heartbreak High*, no *Wildside*, no career for Kylie Minogue or Nicole Kidman because there would be no protective quotas for television and no place to start, no Theatre South, no Melbourne Comedy Festival, no Robyn Nevin at the Queensland Theatre Company, and no Robin Archer at the Adelaide Festival, no National Gallery, no ABC, none of the joy and pleasure we feel as Australians in being us, and being up with the rest of the world as entertainers, musicians and artists. No art to the country, and therefore no heart, and therefore to a great extent no conscience and no seeing eye, no scrutiny of what we are and who we should be, no mockery and laughter at what we do wrong, no decency of purpose, but chaos, complaint, corrosion, no unifying achievements, no recognisable melody, no anthems for our identity, no single nation; a rabble of greedy plaintive rivals instead, eating only steak and eggs and drinking only Lipton's Tea.

There is richness here because we are diverse, there is joy here because we are above all qualities tolerant, or were, and welcoming, or were. And inasmuch as we put long arms around our differences, embracing in one great hug our varieties of endeavour and our difference of purpose, we are blest. And we are Australian.

I welcome Kim Beazley and Bob McMullan here to this declaration of our honourable future, one that will, by the look of it, now come to pass. So this is not a trivial occasion. It is a statement of the lineaments and colourations of what the Aborigines call the spirit of the place. We are here in good company to listen, and respond.

I thank you.

September, 1998

A Preamble to the Constitution

We, the Australian people, hereby acknowledge that like many others our nation was built on theft, murder, unequal conquest, miscegenation, environmental atrocity, the slaughter of harmless animals and the rape, enslavement and brutalisation by forced adoption of indigenous peoples and that, uniquely, it was founded on a prison population, many of whom were transported for trivial offences and some of whom, once here, were hanged for lesser ones. We acknowledge therefore that our civilisation derives from tyranny, error, human folly and abominable superstition, and we ask what ghosts remain of our cruel, culpable and almost unthinkable past for some understanding of our ancestors' ignorance and the shocking pressures they were under.

We vow henceforth to do better, to strive, in a world that may be elsewhere insane, to school our youth and tend our sick and comfort our old and praise our gifted and sow what seeds of happiness we can in our less-than-gifted, to do justly, walk proudly and be a beacon of decent kindness and ordinary commonsense in a darkling world that is more and more in need of a good example.

Let that example be ours.

March, 1999

Kosovo

Like all things the Kosovo blood bath will be solved, of course, by free market economics. New cheap immigrant labour in Albania, Romania, Macedonia, Italy, Austria, Greece, by competing freely on a level playing field with each other's native workforce, will bring down wages, make goods cheaper and so be able to better compete in the global marketplace. Those workers that are surplus to the economy's needs will freeze, starve, suicide or be shot while breaking and entering, and their body parts, I suppose, then sold for cloning or transplanting to those international agencies of merciful human reconstruction, whose prices, too, will mercifully come down.

And the homicidal Serbs will have new farmland to till, harvest, exploit and defend with black-market British weaponry, and because they will pay no mortgages for this land, they too will be able to sell their goods more cheaply and more efficiently compete in the global marketplace, like their newly overcrowded neighbours. And they, and the Balkans, and all 191 countries of the world will prevail in that marketplace, and live happily and profitably ever after. And pigs will fly. And Peter Reith will raise wharfies' wages for the hell of it.

All of the above is nonsense of course, though it is the fashionable theory of the inevitability of how history henceforth must work, and is believed by all who kiss the feet, and fear the lash, of the Chicago School of Economics. But even the most rational of the Chicago School of Economics alumni will be soon admitting there are some things – holocausts, wars, Black Plagues, mass migrations, the sudden liberation of slaves, the sudden slaughter of minorities – that the free market can't solve, the way it can purportedly solve the rural recession, and the health crisis, and the youth suicide crisis, and the heroin crisis, just by letting the market work its magic. Even the experts think Kosovo might be an exception.

Other experts think that it's an exception in other ways. That it, alone in history, can be saved from a persecuting tyranny by aerial bombardment. The way six million Jews were saved by the aerial bombardment of Germany, and the North Vietnamese were converted from communism by the dropping on their paddy fields and beautiful Parisian cities more bombs than were dropped in all of World War Two. And the English were converted overnight to Nazism by the Luftwaffe blitzing London. It worked then, it's bound to work now.

The above examples never happened. A study by John Kenneth Galbraith and his committee on the bombing of Germany found it was either neutral in its effect, or perhaps a little positive in the boost it gave to German morale, just as the German bombings stirred Londoners, famously, to fight back. The rock concerts in Belgrade city square, and the T-shirts with targets on them, showed the Serbs will not be cowed by distant bullies who hope, like fools, for crushing victories that do not cost lives, or American lives at least. Victimless warfare is the new American fantasy. There have been others.

It is costing a lot of Kosovan lives though – to freezing, starvation, death in the old who walk hundreds of miles by night and day or to, in due course, the despair that brings to suicide young immigrant souls who yearn, like the Arabs, for a lost motherland, and live in tents, and throw rocks, and die in border raids or suicide missions. The American strategy has made swifter and fiercer what Milosevic was doing more slowly – the extraction of the infected tooth of the Albanian minority from his body politic, the cleansing from its bloodstream of an alien virus, as Hitler did the Jews.

What should NATO have done? Massed armies in Albania and Macedonia of course, and threatened invasion, and then invaded. Taken losses of half a million, a million, two million, measuring in oceans of blood its strength of purpose, and occupied Kosovo, and secured its people's future, in the way they did South Korea's, with border patrols and threats of massive reprisals by unsleeping armies prepared to die in their mutilated thousands for city blocks or mountain tops or bridges. Wars are never won in any other way. They cannot be played like computer games, with wham-bam explosions and no real casualties. By declaring there would be no ground troops, and reacting like a sulky schoolboy to three American POWs ('America looks after its own.') being taken hostage, Bill Clinton showed his country to be what the Chinese call a paper tiger. It's big, it looks fierce, but close up it's thin, and weak, and likely in any puff of wind to fall down, or rip in two, or blow away.

He has shown, too, what the war he evaded, Vietnam, has done to the petulant American psyche. It was a war they lost, the one war they ever lost, so they're not going to go to war any more, not really, only to wars where you don't get killed.

Only victimless warfare from now on.

Milosevic knows this, and will win every round, unless Belgrade is hydrogen bombed.

That's a good American alternative. It worked before. And it was victimless too. Well, none of the American pilots were killed. They came home safe.

In 1999, it seems, a significant, terminal year, all the great advances of twentieth-century warfare have been shown to be, as Nixon said, inoperative. Poison gas, unused. Germ warfare, unused. Neutron bombs, unused. Rocket-delivered atomic bombs, unused. Stealth bombers, *visible* and shootable-down. Smart bombs, deflectable by the slightest wisp of cloud to where they kill civilians. Precision bombing, pointless, because the human targets pack up and move out, taking their equipment. Aerial bombing of random civilians *encouraging* to the bombed. And all the money spent on these weapons that might have gone to hospitals and schools and curing cancer, vanished forever.

And in the end, at millennium's end, what was always so, what was so in the fifteenth century as it is now, is that it's footsoldiers carrying guns and knives who win battles and conquer countries, and generals prepared to measure in slaughtered young men the price of saving Private Ryan, or the people of Kosovo.

A moron could see this. But not NATO. They have a tradition now, of trusting machines, and of loyally serving their clients' military–industrial complex with more and more wars of attrition and catastrophic experiment, and they will not be deflected from their pointless, baseless, gory protracted purpose, any more than they were by the beautiful vases of Dresden, the paper houses of Nagasaki, the beautiful tropical islands of the Mekong Delta. Not now. Not ever. Blood will follow blood, and after genocidal exhaustion peace of a sort, and neighbours who murder neighbours, more than ever before.

What fools they are. What ignorant fools. Victimless warfare, the latest American fantasy, after a winnable nuclear exchange and Reds under the bed and Christianising the heathen red man and the rest of it. They ought to be ashamed.

Speed the day.

April, 1999

May Day, 1999

A speech in Newcastle

It is May Day again, and there is not much to celebrate. Rights hard won by centuries of struggle have, it seems, in an instant, in the twinkling of an eye, vanished into air, into thin air, or are vanishing fast. The right to strike. The right to collectively bargain. The right to be paid for working back at night, or on weekends. The right to the kind of education for our children that may lift them out of the certain expectation of continued poverty and stress. The right to the reasonable probability for those children of a career that fulfils and is decades long, with security and marriage and home and children and community and safety as part of it. The right when one has worked hard to be paid a bonus from the greater profits of the company. The right to expect to know where we will be nine months from now, where we will be next week, at what home address, in what line of work, with what future prospects, or in what safety net that is guaranteed by our democracy, to citizens, to voters, with ordinary human rights.

All these in a moment, in a twinkling, are suddenly gone, or going, or on the list, as if by the wave of some malign magician's wand, and the too familiar world of the *eighteen* nineties has returned, a shamed and punished working class, an idle, dandified squattocracy, a grimy fearful subculture of crime and alcohol and prostitution and slum despair, the far-off faint hope for some of jobs as waiters and uniformed servants who open doors in flash hotels for their betters, or girls from the chorus line who marry up into the ranks of their betters, or like Kate Fischer at the last moment can't hack it, and the overwhelming waste of talent and potential and human generosity and communal decency that always accompanies the arrival of selfish new money, the crushing of craft and art and small business and the awareness of history, the ending of apprenticeships, the downsizing of the brains of teachers, the weevilling of the integrity of the universities, and the selling off of schools.

How has all this happened? How has it happened so quickly? How is it that the world we knew and for at least *one* lifetime trusted in has become overnight the world of the bruised and baffled young men of *Brassed Off* and *The Full Monty*, where one must become a prancing, bollocky buffoon to pay the rent, for just that week, and give up neighbourhood, and love, and music, and fellow-feeling to survive? And has it happened before? And must it happen again?

These are worthwhile questions, I think.

I last month spent ten days with John Ralston Saul, the great Canadian thinker, whose two books *Voltaire's Bastards* and *The Unconscious Civilisation* tell us, I believe, what it is that has happened in our time, and of the world depression that no-one admits that we have been in since 1973.

And it has happened before. In the fascism of Mussolini, in the British Empire, in the thousands of years of the trade in slaves, there was this same process of a guiltless, blameless, self-righteous elite ruining the lives of the people in the name of efficiency, new technological imperatives, the sainted shareholder, or the godlike Emperor, whose needs for a lavish lifestyle over-rode all civility, all mercy, all Christian kindness, and filled the prison docks with women and children condemned to death by hanging for stealing loaves of bread to feed their families from their *betters*, the all-deserving rich.

And it is May Day again, and all around us, in this one mighty town especially, there is the none too distant reflection of this Dickensian horror, returned and madder than ever, and red in tooth and claw.

As Ralston Saul sees it, our wealthy betters, and their technocratic hit-men, and their grovelling academic servitors, and their rented politicians, never actually admit defeat. We win the basic wage, the eight-hour day, the old age pension, the right to compensation for injury at work, the right to maternity leave and child-care and wages that grow in proportion to the cost of being alive, and we think, we *think* the battle is won and the story is over.

But they know better than we do. They know that governments will change, and new, naive young ministers, yes ministers, like, say, Paul Keating, will yield in a while to a little duchessing, a little linguistic manipu-lation, a little technocratic hieroglyphic and mumbo jumbo, a little flattery, a little elegant propaganda, a little numerical sleight of hand. The world is different now, they will say, it's a global marketplace, and unless we learn to compete with *slaves* by becoming slaves *ourselves*, unless we do those things that Moody's want, or Standard and Poors want, like abolishing social de-mocracy and the tattered remains of the welfare state, and the reasonable security of the average individual from cradle to grave, no respectable world bank will lend us money any more, and no multinational corporation will want to exploit us any more, and then where will we be? It is not our preferred option either, but heck, gee whillikers, gosh, it's *inevitable*, it's the way the world is unchangeably going. There is no alternative.

They know too that the attention span of the average working person is limited, and they do not have the time, between work and children and Brian Henderson and dinner and conjugal exertion and sleep, to address those code words, those deft Orwellian euphemisms – a more efficient work-place, a level playing field, a competitive environment for small business, a Third Way – by which they will see their lives destroyed.

And it is this attack on the meaning of language itself that I as a writer find most frightening, I think. Free trade, which means, in the end, the slave trade. Downsizing efficiency, which means in the end that the phone is never answered, or never fixed, and the counter never served, and the queues lengthen, or a light plane crashes in Berowra, or an ambulance arrives three hours too late, when the corpse that might have lived is already stiff and cold. Affordable safety, which of course means danger. A level playing field, which means if Coca-Cola sets up a great factory on a hundred acres of land with government concessions, you can set up a small soft-drink company on one acre of land beside it without government concessions, and if Coca-Cola spends $100 000 each night on advertising, you can spend your life savings in one night trying to out-advertise them, and you can then go bankrupt. The Third Way, which means, in the end, among those practi-tioners of what I call muscular cowardice, like the contemptible Mark Latham, and the loathsome Tony Blair, a kind of blustering protestatory surrender to Murdoch and Packer and Dupont Chemicals and W.D. & H.O. Wills and Coca-Cola, and the farm lobby of the United States, and a sur-rounding miasma of academic jargon that in England cleverly redefined unemployment twenty-two times in ten years, and rewards the rich, in the usual way, for the dumb luck they had in their parentage and the broken bodies of workers on whom their fortune stands.

I grow more radical as I grow older, the way you are supposed not to do. My father, a Maitland coal miner who escaped into mere commercial travelling, taught me a good deal of what I know still to be the shape of the world. He would rail some nights in his cups of home-brew beer – the greatest legacy, he said, of the Whitlam era – against the sustaining fantasy of the Afterlife, and how the ruling classes invented it in order to keep you content in your lifelong servitude, or at least politically inactive, the glowing promise that *after* your three score years and ten, and your pauper's funeral, and your children's ruin, there would be riches unimaginable for you, and delectable fruits, and choir practice among the seraphim, on the other side. He would rail too against the State Lottery, which was their way of tempting you, he said, with the thought that you might be an exception to the tyranny and you alone might escape your slum and the enslavement you were in and you might ascend on the roulette wheel of a number to Sylvania Waters and a motor yacht of your own and leisure time unlimited, and a first-class seat on Qantas any day of the week to anywhere in the known world.

He taught me in sum that there are con-men everywhere, in politics, in banks, in unions, in churches, in the Labor Party factions, and you should mind how you go.

So I wrote a book in the end, and I am sorry to say that it is not filthy, on the size of the current con of economic rationalism that is washing all our human civility from the planet and our memories, the doctrine that argues, and seems to argue plausibly, that if we sack just a few hundred thousand more *people* there will then be jobs for *everyone*, and prosperity for everyone, and cheap and lovely consumer goods, and big competitive international corporations specialising here in only those things that Australia does best – whatever they are, Akubra hats, fliptop cans – all made cheaply enough to compete, and compete on a level playing field, with hundreds of millions of Chinese now prepared to work fourteen hours a day, twenty-nine days a month, for $1.50 an hour, to compete against them and win, the way every nation will win, all 192 of them.

The level playing field is just another flat earth theory, discuss.

I wrote a book in the end, the way one does, and in it coined a few ideas – like economic anorexia, or less and less flesh on bones till only dead bones are left, and the idea that people who work for a company lifelong are now as expendable as Kleenex, and the title slogan *First Abolish the Customer*, the idea that for every person sacked there are four people who cannot afford to buy things any more, or things other than the price of a roof and mincemeat for dinner and a bus fare to the next job interview, and when as happened in Canberra 25 000 public servants are sacked, there are suddenly 100 000 people not spending money on inessential goods in Canberra, whose small businesses are then put under pressure to sack more people, who like the public servants before them in anguish put on the market houses whose prices go down and down because of all the *other* houses being sold in anguish, and migrate then to the outskirts of Sydney as a new wife-beating, drunken, divorce-prone, undereducated and desolate underclass whose battered children, being rational and desperate, take up crime – of course – and prostitution and the heroin trade as the only profitable options in a universe gone mad.

And it is May Day again, and there is I fear no new Jerusalem coming, or coming soon, to Newcastle, or Lismore, or Longreach or Cobar or Cairns or Fremantle, for a new world view has now arisen in which men in balaclavas with black dogs on chains are the face, and the remorseless face, of the future, if we let them through the picket lines, and the barbed wire and the chanting, and the singing of 'Solidarity Forever' and 'The People's Flag', to decimate for each and every one of us in individual fear of debt and eventual homelessness all our will to organise, to strive, to seek, to find, to hope for a better morning, to do those normal things that in an ordinary democracy of jostle, adjustment, move and counter-move, try-on and back-down, threat and stoush and handshake, we would expect to form the continuing busy fabric of our ordinary democratic lives. It is not possible to overstate the evil that Peter Reith, that humourless Eric Morecombe, now stands for, and hopes to unleash like his black dogs of class vengeance on a nation unprepared, because of its ordinary amiability and good heart, for the scorched earth policy he represents, and the dark core of capitalist corporate greed he speaks for with eloquence and slime and cunning.

And I wrote a book about all this, about the return of empire and slavery under different updated names, and the big lies that are told to us daily, like how foreign investment brings jobs, when it always historically loses jobs, and takes in untaxed profit away from our gutted shores the billions of money that else would make our streets and hospitals clean, and our highways safe, our trains frequent, and our state schools places of honourable encouragement and local pride; and as well the biggest lie of all, believed universally now, that the greed worldwide of a few hundred thousand shareholders will always, always outweigh on the scales of justice the need worldwide of four billion ordinary working people. It's in the book, and I should read a bit of it to you, I suppose, not least because it is sometimes, not always, funny, and you need a chuckle or two on this bleak eve of the workers' holy day. The chapter, perhaps, on the number madness of Nick Greiner, and what became of him, and the dreadful chapter that follows that.

An even more moronic thing was done with trains – by a man called Greiner, who had a degree in economics from Harvard and was for a time, alas, the Premier of New South Wales.

Trains used to travel overnight from the state capital, Sydney, to Australia's favourite tourist resort, the Gold Coast. There were sleeping cars on the trains, with double compartments for couples or family groups, and single roomettes for people travelling alone. Both sorts of sleeper had toilets in them, and the double compartments had private showers. There was also a dining car where you could dine at night, drink wine, observe the darkening scenery and breakfast watching the sunrise.

You could take your car on the train, and drive it off at journey's end and continue on your way through the Gold Coast.

The train left at 6 or 6.30 at night, and arrived at the Gold Coast at 10 or 10.30 a.m. the following day. You arrived refreshed and showered and breakfasted and energetic, ready for your holiday. A steward awoke you with a cup of tea and a biscuit at whatever hour you chose to come to.

Greiner found all this extravagant and wasteful, and determined to improve things.

If there were *faster* trains and fewer people working on them, he argued, the railways would make a profit, whereas now (in part because of the many old people who travelled free) they were losing money.

So he downsized, rationalised and sped things up.

He sacked a third of the staff, including the tea-and-biscuit providers, and the chefs and waiters of the dining car.

He replaced the dining car with a buffet that sold fast food and light beer and peanuts and chocolates.

The buffet occupied only half a car, and the food was terrible.

He sold off all the sleeping cars. Why do people need to sleep? More people, moreover, could be accommodated sitting up.

(By the same logic, hotels without beds could accommodate more people, if only they could be taught to sleep standing up.)

He sold off the sleeping cars, which everybody loved, for about three thousand dollars each. He sold off the platform carriages that the motorists used to put their cars on. No-one could take their cars any more. That was wasteful and extravagant. And he got a whole new kind of train.

This train went faster, and shook a lot, and if it left Sydney at 4.20 p.m. (an hour before the customer gets off work), it arrived at Casino, on the lower Gold Coast, not at 6.30 a.m. as it used to, but at 3.20 a.m. People staggered out at 3.20 a.m. aghast and looking for taxis, and there weren't any.

They didn't have the cars any more, and they missed them.

And those who wished to go to Byron Bay had to get on a bus.

This was inconvenient, and cramped, and frequently stopping, and an enemy of sleep. It was afflicted too by a bus driver who believed himself a stand-up comedian and in the pre-dawn hours told bad jokes loudly over the intercom.

The traveller arrived at Byron Bay at 6.30 a.m. an emotional ruin and, having slept for the whole day, woke up at midnight like one jetlagged, with nothing to do.

So people started to complain that they wanted the sleepers back.

At great expense, having sold off the sleepers, the fool had a whole new kind of sleeper designed. It had glass walls, and curtains and a toilet-and-shower between compartments.

To go to the toilet at night you had to rise, draw the curtain, dress, go out into the corridor, enter the toilet, come back again, undress, and climb a swaying ladder back into bed.

Old people who used to go five times a night found this a trial.

Moreover, because the train was going much faster you couldn't sleep at all. You were flung about like one caught in a cement mixer.

And there were no single compartments. You were stuck with whatever snoring and farting Scientologist you were coupled with.

People stopped travelling by train.

They hated it.

As a result of this fewer people visited country towns, whose economies declined. Fewer people stayed at tourist motels. It was too much trouble. And it could be argued that more people, driving, would be in danger of having road accidents on the shabby highways.

By this means Greiner, the moron, saved maybe fifty million dollars in the first year, then less each year as the rail service grew more repellent to its users. In the meantime, probably no more than forty extra people died on the roads.

In Queensland, meanwhile, a luxury train modelled on the Orient Express, with dining car, club car, gourmet food and plush compartments, started making profits.

Economic anorexia here, economic gluttony there.

And guess which won, and kept its customer base, and so prevailed.

That's right.

At the heart of Greiner's lunacy was his belief, shared by many of his fellow rationalists, that time is only time. And the more you save of it, the more you have to spend in other ways.

But to arrive early in Casino, and so lose the emotional and spiritual benefit of a full night's sleep, saves you a couple of hours of travel but – in tiredness, bad temper and jangled neurasthenia – costs you a day of pleasure.

It is better for you, and more *economical*, in short, to arrive at 6.30 a.m., not 3.20 a.m, at Casino station, or at 8.10 a.m. at Byron Bay refreshed and energetic and have the day in its fullness.

Time is well used, or not well used. It is never saved, discuss.

A shorter, sadder example of the lunacy of this cost-saving tendency occurred at the end of World War I.

The light-horse brigades that had won Beersheba (in the last great cavalry charge of history) and taken Damascus ahead of Lawrence of Arabia, and had been, overall, the best and bravest soldiers in the Middle East, were told that, *in view of the limited space on returning troopships*, they would have to shoot their horses before sailing home.

These were horses from their own farms in Western Australia, horses they had trained with, sailed with, fought with, slept beside, and won their battles with. They had been their companions, fellow warriors and friends. And now they had to personally shoot them through the head.

Just to avoid the expense of bringing to the Mediterranean another couple of troopships to take the horses home.

The men complied, and some, as late as 1998, were still grieving for the friends they were told to kill.

It made a mockery of their valour and a bad joke of their victory. It made them curse their country. It traumatised them like the death of human friends. It haunted their manhood and middle age. It made them feel like criminals, Judases, murderers, fratricides.

And it saved, maybe, some twenty thousand pounds in the chartering of troopships.

The horses had names, and were friends.

Don't think about it. Don't think about it any more.

These horses seem to me a perfect parable of what is happening to all of us now.

It is May Day again, and there is not much to celebrate.

There is some comfort, however, in some things that are happening across the world, in Canada, where an economic rationalist government that brought in as well, poor devils, a GST, had 165 seats in Parliament, and in one election lost 163 of them. In England, the Major government, more Thatcherite than Thatcher in its privatising zeal, lost over a hundred seats and all chance for perhaps a generation of government again. In New South Wales an Opposition promising to privatise electricity, and give everybody a thousand bucks, got less votes for its constituent parties than at any time in seventy years. In Malaysia the tariff barriers once again are up, and foreign companies expelled, and the currency once again local, and jobs are coming back and per capita income rising. You do not hear of Malaysia. They do not want you to hear. And Russia soon, I guess, will default on its debt and Africa will follow and the cruel power, perhaps, of the IMF be broken.

So the word is out, as are the greed-is-good brigade, the Blue Meanies, the men in balaclavas who would be our manifest destiny. And if our future is uncertain as workers and citizens, so is theirs.

It is May Day once again, and it is good to remember, however dire the surrounding patch of history we are for the anguished moment in, what it stands for, and sing in our hearts of what is past, and passing, and to come, that socialism, that belief in community, that anthem of mutual striving and help that is best evoked in Denis Healey's great definition of socialism, which I never tire of quoting.

An obstinate will to erode by inches the conditions which produce avoidable suffering.

We should learn it by heart.

Lift the scarlet banner high.

I thank you.

May, 1999

East Timor

The events of the last month show how far from what is really happening are the words that politicians use to describe it. We hear how a 'peace keeping force' is to 'work alongside the Indonesian military' to 'stabilise the situation' in East Timor, and rescue the sick and starving people there from the 'militias' and 'the rogue elements of the army' that are 'out of control'.

But it cannot go into West Timor 'because that is part of Indonesia', and it would 'need permission to go there'.

Spin doctors are at work here, so much so that practically all of the above paragraph is fantasy. For the peace keeping force is an invading army, and has to be, given the tens of thousands of people being murdered there. The Indonesian military are the people doing the murders, the very war criminals that Mary Robinson is after. There are no rogue elements: they are taking orders. They are not out of control, they are taking orders from the top. And working beside them to stabilise the situation is like working alongside the guards at Belsen to save the Jews of Europe from extermination, the very people sworn to thwart us in that purpose. And you can't stabilise the situation in East Timor because the situation has moved, or most of it has, to West Timor, where 200 000 people, a third of the brutalised population, are starving or being shot or hacked to pieces or drowned or dying of dysentery, and you can't go there. Not without permission. Not soon. Not ever. These are the bitter fruits of the airbrushed words our diplomatic spin doctors use, a Holocaust. The Final Solution is another spin doctor's phrase, a spin doctor called Goebbels, famous for phrases like 'stabilising the situation'. Both phrases have the same effect, the coded condoning of slaughter.

The peace keeping force will arrive. It will wade ashore unresisted. It will find an empty, smoking place with nine tenths of its people missing. There will be no militia, and only a few smiling army officers adept at PR, and burnt and empty houses, and no bodies. And a stable situation, with nobody in it. And the peace keeping force will declare victory, and brew a cup of tea.

And across the border the killing will commence, the Final Solution of 200 000 people, and no-one will be there to stop it. We will need the permission of the killers, the hackers and shooters, to be there to stop it. So we can't stop it.

We would not be in this fix if the language of war had not been so purged of its bloodiness. We would have talked of killers kidnapping the innocent and a corrupt government with blood on its hands assisting them in their acts of slaughter. A corrupt government pretending it was rogue elements who were out of control when the rogues were taking orders from the top to end a young democracy with wholesale murder.

And we would not be tied up with the idea that catastrophes take place inside particular borders. We would know they can be moved across borders into other countries, in the same way as Jews from all parts of Europe were taken in trains to Poland, and murdered there. We would know this was happening, because we would be using these words. We would not be saying we *can* save the Jews of Italy, but not if they are moved to Poland. For that we would need permission. And we would be talking of war with Indonesia, because it is an evil regime, run by a man who sings 'Feelings' and permits massacres. And we would be calling for the breaking up of Indonesia into its component regions, as the Soviet Union broke up, because this was a good idea, and what its peoples want.

And we would be on the side of history, instead of maundering about permission and co-operation and working beside a tyranny. We would be dropping food and not talking about 'technical difficulties' while people starve.

Words take you so far from truth that you can die in them, like gas chambers that are supposed to be showers.

Thousands of Timorese are dying as I write this, inside the wrong words, the words we have built up between us and their fate.

September, 1999

Goodbye Kennett

Last Saturday night, unlike the rest of the world, I got it about right. A hung parliament, I said at 6.30 in the Tally Room to 3LO, as I had to Sandy McCutcheon the day before. Then weeks, maybe months of confusion, and an *eventual* Steve Bracks government in Victoria. When asked by a stunned compere why I had made this outlandish prediction, I said, 'Bad policies lose votes. And the people are not fools.'

I didn't add, and I should have, that the Morgan Poll had given the preferred vote at fifty-fifty for months, and Newspoll that morning had said Labor 51, Coalition 49, and five people out of a hundred voting against policies that hurt them wasn't too hard to imagine. I instead said sourly I'd been right in twenty of my poll predictions, and dead wrong in five poll predictions. I later counted these up, and I was right, I'm sorry to say, only sixteen times, within four seats, and got five elections dead wrong. Though it is probably still the best track record on earth (and incudes Keating's win of '93, Harold Wilson's surprise resurrection of '74, the New South Wales hung parliament of '91 and Tony Blair's huge margin of '97) it is not as good as I said. And I'm sorry.

Bad policies lose votes. I think now this is all that happens. A set of policies that hurt people cause a party to lose government. A new government is then installed, whatever its leadership. Kennett. Keating. Howard. Court.

That party is then re-elected because people think all governments need two terms to prove themselves, and then the bad policies hurt, and the party is voted out. Or their good policies don't hurt, and keep them in office. And when, eventually, other, later policies hurt, they're voted out.

And leadership has nothing to do with it. Or personality. Or eloquence. Or campaign imagery. Or spin. Anyone could have won the Victorian election of 1992, given that state's financial disasters. Anyone could have lost last Saturday's, given the sold-off schools and the rundown hospitals and the cancelled ambulances and the money spent on casinos and racetracks, money that was needed elsewhere. And the stifling of democracy itself by a twenty-five-day election campaign hidden under football and gagged ministers and censored reports. Anyone.

Personality and leadership and eloquence didn't save Keating after he sold off Qantas and the Commonwealth Bank and caused a recession and failed to staunch the bleeding of the country towns. They didn't save Whitlam after his tariff cuts wrecked so many small businesses, and his petulant sacking of so many of his ministers rattled everyone. They didn't save Churchill from the wrath of the servicemen he had put, with his addled strategies in Crete and Italy and the Far East, in harm's way. They didn't save Piggy Muldoon from a man, David Lange, half as popular as he. They didn't save Joan Kirner from a man, Jeff Kennett, less popular than she. Because personalities have nothing, or very little, to do with it. With personality, charisma, eloquence, image management, you can get away with jay-walking, but not murder. Policy is all – plus the electoral habit of the second-term fair go.

Thus I was sure in 1983 that Fraser's policies were hurting, and Hawke could be elected, and I called his exact majority, 25. And in 1987 and 1990 I knew that Hawke's policies were good enough, and he would narrowly survive. In 1993 I, like very few others, was right because I felt that the hurt of Keating's policies, which was considerable, was less than the feared hurt of Hewson's.

Guessing the margin is harder. I do it by reading the opinion polls, especially Morgan, who don't phone people but stand at the front door, or sit in the front room, till a lot of the Undecided, not all of them, decide. And if the Undecided are, say, 12 per cent, I ask how many of those 12 per cent are really hurting, and add them in. And that I admit is a guess, with some telepathy in it perhaps, perhaps not, based on talkback radio and letters to the editor and the number of jobless and garage sales and businesses for sale, and the number of drunks on the street. And if, as in Victoria this month, the number of Undecided is huge, around 30 per cent, that probably means there are a lot of people hurting, and not wanting to think about it yet. But they will by polling day.

And so it is that Howard cannot, I think, survive. His fair-go second term will end, and at that point the Timor cock-up, the GST cock-up, the IR cock-up, the education crisis, the hospital crisis, the starving of the ABC, the ongoing punishment of migrants and Aborigines, and the widespread wrecking of the morale of Australian families will take him – or his chosen successor, Nick Minchin – out in a punitive landslide. Carr, I think, will survive because of his adequate management of smaller suburban issues and the larger Olympic Games. Beattie and Bacon will get their second terms, and Bracks his two terms. Olson and Court have had two terms and will go, because of their policies on trees and privatisation, in landslides that, like Chikarovski's, will bring into doubt the Liberal Party's very survival.

Because the Liberal Party's current philosophy of greed before all, and individual profit before the common good, is a philosophy only 10 or 12 per cent of people now support. And it is therefore likely that they will vanish altogether, and a more voter-sensitive mix of Democrats and Nationals will take their place, on either the right or the left of Beazley's Labor – which will have two terms till people hurt, or not, and go, or not.

See if I'm wrong. I sometimes am. Bad policies lose votes, and the people are not fools. And a big Undecided vote nearly always means a government will go. And governments usually fall after campaigns that the commentators find wearisome – those experts we pay so much to get it all so wrong, as they did last week.

They should bone up on the rudiments of politics. But they won't, of course, for they're the experts, they study 'image' and 'spin'. And I'm an amateur, and a dilettante, and I wouldn't know.

But I was the one who was right.

Bad policies lose votes. And the Undecided eventually decide. And they have reasons.

And it's not that unusual for five people in a hundred to vote against policies that hurt them.

It happens all the time.

September, 1999

1968, Where Are You?

No-one who did not live through it will ever know, *precisely*, what it was like to experience 1968 or to be, as I was, young and keen and alive in that epic, vivid, abrasive, abusive, tumultuous year. Few know now, for instance, that after Bobby Kennedy was shot he did not die immediately but lingered for a day and a half while hearty, bullying commentators inquired of shifty doctors how soon he would be back on the campaign trail and running again for President. Few recall that there was a number of weeks when the Prague Spring of Alexander Dubček – a dress rehearsal for Gorbachev and perestroika – looked as if it had worked, when the Soviet Union announced (before it came in with tanks to smash it to pieces) that it would not interfere. Few remember the stark, strange, dumfound half-*amused* emotions that came with the drowning of Harold Holt, or the quiet thrill of the sudden emergence of John Grey Gorton, Spitfire pilot, scarred war hero and 'Waltzing Matilda' singing man of the people (dirt farmer, illegitimately born), as our new Prime Minister. Or the full devastation of Martin Luther King's death, or Bobby Kennedy's speech, impromptu and quoting Sophocles, when he heard of it. Or the hours of hope when Paul Newman and Shirley MacLaine and Jane Fonda and Norman Mailer and others arrived at the Chicago Convention and it seemed for a moment that Eugene McCarthy – poet, former priest, man of deft, ironic, self-mocking Whitlamesque resolve – might yet be President, and the troops in Vietnam home by Christmas. Or the awe we felt when man first flew round the moon.

Some of the rich indulgent vividness of that watershed year survives, of course, in the miniskirts and flares and granny specs of Carnaby Street's brief interregnum, in the cover photo of *Sergeant Pepper's Lonely Hearts Club Band*, the first LP to be structured round a theme; in the hairy, naked, in-your-face opening night of *Hair – The Musical*; in the legalisation, in Britain, of abortion on demand. Or the exhilaration attendant on the cancellation by Roy Jenkins, the British Home Secretary, of those hoary bans on books and plays that would have kept *Lady Chatterley* off our shelves (because of bad language) and *Jesus Christ Superstar* off the public stage (because it dared to represent the Deity in human form).

Nineteen sixty-eight was my first year overseas, and I was probably too cautious at times. I stood on Prague railway station the day the tanks rolled in, and I got back on the train and went on to Vienna, where a girl was waiting, and missed it all. I was part, but not for long, of a plan to smuggle across the Channel the family wealth of an aristocratic French acquaintance while Paris swarmed with barricades and tear gas and rotting food and Charles de Gaulle in panic fled the city. I planned to see Bobby Kennedy crowned at Chicago as presidential candidate but delayed my departure and instead was able to visit his grave. I spent election night in New York and went to bed believing Humphrey had won and woke to find with amazement the dark, fraught, fevered years of Nixon beginning, and all the dreams of our one brief shining year of shaggy-Camelot hope and glory (and it was little more than a year, before the mud of Woodstock soiled it and the Manson murders bloodied it, and the Beatles broke up and Hendrix and Joplin died) beginning to sluice down sludgily into anticlimax and futility and a kind of shame. I couldn't believe it. It was all, all over so soon – an end so well portrayed, with bong and epilogue, in the final scenes of *Withnail and I*.

In a few months, stirred by everything I had seen, in particular the unceasing miracle that was (and is) London theatre, and a silly little film I'd appeared in, made by Philippe Mora, with Richard Neville and (yes) Germaine Greer, I wrote with Michael Boddy a musical play about King O'Malley that unleashed the Australian renaissance (most historians say) in theatre and film and sped our nation, so long pent-up and cringing, gamely and belligerently on its way.

. . . Some things, as I write this, come roaring back into memory, not all of them good. A car trip with Les Murray and our then and future spouses Val and Annie through Spain and France, full of quarrel and contention, that all but ended our friendship. A long dreary yarn in Chelsea with Martin Sharp as he proudly invoked his first LSD trip, when the trees in Hyde Park were melting and a brass band played Rogers and Hammerstein and he *knew, just knew*, what the universe was like. The moment of our arrest in East Berlin, hard by the bullet-pocked sandstone of Checkpoint Charlie, for having unwittingly brought into Bert Brecht's utopia 102 contraband paperbacks. A trip on a Greyhound bus to Chicago beside a man who said he was a serial murderer specialising in honeymoon couples. A Nixon election meeting I was thrown out of four times because I had a beard. It seems amazing I went back in. We were game then, but so was the era.

Eight young heroes, for instance, stormed and took the American embassy in Saigon and ran up the Vietcong flag on its roof and held out for nearly a day till the helicopter gunship missiles of the Free World cut them down. Never such courage again. These young men won the hearts and minds, I think, of those in the West who were young like me; never such courage again. And when only six weeks later other young men wasted the women and children and old men of My Lai, destroyed a village in order to save it – as a general said with Orwellian precision of another place – that battle, probably, for the mind of the West was won, and the New Agnostic Pacifism began that has not ceased.

Few who write of 1968 have mentioned its religious dimension, or the seedbed planted that year of what I suppose will be finally known as the post-Christian age. For a year that saw the death by a shot to the brain of a second Kennedy and the death, at thirty-nine, of a man as good and brave as Martin Luther King, and the political crippling of a man as fine and brilliant as Eugene McCarthy, and saw exalted into kingship of the world in their place a man as creepy and mediocre, as vengeful and shifty and slimy, as Richard Nixon, is one that challenged for all of us the notion of a caring Christ and an all-knowing God. These mortalities, that victory, and our desolation, did not stack up beside the power of prayer, or the court of heaven, or the promised good. It did not, as HAL in *2001* said, compute. That film was made that year, too, and it bespoke the need we all of us felt for a better God, a better universe. So too did a shrewder hit of 1968, *The Graduate*. Where was the promise, oh Benjamin Braddock, of a greener spring?

Some of us (though not me or Annie, thank Christ) thought they had found that better place, that greener spring, in drugs, and minds that might else have been good and great were spent and wasted on this youthful fool-ishness, this chemical breath of a mysticism yearned for but not had, in the belief that it was a worthy cause (they would not, I once wrote, have spent so much of their strength in trying to legalise, say, Bacardi and Coke), and brain cells bruised and swollen by that subtlest ally of paranoia, marihuana, and perspectives distorted and lives made marginal and pointless, and a sig-nificant fraction of a perhaps worthy generation left on the junkheap of history, playing guitars and saying Om. 'While we were drunk at the post,' Norman Mailer wrote eloquently after *Apollo 12*, 'the WASPs were taking the moon.' Few have looked frankly at this waste of potential, or the unwor-thiness of the drug (as emotionally unremarkable in its way as a Bex and a cup of tea) for which so much was sacrificed. 'If I were the CIA,' I once wrote, 'I'd get the Left stoned on pot. I think they probably did.'

(I differ with my contemporaries on this. I always have.)

And so it goes, and so it goes.

Out of 1968 came ... what? Well, a great democracy of thought. A fifteen-year fashion for casual sex that AIDS ended. A tolerance for abortion that saved a lot of souls and ended a lot of tiny lives, and rendered a good few unknowing girls (maybe no more than a million) incapable of child-bearing. A wistful need for new religions to replace the drugs that had in turn replaced the ones that were gone. A lot of excellent popular music (Bob Dylan, Frank Zappa, Rolf Harris) and intricate clothing design and backyard careers in pottery and surfboard polishing and abstract sculpture. A tidal retreat from threatening grey metropolises into green and welcoming arcadias of drugs and quarrelsome promiscuity and art and poetry and deaths by overdose and good companionship. Oral sex. Tarot cards. Khalil Gibran. Don Maclean at the Coolangatta RSL. A lot of toying with Buddhism. A lot of divorce. A lot of blameless children wrecked, or buffeted, by divorce, and now hanging out for a fix or an act of violence that will fill the loveless darkness of their hearts. Sex shops. Encounter groups. Acupuncture therapy. Holistic dentistry. Aerobics. Chiropractics. Vegetarian cafes. Stand-up comedy. Performance poetry. Andrew Lloyd Webber. Bob Dylan, lapsed Christian. The Australian film renaissance. Hemp in pot plants for personal use. Daily deaths by heroin in our better cities. Campaigns to legalise it, and make it free. A tendency to foreign travel, and Third World journeyings, and religious and political comparisons that have brought a perspective into our lives, I think, that is a considerable improvement on the way we were. Without 1968 we would still be stifling (perhaps) in the buttoned-up world that *Grease* so pungently shows – of short hair-cuts and lying to parents and hypocritical religiosity and fraught careerism and tedious life-plans and souped-up cars and censorship and tight communities and sexual ignorance, a world some still yearn for, I too some nights.

I remember in particular a designed postcard of Martin Sharp's, for 1968, that year when all things changed.

These ARE the good old days, it said.

They probably were.

April, 1998

BOOK EIGHT

And So It Goes

The Forty-year Christmas Dinner

From 1947 when Dad first bought the land till 1992, last year, when so many of us were dead or away across the world that it wasn't the same any more, I and my varying relatives (parents, grandmother, sisters, brother-in-law, nieces, girlfriends, eventual wife and eventual children) converged in tents and caravans round the same shabby concrete shack by a muddy lagoon with great blowing sandhills and a roaring surf at its back in Fingal, near Tweed Heads, up north, contentiously, at Christmas, among the sandflies and the family quarrels and the pet frogs and the perilous, unpatrolled beach, the shark scares and humid bickering and looming divorces and broadcasted cricket and adolescent rebellion and home-brew and broken motor boats and fractious nights of Scrabble and theological contention that we, like so many others (I guess), had instead of the intended happy family time in all those years, on a quarter-acre block between river and sea bought for seven pounds and nearly sold (but, after a family conference, not) for $250 000 to a developer, later named in the ICAC, in the fraught nostalgic year of 1987.

I roved all over Fingal that bad year, putting down on videotape the quiet streets and wooden and fibro houses among the banana plants and motor boats, knowing it would soon be a luxury tourist resort with skyscrapers full of hearty Japanese playing roulette above the mild and buzzing village that formed and flavoured my testy infancy and mournful youth. A few fool Greenies and some glum black activists were fighting to save it, taking the millionaires to court, but I knew they had no chance. So I got it all down on videotape, that and my tiny children and Auntie Glad, incontinent now, and Paddy, her dying alcoholic son, in the immemorial green and flyblown settings soon to go.

But it didn't happen like that. The Greenies, to everyone's admiring astonishment, prevailed before the ICAC in one of the first cases fought, the millionaires went broke, and Fingal, miraculously, remains as it was, un-changed. The videotape, on the other hand, burned in a fire. Which goes to show. You *can* go home again, sometimes. I wonder if that is so.

Christmas holidays, I once wrote, are what Australians have instead of psychoanalysis. They may be why, in the southern hemisphere, where summer heat and Christmas reunions coincide and because of the extra weeks are prolonged, there is so much less of mental illness than in the fraught and frozen brevities of the European north. Here we have time, and beaches to walk on, and rivers and surfs to swim in, while sorting things out.

All those Fingal summers, forty-four of them I suppose (I missed 1971 because I was working and 1974 because I was in England), merge in my mind. Keith, my father, always presided. Ill-tempered, charismatic, full of political quarrel, up fishing at all hours and catching little, fighting with the innards of his various recalcitrant motor boats, dismayed at his children and grandchildren, grieving over the cricket, uncorking his home-brew and despite its ghastliness making us drink it . . .

Ah yes. All that. I put it all down on videotape and the videotape burned. In 1976, I think, I instituted our Annual Beer Tasting. All sorts of foreign beers would be bought and, after Christmas dinner, sampled and given a mark out of ten. Mum, the only surviving Seventh Day Adventist (we were all that way once, but times change), eventually joined in, in 1980, but her judgments were unreliable. Lately after Jack, my teenage son, joined in, the labels were concealed but the result was always the same, for sixteen years: Heineken: eight and a half.

One year it pelted with rain every day for six weeks. One year Jack and his playmate Ben Hollows went missing overnight for five hours and I frantically walked the length of the six-mile beach to Cudgen Headland in the dark, yelling out their names. I found them at midnight calmly playing pinball. Each year with diminishing gusto we took the kids to Surfers, and Sea World, and Dream World, and Warner World, as the Gold Coast megalopolis grew and the old verandahed houses came down, and to *Home Alone* and *The Addams Family* at the Coolangatta cinemas, bumping down the waterslides behind them and hovering over them fretfully in the video-game arcades – and always, nostalgically, fearfully, surfing with them on the unpatrolled beach (the shark is waiting, I thought, it is out there) and climbing the Fingal Causeway, a unique formation of rocks with prehistoric trees and a lighthouse on it that seemed drawn out of race memory, and the first dawn of the world. Here, we knew, Captain Cook was nearly shipwrecked and white Australia, therefore, nearly didn't happen. We showed them where the Aboriginal caves were before they became a blue-metal quarry (Mum remembered the caves, and tiptoeing through them in the 1920s) and the Aboriginal midden beside the burial ground and the massacre site where still, some twilights, you could hear the dead screaming out, very distinctly, *my land, my brothers, my home*, and where the sandhills were before the miners came. We told them this was history, and we were part of it, a movement of people towards these waterways, these hills, these trees, and past them. The first cane toads arrived, harbingers of the grosser future.

Each year Christmas dinner grew more sad, as the oldies grew more frail (Auntie Glad, last year, had lost the power of speech) and the children more desirous to be home among their friends in Sydney, and Yarrawonga and Melbourne.

It was when Dad died in 1989 – correctly and conveniently over the Christmas break – and we all went back, after burying him, to the shack he had built and extended, and watched the cricket that he was determined, even in his last days, to see out, that the heart went out of Fingal I think. It wasn't the same after that. Peter, my bearded brother-in-law, the Yarrawonga teacher, fished with Dad, and he missed him. No-one else would go, disliking the torture of yabbies and the decapitation of our fellow creatures. Peter would brood alone by the boat on its trailer, and clean and scrape it sometimes, but never take it out. Then his daughters Leisa and Lettie got jobs and started to travel overseas and Paddy died first and then, last month, Auntie Glad, and this year . . . well, the decision was made.

We're converging, those of us that are left, in Avalon, Sydney, a little before Christmas, and then Peter and Kay, my sister, will go north to Fingal alone. Peter is retiring and will live there alone next year, all year, while Kay works on another year at Yarrawonga.

Nothing lasts. It's the most ordinary of life's lessons and perhaps the only one. No sense of ah-well-forty-four-years-is-a-good-innings, or Fingal-was-never-much-chop-anyway will ever make up for the feeling of foreshortening, of spiritual bereavement, I am feeling now, in the aftermath of all those years in that ordinary place among those ordinary people, my blood group, my gene pool, us.

We might make it back next year. I'm feeling the need already.

September, 1993

The Lismore High School Reunion

You know: there are people you love, and you never see them.

And there are people you can't stand — and you see them all the time.

Sandy Stone, 1990

The Lismore Workers' Club, a dull white concrete temple of small-town banality, was packed to the poker machines on this one night, the seventy-fifth anniversary of the public school (*Spectemur Agendo*: by our actions let us be judged, oh let us sing of Lismore High, and sing of it with pride, yah! yah! ibba! ibba! Wagga! Wagga! whiskers on your gobba! gobba!) with a dozen successive perspiring generations of the black and gold, all of them mutually dubious, some of them outside in the foyer pleading to get in, *I've just flown in from Leningrad, let me in*, as up on the stage Norm Robinson, the current retiring headmaster, with magisterial rectitude transformed an evening of potentially warm remembrance into a slow mud-slide of ornamental praise for the proudly remembered school traditions, and school spirit, of yore.

Spirit? Traditions? What traditions? we wanted to know. What does he mean, the torpid old fool — four years older, I noted with a twinge, than me. Our lot, squeezed between tables on the upper level for three hours of stupefying corpulent oratory, which efficiently prevented our first bodily contact in thirty-seven years (Can that be Delyce Johnston? And Helen Brown? My God! They're old! Funny how you only remember the girls you were keen on.), were uncertain there *were* school traditions, unless you counted losing every football game to Woodlawn and annually carrying Mr Marwood's little car up the stairs to the second storey and leaving it in the corridor on break-up day. Headmaster Robinson apologised for there being no twenty-fifth anniversary (the War) and no fiftieth ('I can find no adequate explanation for this'), 'but better late than never', he added, coining a phrase. A graduate school captain, female, then sang 'The Way We Were' with a kind of breathily tuneful, gasping nullity, and a bevy of swaggering virgins, still at school, sang 'Summertime' with sassy negroid vigour, to our growing dismay. Serious damage, I inwardly moaned, is being done to two of the century's better songs in my hearing and it's 9.35 already and we're still not being permitted to *talk* to each other, clutch at each other, kiss . . .

> Oh let us sing of our Lismore High
> And sing of it with pride,
> The school where we by work and play
> Our future lives decide,
> By working hard and playing fair
> We guard its noble name,
> Oh, Lismore High, as the years slip by,
> We help to build its fame.
>
> *Traditional (to the tune of 'The Lincolnshire Poacher')*

The occasion's famous guest of honour, one Peter Arnison, who bore a startlingly close resemblance to his former youthful self, we his classroom peers remembered as a jovial ebullient hoon. He was a Major General now, the one in charge of the defence against foreign invasion of the entire land mass of Australia. This, we all murmurously agreed, was a bit of a worry. In his dashing regimental scarlet and jaunty yellow sash he looked, as he adjusted the microphone, like one about to sing a bracket of songs from *The Student Prince*. He spoke, instead, of the school traditions. Murder grew in our ancient adjacent, heaving hearts.

I came back like a ghost on sabbatical to Lismore in those intervening thirty-seven years, rarely looking anybody up, seeing only my parents, my cousin the church elder and underwear salesman, and my immediate neighbours, avoiding the Adventist Church and those few school fellows I might have rubbed words with, afraid I suppose that I would be mocked or judged by people whose language I no longer spoke, or be tempted to mockery or judgement in return, and slowly as over the dwindling decades the unremarkable city emptied of old acquaintance it became like a phantom too, a mist in the shape of a town, a fading Brigadoon, yet one in certain twilights luminous with memory. Each house, untenanted now by friends long since moved on, appeared to glimmer with their absence. Each row of fibro houses, each street sign grew eloquent with remembered pleasure or hurt – here it was I came off my bike and skidded for a yard on my chin, here it was I knew I would never play cricket well, and here it was I stood all night and looked at the girls' dark bedroom windows – as though Lismore was already a legend merely, something that never really happened in time, a forged map of my beginnings, a counterfeit presentiment of my history, a town in which occurred a boyhood that never was, among friends that never actually existed – rumours, vague rumours, not real people at all.

Bob Ellis, diary, 7 September 1994

The mud-slow drip of appropriate public utterance dimmed our hearts and then, at 10.35, ceased. The mayor, it seemed, the MLA, the MHR, the neighbouring MHR, the rightly apprehensive representative of the abominated and shrewdly absent Minister for Education Chadwick, the School Council President, the Assistant Director of Local Education, the present delectable shapely school captain, female (be still, my heart), the first school captain, female, now eighty-four, who sang unaccompanied in a fraying soprano a song of her own composition to the tune of 'Galway Bay' amid much applause – all agreed with Norm that it was a fine school, a good school, a much underrated school, a model school in its way for its time, while across the crowd of half-familiar shoulders and necks and turned-away faces I ached to reach out and stroke the cheek of Judith Rothery, my first hope, vain of course, of romantic love in the secondary school (Betty, I thought of her, to my Archie, and Helen Brown as Veronica), or maybe Rita Norton, my last, or Deanne Bishop, whom I loved when I was six and dreamed of rescuing heroically from a fire when I was six and a half, or serene blonde Diane Bartlett, who looked, amazingly, there in the distance, no different . . .

> Hereto I come to view a voiceless ghost;
>   Whither, O whither will its whim now draw me?
> Up the cliff, down, till I'm lonely, lost
>   And the unseen waters' ejaculations awe me.
> Where you will next be there's no knowing,
>   Facing round about me everywhere,
>   With your nut-coloured hair,
> And gray eyes, and rose-flush coming and going.
>
> 'After a Journey', Thomas Hardy

Major General Arnison then came on again and controversially asserted without fear or favour that it was a fine school, a good school, a model school in its way for its time, and while our fingernails clawed at our knees and our separate nostalgias grew more erotic Norm Robinson, lugubriously and alarmingly recycled, took twenty-one more minutes by my watch to instruct us to leave the building in an orderly manner when the happy foreshortened rejoicing was, by his rigid command, soon over. Only once, when Arnison with a gleam of his old playground mischief led us in the school war cry (Yah! Yah! Ibba! Ibba!) and we then immediately sang the school song, did the desired authentic soaring and purging of our hearts take place, and our minds winged back to a time when life was simpler, by the white picket fences against which the pushbikes leaned and the blue jacarandas bloomed and the glittering waters of the Memorial Pool lapped round nimble bodies unhad, never to be had, but ever recalled, a time of unfinished business, never to be finished now, so sundered were we from one another by career, Australian distance and time's derision, lost, regretted, oh well . . . so it goes.

> And maybe what they say is true
>   Of war and war's alarms,
> But O that I were young again
>   And held her in my arms!

Free at last, glory hallelujah, we moved with daunted, tense and tired excitement towards one another. Ken Buttrum's lank hair, thank God, was not a wig. I greeted to his annoyance Adrian Bryant as Bob Sillar, a mistake I'd also made in 1954, and Rita Norton, initially and shamefully, as Judith Rothery. The faces came at me like a special effect in a Schwarzenegger movie, morphing out of puddingy middle-aged nonentity into sudden teenage clarity, the intimate acquaintance I always knew. Lifetimes ran by in melting fast-forward – the retarded child, now twenty, the long-loved farm lost now to rural recession, the years of angry urban solitude and the Filipino bride. The death by mauling shark of a younger brother, long beloved, long mourned. The death in road accident of two long-grieved and in dream recurring children. The abrupt death at thirty-two, by coronary occlusion, of big, healthy, hearty Ian Havilah. The eerie triumph of Bruce Watson who departed school a perceived dunce at fifteen, and was now a millionaire.

Helen Stacey was still missing, murdered probably while hitch-hiking, but Rex Bartlett, who had strangely not turned up at school one morning and never came back, was alive and visible, a lecturing academic, belatedly qualified, in Brisbane, his unchanged smiling blonde beautiful sister Diane revealed. Why was she so unchanged? I wanted to know. I did ballet seriously, she said, for twenty-five years.

> Yes: I have re-entered your olden haunts at last;
>   Through the years, through the dead scenes I have tracked you;
> What have you now found to say of our past –
>   Scanned across the dark space wherein I have lacked you?
> Summer gave us sweets, but autumn wrought division?
>   Things were not lastly as firstly well
>   With us twain, you tell:
> But all's closed now, despite Time's derision.
> 'After a Journey', Thomas Hardy

All but a few (Harvey Lee and Heatherbelle MacLeay, Ray Gooley and Helen Brown) had committed the mortal sin of exogamy, marrying outside the tribe, in Sydney, in Brisbane, far away, finding other priorities, other dreams. The spare spouses gloomily smirked at the edges of our hearty alien conversations, like poor relations at the baron's table, as never before. I looked round the faces, missing them already: David Lowe especially, hunched, sallow, villainously-handsome-or-perhaps-no-longer, like a Shakespearian Fool with a dry wit and a sly warmth, once my best friend, or was he, a surgeon now in Gold Coast City. I could have seen him every Christmas, for these fifteen years, I realised, and I hadn't. The ebullient, tiny Ken Buttrum especially, with whom I had run a threepenny cinema of Charlie Chaplin silent comedies in a garage in Oakley Avenue, and a street fair (the Bonaparte of Oakley Avenue he was known as), and co-starred with in a wobbly production of *Julius Caesar* on a front verandah, in Oakley Avenue, long ago. (Ken had found out at last what we all had long known or thought, that his older, much older sister was in fact his mother and he was her illegitimate son and lately by her deathbed weeping had said of course he forgave her, there was nothing to forgive, and she didn't quite believe him, and so died.) He'd lived round Sydney these thirty years, and I hadn't seen him since 1961. We had a phone conversation in 1966, another in 1992. Why was this? I asked him. We get other priorities, he said, and we move on.

'It is now midnight,' said Norm Robinson. 'Will you all move quietly and in an orderly fashion toward the several exits . . .' Ken and I looked at each other, swiftly, mortally afraid. *See you at the service tomorrow? At the memorial service.*

I cannot tell
why He whom angels worship,
should set His love
upon the sons of men,
or why as Shepherd
He should seek the wanderers
to bring them back,
they know not how or when . . .

John the Beloved, A.D. 71

The enormous, unfamiliar hymn to Danny Boy's melody soared to the concrete roof of the new big vulgar school's assembly hall on the fibro outskirts of town. Deferential bored youngsters in the changeless yellow-and-black of the ever ghastly uniform steered groggy latecomers through the concrete portico to the Standing Room Only. In heavy-framed spectacles now, her face deep-lined, Barbara Brockington, whom I'd asked out in 1957 and who said no, a long rankling memory (be still, my heart), stood unperturbed beside me, called me Robert, and sang with uplifted chin each piercing word by rote in perfect pitch. With apologies then to the accidentally unhonoured,

Major General Arnison, lifting his voice in the wake of a defunct and briefly pinging microphone, unveiled a modest marble plaque to the Vietnam War veterans of the Lismore district, of whom he of course was one, and spoke with dwindling warmth of school traditions.

We swim, we run, we hit a ball
We always play the game –
Oh, Lismore High, as the years slip by,
We help to build its fame.

Few among the sombre churchy witnesses of this overdue solemnity were people I knew – a corpulent, gravid right-wing bunch of sluggards I decided, National Party fatheads and armchair war buffs and plaintive rednecks, woe unto ye scribes and pharisees, hypocrites, ye strain at a gnat and swallow Red Menace, gripe, mumble, not like the Lismore I want to remember, or is it? How little we know our home towns, I suddenly grieved. We are sojourners all, and strangers ever, so slim a wafer are we in the life of a town or a nation. We pass on unknowing, and never know.

'Would you please file out,' boomed Norm Robinson, amazingly recurrent and dominant once more, 'in an orderly manner, starting with the left-hand rows ...'

BLACK MAN: *As Henry Miller correctly said, the purpose of life is to remember.*
Bob Ellis, The Nostradamus Kid, *1979*

With practised courtroom acerbity and the unaltered sly sweet grin on the exact same face Bob Stitt, our contemporary school captain, mocked *The Nostradamus Kid* before our class of '58 on the sunlit concrete verandah of the Goonellabah Leagues Club. 'This guy was *irresistible* to women!' he chortled. 'Mouse Ellis! Completely irresistible! Think about that!' Laughter, some of it forty years in the making, ensued and with mingled grief and scaldedness I looked round the already thinning crowd. Photos had been noisily taken on the verandah in the sun and somehow, on that ritual signal, after only two hours and a boozy buffet lunch and the shy beginnings of restored affection of people newly known, we were beginning to leave. *Come back!* I was crying inwardly. *There's still so much to say. It shouldn't be like this.*

We're young today in hearts and minds,
We always will be so,
For members of the school we'll be
No matter where we go ...

Old teachers had been satirised and mourned – Miss Waller, Miss Willkie,

Mrs Oakes, Mrs Murphy, the Bills Marwood, Maiden and Newling, Bob Muggleton, Des Davis, the red-faced angry Cyril Butcher, of late a suicide in England, 'Arfie' Edwards whom the kids' chiacking one morning killed with a heart attack, Selby Jenkins, Bob Sykes ... One of them, Noel Rumble, who ran the cadets, communed at the main table with Major General Arnison, as eventually did I, swapping views on the seventeen-year Eritrean insurgency and the patient ingenuity of subject nations, Vietnam of course among them, who have no choice but to win. The major general's easy disarming grace, that of a self-taught barracks aristocrat, charmed me too, and we agreed to have lunch, eventually. He had done well, old Arno, the former playground wide boy. Australia is probably in good hands.

And so had others, not all of them present, not that it mattered. Bob Stitt, Q.C., the perpetual guardian of the courtroom fortunes of Ian Sinclair. Ken Buttrum, Head of Children's Services, whose wisdom and mercy, derived not only from Solomon but his own genesis and revelation, restored to their sorrowing parents the sequestered Children of God. Roy Masters, the columnist, broadcaster and football coach. Phil Wilkins, the *Herald*'s perpetual sports writer. Professor John Niland. Lots of doctors and social workers and accountants and newsagents and road workers and beloved nurses and still revered teachers, like Brian Batterham, my best friend once, or was he, who'd taught at Lismore High unceasingly for thirty-three years. Excluding four years away at uni he'd been there thirty-nine years in all, a chubby, balding happy man. And why not. It was a good town, with or without us. We should have stayed.

And when we leave behind our youth,
We'll still in song proclaim,
Oh, Lismore High, as the years slip by,
We help to build its fame.

The girls had done especially well, unlike, I thought, the liberationist, cliterocentric, exhaustively aborted, fist-high generation immediately after them. They'd had their careers, and then their children, and then went back to their careers, and kept their marriages, and found, on the whole, a measurable happiness of an ordinary sort on this imperfect earth. It was an era of full employment of course, and things were easier for us, and conformity was easier too. We were lucky in a way, a big way, the lot of us, in all things. No war. No truncating Depression. A good state school, in an era when there were such things. We had much to be thankful for. And here we were. And now we were leaving.

I wish there was some way of passing on what I've learned, though. I was learning fast there at the end. I know now there is no one thing that is true. It is all true. Pretty soon with many vain promises the party broke up.

I thanked Harvey Lee from my heart for bringing us all together again and drove on down the hill to the old school, now a college of art, and loitered round the asphalt yard where the basketball hoops were once in the slanting summer light, and walked down a chalky corridor or two among strangers from other years; with a few of whom I then got seriously drunk. I found as I talked to these strangers that we shared a common dialect, a literary, ironic and yet colloquial ease of self-mocking discourse that is very North Coast, very Lismore, very much the way we were brought up and taught, a mixture, like that of our fellow North Coasters Les Murray and Tom Keneally and P.J. Hogan and Doug Anthony, of innocence and cynicism.

It didn't matter any more who had done well, we conjointly and slurringly decided in our cups, we were fifty now and knew how accidental it all was, now our playground competitiveness had shrunk with our sexual desire. We were all one family, one we could book back into at any time. Now we had gone back to Lismore as, in their forties, so many now had. Gone home. We had another drink.

It was hard to say goodbye, even to a pack of tottering strangers. I meandered slowly and sorrowfully home to Mum's, lay down at sunset in my unchanged boyhood bedroom, and slept. My dreams as always were populated with everyone I ever knew, but the town, the landscape, as always, was Lismore.

> Ignorant of what there is flitting here to see,
>   The waked birds preen and the seals flop lazily;
> Soon you will have, Dear, to vanish from me,
>   For the stars close their shutters and the dawn whitens hazily.
> Trust me, I mind not, though Life lours,
>   The bringing me here; nay, bring me here again!
>   I am just the same as when
> Our days were a joy, and our paths through flowers.
>   'After a Journey', Thomas Hardy

The fortieth anniversary of the Class of '58 is next. Buttrum and I are organising it, or that's the plan. I had arranged to spend last weekend with him, out at Penrith, but something else I had to do got in the way.

November, 1995

Childhood

Childhood is not what it was. I lived in two towns in mine, and in each I had uncles, aunts and cousins in the same street. In one of the towns was a grandma and grandpa, and a mother always home.

We had set meals and family games of Scrabble, and games of neighbourhood cricket, and gatherings of the whole extended family at the beach. Church, too, we had, and the interlacing gossip and loyalties and feuds and picnics religion brings.

Childhood was more *populous* then. You might have three or four siblings, and five kids in the next yard, and six in the yard beyond. You might have twenty cousins, some your age, in the same district. Blood loyalties were strong, and there was always a favourite, forgiving auntie you could pour out your heart to, then sleep a night on her couch. Neighbours were like aunties, and were called Auntie. If your parents weren't there, you could go next door and she'd feed you.

Some societies are still like that. Ireland. Calabria. Eritrea. Nepal. Poverty mattered less because there were blood ties and neighbours and an ethic of love. Between a child and hunger or danger there were a lot of adults, adults who really cared.

It's not like that now, or not very often. Smaller families, working mothers and the commonness of divorce mean childhood is more solitary now. Television makes it less verbal. Computers make it less physical. Children who once would have spent all their daylight hours outdoors playing now spend them in front of a screen, murdering aliens with special weapons or pestering strangers in other hemispheres. They change address more too, as their dads lose jobs and move on, or their mums divorce and move on, and neighbourhood friendships that once lasted lifetimes are episodes now. There are fewer kids on the street, because fewer get born in the first place. Kids stay in more because they feel safer at home. They wait for Mum there, behind a closed front door, for Mum to come home from work, at the deli or the insurance office.

Because of television, kids know more now. The AIDS campaign revealed anal sex to them, the Lewinsky scandal revealed oral sex. The murder and starvation of Rwanda, the war in the Gulf, made real to them what to us were fuzzy, abstract concepts. War. Death. Famine. The death of children.

Childhood used to be a time of dreaming, of the imagining of infinite possibilities. Reading was a sensual delight in childhood then. You imagined your heroes' faces, and their mighty deeds. Radio let you do that too. The mind was activated. Dreaming had an edge of amazement to it.

Now the dreams are all prefabricated, put in a blue chip, standardised. Disney dreams. *Star Wars* dreams. Japanese warrior dreams. Reading is a task, not a pleasure. Not now.

There is, too, a feeling that we never had, a feeling that the future has little hope in it. Because the jobs aren't there, and the money is less and less, and love won't last, and a nomad life, moving on and on from job to job and marriage, maybe, to marriage, is maybe all there is. And then there's the crematorium, and that is that. No heavenly choir. No loved ones waiting beyond the Pearly Gates. Hope gone. April fool.

In the first biblical story Eve and Adam learn too much, and are ashamed, cast out, and they come to know, in grief, of their mortality, because the Tree of Knowledge is full of bad news in the end. Knowledge likewise has polluted childhood, slimed it, in the same way as the apple of knowledge did for Eve. Knowledge is like champagne at first, but it comes with a hangover.

Many children now fourteen have already (amazingly) been through sex, drugs and rock'n'roll, and are wiser for it I suppose, but it's too early. Many children of eight have already, through *The Simpsons* and *South Park*, learned too much disgust with the world. It improves their sense of humour, but it makes more desolate their little souls.

I hope I'm wrong. I don't think I am. Sometimes, at Christmas, among the extended family I see them as children ought to be, opening presents, playing with the baby, curled up on the bed with grandma, lighting candles, singing carols and putting on puppet shows, squealing down the waterslide. There should be more years of this, not less.

But the information revolution and economic rationalism is ending all this, and much else too. Soon – it is pretty certain – as the laws of employment slacken and competition heats up, child labour will be back, overt and covert, as it was in the days of the cotton mills and the chimney sweeps, as it is now on the few small farms remaining and the seven-day-a-week small family stores, slavery in all but name.

Kids are tougher now, but scareder too. They see their role models daily get the sack, their overworked teachers haggard in the street. They hear of pederast priests and incest and youth suicide and Stolen Children and computer crime and a Global Economy where the rich, the lucky, the crooked survive. They have no belief now, as we did, in the power of prayer. They have no belief in the wisdom of their elders. They can operate a computer, their elders often cannot. They have no eternal scenario they can book into, in this world or the next. They can get the same rush of joy from a drug or a song or a movie, they know that. They live for the moment. The moment may be all there is.

I mourn all this, and I yearn for better times. I wish there were some place in my country, and maybe there is, in Burringbar perhaps, or Boonah, where things are roughly as they were. But I fear for our children, and the Great Bust that is coming, that will overwhelm so many of them, and convince a lot more not to have children themselves. The ghost of that certainty is reaching its bony hand back into their childhood, even now. They know there is not much out there. The door is locked, and the computer busy, and the aliens hurling themselves before the zapping weapons that will provide a little victory, just this once.

March, 1999

Lolita

Adrian Lyne's *Lolita* is a fine compelling film of a great, abundant, evocative book, one of the better novels in English of this century, an adventure in language that rivals in its gorgeous rainbird raiment the sonnets of Shakespeare, and like them sings of love's rapture, love's loss, its torment, its tyranny, its likeness to a prison, and the agony of its remembrance and aftermath.

The love, in book and film, is *almost incidentally* that of a thirteen-year-old girl by a man in his forties. The girl is cheeky, provocative, aware of what she's doing, a collaborator in her seduction, a penny-wise manipulator of her sordid situation, a young, very young adventuress ruined by her adventurings, and so is he. Book and film end in pain, regret, remorse, repentance, the black comic murder of a rival pederast, and the premature, comfortless death of both lovers, both partners in perversion.

Does the film offer dignity to male pederasts? Almost certainly. Does it bring them solace, understanding and forgiveness? Yes. Will it encourage them to further acts of pederasty? I would say so. Will it encourage a man so inclined to begin stalking young girls? I'm not sure. It's possible.

Should the film, then, be banned? I don't think so. Others will differ. We should argue it through.

Deep breath.

Our society and our democracy are built on limited freedoms, despite the dangers these freedoms bring. We are free within limits to travel by car, though we may die at the wheel. We are free within limits to smoke tobacco, though we may die of lung cancer. Free (at a certain age) to have sex, and also to die of AIDS. We are free to join the Moonies, or the Children of God, and impose that system of belief on our gullible children, and ruin, perhaps, their lives.

We are likewise free to see *Pulp Fiction*, and *Die Hard*, and *Lethal Weapon*, which *to some extent* celebrate the joy of slaughtering our fellow human beings; free, if we will, to imitate their heroes and take the consequences. We are free to play video games which evoke and celebrate violence, and be so stirred to hurt our fellow creatures. We are free to read *American Psycho*, about a serial killer, and *The Silence of the Lambs*. We are free to read that compendium of rape, crusade, human sacrifice and murder, the Bible. We can still, unpunished, read *Mein Kampf*. We can still see *The Simpsons*, which eloquently disdains all aspects of human behaviour and modern capitalist society.

It is thought, *perhaps wrongly*, that these freedoms are worth it. We base the very idea of a free society on these risks, these temptations, this unfettered freedom to choose what harm is to our taste. It is assumed that most of us, enough of us, will choose right.

This, of course, is arguably not so. Twenty-nine thousand Americans a year die by gunfire. Thousands of Australians each year inject heroin, unpunished and unimprisoned. Dozens of children born of unprotected sex are abandoned on doorsteps and rubbish tips and at adoption agencies. Hundreds of young men die of AIDS. And yet, almost religiously, we believe in freedom, freedom within limits. Speed limits. Age limits. Blood-alcohol limits. And so on.

So is it a reasonable limit, perhaps, that one can read *Lolita* but not see it? Some would think so. You are not by the novel so vividly shown the many provocative slouches and pouts and wriggles and face-pullings of Dominique Swain, nor the teasing use she makes of her tooth-brace. We may add our daydreams to our reading of the book, but they at least are ours, our private readings, not Adrian Lyne's. Just ban the film.

... Well, the emotions may lead us that way, but the logic is different, at least for a while. A dramatisation of the life of Lee Harvey Oswald may lure some to murderous emulation, but none of the many versions have been banned for that reason. *The Godfather*, where Al Pacino *comes of age* by shooting two men in a restaurant, may likewise tempt imitation, and yet was never banned. A documentary on Hitler, or on Idi Amin, or on Milosevic, may stir some souls to hero worship and genocidal mimicry, and yet is shown most months on Foxtel. *The Silence of the Lambs* may tempt, I suppose, some to cannibalism, *Taxi Driver* to random killing. *Ben Hur* may tempt a few to cheating in chariot races. And so on.

But it may be argued that *Lolita* will unleash more likely harm, and do more human hurt to more *young* people than any of the above – because, if the research figures are right, a million or so Australian men are already pretty keen on the idea. How do you argue with this potential level of harm, asserting against it, what, artistic freedom? That a masterpiece is worth the cost of, what, three hundred, five hundred, wrecked human souls?

Well, you can't. But it follows, if you proceed on the basis of this preventive logic, that all the fourteen- and fifteen-year-old models who pose for the covers of teen and adult magazines, and whose appeal is in some part pederastic, should be put out of work, and the magazines banned, back numbers and all, since their effect, over time, is probably worse than *Lolita*. It follows that all male teachers be barred from teaching classes with girls in them, girls likely to daydream about them, or fall under their sway, or to make the cheeky offers that girls of that age sometimes make to teachers they fancy. It follows, if you are to be logical about it, that many fathers should be evicted from the houses they share with their fourteen-year-old daughters lest the worst, one night, occurs.

Like Kosovo, the question is difficult, and any action's result is hard to predict. It may be that this fine film will purge from some sad souls the desire to do what it shows and cause them to heed its appeal, at the end, to let childhood be. It may be that, over and over, they will watch the videotape instead, as many troubled young men watched *Taxi Driver* over and over and did not shoot anyone. One young man, however, shot Reagan because of it, and that's a worry.

Overall I think more good is done by *Taxi Driver* than ill (though not to Ronald Reagan, or Jodie Foster) and *Lolita* is much the same. But what would I know. See it for yourself, and decide.

April, 1998

Habit

I worry less that the old get set in their ways than that most people do, and I do too.

I've lived near a beach for twenty-three years, and I swim there maybe twice a summer. My story is that round Murwillumbah and Coolangatta, where I swam as a boy, the water was warmer than Sydney and I've never adapted. But that's not the reason. Some days are brutally hot down here, and the water warm enough. The reason is, I'm in the habit of not swimming, and habit has the force of principle.

I don't go to the races either, though I had a terrific time the five times I've been in my life, and always won money, because I'm not in the habit. Nor to the opera, or modern dance theatre, or the football, though I know I'd like it. Nor have I learnt computers, or surfed the Internet, though my sons are zapping aliens and e-mailing Icelanders with abstruse questions long into the night most nights of the week. I communicate with a fountain pen, filled with blue-black ink, and that's the way I am. New-fangled things like telephones, or phone pagers, or phone cards, or EFTPOS, I'm still a little shy of. They seem too big a step to take now in my middle age. My late middle age.

This universal human tendency to stick with what you know can be bad for you, of course, occasionally fatal. Smoking is just the most obvious, and perhaps most forgivable, example. Bex. Black coffee. Overproof rum. I know people cured of life-threatening conditions by chiropractors who never go back to the chiropractor again because they did not, for fifty years, *believe* in chiropractors and they're not going to start now. I know old people stuck in the meat-and-two-veg diet of the 1930s who need better food and can afford it and never try it because, well, habit has the force of principle and bad food is their principle now.

My mum is eighty-eight and has all her faculties and refuses to visit the few old friends she has left because she thinks she won't survive the journey. I put it to her that twenty minutes in a car that somebody drives down a road and helps her out of can't be mortally dangerous, and she says, 'You don't know what it's like, Robert, you've never been *sick*.' The joy she'll get from face-to-face contact with friends she's known for eighty years, friends who love her, share memories and want to see her, doesn't weigh with Mum. She's in the habit of *not travelling*, and that's that. She's staying put.

She'll bestir herself, maybe, to get to their funerals.

They're welcome to visit *her*, of course. Be glad to see them.

. . . I'm not sure what to do about all this. I see so many people chucking away happiness with both hands ('England? Why would I want to go to England? Too cold for me.') that something more than mere habit seems to be involved, somehow. Something like masochism. A taste for self-punishment. *Japanese food? Oh no, I couldn't eat raw fish, ever. It'd turn my stomach. Why don't I fix us a corned-meat salad?*

I remember one week trying to force two old women to see *Titanic*, a film they would have adored, at any session they chose. They worked out hundreds of reasons why they couldn't, and so they stayed home, and a thrill, a joy, a marvellous, glamorous, terrifying purgation was lost to them. Forever.

I remember, worst, one night acquiring five tickets to see my favourite writer, Gore Vidal, appear on stage for the last time in Australia. I rang round maybe fifteen of my friends, begging them to come, *at no cost*, and experience the wit and wisdom of a writer *they themselves loved*, on a great irreplaceable night of the world. But all, or nearly all, had better things to do, or unavoidable obligations (dinner with their idiot cousin and so on), and I gave away three tickets at the front door and myself underwent a monumental, indescribable, triumphant night I will remember all my life and desperately yearned to share. *Why didn't they come too?*

Fear of excellence, maybe. Fear of the kind of showy genius that unnerves the kind of person that doesn't have it.

Fear of the big world outside the nursery, maybe. Fear of the light. My mum won't let me get her Foxtel either. She's gone off television, she says, ever since they stopped *The Midday Show*. All the *I Love Lucy*s and Bette Davis and Ingrid Bergman movies, all the *Eastenders* and *Alfred Hitchcock Mystery Theatres* and *Twilight Zones* she'd love to see again she won't see now, and in her eighty-ninth and ninetieth year will instead do . . . what? Beats me.

I have very few rules in life, but one of them is to accept invitations, if I possibly can. For there will always be someone at the new place – Gundagai, Cobar, Hanoi, Reykjavik, Boonah – that I'm glad to have met, and things I've never thought of that will stir and absorb me thereafter. A school play, a municipal council meeting, a street fair, a bushwalk, a night of Swiss dancing or political speeches or Balinese music, have particular joys that a Mel Gibson movie doesn't. A day on a boat doing nothing but look at the rippling sun on the water is unrepeatable elsewhere.

We are creatures of habit, sure. But we are challenge-seeking animals, too. Foragers, questers, experimenters. We like to sniff out new areas of pleasure like dogs in a paddock. We *like* new things, if ever we get to experience them.

But tell my mum that and she won't believe you. Tell most old people that, and most middle-aged people, and I am one of them. Happiness? No way. Novelty? Pleasure? Diversion? Not a chance. I'm perfectly comfortable, thank you, here in my routine. My old set of clothes, with Channel 9 and a cup of tea. My rut. Happiness? Don't give me that. There can't be any happiness more than I know, or I would have found it already.

Turn out the light when you go, dear. I'll just lie here a while in the dark. Remembering all the days of my life.

May, 1999

Queuing

In the 1950s we were all disgusted by Soviet Russia, and the sorry spectacle of its queues. Grim-faced old squat women would line up for days, we were told, to buy spoiled fruit and mouldy bread, and this was evidence, and a symbol, we were told, of a society in decay. Queues were a sign of a political system that was evil.

Today there are queues everywhere. *Your call is important to us, and you have been placed in a queue. All our operators are busy at the moment, and your call has been placed in a queue. Thank you for waiting, one of our operators will be with you shortly. If you wish information on session times, press one.* And they play sometimes pleasing music, or the ABC or 2UE. And they thank you for your patience, whether or not you are kicking the wall.

People queue for twenty minutes to buy a stamp in a post office, or to put money in a bank. Forty minutes, sometimes, to put luggage on a plane. An hour to see a doctor. Few phone calls reach a human any more. You talk to a machine, and wait. The upshot of a more efficient economy, a booming, expanding economy, it seems, is that the customers must wait.

Is queuing, then, a sign that our society is in decay? Or evil?

Let's closely look at what queuing means.

It means, first up, quite simply, quite obviously, that not enough people are working, not enough people are there to handle the current volume of customer demand. If there were more people working, there would be more customers dealt with every day, and more customers, therefore, probably, likely to line up for service. If there were more people working, too, there would be more people with money to spend, who would join the queue.

It also means that the people queuing up are wasting their time. Time that they might have spent elsewhere in productive work. Somewhere down the line, an hour from now or whenever, people are not doing productive work, or enjoying themselves, or caring for their children, because of the time spent queuing.

The third effect is a spiritual one. An impatience, then an anger, then a sigh, and then at last a despondency creeps over everyone. The repair man doesn't come for two weeks. It's not a big job, he reasons, so it goes to the end of the queue. You do without the dishwasher, or the phone, for those two weeks, and that's depressing. That's the way it is now, people say. We're privatised now; we have to make economies. A train is cancelled. A bus is late. You wait for weeks, when it used to be hours, to get a small bank loan approved, or maybe not approved. And the feeling that things are getting worse begins to settle over you, and sooner or later you get used to that.

It all comes, probably, from computerisation and various electronic revolutions. Now things will happen faster, we were told. Everything will be really quick.

And some things are. You can dial overseas instantaneously, and get an answering machine and a recorded message. You can get at all hours from an automatic teller money you then have to queue up to spend at a supermarket. You can get through straight away to a machine that tells you the person you want is unavailable, but your call is important to it, whoever you are. You can fax to him immediately a letter that goes in a pile and remains unread for the rest of its life. It's quicker, sure, but not too helpful.

The new time-saving machines, you see, meant people could be sacked and replaced by those machines. And the trouble is, most trade, most business, most shopping involves a conversation, a conversation with a person, not a machine. Because you cannot talk to a machine. Everyone knows that. A machine can do everything but listen. And so you wait, as the machine has beautifully and delicately asked you to. And you listen to the music. And you queue.

In some places this doesn't happen. There are some all-day/all-night Chinese restaurants, like the B-B-Q King in Sydney, with dozens of cooks and waiters and cleaners shouting and rushing about, where within five minutes of sitting down you can begin to eat the luscious meal you want. There are McDonald's restaurants all over the world where the queues are short and the smiling service rapid, because there are lots of people working there.

There are inexpensive resorts in Asia where waiters and porters swarm all around you. They are in work, and happy. You are served, and happy. And not queuing.

And their economy is booming, because people want to go there. They have budgeted for abundance, an abundance of people in employment, and no queues. And it works. It always did. They have not budgeted for frugality, which leaves everyone mean-minded and surly. And queuing. And the company, oh yes, in profit, for the moment, but not much liked by its customers. Not any more.

Queuing is indeed, as it was in the 1950s, a sign of a society in decay. Because it is a sign of a society that puts some other factor ahead of people. The profit margin, expressed in billions. The golden handshake, expressed in tens of millions, of the latest cost-slashing American trouble-shooting executive. The price of John Laws' golden words of approval, of a method that is short-changing everyone. The new expensive computerised machine that will do less kindly, and less quickly, what people have been doing for thousands of years.

A society careless of its people, and calling that carelessness efficiency, is a society in decay. Discuss.

A society with queues is a bad society. A society in decay. Discuss.

An evil society, perhaps.

If it is a better society than the one we used to have, I want to know why.

July, 1999

Dead Heart

To the premiere last night of *Dead Heart*, Nick Parsons' film (from his lacerating play) on whites and Aborigines in the Outback, and the difficulties experienced by a racked and honest copper, played by Brownie, in administering Stone Age customs of payback, bone-pointing and blaming selected males for illness, death and sandstorms and murdering them therefore. It has the same impact – an elbow to the bridge of the nose and a knee to the groin – as *Breaker Morant*, two of whose cast appear in it, and it leaves you pretty shattered all in all, especially when the old Aboriginal Godfather won't let the black kids go to school or learn English and you end up convinced it's their country and maybe we're only an episode in their 120 000 years of residence here and they may see us out and wave us away at last from the fatal shore. Brownie was particularly good in a performance of such truth and jovial pain and ferocious Australian puzzlement it left me gasping.

'You're very good,' I said to him over a lot of beer, 'in roles with a touch of masochism in them. You give good crucifixion.'

'Mate,' he said, 'I give great crucifixion.'

'What Kirk Douglas role,' I asked innocently, 'are you looking to remake next? *Spartacus*?'

He looked at me in that lovely, leery, evil, hateful, loving way he has. 'Get fucked,' he said.

I talked with Nick and we agreed that Brownie was a great script editor, not just an ugly face, and a brave producer too. Self-made and like Keating a Bankstown boy, streetwise and alert to nuance, disguising under the chiacking bumptiousness of a Ginger Mick a civilised soul. It may be so that much of Australia is like this. Fred Daly. Chips Rafferty. It's possible. It may be so.

This fine, no, bugger it, great film underlines the craziness of the present AFI award system. That Brownie with a performance as good as George C. Scott's in *Patton* didn't even get a nomination from its jurors argues that the jury system, which was always pretty dodgy (claiming as it does that the vote of seven or thirteen out-of-work film people is fairer than the vote of seven hundred out-of-work film people), is a system that is now fucked.

Because, you see, it doesn't make any sense that *In Search of Anna* has an award for script and *Dead Heart* doesn't, or *The Custodian* or *Stir* or *This Won't Hurt a Bit*.

We're in a situation roughly akin (with some differences in quality) to Hollywood in 1939. In that year the films made included *Wuthering Heights*, *The Wizard of Oz*, *Goodbye Mr Chips*, *Gone With the Wind*, *Young Mr Lincoln*, *The Grapes of Wrath*, *Stagecoach*, *The Front Page*, *Snow White and the Seven Dwarfs*, *Dr Jekyll and Mr Hyde*, *Bringing Up Baby* and *Mr Smith Goes to Washington* and, if you think about it, any one of them could have won in most categories in any other year; and though there was some justice in *Gone With the Wind* (at that point the most expensive film ever made) getting up in most categories there was less justice done to eight or twelve other masterpieces.

It's a bit like that here now. *Shine* is a lovely film but *Dead Heart* is just as good and may be more important in its theme and *Children of the Revolution* is not to be sneezed at either, or *The Quiet Room*. And the leaving out of *Love Serenade*, whose shelf life is clearly as long as those beaut dark Ealing comedies it so resembles, merely because (or so I suspect) it had already got a gong in Cannes and cost three million more than (the admittedly splendid, but not that splendid) *Love and Other Catastrophes* or merely because some moron found unease in the notion of two nominees with 'love' in the title. And the omission of *Rats in the Ranks* is a fucking joke.

I'm sorry if I sound like Brownie but he gets to you that way.

The solution is both desperately simple and stupendously cheap. All you have to do is abolish the jury system and let everyone see all the films (we got the jury system back in the 10BA days when blue movies and stark rubbish were among the forty or fifty films made as tax dodges by shady dentists and shown for weeks on end); and have (by a committee vote) either six or, in a very good year, eight finalists in each category. It will both cost nothing and boost to buggery all the films that are nominated with the punters. It will in fact cost less than what happens now because all the money spent flying all the films around to all the jurors before they're flown around again for the final screening will thereby be saved.

A few retrospective awards wouldn't hurt while we're up either. Like to Elfick for *No Worries* and Wallace for *Stir* and Norman Kaye for *Man of Flowers* and Mel for *Tim* and Noah Taylor for *Flirting* and *The Nostradamus Kid* and *Shine*. As one of the best three or four screen actors in the history of the world, he arguably deserves something.

The AFI as it's currently run should now, I mildly suggest, be burnt to the ground and the ashes sown with salt. If anyone's got any other ideas I suggest they be taken into care.

October, 1996

Dead Heart *Reconsidered*

I saw *Dead Heart* again and regard it now as one of our most important films. It goes to the heart of our history and the soul of the land we conquered, and the strange, very strange people here for 120 000, maybe 170 000 years, to whom (or to some of whom) we are only a passing chapter.

And what big questions then arise. Like, should the tenets of a Stone Age religion govern how we deal with its true believers? The Indian habit of suttee, for instance, that is, the burning to death of squealing young women on the funeral pyres of their old dead husbands, though a big part of the local religion, was outlawed by the uncaring imperial British conquerors, the bastards, and a few young widows rejoiced but the communities were devastated and felt themselves defiled and this is a pity; or is it? The banning of clitoridectomies in Bankstown would have the same effect. Do we have a right to change a culture? And how much?

Payback, likewise, the blaming of a chosen enemy for illness, death or bad weather, and the spearing of him in the leg, or the killing of him, is a similar bad old habit and maybe it should go – however politically correct it is to preserve old ways and to give dignity to tribal practice and sit at its witch doctors' feet and learn from them. And maybe the kids should be taught English, and educated anyway in the dull old white way, whatever the upshot. I don't know.

That these and attendant questions can be dealt with in what looks and feels like a mainstream western or a small-town murder thriller is a measure of the ambition and success of Nick Parsons' art. I saw the play twice and the experience was enormous (it was the first play I'd seen thus far with car chases in it), as great as *King Lear* well done in a quarry, and the film, though different, slimmer and clearer, troubles the heart as much.

That its humour can be so black and so enticing is also remarkable. The ban on liquor, for instance, leaves the conscienceful, guilt-racked whites to cope with a dreadful situation – the death by bone-pointing of one wife's black lover – by drinking lemon cordial. The language of police corruption and investigative journalism enters a situation that is infinitely more complex than the lexicon of either. The best scene in the film, possibly, is a television interview where Brownie is silent and surly and evasive and, when the camera turns off, strong-arms the interviewer into a store room and threatens him with slow death in an ant's nest.

It's also about the nature of commitment. Is an anthropologist right to walk out of his new tribal brotherhood for a better wage in a far-off university? What does a cop owe his Aboriginal deputy? 'He don't like me,' the deputy says (an amazing performance by Lafe Charlton) after being roughed up and locked in a cell: 'I'll just be a poor blackfeller now.'

The supporting performances are superb, and at levels one normally expects from, say, Anthony Hopkins or Meryl Streep or Ken Branagh. Anne Tenney and John Jarratt prove to be an adulterous couple bound by common interests in the end, and bound to split up in any other place, and we don't know this at the start, but somehow, in performances as three-dimensional as any you'll see, they signal its possibility. Lewis Fitzgerald and Angie Milliken are racked and Strindbergian, and Fitzgerald in particular does a scene where he learns of his wife's adultery with a dodgy young black beer-smuggler (Aaron Pedersen) and tries to keep face while weeping and confined to lemon cordial, a scene that should be a benchmark for acting classes worldwide. He looks pathetic, justified, weak, disciplined, admirable, foolish and sensible, tragic, doomed and resourceful all at once.

And Ernie Dingo and Bryan Brown could be booked into a great buddy movie any time. Ernie's impersonation of the man of two cultures (three, if you count the Lutheran Church) is as economical as the dialogue and as eloquent as Hamlet. He is among our greatest actors, up with Quast and Roxburgh and Howard and Hardy, and I'm glad to have said so before, in my first column I think.

And Brownie. In this film he's as good as the best of Brando, or Kirk Douglas when he was young and great, in *Detective Story*, say, or *Out of the Past*. Like Douglas he has a masochistic quality that reaches out and grabs and scares you. Like Paul Hogan he has a candour that leaves you helpless with laughter. He says 'get fucked' better than any living actor. Think of Nicol Williamson in *The Reckoning* and you get a measure of his speed.

There's a turd on earth called David Dale who ran once a Dubious

Achievements Award page in *The Bulletin* where under a portrait of Brownie appeared the caption, 'Someone, somewhere, thinks he can act'. I ask this worthless moron (an old close friend of mine actually) now to apologise in print; how fucking dare he.

Dead Heart has the impact of *Breaker Morant*, and the moral complexity, and like it will prevail critically across the world. Like *Jimmy Blacksmith* it is both exciting and upsetting and therefore may not do as well here as it should. Films about cruelty to animals and films about Aboriginals, Ken Hall repellently said, put ordinary Australians right off, and maybe things haven't changed too much, as Pauline Hanson daily reminds us.

If the Film Finance Corporation had funded no other film, this one would justify its past eight years. It may not be the end of our cinema's story but it is, thus far, a kind of interim climax. See it if you can.

December, 1996

Courage

Courage in the old way of battle is easy to recognise. I think it was there, for instance, in the eight young men who stormed and took the American Embassy in 1968 in Saigon, and ran up the Vietcong flag and died one by one on the roof under gunship bombardment, as they knew they must. Before they did that, I later found out, they crawled down a tunnel barely wide enough for a human body *for thirty-seven hours*, knowing they were on a journey that would end in their deaths, with a view of the moving hind-quarters of the hero in front of them as their only comfort in the last hours of their lives. That took courage, and discipline, and patriotism, like I for one cannot imagine.

And they were volunteers.

Never such courage as this. Never such courage, I think, again.

In Eritrea, too, I met a woman whose seven children – six sons and a daughter – were away *for seventeen years*, fighting the great patriotic war against the Ethiopians and she did not know until Asmara fell in the eighteenth year of the war if any of them were alive. Six came back, including the daughter. 'My only regret,' she told me, 'was I only had seven children to offer my country.'

That takes courage.

I know a man in Kiev who was the one survivor of the slaughter of Jews at Babi Yar, the first such mass execution of the Second World War. Slowly, lining up naked in the falling snow, they were shot one by one till 130 000 of them lay dead in piles and he crawled out from under the bodies by night and so at eighteen survived, and lived to be middle-aged, and old. He works now as an optical technician in Kiev, *just three kilometres from the site of the massacre*, where all his fellow victims lie under a big green hill and a monument commemorates their extinction.

That takes courage too. Merely living on in such a way takes courage. 'Why do you live here?' I asked.

'It's where the work was,' he said.

It is easy to say that we in our mere Australian lives are not called on to show such grace under pressure, as Hemingway once called courage, but this is not so. Fred Hollows, whom I knew and wrote a film about – soon I hope to be made – gave the last three years of a life that he knew would end very soon in cancer to curing the Third World of cataract blindness, and lived to see much of it happen. He left behind his infant children for weeks, months, to argue with foreign bureaucrats and politicians and operate in tents on mountainsides on the eyes of old people and young people, replacing their cataracts with five-dollar lenses and then drink whisky afterwards and sing old revolutionary songs and recite the best Banjo Paterson. He was, if not an Australian, an Australasian. He did such things as we would never contemplate, in the Eritrean way, for a larger Cause. And he was a man I knew. Never such courage again.

For courage is out of fashion in these pale number-crunching latter days of Economic Rationalism – whose secret names are Cowardice and Avarice, Hit And Run – and that all-pervasive milk-and-water agnosticism that looks now beyond our death and sees there no reward, no medal, no laurel, no Extra Time, no shining city on a hill where the brave are praised and live millennia in good company. Bravery has gone from so many of us, and been replaced by counting the odds. And meeting misfortune by suing the doctor, and the Water Board.

But not from all. I know Noel Pearson, whose life is an ongoing nightmare of aeroplanes and oratory and red-eyed exhaustion and hope and cajoling and calculation and despair. He sometimes speaks in three different states in one day. I have seen him wretched and tottering and at 10 p.m. rise to his feet and speak, and, majestically unfurling his cadences, hold a white indifferent audience bewitched for a further hour – in orations every night as good as Churchill or Bevan or Jesse Jackson or Gladstone or Macaulay – uttered without notes and bringing his listeners to their feet in amazed applause, then seen him asleep soon after in the cab that whisked him away. That, in these awful, dreadful times that lately dog and sully his Cause, takes courage too. He is thirty-three now, with miles to go before he sleeps, or a bullet takes him, or a heart attack, or despair.

I find courage likewise in other heroes of belief like Ian David, whose television series *Blue Murder* named the names of corrupt and homicidal police and brought himself, sooner or later, into the cross-hairs of the gun-sights of those named and led to the trashing of his home and the theft of all his irreplaceable computer discs. He wrote the film, too, on Joh's jury and is essaying another now on East Timor. We owe him a lot. He has given us much, and has risked his all.

To this list I suppose must be added Pauline Hanson, whose risk has been as great as Pearson's, and whose possible killing was on the lips of ordinary Australians last year for months. She, too, pursues her cause unflinching. She, too, is risking her all.

It seems of late, however, that our culture is fast becoming one of meas-ured and calculated cowardice as it never was in Anzac or Light Horse or Kokoda times – in even that field, athletics, where courage out-running pain was once the rule you lived by, the race you ran, for there are dishonest drugs now to ease you through it, and lessen the need for courage, and that is sad.

There is courage though, I think, in the young of Australia that I for one cannot conceive – going daily to their hundredth, and hundred and first, and hundred and second, vain job interview and going back at night to their shocked and baffled parents and later at night, on the point of sleep, looking down the coming years, and somehow finding humour, and comradeship, and roisterous company, and things to read and do, and attempt and mock, and going on.

I find it in the old who are dying, and the young men dying of AIDS, who on their deathbed find politeness and kindness and concern and humour *and time to spend in conversation* with even their most unwelcome visitors.

I find it especially in women.

I knew a woman who at thirty-five purposed to have children and married a man who proved to be infertile and stayed with him, lovingly, nonetheless. I know a couple who had a baby that died and stayed together afterwards in childless comradeship and a kind of loving studiousness and intellectual playfulness and are together still. I know women who lived through five miscarriages, stoic and scared, to have, at last, a healthy child. My wife did that, and calmly waited six weeks once to give birth to what she knew was already a corpse. That took some doing.

My mother-in-law waited out two years of the Second World War, with two baby girls, for a husband who worked behind Japanese lines to survive his continuing peril and at last come home. Women who wait like that, often pregnant as they wait, or tending little children, are extraordinary – the wives of Fastnet sailors or bushfire fighters, or policemen, or the soldiers who went off to the Gulf War and Rwanda, and the volunteers who battled the summer holocausts of '94 and '83, not knowing what the day would bring. Imagine *waiting*, waiting like that. Imagine waiting as the wives of Apollo 13 waited. Imagine that.

On the other side of motherhood I find courage likewise, courage unimaginable, in each and every one of the Stolen Children, and the British children taken from their families to far, strange, brutal Australia, in merely getting up every morning, and facing the day. Courage, too, in the homosexual men who declare themselves with their dress and make-up and pouting swagger on the streets of Surry Hills and take each year – in mockery, in bashings, in death by murder or AIDS – the consequences. Courage, dauntless courage, in most of our stand-up comics, especially Hung Le, the flame-haired joshing Melbourne–Vietnamese.

Courage, amazing courage, in women who each night face an alcoholic husband and his brutish moods or cope down years with a heroin-addicted son. Or with a son in gaol, and welcome him home, and dodge round his battered pride, and see what then befalls him. Courage, always, in divorce, and starting out again, with one child and a small room, and imagining the worst of loneliness, and going on.

Some courage is hard to pin down, and may seem for a time like its opposite. Was Kernot courageous in leaving her party's leadership and her Senate seat, or was she merely ambitious, or scared of losing her Senate place to the Hansonites, and therefore merely calculating? Is Katter in his rage against his party courageous, or only shoring up the vote he would otherwise have lost? Is Howard in his onrushing stubborn pursuit of the social revolution that nobody wants now being brave, or politically blind and tactically dull-witted in staying his course of certain political self-destruction? Was Tim Fischer's pursuit of deeply felt philosophies and policies that will cost him his seat now brave, or didn't he think it would come to that? Was Beazley weeping for the Stolen Children brave, or was it so much in his nature that no choice was involved? Is Harradine in his daily contortions brave, or shoring up his vote, or merely hurtling fearfully and choicelessly on, away from the wrath of his God and his purgatory? When there is no choice, can there be bravery? Discuss.

Mass bravery is all around us in Australia, I think, in every migrant group. Imagine leaving your village, your extended family, your culture, your nation, your *language*, and coming to a region of brutal new rules and subtle hostilities with children who will grow up into strangers you cannot fathom. Imagine being so disadvantaged, and applying for a job. Imagine driving a taxi, and hoping your boy will make it through medical school, and your daughter will marry, somehow, one of your tribe. Imagine bringing your old mother out, and giving her the small back room, and trying to settle her into a place that she finds unimaginably alien and unsuitable. I find these ordinary common crises, common to all migrants, daunting to contemplate. What daily bravery is there.

Imagine, on top of all this, meeting Hansonites in the street. Go home. Go back where you came from.

There is I guess a lot of courage in merely being alive. People abort their babies in fear of how badly they will fare among our modern metropolitan cruelties and confusions, and this is a measure of how hard it all is these days. Many find solace in ethnic origins, in old songs, and sex and boozing up and gamesmanship and sporting occasions, in festivals and birthday gatherings and *The Simpsons* and *Seinfeld*, but gnawing at the back of all of us, I think – in every plane taking off, in every farewell at the door – is the knowledge that life is impermanent, and love and friendship finite, and the family name uncertain and posterity never assured. To know all that, and all of us do, and to go on uncomplaining, or not complaining too much, is bravery too, getting up in the morning and seeing the face in the mirror and going on through the day and its treacheries, its hundreds of little deaths, its disappointments and betrayals and hopes that run dry and dreams that sour. And that is bravery, that is courage too.

We are probably better people than we know, or are told by the sardonic, prying media, and capable of much, as every bushfire season shows. We have good brave things about us to be proud of. And we should think on these things.

Bravery is everywhere, and should be recognised. Courage is universal, and should be praised.

August, 1998

Right and Wrong

Some words we once heard a lot we don't hear much any more. Right and wrong, for instance, and good and bad. And evil, come to think of it. Not in the newspapers anyway.

No-one says it's *right*, for instance, to hurt or impoverish ordinary people or wreck their lives or destroy their confidence, but they find other words, other adjectives, to say or imply the same thing, that bad is good, or excusable.

For there may be no editorials that praise our part in the Greenhouse Effect (the world will end sooner because of us, but we have our reasons) or our high youth suicide rate, one of the highest in the world, but there are many, many words we have found to excuse them.

And there are no editorials, for instance, that say it is *right* that the coal miners of Lithgow and the clothing workers of Lithgow and the steelworkers of Newcastle should lose their livelihoods and their neighbourhoods after thirty or forty years of tedious toil when a few shareholders, already rich and already making a tidy profit, feel like getting a little richer. There are no leading articles that say landmines sold in Africa to blow little children's arms and legs off made a profit for British investors, and this was good. Or that two hundred closed coal mines in Britain have destroyed their local communities and shattered the hopes and saddened the dreams of blameless exuberant young men of the sort portrayed in *Brassed Off* and *The Full Monty*, and this was good.

But there are plenty of editorials calling these things *historically inevitable* or *politically unavoidable* or *economically rational* or *building a more efficient industrial base* or *the free market responding on a level playing field without needless government interference* or *changes that have been long overdue*. None to call them, simply, wrong.

Or evil.

When asked, 'What is the first necessity?' Confucius answered, 'The rectification of the language.' And the language in which we talk of our society now has been rectified, in a most Orwellian way. War is peace-keeping. Ignorance is comfort. Freedom is the freedom to enslave.

No-one said it was right, for instance, when Telstra posted a $2 billion profit and then sacked twenty thousand of its workers (in the old days the workers, as part of the company's laudable success, would have each got a bonus). But lots of people said, the Prime Minister for one, that the company was thereby made more 'efficient' and 'streamlined', and 'competitive', and so made more attractive to future investors when it was privatised, investors greedy for billions, and tens of billions. Those 20 000 sacked meant, probably, ninety thousand broken lives, and a hundred bruised and wounded country towns. No-one said this was simply wrong, and the greed of a few shareholders should not outweigh the need of 100 000 people. Right and wrong. Efficient and competitive. Coalmines out, landmines in.

No editorial writer has said that the core belief of economic rationalism, to wit, that by sacking people in their hundreds of thousands you thereby create employment and stimulate spending, is not only wrong but crazy. They have mostly said we're not being hard enough (translation: sack more people), we're 'avoiding the tough decisions'. Tough decisions mean, mostly, doing irreparable evil to ordinary people. Evil is often bad economics, I suspect. Not always. Not instantly. But after a few plane crashes due to cheap spare parts or 'affordable safety' (translation: danger) your airline soon goes bust. One dead princess and the price of celebrity photos quickly plummets to nothing. One lawsuit from lung-cancer sufferers and cigarette companies are quickly in strife, and their products banned indoors.

Tony Blair speaks with crisp warmth of 'the radical centre' and 'compassion with a hard edge' and 'tough love' and 'New Labour for a new Britain' when all he actually means is taking money away from people already poor, like black single mothers and slum-bred students with inconvenient brains. This I think is wrong. But right and wrong are words that don't suit him, any more than they suit John Howard when he speaks of 'wider choice' or 'the free market initiative' or 'the user pays', when all he means is taking money from child care and universities and old age homes. If the user-pays idea is fair then Stewart Diver should get a bill of seven million dollars for his rescue, or whatever it cost. It wasn't his fault, but it mostly isn't any user's fault. A user is merely someone in need.

The user-pays is a really bad idea, a wrong idea, and someone should say so. It means, at its heart, that you pay $500 000 for your bone-marrow transplant, and your family goes to the wall. Or you pay a quarter of a million dollars to go into a nursing home, and your family goes to the wall. A little consideration of right and wrong would have saved John Howard a lot of trouble. And his coming ignominious end.

(Tony Blair also said of New Labour, 'we had the courage to change', when what he meant was: 'We had the contemptible cowardice to fellow-travel with the fashionable Thatcherist brutalism of the day. We let our side down, and it worked.' He doesn't believe he did this, of course, he is far too entangled, far too seduced, by his own delicious abuse of the language.)

Words aren't what they were. Language, as Harold Pinter said once, is more often an instrument of concealment than revelation, in particular for the English. 'Yours is a very interesting point of view, Mr Hoskins,' means, as a rule, to an Englishman, 'Get out of the room. I don't wish to see or hear from you again.' And 'Won't it be inconvenient to come all that way?' mostly means, when said by the English, 'I do not wish to see or hear from you again. I really dislike you. Go away.'

But it's not just the Poms who are steeped now in vengeful euphemism. Some of their colonies do it very well. California works, as *The Larry Sanders Show* reveals, on saying exactly the *opposite* of what you mean. And the trick has caught on in Sydney, where 'let's do lunch sometime' now means 'bugger off'.

We all used to laugh – or some of us did – at the words America's Vietnam generals used, like 'collateral damage' or 'friendly fire' or 'anti-personnel weapons' or 'terminate with extreme prejudice' or 'winning the hearts and minds' for bombing, torture, summary execution and fratricidal slaughter.

But the whole world now has picked up the same Orwellian melody.

And wrong and bad and evil are back in their many artful disguises. War is peace-keeping. Wage slavery is a free-market workplace agreement. Racial plunder is land management. Racial enslavement, rape and kidnapping the well-meaning errors of a previous generation. Youth's grievous plight is dole-bludging. And daylight robbery by nursing-home owners the inevitable cost of structural improvement. The slaughter of unborn children, children who would have loved you, is the right to choose.

Right and wrong are not bad concepts overall. And good and bad and evil. It is not too hard, I find, to uncover what they mean. Not too hard thereafter for the government to buy up Newcastle Steelworks for a lousy $100 million and re-employ sacked workers and rebuild, perhaps, a great city. The words should be used again, good and bad, right and wrong, by newspaper editors and politicians. All else is cowardice, or the coded phrases of tyranny.

January, 1998

Epithalamion for Lu and Sid

On the occasion of the wedding of the former chief-of-staff of Kim Beazley, Sid Hickman, and the principal speechwriter for Kim Beazley, Lucinda Holdforth, in the Skeleton Room, Sydney Museum.

Time was when one in such a place as this
Could make a pun in French, l'amour, la mort,
On love and death, and conjure skulls that kiss
And ask of rattling bones what life is for,
And mock with death's mad grimace each love's day,
Spin-doctoring the joy from bride bed's bliss,
Proclaiming it is nought but vulval friction,
Man's death is fact, man's love a fleeting fiction,
And all the warmth from such an hour as this,
Though he in lover's hymn to her might say:

Forbid me not to love thee as I must,
For love will have its morning and its day
And by rude August winds will not be swept away,
Nor any whimpered word 'tis but my lust.
No harlot stirs the midnight as thou dost,
Nor fires to hot ceramic all my clay,
With angel trumpet summons up my dust,
Restores to sour October all of May.
I cannot hope that thou wilt love me just
Because my love is love I cannot stay.
I know by inches I must earn thy trust,
With wooer's verses keep thy fear at bay,
But, lady, I am true and love thee well,
And wait thy resurrection from this hell.

The sonnet form, I find, best fits new love,
But love at second sight, which here we see,
Draws on more deeps of heart's inconstancy
Than youth's hot noisy hour of rush and shove.
We see among these bones a pair halfway
To being bones themselves, who well know how soon time
Will moss and crack love's headstone-sculpted rhyme
That says forever love, tomorrow as today,
Till all the seas gang dry, my dear − that soon −
Shall we protract this south coast honeymoon,
This bridal dance among forefathers' bones,
Old lovers' moody glance, and mobile telephones?

A sunburnt western heart was dry as tinder
When first his lazy eye fell on Lucinda,
And hers was brimming, though she kept that hid,
When first she took an office job from Sid,
And love bloomed in the wide round shade of Beazley,
And though the wage Sid paid her was quite measly,
And though love's words at first were pretty weaselly −
'Miss Holdforth, there are errors in this speech;
Come share a pie at Ozzie's, I have so much to teach' −
She took them as he meant them, i.e. sleazily:
'Mr Hickman, I do fear I get your drift,
And I shall not travel with you in the lift.'
And so it was, for four years' thrust and parry,
And thus do maids get haggard swains to marry,
And so it goes, for love goes never easily.

It was a contest wiser heads have seen
As Annie Hall at war with Steve McQueen,
For though they still dispute the worth of Keating
On long nights when the white wine takes a beating,
And though he cooks than her a better pasta
And mocks her as she reads her Woman's Day,
Though some have thought their union a disaster –
He's fond of Wilde, she loves her Hemingway –
And though they differ on the might of Plugger,
And he's a Democrat, and that's a bugger,
And she in thrall to Tony Blair's Third Way,
And though they talk in different football codes,
And fell to blows once over Cecil Rhodes,
And though they are both writers and compete,
They are at one most nights when touching feet,
They are one flesh, when seasoned love o'erspills
The master bed most nights in Surry Hills.

But stay, my tongue. The holy hour draws nigh,
For these brave banns this Nostradamus year,
The planets lining up, the Dow-Jones high,
The dollar upward, Stott-Despoja shy,
The Howard government, both dread and drear,
Proclaiming she'll be apples by and by,
The ocean warming, and the Maldives dwindling,
The jarrah forests daily turned to kindling,
Tim Fischer in the sunset waving his Akubra,
Bob Carr chin-deep in Proust in far Maroubra,
Mal Colston lumbering home with pockets laden,
Psychiatrists advancing on Bill Hayden,
The West Australian *greeting with abhorrence*
A small fib told years back by Carmen Lawrence,
Milosevic rat-cornered in Belgrade,
The wide world anorexic on free trade,
The pundits going down on craven knee
To hail the phyrric triumph of the GST,
My mate Costello nightly smirking at his brilliance,
And The Spy Who Shagged Me *coining millions,*
All this finds Sid and Lu abloom, and smiling at all fear,
Prepared to cop it sweet, whatever comes
Of two confetti-strewn millenniums,
And consummate at last at Bawley Point
This tardy love that heaven doth anoint,

And we with them rejoice that love's conjunction
Precedes by some few years their final unction,
And glad among these bones, in fine home-brew,
We toast the happy oldyweds — to Sid and Lu.

July, 1999

The Con Con

I'm not sure how other people saw it (some of my fellow dog-walkers on Palm Beach have called it a wank and a waste of money), but for me the Constitutional Convention was a great affirming experience, one of the best of my life. By the time it started, John Howard had got us just about convinced that the country we were living in was a grubby mean sub-racist footnote of dead Empire like, say, Southern Rhodesia; by the time it ended we knew again with pleasure — or those of us who went to it knew — what it was to be Australian. It reminded us of our comradeliness, our decency, our wit and fellow-feeling. It wasn't his country at all. It was ours.

I made some new friends — Phil Cleary and Jason Li and Mischa Schubert and Moira Rayner (When, said Mungo, is she going to tend her head-wound?) and Tim Costello and the furious, formidable, fuckable Sophie Panopoulos — across the political spectrum and got to know again some old ones, principally Sir James Killen (whom I have described elsewhere as a shaggy-drover's-loaded-dog in whose grey and snaggly bicuspids is clenched not a bomb but a Latin concordance) and Janet Holmes à Court, who was furious (she said) at having been described in these columns as an *ageing* sex symbol, she did not *age*, and Nifty and Peter Bowers and Peter Cole-Adams and Bill Leak. Bill did a cartoon of Howard sloppily fellating Bill Clinton who is simultaneously telling a number of pointed microphones, 'What he SAID was, Australia is a proud and independent nation and it doesn't NEED to become a republic,' and though it wasn't printed it scored a good few laughs — and one near cardiac arrest — when it was passed round the parliamentary chamber. It was good, too, to hang round with Mungo again in the old place, and see the crowded corridors of a true democracy such as it hasn't been since our politics moved up the hill to its mausoleum. And so on. So it goes.

As television the Convention had the irreplaceable ingredient of suspense – suspense, as in one-day cricket, in real and present time. Like a good soap series it had a swag of attractive young people and crusty older and wiser ones (Jonesy and Sinkers like a pair of motheaten old MGM lions, avuncular, catarrhal, self-knowing), and cliff-hanger episode endings (Will Turnbull again stuff up? Is dictatorship imminent?), and the rest of it. A theme tune as unlikely (yet somehow successful) as 'Advance Australia Fair'. Cleary reviving that almost legendary figure, the Red Under the Bed. Ruxton as Barney Rubble. Mike Rann as Mickey Rooney saying we've got a barn, let's put on a show. Geoff Gallop *exactly* like Superman in *Lois and Clark*, saying up, up and away. Neville Bonner as Geppetto. Flo as Ma Kettle. God, I'm glad I was there.

It told us again how good it is to see someone standing up in a public place and speaking from the heart. We thrilled again, most days, as we did when Spencer Tracy gave his Big Speech at the end of *State of the Union* or *Judgment at Nuremberg* or *Inherit the Wind*. It's a basic tribal experience, I think, that is regaining popularity. As the movies get more technologically miraculous, with people turning into mercury and flowing under doors, a countervailing need for something more primitive, more Cro-Magnon, is revisiting our hearts, the returning pilgrim telling his adventures round the log fire on a winter's night is recurring in our spiritual structure. The current love for stand-up comedy is part of this, for ABC debates, and *Late Night Live*. The spoken word matters, and the more it is elbowed aside by technology, the more important it becomes.

I spoke of these and other things to Tim Costello at the piss-up in the Members' Bar when it all was over (carefully avoiding my puce-faced foe, John Howard, a few feet away). Tim's a fan of *The Nostradamus Kid* and we compared our miserable fundamentalist upbringings. He agreed that his brother Peter's hortatory speaking style ('And why do I say that? I say it because it's true.') involves him all the time in Baptist preacher's cadences ('And why does Jesus do that? Because Jesus loves you.') and agreed it was 'a mystery' that the two of them had shared a bedroom for nineteen years and yet turned out so differently. What an Irwin Shaw novel, or a Jeffrey Archer novel, their two careers to this point would make. And so it goes.

The party went on to the Press Club where Panopoulos tried to recruit me for the monarchists and then handed me a camera so I could photograph, with flash, the moment when she kneed Mungo in the balls, and Mungo hit her with the flat of his hand across the side of the head, and I photographed this too. I'm not sure what the quarrel was, or the joke, and I had no idea of what she was going to do, but I enjoyed the spectacle, I must admit, of the working out of the differences of two highly intelligent people in this even-handed and civilised manner, the way one does in these jaded times.

It was a good gig. The best of it was, I think, the communion across the generations (Alamein, silverchair): the old lions and the lion cubs on the grassy upland in the summer twilight gnawing old bones together, the sad old wisdom of the scarred survivors and the fresh impertinence of youth. It was good to be here. Like Halley's comet in my lifetime, I shall not see its like again.

February, 1998

Freudy's Wager

I share a poky little office full of cardboard boxes on the Premier's floor above the harbour with Graham Freudenberg, the famous ash-stained speechwriter of Calwell, Whitlam, Wran, Hawke and Carr, who works there at nights because he can smoke then unpoliced, and I occupy it one day, or two half days, each week, an arrangement Freudy arcanely describes as 'Box and Cox', and I always leave at sunset lest I encounter him, and then drink with him, which Mick Young sternly warned me is 'bad for the liver'.

It was with a sort of pleasurable dismay, therefore, that I found him present when I dropped in one August afternoon at 3 p.m. to pick up some papers, and was quickly persuaded across the road to the Bar Luca for a VB or three and one for the road. He'd just completed a mighty speech for Carr on the cruelties and the murders white Australians had wreaked on Aborigines last century and since, and his colour and eloquence heightened as the shouts and the hours flashed by and we spoke of Whitlam's health, and Calwell's cowardice, and Evatt's madness, and the luck of history that felled Bert Milliner and so gave the Tories their majority just in time for the Whitlam sacking in 1975, and attendant matters like the Watergate series on Foxtel and how it was better than any book, and how the film *Dr Strangelove* got so accurately the bizarre suspense of the Cold War arms race that so warped and crazed so many days of our youth: will atomic war happen now, or next year? For it surely must come.

Eventually, as often happens, we made a five-dollar bet, signed with my pen on one of his cigarette packets. The wording of the referendum on the republic had been decided that day and Freudy reckoned, with lots of powerful precedent, that no referendum would pass without the support of all the major parties, quoting in particular the second referendum question in 1967, one that would unlink the numbers in the Senate from the numbers in the House, a proposition supported by both Labor and Coalition and yet defeated by the DLP's three-word campaign, 'too many politicians'. In 1999, he said, the parallel proposition by the direct election zealots of 'too much power to the politicians' would likewise carry the day. I winced at this, but held to my moody belief that the Malcolm Turnbull slogan '1999 is no year to pass a vote of no confidence in ourselves' was good enough to carry, well, 57 per cent of the people and five of the states.

'Only one state will vote for it,' said Freudy firmly, 'New South Wales.' And he placed a pendent five-dollar bet on the cigarette packet that this would be so.

Now, Freudy's judgment of most things, as all round politics know, is pretty God-like. Assessments he made twenty years back of, say, Cairns, or Kerr, or Fraser, or Evan Williams, feel as monumentally accurate now as any Macaulay made on Fox or George III or Pitt the Younger. Predictions Freudy made of a Keating massacre differed with mine of a narrow victory, and so on. But he is wrong this time, and I'll tell you why. (The date as I write this is 14 August 1999, though you, the reader, months ahead of me, already know the outcome.)

First, because the republic is not the trivial issue John Howard has always called it, and always wished it to be. It crowds the letters columns and the talkback shows every day. Like the Constitutional Convention, it's stirred up more energy and more absorbing quarrel than anyone foretold. It's a transfixing argument. It's about our sense of national self, our tribal meaning, and all Australians find that interesting. The level of interest is huge. And it's still three months away.

Second, the number of voters who want a republic of one sort or other is round 62 per cent. The idea that one in six of these republicans will vote instead for a septuagenarian queen, her centenarian mother, her tactless vulgar husband, and her mocked and humiliated son, and for a future Queen Camilla, and do so on the eve of the year 2000 is a pretty unlikely supposition. One in twelve might, not one in six.

Third, five Premiers, two Chief Ministers, eight Leaders of the Opposition, the Leader of the Labor Party, the Leader of the Democrats, the Leader of the Greens, the Lord Mayors of most big cities, and the next Liberal Prime Minister, Peter Costello, want a republic. Only one Premier, Richard Court, a widely detested lame duck, and one ever-shrinking Prime Minister, and Tony Abbott and Bronwyn Bishop and Pauline Hanson want to keep the Queen. Their following is just not big enough. Most celebrities moreover are on the side of the republic, and that must count. And every day there are fifty monarchists dying, and sixty republicans acquiring the vote, and that must count.

The fourth argument is more contentious, and it's to do with Howard's credibility. The election he lost on the numbers. His candidate Chikarovski went down in catastrophe. His Preamble was greeted with derision. He looked like a goose in America, a bad joke in Downing Street. The GST he backed down on, after saying he wouldn't. He just scrambled through, to unapplauded victory, but won no votes with it. He's backed Reith's betrayal of the miners' just entitlements, a bigger issue in middle Australia than he thinks. He's lost the valuable Tim Fischer, his one acceptable face.

Anything he touches therefore will be stained. People don't trust him that much any more. If *he* believes in something, they think, then it could be wrong.

Fifth, Kennett's re-election in October, moreover, will exalt and celebrate a republican. And Howard has to win Victoria to have a chance. He can't win only Queensland, with its prickly loonies, and Western Austalia with its Poms. He needs another state. Where is it?

Sixth, there's a big multiculture now. Italians, who discarded their king. Greeks, who discarded their king. Indians and Pakistanis, whom the present Queen's husband vilified last week. Chinese, who discarded their last emperor, and whose memories of England are of the Opium Wars and the weaklings who sold out Hong Kong to the communists. Germans, who recall the Queen's uncle, Edward VIII, and his fondness for Hitler. And, yes, a few Dutch, Scandinavians, Hispanics, Japanese and Cambodians whose view of monarchs is fonder. But not many. The ethnic republican vote must on its own be worth 15 per cent.

Seventh, a small but significant factor, which is female and to do with Princess Diana. A vote for the monarch is a vote for an eventual King Charles, and a de facto Queen Camilla, who humiliated Princess Diana and sped, in many eyes, her accidental death. There are women who would have voted without question for King Charles and Queen Diana, but they feel betrayed, let down, made fools by the monarchy now, as witnessed by the lack of excitement over the wedding of Edward and Sophie. And if the monarchy vote is not among women, where is it?

John Howard, moreover, refused to meet with Princess Diana when she was here, or to go with her to a dinner for Victor Chang, lest he offend the Queen. And this by some will be remembered.

So: if we take as a starting point, and I think we can, the Newspoll figures of 46 per cent for the republic and 34 per cent for the monarchy and 20 per cent undecided, the monarchists must win 16 of that 20 per cent to be in with a chance. And they can't. They can win 12 per cent but that is not enough. It's likely, pretty likely, they'll win only 8 per cent and lose the day.

For the Beazley argument of one step in the right direction and then, if need be, another step makes more sense than the hectic, entangling argument of the ex-monarchist Reith that a vote for the monarchy now is – a vote, somehow, for a true republic later on. A Barry Jones, perhaps, could argue this effectively. A Peter Reith with his black-dogs-on-chains associations, and a bolshie bearded Phil Cleary beside him, cannot.

The vote will be 55 to 59 for the republic, with one state, probably Queensland, maybe Western Australia, for the monarchy. Fifty-one per cent for the new Preamble. A scalded and petulant John Howard, under mortal threat from his smirking deputy, will not be there, I think, to open the Olympic Games.

I write these things on 14 August against a background of pundits hailing Howard's triumphant wiliness on the issue, pundits who believe there is no way now the republic can win.

What fools they are.

August, 1999

The Whitlam Question

I arrived with my daughter Jenny at the Sydney Film Festival opening night, for the premiere showing of John Sayles' *Limbo*, and there was no-one in the mezzanine bar area but Gough Whitlam, who in his famed emphatic breathy contralto said, 'Welcome to Limbo. I'll be your waiter for this evening.'

And I said, 'Good evening. This is my real daughter.'

And he said, 'Yes, I knew there had to be one.'

And we talked of a number of things, the way we sometimes do, including the love of language, and how those in politics who have it are remembered by history, whatever their legislative achievement – Lincoln, Disraeli, Churchill, Kennedy, Reagan, Dunstan, Whitlam, Keating, Clinton – and those who don't have it – Atlee, Eisenhower, Nixon, Ford, Fraser, Hewson, Major – are forgotten by history, or neglected by it, whatever their political success.

Gough, I had written in the *Australian* the day before – it was the week of his great triumphal celebration among his adoring disciples at the Sydney Entertainment Centre, one of a few such bashes this year – had 'enlarged a career of considerable political failure into the noblest stand-up comedy act of the century' and would be remembered, I said, because of his love of language and his artfulness with words, whereas John Howard, 'an already forgotten leader', would go down in history as 'a black hole around which the language beats in vain'.

We talked of Paul Keating and his considerable pugnacious verbal gifts 'at the C.J. Dennis end of town', and how he, and Judy Davis, and Phillip Adams, and Woody Allen, and Ingmar Bergman, and Alfred Hitchcock, and Winston Churchill, and George Orwell, and Charles Chaplin, and Tom Stoppard, and John Osborne, and Noel Coward, and Charles Dickens, and Will Shakespeare had got by without a university education, and whether the lack of it helped or harmed them. And so it goes.

Jenny was astonished that she had actually met him, and had come so close to legend. I gave her my useful transferable one-liner, that Gough Whitlam may not be the answer, but he is the question. And so it went.

In the days and nights thereafter (and now past midnight as I write this), it struck me with Tennysonian force that the good old days are dead, and we live now in an era that, in John Osborne's phrase, might best be described as the Mean Time, an era that Whitlam haunts like a mocking Puck, a Robin Goodfellow darting from gum leaf to gum leaf with his wand and fairy dust and one-liners, tormenting us each midsummer night with how it might have been. A decent Swedish outcome. A golden age.

The Mean Time. Limbo. Few will believe in a hundred years from now just how readily and meekly we submitted to the cold, grey, merciless dullness that engulfs us, at this millennium's end, like airport fog. Or how we believed, or even half believed, that sacking people in their hundreds of thousands, and terrifying those who still had work, was good for Australia. That the arts must be starved, and the old and the black and the jobless persecuted, and hospitals made cheaper and dingier, and queues longer, and some country towns deprived of public phones, and all country towns of phone technicians, and many of doctors, and banks, and schools. That prisons must be run for profit, and kids on the dole press-ganged into slave labour while banks make billions by firing tellers and penalising customers for daring to presume to deposit money or take it out.

And this is good, we are told, good for Australia.

And, amazingly, we believe this. Or we half believe it. There seems to be a self-punishing streak in all of us, and we tell ourselves we deserve no better, and we half believe that Kerry Packer deserves his billions, and his big nights playing roulette, and we do not. It's a belief our rulers play on. And when a person like Whitlam comes on the stage – one who believes and tells us forcefully that things can not only be better, they can also be *excellent* – he has to be cut down, got rid of, made to seem a fool or a tyrant or a madman. Like Allende. Or Castro. Or Palme. Or Rabin. Or Kinnock. Or Clinton. Our rulers must keep us believing in the inevitability of misery, or they would be less rich, and that would never do. They might have individual fortunes of eight, not ten billion dollars. And that would never do.

I get more radical as I get older. I want to smash things up, do damage to the persecutors of our young. I want to elect Gough Whitlam President, with dictatorial powers. I want the world to know that Gorbachev was a good man, and Yeltsin a monster. That Gorbachevism worked, and Yeltsinism is a catastrophe, a catastrophe because of, not in spite of, his free market reforms. Because the free market doesn't work, any more than unleashing a thousand hungry crocodiles into Martin Place is good for the economy. It never is. I want to shout out loud and frequently that the level playing field is just another flat earth theory. And protecting our country is a better idea than not protecting it. We protect our children from harm. It's the same idea. And I want people to know that.

I want too many things, I guess, and I should be sedated. I look out over my country, and I am not content.

The time is mean, and we all are shrivelling, and scared of the morrow. And I am not content.

August, 1999

City Lights

A speech to the Australian Society of Authors

I've been troubled by the topic of this, the opening speech, for a few days now, because like many an Australian writer – Buzo, Williamson, Murray, Moorhouse, Hewett, Hibberd, Masters, McKie, Malouf – I came at a certain stage from a country town that I sort of *knew* to a city that, forty years on, forty years on last March, is still a mystery to me, and a maze and a puzzle and a run of the arrow, an unwinnable game of unknowable rules in which I still feel a stranger, an unwelcome fool, a bumpkin, a country cousin.

And it's fair to say, I think, that in all big cities – cities larger than, say, Newcastle – there are never really natives, only ever migrants, migrants of one kind or another – from country towns, from lesser suburbs, from Greek islands, from genocidal wars of Africa or Alice Springs, and they have always the symptoms of migrants, paranoia, fear, suspicion, wariness, not knowing the rules, a great unease with the spoken word, an admission into our conscious lives of other selves we may be true to or not — or is it a *single* self that divides and divides like an amoeba with each new job or affair of the heart or emotional trauma, and most nights turns to self-disgust or its mirror image, bluster, or to bullying or nouveau snobbery or cruelty to waiters, or alcohol, or drugs, or cult religion, or a series of arbitrary habits, infinitely reiterated, that take on the force of principle, from fear of the dark, the unknown; plus a dream of the one good village we may find if we are good, or have left behind and may never find again. Some of this fear of cities and how they soil the old good self that we once had, or think we had, is delineated well, I think, in a verse by Lawson that appeals to me in particular for a number of reasons.

I met Jack Ellis in town today —
Jack Ellis — my old mate, Jack —
Ten years ago, from the Castlereagh,
We carried our swags together away
To the Never-Again, Out Back.

But times have altered since those old days,
And the times have changed the men.
Ah, well! there's little to blame or praise —
Jack Ellis and I have tramped long ways
On different tracks since then.

His hat was battered, his coat was green,
The toes of his boots were through,
But the pride was his! It was I felt mean —
I wished that my collar was not so clean,
Nor the clothes I wore so new.

He saw me first, and he knew 'twas I —
The holiday swell he met.
Why have we no faith in each other? Ah, why? —
He made as though he would pass me by,
For he thought that I might forget.

He ought to have known me better than that,
By the tracks we tramped far out —
The sweltering scrub and the blazing flat,
When the heat came down through each old felt hat
In the hell-born western drought.

The cheques we made and the shanty sprees,
The camps in the great blind scrub,
The long wet tramps when the plains were seas,
And the oracles worked in days like these
For rum and tobacco and grub.

Could I forget how we struck 'the same
Old tale' in the nearer West,
When the first great test of our friendship came –
But – well, there's little to praise or blame
If our mateship stood the test.

'Heads!' he laughed (but his face was stern) –
'Tails!' and a friendly oath;
We loved her fair, we had much to learn –
And each was stabbed to the heart in turn
By the girl who – loved us both.

Or the last day lost on the lignum plain,
When I staggered, half-blind, half-dead,
With a burning throat and a tortured brain;
And the tank when we came to the track again
Was seventeen miles ahead.

Then life seemed finished – then death began
As down in the dust I sank,
But he stuck to his mate as a bushman can,
Till I heard him saying, 'Bear up, old man!'
In the shade by the mulga tank.

He took my hand in a distant way
(I thought how we parted last),
And we seemed like men who have naught to say
And who meet – 'Good-day,' and who part – 'Good-day,'
Who never have shared the past.

I asked him in for a drink with me –
Jack Ellis – my old mate, Jack –
But his manner was no longer careless and free,
He followed, but not with the grin that he
Wore always in days Out Back.

I tried to live in the past once more –
Or the present and past combine,
But the days between I could not ignore –
I couldn't help notice the clothes he wore,
And he couldn't but notice mine.

He placed his glass on the polished bar,
And he wouldn't fill up again;
For he is prouder than most men are –
Jack Ellis and I have tramped too far
On different tracks since then.

He said that he had a mate to meet,
And 'I'll see you again,' said he,
Then he hurried away through the crowded street
And the rattle of buses and scrape of feet
Seemed suddenly loud to me.

And I almost wished that the time were come
When less will be left to Fate –
When boys will start on the track from home
With equal chances, and no old chum
Have more or less than his mate.

'Back Then'

Jack Ellis was the name Lawson used for his younger self, the purer youth he was in cleaner air before the city grimed him, before he came to that awful realisation, common both to Hitlerism and economic rationalist theory, that people are *replaceable*, and even mateship is expendable when the situation changes and times get to be as hard as they can be in the cities, times like the nineties, his nineties, and times like ours, and of this he famously wrote:

Turn the light down, nurse, and leave me while I hold my last review,
For the Bush is slipping from me, and the town is going too.
Draw the blinds, the streets are lighted, and hear the tramp of feet –
And I'm weary, very weary, of the Faces in the Street.

I was human, very human, and if in the days misspent
I have injured man or woman, it was done without intent.
If at times I blundered blindly – bitter heart and aching brow –
If I wrote a line unkindly, I am sorry for it now.

'My Last Review'

There are cities and cities, of course. Melbourne is a very European city and Sydney, these days at least, is a very Asian one, like Hong Kong, or Singapore, in the sense of it being a stopover city, a transit lounge of a city, a plush hotel you go to for a night on the way to somewhere else. Sydney, I once wrote, is the town of the one-night stand, and Melbourne the town of the poisonously durable marriage, where twenty-five years later the same faces in the same order round the same dinner table are having the same who's-afraid-of-Virginia-Woolf quarrels in front of yawning witnesses, and all is well.

These differences are important. In Melbourne that ultimate test of friendship, whom can you ring up and ask to pay your bail at 3 a.m., is likely to find such a friend. In Sydney there is no-one who can be trusted to be there for lunch on Thursday let alone to be your friend for life. All acquaintance in Sydney is lost in the numbers of other acquaintance, and our capacity for friendship is therefore downsized, or do I mean asset-stripped, and we begin most conversations in Sydney not knowing where we stand, or if we have been superseded in the mind of our companion since our last encounter. The destiny of every Sydneysider is to be an also-ran, discuss. The destiny of every Melbournite is to be a loyal, reliable and knowing pest. The classic Sydneysider is Leo Schofield, being sued for a restaurant review. The classic Melbournite is B.A. Santamaria, who in his eighties, and even in the hour of his death, was still at it, still grinding away, having stayed the course, and not been found wanting in his jerry-built faith; his zealous constancy made him an iridescent anachronism, a mesmerising, convincing, irresistible bore. In Sydney, the town of the eight-second sound grab, he would not have lasted. In Sydney he might not even have got his start.

Cities declare themselves, and their emotional priorities, in the lines of their greatest writers. Melbourne is always and ever C.J. Dennis, in 'The Sentimental Bloke', that essay in the vernacular language that gave birth to other Melbourne-bred adventurers in language, to Barry Humphries and John Clarke and John Hepworth and Michael Leunig, and the writers like Don Watson who wrote for Max Gillies, and all the better stand-up comedians – Harmer, Vizard, Fahey, Hung Le – of our urban story. And Sydney, I think, or my generation thinks, is always and ever preserved in the great spare poems of Kenneth Slessor, and these lines in particular.

The red globes of light, the liquor-green,
The pulsing arrows and the running fire
Spilt on the stones, go deeper than a stream;
You find this ugly, I find it lovely.

Ghosts' trousers, like the dangle of hung men,
In pawnshop-windows, bumping knee by knee,
But none inside to suffer or condemn;
You find this ugly, I find it lovely.

Smells rich and rasping, smoke and fat and fish
And puffs of paraffin that crimp the nose,
Or grease that blesses onions with a hiss;
You find it ugly, I find it lovely.

The dips and molls, with flip and shiny gaze
(Death at their elbows, hunger at their heels)
Ranging the pavements of their pasturage;
You find it ugly, I find it lovely.

'William Street'

You find it ugly, I find it lovely.

This adoration of the shabby, the not quite legal, the morally ambiguous, the corrupt jockey, the colourful racetrack identity, the Premier with shares in the crooked roulette table, the football star on a charge of assaulting a waiter, the what-it-takes Richo, the take-the-money-and-screw-them Singo, the certainly-I-charge-big-but-I'm-worth-it Leo, the Italian-suits-and-silk-tie-and-monorail Laurie Brereton, the Paul Keating who in certain of his moods reminds you of the kind of man who would sell you a watch in a pub, is very Sydney still, just as it was when rum was currency and only certain people could sell rum, and wives were *selected* from the grimy convict girls who came off the boat, girls who had themselves little choice in the matter of a spouse, just as it is in *Blue Murder*, a show that you are supposed not to have seen, but *you* bend the law too, don't you, like every Sydneysider, a show whose hero-as-murderer is still at large, a celebrity, a star, like a mafia don, in another Big Apple, or do we call it here a Big Choko, somewhere quite close to here.

Cities differ, and the truly great cities, as the Russian general in *Fail Safe* remarked to the American general on the eve of their short, sharp nuclear war, 'The truly great cities are where you can walk', and Sydney is *not* such a place, for it is built on hills and hollows and costly water views, and these differentiating altitudes, as is well known, breed neighbourhood loyalties and local chauvinism and local snobberies; those on the hill do not speak very easily to those in the valley, those by the water do not feel very comfortable, or identify very readily with those in the dingy landlocked suburbs of the west, those who go to the Wharf Theatre would never dream of going as well to the Marian Street theatre, for this means climbing too many hills – and these geographical wearinesses add up, in the end, to something very like class feelings – does Anglo-Saxon Bellevue Hill really want to mix with

Jewish–Hungarian Double Bay? – in ways that do not trouble the flatter cities of Melbourne and Dublin and Paris, cities where you can walk, and find friends across educational boundaries as you never do here, in ways that make us in this metropolis pretty shifty, and encoded, and suspicious, and clubby, and litigious, and money-grubbing.

No two Sydneysiders meeting will take more than three and a quarter minutes now to begin to talk of real estate prices, and the current valuation of their cheap-bought house, or to ruminate autobiographically in the way that Los Angelinos do, defining themselves by geography, *when I lived in Bondi, when we lived in Birchgrove before the divorce, now I and my new wife have moved to Killara, it's for the sake of the kids, the schools are better, they really are,* and so on. In a city of hills and valleys and water views you get skyscrapers too, and the dwarfing of individuality and that censoring, that erasure by architecture, of community and conversation and democracy as the little stone pubs come down and the tall glass towers full of careful courtiers and bureaucrats rear up in their place.

Human beings, Robert Ardrey wrote in *The Territorial Imperative*, human beings seek, in no particular order, (1) Identity, (2) Stimulation, and (3) Security, and so most of us try to get by with only two of these three things, and most of us end unhappily. And it is the work of cities, of course, to give us the other two but always to challenge the stuff of our identity. Who am I this week? Which of my three girlfriends am I truly committed to? Do I really believe Tim Fischer, who promised 'bucket-loads of extinguishment', is a good bloke this week, or has my opinion been lately changed for me, without my knowing it, by Sydney journalists? Woody Allen, in his lovely New York film *Manhattan*, has a scene where Diane Keaton is scornfully deriding the books of Saul Bellow and Norman Mailer and Philip Roth and Joseph Heller, and Woody is nodding along with her because he's attracted to her, until he suddenly realises that these are his favourite writers, and she is a moron he must urgently tame.

Cities get to you like that, they conscript you into schools of opinion, like Scientology or its intellectual equivalent, economic rationalism, and march you off – hup, two, three, four, sound off, sound off – into opinions you may not really hold, like how Woody Allen is an incestuous, predatory, bisexual pederast and you should therefore never go to any more of his films if you are a *truly caring person*; or Bob Ellis is the most poisonous living Australian because he leaves swear words on answering machines, and he should therefore be deprived of his livelihood or permission to eat occasional Chinese food with Kim Beazley; or Les Murray is a racist, fascist ratbag with nothing to add to our national consciousness or its emotional vocabulary. It's almost possible to *believe* rubbish like this – or past rubbish like how Lindy Chamberlain *certainly* cut the throat of her baby and yet was somehow simultaneously fit, and safely qualified, to look after her other children, including her subsequent baby, while she was out on bail – because of that hectic abundant confusion of city life that crowds out those thoughts, with noise and headlines and commercials and junk mail and alcohol and one-night stands in the De Vere Hotel and Brian Henderson and Alan Jones, crowds out those logical, sensible thoughts that you might have come to on your own.

Your identity is always under assault in cities – are you thin enough? are you tough enough? are you beautiful enough? are you computer literate enough? have you truly considered the career advantages of a breast implant? will you go blond this summer or only streaky? or put rings on your nipples? or bells on your toes? – in ways that in country towns, where faces are clear and focused and relaxed in the certainty of who they are, it rarely is. A city is a breeding ground of a divided self, of a kind of house-trained schizo-phrenia – it has to be, to be as abundant as it is, and from Philip Pirrip and Becky Sharp to Holden Caulfield and Portnoy and Sophie and Joe Lampton and Jimmy Porter and Travis Bickle and Prendergast and the glum young hero of *Praise*, it has been the business of literature, and drama, and film, and song, *Hello darkness my old friend*, to find it out. Samuel Johnson in terror of hellfire from his masturbation, and James Boswell out in Cheapside in the small hours in search of strumpets, and James McAuley nightly shrieking at his vision of a man in a stovepipe hat who has come to claim his soul and stands in the dark of his room, and Virginia Woolf decorously growing suicidal in her Bloomsbury room with a view, and Henry Lawson begging behind his hat in Circular Quay, and Chidley in his toga extolling natural coition in the Domain, and Barry Humphries playing his hilarious tricks on his amazed fellow passengers on suburban trains, and Les Murray shoplifting long peppery sausages that went up the sleeves – thin food – and wide flat cheeses that went under the belt – flat food – and eating for one more day, and Dorothy Hewett's heartbreak boarding houses at the end of the universe, and Lennie Lower's punters betting on the burning house – all are one with this question of how do we cope with the numbers of selves that are daily offered to us by city life, the infinite pilgrimages to nowhere much, and how do we stay true to friends and beliefs and states of origin and home towns when we are so assaulted by so many numbers of alternatives and realities; how do we hold ourselves in our hands like water without parting our fingers and spilling ourselves forever away? And how do we choose between the boredom of stasis in the dusty country town and the certainty of change in the big noisy city? How can we know when that change is good? How can we?

Cities vary too, I think, in time, and here in Sydney it is different now from when there were orchards in Wahroonga and Clive James grew up in a suburb not much different from a country town. There was a time when you could leave your door unlocked and walk home unmolested through parks and streets at three and four in the morning. It is different now.

In a musical play I've been co-writing for ten years now, called variously *Man – The Musical*, *Neon Street* and *City Lights*, and set in Kings Cross in 1951, about a returned soldier who works as a writer and sub-editor for *Man Magazine*, and a war widow who works as a writer and sub-editor for *The Woman's Weekly*, each of them in their hackwork subserving the male and female imagery of the time – loyal housewife and great white hunter, dizzy blonde chorus girl and French Foreign Legionnaire – while trying after hours to write the novels they really care about, I deal with this question of the unbreachable, urban, squalid, undecipherable mystery of the Big Smoke and its coexistence with the dream, the unreachable dream, of the country town you will never return to, and might not even like, and I deal with a Sydney that no longer exists and is much more real to me that what has followed. I thought I'd end by reading a few of the lyrics as the men come out of the bars at six o'clock and start to walk home and the hero, Tom Rayner, sees the girl with the up-town face hanging out her underwear on the roof of an apartment block in Kings Cross and knows he is cruelly in love with what he clearly, surely, will never have.

> *Time, gentlemen, please! Time, gentlemen, please!*
> *Time . . .*
> *Drink your last orders and home you go*
> *To the little woman and the mantel radio,*
> *To the curled-up lino and the leaking fridge*
> *And the outside loo*
> *With the interrupted view*
> *Of the Sydney . . . Harbour . . . Bridge.*
>
> *It's six o'clock closing in my baby's heart,*
> *And the red-headed barmaid and I must part,*
> *And under the Southern Cross I'll stroll,*
> *Where I've . . . mislaid . . . my soul . . .*
> *The moon is full . . .*
> *The night is dry . . .*
> *And what to do?*
> *And who . . .*
> *Am I?*
>
> *Time, gentlemen, please.*
> *Time . . .*
> *Time . . .*
> *Time takes you where you should not go,*
> *Down the Hasty Tasty where the passing show*

And the winos and the riff-raff and the ratbags meet
Underneath the Dunlop sign on William Street . . .

I wish there was a better place to be,
Where everyone I knew was glad that they knew me.
I wish I was the man I pictured then,
When everything was simple –
Can it be that way again?
And far back in the boy I used to be,
A man began to grow who isn't me,
And walked off down the road the other way,
When everything was simple –
But that was yesterday.
And down the streets and through the neon light
A kind of life is glimpsed, then out of sight . . .
We yearn to be the folk we looked for then,
When everything was simple –
Can it be that way again?

Hey, girl in the moon, are you moth or are you flame?
Will the dirty washing you hang out ever bear my name?
And will there ever be a smell of me in so ladylike a nose?
And am I what by any name might then be called a rose?
Hey, girl in the moon, are you real, or just a back projection
Of the way I used to feel
When love was up there in his castle
And I in the mud below
And there were many ways,
Or so the legend says,
For love to say hello?

I haven't said the word yet, and now the summer's near
I haven't felt as bad as this all through the bleeding year
And every girl I see does something worse to me,
But this one hurts me so much that I know it has to be.

Ah, who cares what I think?
Who knows that I'm alive?
Who'll say, 'Come up and see me some time',
After six-oh-five?
Or say, 'Hey, big boy, got a light?
You have such knowing eyes.'
Or, 'Are you still a small boy really

399

And has the world got wise?
Where have you been all my life?'
Is it your place now or mine, I wonder,
Where we can hide away,
And play our sweet games unencumbered,
All innocent and free,
And I will say to you,
Please for tonight be true,
And then . . . at dawn . . . we'll see . . .

There's Gable at the Mayfair and Bogart at the Star,
Tooheys at the Journos' Club, and the all-night baccarat,
A parting toss at Thommo's, a strip club for the lonely,
Fat girls with blue eye shadow who'll swear they'll love you only . . .

Downtown in the night,
When the night consumes the soul,
And there is nothing left on earth
To uplift and make me whole,
Rough trade and Johnny Walker bring
Many starts to many ends,
The girls are out on Neon Street,
But the dark and I are friends . . .

Hey, girl in the moon,
In the dark I see my old addiction,
When I was just a man,
And your hair descended from the tower,
But the tower was too high,
And there were many ways
While love's old music plays
For love . . . to fade . . . and die . . .

There are things I might have added, I suppose: the man who wrote
Eternity on the pavement, Sandor Berger and his pamphlets against psycho-
analysis, the Royal George, the Newcastle, the bookshops in Rowe Street,
Lorenzini's, Repin's, the Greek Club, the Broadway Theatre, the Lalla
Rookh, the Forum, the Tivoli, the Regent, the Phillip Street Theatre, the
Minerva, the Embassy, the Mayfair, the Town, the old Royal, the old Her
Majesty's, the Elizabethan, the Q, the Macquarie Auditorium, the Eisteddfod
Theatre, Romano's, the particular atmosphere of the steam platforms at
Central Station, the nights I slept in a park across from Central Station and
with Les Murray on the golf course at Bondi and in the cemetery at

Waverley, and did shouted recitations from *Moby-Dick* on the Manly ferry, and the Tai Yuen when it was the Tai Ping – all these abide in the festival of memory while still the brain cells of some of us now dying resonate with bits of the past, a memory of the rites of passage into the mouth of the unbreachable mystery of our city in our youth, a city at one now with Nineveh and Tyre and, unlike Old Jerusalem and Petra, that rose-red city half as old as time, gone from all retrieving, insensible of our grief. I mourn what it has turned into – all modern cities tend towards the condition of car parks, discuss – and the computer-radiated lurk men we have turned into, and our children and our children's children, but there it is. We must remember, while we can, how it was, and close the book, and visit better cities sometimes, Dublin, Kiev, Dubrovnik, Prague, Hanoi, and kindle again if we can the young courage we had then, back in Port Jackson when the future was big, and the world was wide.

I thank you.

July, 1999

FIRST ABOLISH THE CUSTOMER

202 ARGUMENTS AGAINST ECONOMIC RATIONALISM

BOB ELLIS

'Economic rationalism at its heart is a refusal to spend money on the unnecessary . . .' But what is unnecessary – and who decides?

With eloquence, passion, wit and humour, Bob Ellis explodes the myths of economic rationalism. In this incendiary, life-affirming book, he reveals it to be, at best, little more than an empty fantasy which, as a guiding principle, has more flaws than a factory second. And, at worse, a self-serving and destructive strategy of greed. Along the way, he demonstrates why the economy of unemployment doesn't work; why it is better to spend than save; why a level playing field won't help; and why economic rationalists never practise what they preach.

With all this and much, much more, *First Abolish the Customer* is a sweeping, swashbuckling account of why economic rationalism is *not* the answer for Australia.

NAVEL GAZING
ESSAYS, HALF-TRUTHS AND MYSTERY FLIGHTS
PETER GOLDSWORTHY

Funny, wise, idiosyncratic and original, these occasional essays chart a course through the various genres of writing that Peter Goldsworthy has investigated: fiction, science fiction, poetry, opera and film.

Spiced with often hilarious personal anecdotes and references to the wide-ranging reading of a self-confessed 'hick autodidact', Goldsworthy offers a book that is at once a writing manual for various literary disciplines, and a loose, extended exploration of his key themes and obsessions: death, humour, the limits of language, the relationship of biology to thought and culture, and the role and responsibilities of art. And first love gets a look in . . .

TWO WEEKS IN LILLIPUT

BEAR-BAITING AND BACKBITING AT THE CONSTITUTIONAL CONVENTION

STEVE VIZARD

Two Weeks in Lilliput is a hilarious and penetrating personal journey through the 1998 Constitutional Convention held to debate whether Australia should become a republic.

Steve Vizard, writer, lawyer, producer and elected delegate to the convention, applies his needle-sharp wit and eye for detail to this side-splitting, fly-on-the-wall, rollercoaster ride through Canberra's corridors of power.

Here is the insider's account of the backroom deals and excesses of some of Australia's most colourful characters – the *60 Minutes* dinner party from hell, an assault on Janet Holmes à Court, Jeff Kennett's late arrival, Hazel Hawke's return to Canberra, and an evening with the Governor-General.

A must-read for anyone interested in Australia's future as a republic.

DUCKS ON
THE POND
AN AUTOBIOGRAPHY
1945–1976

ANNE SUMMERS

Ducks on the Pond is the unflinching personal story of a woman who challenged the world she was given. Anne Summers grew up in a postwar Australia where Catholic schoolgirls learned their only options were to be a mum or a nun – or to end up on the shelf.

In this startlingly frank account, she tells the story of a suburban childhood marred by her father's rejection, which forced her to strike out on her own at an early age and discover that there were other destinies. But she had to make them happen. It was to be a long journey through unfamiliar cities and a succession of low-paid typically female jobs for this gawky, unconfident convent girl before she emerged as a founding member of the Women's Liberation Movement, an award-winning journalist and ultimately a key adviser to prime ministers Bob Hawke and Paul Keating.

Her book *Damned Whores and God's Police*, written before she was 30, became a publishing sensation and helped to change the way Australians see themselves and especially the role of women in this country.